Emerson AND Power

Emerson AND Power

Creative
Antagonism
in the
Nineteenth
Century

Michael Lopez

Northern
Illinois
University
Press
DeKalb
1996

Published by the Northern Illinois University Press,
DeKalb, Illinois   60115
Manufactured in the United States
using acid-free paper ⊕ ∞
Design by Julia Fauci

Library of Congress
Cataloging-in-Publication Data
Lopez, Michael, 1951–
    Emerson and power : creative antagonism in
the nineteenth century / Michael Lopez.
          p.   cm.
    Includes bibliographical references and in-
    dex.
    ISBN 0-87580-196-X (alk. paper)
    1. Emerson, Ralph Waldo, 1803–1882—
Criticism and interpretation.
2. Emerson, Ralph Waldo, 1803–1882—Philosophy. 3. Power (Philosophy) in
literature.
PS1642.P5L67   1994
814'.3—dc20   94-10716
                    CIP

Portions of chapters 1, 2, and 3 originally appeared
as "Transcendental Failure: 'The Palace of Spiritual
Power,'" *Harvard English Studies* 10 (1982):
121–53, used with the permission of Harvard University, Department of English; an early version of
chapter 6 appeared as "De-Transcendentalizing
Emerson," *ESQ: A Journal of the American Ren-
naissance* 34 (1988): 77–139, used with permission;
and an early version of chapter 7 appeared as
"Emerson's Rhetoric of War," *Prospects: An Annual of American Cultural Studies* 12 (1987):
293–320, reprinted with the permission of Cambridge University Press.

for Clare

C O N T E N T S

Acknowledgments   ix

Abbreviations   xi

Introduction   3

1   The Anti-Emerson Tradition   *19*

2   The Doctrine of Use   *53*

3   The Uses of Failure   *106*

4   Extravagance   *117*

5   Working and Being Worked Upon   *132*

6   Detranscendentalizing Emerson   *165*

7   The Rhetoric of War   *190*

Notes   *211*

Works Cited   *237*

Index   *249*

ACKNOWLEDGMENTS

This book must begin by acknowledging the brilliant teaching of a tough subject. It was Joel Porte's courses on American Romanticism that first inspired my interest in Emerson and helped shape, in ways I am still learning to appreciate, my understanding of American literature generally. His work continues to provide the context for my thinking about Emerson.

For over twenty years now, I have relied on the advice and encouragement of Gerald Jay Goldberg; I remain indebted to him for more acts of friendship than I can begin to list. I thank Steve Arch, Sheila Teahan, and Robert A. Martin—colleagues at Michigan State University—for reading parts of the manuscript as it neared completion and Clint Goodson for his belief in this book since I first arrived in East Lansing. The English Department and College of Arts and Letters generously granted me leave time to complete the manuscript and funding that assisted in its publication. Acknowledgments to fellow faculty and administrations are commonplace; the supportive environment that Michigan State University has always provided me is not. I am grateful as well to Julie Ellison and Peter Hawkes for inviting me to participate in special MLA panels on Emerson. Both panels helped me clarify the argument presented here. At Northern Illinois University Press, I thank Dan Coran, for his support for this book, and Susan Bean and one anonymous copyeditor, whose careful labors considerably improved it. My greatest debt is to Clare Cavanagh. Her love, companionship, and continuing interest in this book—and her faith in me—made it all possible.

Some sections have appeared previously in different form. I am grateful to *Harvard English Studies*, *Prospects: An Annual of American Cultural Studies*, and *ESQ: A Journal of the American Renaissance* for their permission to use material they originally published.

ABBREVIATIONS

For Emerson's and Nietzsche's works I use the following abbreviations and editions. Nietzsche's works are cited by volume and/or section number; "Pref." refers to Nietzsche's prefaces.

BGE   *Beyond Good and Evil.* In *Basic Writings of Nietzsche,* translated and edited by Walter Kaufmann. New York: Modern Library, 1968.

BT   *The Birth of Tragedy.* In *The Portable Nietzsche,* translated and edited by Walter Kaufmann. New York: Viking, 1954.

CEC   *The Correspondence of Emerson and Carlyle,* edited by Joseph Slater. New York: Columbia University Press, 1964.

CW   *The Collected Works of Ralph Waldo Emerson,* edited by Robert Spiller et al. 4 vols. Cambridge, Mass.: Harvard University Press, 1971–.

D   *Daybreak: Thoughts on the Prejudices of Morality,* translated by R. J. Hollingdale. New York: Cambridge University Press, 1982.

EH   *Ecce Homo.* In *Basic Writings of Nietzsche.*

EJ   *Emerson in His Journals,* edited by Joel Porte. Cambridge, Mass.: Harvard University Press, 1982.

EL   *The Early Lectures of Ralph Waldo Emerson,* edited by Stephen Whicher et al. 3 vols. Cambridge, Mass.: Harvard University Press, 1959–1972.

ET   *English Traits,* edited by Howard Mumford Jones. Cambridge, Mass.: Harvard University Press, 1966.

GM   *On the Genealogy of Morals.* In *Basic Writings of Nietzsche.*

GS   *The Gay Science,* translated by Walter Kaufmann. New York: Random House, 1974.

HH   *Human, All Too Human: A Book for Free Spirits,* translated by R. J. Hollingdale. New York: Cambridge University Press, 1986.

JMN   *The Journals and Miscellaneous Notebooks of Ralph Waldo Emerson,* edited by William H. Gilman et al. 16 vols. Cambridge, Mass.: Harvard University Press, 1960–1982.

L   *The Letters of Ralph Waldo Emerson,* edited by Ralph L. Rusk. 6 vols. New York: Columbia University Press, 1939.

SE   *Selections from Ralph Waldo Emerson,* edited by Stephen Whicher. Boston: Houghton Mifflin, 1957.

TI   *Twilight of the Idols.* In *The Portable Nietzsche.*

TN   *The Topical Notebooks of Ralph Waldo Emerson,* edited by Ralph H. Orth, Susan Sutton Smith, and Ronald A. Bosco. 2 vols. Columbia: University of Missouri Press, 1990– .

UM   *Untimely Meditations,* translated by R. J. Hollingdale. New York: Cambridge University Press, 1983.

W   *The Complete Works of Ralph Waldo Emerson,* Centenary Edition, edited by Edward Waldo Emerson. 12 vols. Boston: Houghton Mifflin, 1903–1904.

WP   *The Will to Power,* translated by Walter Kaufmann and R. J. Hollingdale. New York: Random House, 1968.

Z   *Thus Spoke Zarathustra.* In *The Portable Nietzsche.*

Emerson AND Power

INTRODUCTION

William James was probably right. Philosophy *is* a matter of personality. The history of philosophy, James once remarked, is the "clash of human temperaments"—and temperament gravitates either to the "idealistic" or to the "materialistic" pole:

> Idealism will be chosen by a man of one emotional constitution, materialism by another. . . . [I]dealism gives to the nature of things such kinship with our personal selves. Our own thoughts are what we are most at home with, what we are least afraid of. To say then that the universe is essentially thought, is to say that I myself, potentially at least, am all. There is no radically alien corner, but an all-pervading intimacy. . . . That element in reality which every strong man of common-sense willingly feels there because it calls forth powers that he owns—the rough, harsh, sea-wave, north-wind element, the denier of persons, the democratizer—is banished because it jars too much on the desire for communion. Now, it is the very enjoyment of this element that throws many men upon the materialistic or agnostic hypothesis, as a polemic reaction against the contrary extreme. They sicken at a life wholly constituted of intimacy. There is an overpowering desire at moments to escape personality, to revel in the action of forces that have no respect for our ego, to let the tides flow, even though they flow over us. The strife of these two kinds of mental temper will, I think, always be seen in philosophy. Some men will keep insisting on the reason, the atonement, that lies in the heart of things, and that we can act with; others, on the opacity of brute fact that we must react against.

Until recently, the traditional scholarly response to Ralph Waldo Emerson has been to place him squarely in what James defines as the "idealist" camp. This is not to say that quite contrary emphases in Emerson's thought have not been noted and duly catalogued. I mean only that scholarship has almost universally concluded that Emerson can, on the whole, be most justly classified as an idealist in the large but eminently useful terms James supplies in the above passage.[1] And there is, indeed, much in Emerson that would appear to offer obvious evidence for that decision. He certainly speaks of a desire for atonement, of a longing for some all-pervading intimacy with the universe. He prophesies, at memorable junctures, the disappearance of life's harsh "north-wind element." He remains resolute in his belief in the absolute law of the Over-Soul (a vision of cosmic Oneness he more routinely refers to as "the divine," "moral," or "universal sentiment," the "universal soul," or simply "Unity").

But the Emerson I argue for here belongs in the opposite camp. He searches always for something to react against. This is what we might call a deep structure, or elemental pattern in his thought, a pattern that can be found underlying even those passages in which he seems most monistic, most in love with the idea of atonement. We err when we speak of him as a "Transcendentalist." For his psychology and philosophy (the two are, for Emerson, really the same, just as they are for Nietzsche) are founded on a conception of *resistance* and *overcoming* that Nietzsche incorporated, with at times notorious results, into his own work. Emerson never turned away from brute fact or the rough sea-wave world we must react against— though a century and a half of commentary would have us believe so. His essays are born and take shape in that rough world. It is only, Emerson insists, within the limits, only from within the pain, the poverty of the real world, that we can find what the soul always seeks: some form of power.

Only that real world, that world against which we must react, is capable, as Emerson would say, of calling forth all our latent powers. It is the drama of this continually undertaken process that is documented in most of his prose. "What activity the desire of power inspires!" (W, 10:129). That is the chant resounding through almost every essay. Life, for Emerson, was the unfolding of "the active faculties of men"; the boon of all human activity was the accumulation of power (W, 10:129). Each of his major essays can be read as a fable of the self, the soul, the mind, man, or humankind in the process of struggling for, gaining, losing, or rewinning some form of power. The Emersonian universe is thus, of necessity, a "stupendous antagonism," a ceaseless play of conflict and reaction. His verdict on Webster or Thoreau applies equally to himself: he does not speak without an antagonist; he does not feel himself except in opposition (JMN, 13:183).

Nature is thus postulated not as some superior object of atonement but as a powerful adversary, a "beautiful enemy," the stepping-stone, the catalyst to man's inborn energies. Failure is not transcended but courted as an opportunity for triumph. Evil is not denied but welcomed as the negative force necessary for any act of mastery or overcoming. Individual identity is defined not in terms of some absolute, presocial self but as the result of contention and suffering, as the reward for daily acts of psychological "counterbalancing." National identity is likewise defined as the product of the energies of war—war in either its overt or its sublimated forms.

If such acts can in any way be considered acts of "transcendence," then they are not the kind of transcendence Emerson's critics generally have in mind. (The kind of transcendence traditionally ascribed to him amounts to a kind of escapism critics usually treat with contempt.) Such acts of mastery are, rather, what Martha Nussbaum distinguishes as acts of strictly "human," as opposed to Platonic, "transcendence." They are "transcending by descent, delving more deeply into oneself and one's humanity, and becoming deeper and more spacious as a result."[2] (The very language of that description has a decidedly Nietzschean/Emersonian ring. Nietzsche calls such transcendence overcoming by "going under." Emerson invokes the same criterion when he defines "the complete man" as the being capable of "traversing the whole scale," of soaring higher and sinking deeper than other men.)

Let me suggest the same point in slightly different terms, the terms Nussbaum employs in a trenchant essay on the perennial human aspiration to "transcend humanity." There is, Nussbaum argues, a type of philosophical thinking that gravitates toward the ideal Calypso upholds when she offers Odysseus the chance for a life of godlike transcendence, a life in which the brute facts of death and sea-waves can be left behind for a life of Olympian detachment. Calypso represents an otherworldly life, a life apart from the painful boundaries of human existence. Her name, appropriately, means "she who conceals." She offers Odysseus, as Nussbaum notes, atonement with a transcendent, ideal, or "true world." (It is, in other words, a world very much like the kind of Platonic or Christian "otherworld" Nietzsche scorned because it leads to a denigration of our actions in this one.) But Odysseus chooses a different course, one more in keeping with his own name, with its suggestions of suffering and struggle. He decides, finally, not to transcend his humanity. He willingly returns to a world against which he is compelled to react. It is a world of risk, incompleteness, and conflict—but it is the only world in which human action, virtue, or heroism is possible.

Calypso and Odysseus inhabit different worlds, worlds that represent two fundamentally opposed intellectual tendencies. One represents a Platonic aspiration to transcendence ("the aspiration to transcend one's humanity as a coherent and valuable ethical aim for and in a human life"). The other represents a rejection of any such transcendence in favor of a commitment to those very human limits that "structure the human excellences . . . and give excellent action its significance."[3] (As one example of this commitment, Nussbaum suggests athletic excellence: it can never be found in the transcendence of human limits, only in the acceptance of, and struggle against, the natural weaknesses of the body.[4]) If these two contrary aspirations can be taken as one broad context for locating primary philosophical tendencies, then the general aim of this book can be simply stated. It is to argue that Emerson belongs not in the transcendental, Platonic (or quasi-Platonic) school in which he has been so often placed but in an opposing tradition.

This is to claim something more than that Emerson's pie-in-the-sky image has been overblown, that he is relevant to everyday human life in ways that have hitherto gone unappreciated, or that he actually lived a life of greater vulnerability than is popularly believed or was more actively supportive of social reform than has been recognized. All of these are certainly worthy claims. What I wish to argue here, however, has to do with an extraordinarily consistent pattern in Emerson's major prose, a characterizing pattern that might be called (borrowing lines from F. R. Leavis) the "deep centre of life" or "deep animating intention" that defines a distinctly Emersonian way of thinking.[5]

I use the phrase "distinctly Emersonian." Yet the kind of agonistic thinking to which I refer was so successfully absorbed by Friedrich Nietzsche, two generations later and an ocean away, that from our perspective the most appropriate description for this originally Emersonian kind of thinking must now be "Nietzschean." It is Nietzsche we now consider the nineteenth century's "philosopher of power." It is Nietzsche we identify as the originator of a philosophy of "overcoming" and "will to power," a philosophy of conflict, struggle, use, tuition, incorporation, and war. But these were, in ways I shall investigate, Emersonian principles as well.[6]

"Power, "force," "energy": these three words seem to recur on Emerson's every page. If they do not appear themselves, then the idea of them does. "Life is a search after power" (W, 6:53). "Power is the first good." "Power is in nature the essential measure of right" (CW, 2:40). "Power, new power, is the good which the soul seeks" (W, 8:63). Watt mastered electrical force, Emerson tells us, because he knew "that where was power was not devil, but was God" (W, 6:33). At times, his vision of human (and national) power swells to universal proportions—anticipating Walt Whitman's cosmic giant or Zarathustra at his most dithyrambic:

> There is a moment in the history of every nation, when, proceeding out of this brute youth, the perceptive powers reach their ripeness, and have not yet become microscopic, so that man, at that instant, extends across the entire scale, and, with his feet still planted on the immense forces of Night, converses by his eyes and brain with solar and stellar creation. That is the moment of adult health, the culmination of power. (CW, 4:27)

(George Santayana once dubbed Emerson the "champion of cheerfulness," and for some readers that is what he will always be.[7] But notice the way in which even this brief passage, from Emerson's essay on Plato, belies the popular misconception of his work as merely the cheerful expression of an innately sunny disposition. Emerson's fully empowered man requires, like Nietzsche's "overman," the inclusion, the overcoming, the bridling— not the evasion—of "the immense forces of Night." Nietzsche's overman is an overcomer; to attain that condition the all-too-human man must become "a rope over an abyss." As Zarathustra declares: "one must still have chaos in oneself to be able to give birth to a dancing star" [Z, 1:Pref., 4–5]. Emerson's central man similarly has both feet firmly grounded on what Emerson elsewhere calls "negative force." As he puts it in the journal entry from which the above passage is taken: "There must be the Abyss, Nox and Chaos, out of which all come, and they must never be far off. Cut off the connection between any of our works and this dread origin, and the work is shallow and unsatisfying" [SE, 283]. Emerson's projec-

tions of man empowered are, like Nietzsche's, always intended as sublima-
tions—not rose-tinted circumventions—of the resisting force of "Abyss,
Nox and Chaos." And they imply a similarly Nietzschean respect for the
"hardness," the "discipline," necessary for any act of creation. Why have
we been able to appreciate Nietzsche's philosophy of "adult health" and
"affirmation" while reducing Emerson's to a case of "optimism"? Recent
criticism has reopened that question, and I shall return to it often.)

Like Nietzsche's will to power, Emerson's search for power is ubiquitous, all-inclusive, "omnific and thousand-handed." It underlies all aspects
of life and art. What seems to shine beneath his prose, in the flow of images of destruction, creation, liberation, metamorphosis, melting, dissolving, pulsating, bursting, unfixing, upheaving, and unsettling, is a vision of
"pure power" and the universal quest, the universal struggle for that
power. That vision illuminates his pages like the spiritual-cosmic light that
radiates through the canvases of his contemporaries, Sanford Robinson
Gifford, Martin Heade, Fitz Hugh Lane, Frederic Church, or Thomas
Cole. "Through his words we intuit," Stephen Whicher writes, "almost in
spite of any intention of his own, a primal realm of being—pure energy,
naked spirit, unincarnate life—which lies barely within the reach of
thought" (SE, xxi).

Such descriptions may suggest that power for Emerson means purely
spiritual energy, that the Emersonian search for it is a Platonic search for a
purely transcendental realm of being. But this is demonstrably not the
case. Emerson was always attracted to *all* forms of power, even those that
repelled him morally. He lost respect for a Cromwell or a Bonaparte when
he considered their immoral ends, but he could not help admiring "the
simplicity & energy of their evil" (JMN, 3:277). He was drawn to spiritual
force as well as brute force, the force of mind and the force of sex, the anarchic energies of the mob, the power of armies, gunpowder, steam,
sawmills, electricity, the power of genius, eloquence, great men, dema-
gogues, and tyrants. He was drawn to beast power, dream power, and the
power of race, the powers of water, lightning, and the vastness of the
American landscape, the energies of evil and vice, as well as the pacifist,
moral force of martyrdom. "The ecstasies of devotion," he once remarked,
"appear with the exasperations of vice. Get energy & you get all" (JMN,
11:45). "All kinds of power usually emerge at the same time; good energy
and bad; power of mind with physical health; the ecstasies of devotion
with the exasperations of debauchery" (W, 6:64).

Criticism has, until recently, been too eager to downplay this conspicuous "Nietzschean strain," as Whicher labeled it. Scholars have been too
eager to remind us of the limits of the Emerson-Nietzsche comparison, or
they have simply chosen to ignore it altogether. There are reasons for
this—some of them good, others increasingly outdated. There are, as I
shall note, fundamental ways in which Emerson can never be mistaken for

Nietzsche. Yet one cannot help but feel that Emerson scholarship has all along been handicapped by an unfair, now quite obsolete, anti-Nietzsche prejudice. Unfortunately, it is a prejudice that still seems very much alive and well within the local confines of "the Emerson industry." The Emerson-Nietzsche connection seems still to be regarded by many scholars as a slander from which Emerson's good name must be vindicated.

This state of affairs is regrettable for several reasons. It has, for one thing, helped to keep our appreciation of Emerson on relatively parochial grounds, when the work in question is of such unsurpassed quality and influence that it cries out for a far more cosmopolitan approach. This parochialness has, in turn, helped to insure the scholarly condescension that has always characterized Emerson's academic reception. Most significantly, however, it has helped to keep suppressed what are major and omnipresent patterns in Emerson's thought. For if there are, indeed, limits to the comparison to be made between Emerson and Nietzsche, there are also fundamental connections that have still to be recovered. And the connections are crucial. For the more we begin to recover the strongly Nietzschean nature of Emerson's imagination, the more we must begin to question many of those Transcendentalist/Idealist chestnuts that scholarship has settled on as the virtually unchallengeable features of his thought.

I mean by this those putatively defining characteristics that most introductory college lectures on Emerson continue to stress: his organicism, his monism, his pantheism, his philosophical absolutism, his unyielding belief in the moral law, his reputation as an optimist and a seer of unity, his yearning for *atonement with* rather than *reaction against,* his indifference to evil, his escapist naïveté, his desire for transcendence of this world rather than struggle within it. Add to this list the perception (one that runs from Santayana through the work of Perry Miller, Charles Feidelson, Stephen Whicher, Bruce Kuklick, and, most recently, Michael Colacurcio) that Emerson was an intellectual anachronism, holding out for a shopworn idealism in a century already moving toward new (and, according to some, more respectable) forms of "realism." Add also the common perception that Emerson disappears, at last, into his "mystical tendencies"—or the mantle that has been hung on him as a fundamentally theistic thinker, a God-intoxicated provider of primarily religious insight. (Emerson advocates, Robert Richardson concludes, "not anthropomorphism, but theomorphism."[8])

Of such virtues is the traditional (canonical) "Emerson image" made. Yet criticism over the past two decades has steadily been abandoning that image, and one can only hope that those who subscribe to it will eventually find themselves in a largely defensive position. One hopes that this may come to be not because the scholarship that has portrayed Emerson in this way has not been valid or enormously valuable, not even because this approach will not continue to be of value, but because those readers who see Emerson this way have generally concluded that there is really nothing particularly virtuous, nothing of much contemporary interest, in those transcendentalist virtues they find. Those who have presented an Emerson who adheres to the lines of the traditional lecture described above have, again and again, wound up finding little use for him beyond the purely historical. This is the topic of my opening chapter: a critical tradition that has successfully enshrined its subject as a monumental museum piece while failing, on the whole, to find more than secondary value for his achievements as an artist, a philosopher, even as a still vital religious thinker.

I must now, however, state emphatically that I am not suggesting that the familiar features of the Transcendentalist Emerson are not there or that they are merely critical constructions imposed on him. They *are* there. And they define a major strain in his thought. There is much recent work (like that, for instance, by Philip Gura or John Irwin on the Transcendentalist commitment to the recovery of a universal Ur-language of nature) that makes clear the depth, the extremity, of Emerson's organicist and syncretic tendencies. The problem is not that defining Emerson in these terms is wrong, only that it is radically incomplete. For this way of approaching him leaves out radically contradictory tendencies, tendencies that seem to me not only equal but ultimately greater in extent and importance.

We have always been aware of a Nietzschean strain, a pragmatic strain, in Emerson. But generally we have tried to approach him primarily in terms of his organicism, his monism, his Transcendentalism. This is, however, somewhat like trying to understand the secondary, composite color orange mainly in terms of only one of its contributing, primary colors—by focusing, say, on yellow and downplaying red. The uncanny complexity of Emerson's essays demands that they be approached in equally complex terms: as examples of an unwieldy but singularly mid-nineteenth-century composite or synthesis—one that looks backward to Schelling, backward to idealist, organicist, and theistic traditions, as it concurrently looks forward to the power philosophies characteristic of the later nineteenth century. The weaving together of these two strains takes on, in Emerson's hands, a formidable rhetorical power, one that seems to shimmer mysteriously, attracting widely diverse kinds of readers while defying explanation.

This composite (and uniquely mid-nineteenth-century) nature of his prose helps to account, I think, for that phenomenon critics have often noted: the way in which his lines can be so slippery, like lines of verse that mean one thing when the emphasis falls one way but imply the contrary when the emphasis changes. Thus Jonathan Bishop speaks of Emerson's "doublings of tone" or "tonal puns," and Donald Pease notes that Emerson's "propositions are at an equal distance from one another, so that it is impossible to affirm without denying or the reverse."[9] This elusive "doubleness" in Emerson's thought requires that we approach him in terms of some more cumbersome third category. His essays present something that

stubbornly evades classification under any pure or single philosophical category. (One may respond, of course, that no text can really be reduced to
any single philosophical category; my point is that scholarship too often
acts as if Emerson's texts can be.) His essays may have idealistic roots, but
they offer something quite other than "idealism" ("post-idealism" is the
rather awkward tag I shall suggest). They may seem to approach a Platonic perspective but do not end up endorsing Platonic transcendence.
They may seem to move toward atonement with nature, yet they depend
on a vision of universal antagonism, not cosmic unity.

Emerson should, in short, be approached in terms of the philosophical
contradictions indigenous to the middle decades of the nineteenth century.
Yet his case is more extreme than this, and it will not do to leave matters
there. Emerson's imagination, it seems to me, leans so habitually in one direction that it is finally not enough to describe his work as a balanced synthesis (an empiricist idealism, say, or a monistic dualism—descriptions that
have been used before). It is something more extreme, even, than an unbal-
anced, always shifting amalgam. The deep, animating intention, the recurring, agonistic pattern beneath his prose, seems to fall, ultimately, toward
Nietzsche—toward the "search after power," toward what is usable and
empowering, toward pragmatism, toward a philosophy that sees the
world, the self, as something to be "worked up," toward a Nietzschean
"aestheticist ontology" and "creative nihilism."

W hat, then, is Emersonian power? And in what kind of historical context can this preoccupation with power be located?

These are closely related questions. Emersonian power is, as I have suggested, not a single subject. It functions, rather, as an umbrella term. It encompasses a family of intertwined but different and at times contradictory
meanings. Power, Richard Poirier writes, "has a variety of meanings for
[Emerson], and they can on occasion cancel one another out." His extraordinary, fluctuating reliance on the word "can be confusing . . . because he
does not always indicate the kind of power he has in mind."[10] The search
after power, the goal of empowerment, remains consistent through Emerson's essays. But the kind of power he has in mind, the kind of energy that
inspires or intimidates him, changes. And this very looseness or inclusiveness that characterizes his use of the word is characteristic of the nineteenth century as a whole. For if it is true, as Emerson once claimed, that
"Certain ideas are in the air," then power was one of those fluid, ever-
adaptable ideas, one of those "master signs," as one historian refers to
them, most in the air throughout the century.[11]

That continuing fascination with power is, as a subject in its own right,
endless. To trace the history of the idea of power in the nineteenth century
is to write the intellectual history of the century itself. Whatever corner of

the carpet one raises, it leads to an unending series of affiliated theories.

One might begin with the obvious: the characteristic, Romantic attraction to power in every form, divine or satanic. For William Blake, energy was "eternal delight," the redemptive force in the universe. For Samuel Coleridge, "Imagination" was an "indestructible power." Nothing was sublime, Edmund Burke argued (a thesis that would prove massively influential), which was not at root "some modification of power." The association in the Romantic mind of natural, creative, and revolutionary forces accounts for the "self-identifying" admiration for Napoleon shared by so many minds of the century—Emerson, Byron, Shelley, Blake, Hazlitt, Carlyle, Henry James, and Nietzsche among them—generally despite their own disappointment that Napoleonic energy turned out to be only destructive.[12] Even William Ellery Channing, Unitarianism's opponent of religious or political enthusiasm and the last one to be impressed by military fame, could not withhold his admiration for Bonaparte's dazzling "energy of will."[13] That "sense of vehicular energy," which Northrop Frye has discerned propelling so much of Romantic poetry, is another expression of the age's reverence for the inward creative power.[14]

The Victorian age was no less venerational of power. "The Worship of Force" was, as Walter Houghton suggests, one incarnation of the "Victorian mind."[15] "Knowest thou," Carlyle asked, "any corner of the world where . . . FORCE is not?" "The Gospel of Man's Force" (the belief in man's "dynamical nature," his "inward primary powers") could, Carlyle hoped, withstand the proliferation of "Iron Force, and Coal Force."[16] For well before midcentury the idea of "force" had come to imply not only poetic or psychological power but also the power of the machine. It would come to include the evolutionary force Darwin proposed in *Origin of Species*—or that inevitable, social force Herbert Spencer championed as the brute but "benevolent" energy that allows the strong to prevail over the sickly.

We are only beginning to scratch the surface of a subject that branches out in every direction, making any attempt at chronological overview difficult, if not impossible. The century's search after power was ubiquitous. "The scientific laws that each sought for," as Jacques Barzun writes of Darwin and Marx at midcentury, "was that of the motive power within a world which everybody agreed was a dynamic one." But this "intoxication of power," as Bertrand Russell notes, is nothing new to the nineteenth century—it "invaded philosophy with Fichte." So we must move backward again, at least a half-century, to include, under the broad rubric of the age's hunt for the key to a dynamic world, such German precursors as the Kantian conception of power as an a priori idea, Fichte's notion of *Selbsttätigkeit* (self-activity), or Schelling's search for "an inner connection between all forms of life and expression on organic and dynamic principles." By Hegel's time "Force" had become, Robert Solomon writes, "a metaphor for any below-the-surface activity which could be used to explain movements and transformations." (It had become, by the turn of the eighteenth century, "the dominant explanatory principle of science," "one of those words—like the key words in science ever since—that had captured the popular and philosophical imagination.") "It may appear pure fantasy," Maurice Mandelbaum concludes, "to hold that the entire phenomenal world is a product of some force within us, identified as Will; yet if this represents a fantasy it was not unique in Schopenhauer, as Fichte's theory of knowledge serves to suggest": "a tendency to explain all external manifestations in terms of inner forces was a trait characteristic of the *Naturphilosophie* of the whole idealistic period."[17]

John Kinnaird attempts to provide some kind of general background for Hazlitt's fascination with "the idea of a primal power-urge in man," and his description suggests the extensive, if amorphous, attraction the idea exerted as the new century dawned:

> "Power," wrote Coleridge in 1800, "is the sole object of philosophical attention in man, as in inanimate nature." A novel fascination with "power" was inevitable in an age not only of war and political revolution, but of new class mobilities, of the scientific discovery of unsuspected electrical energies in nature, of the meteoric rise and fall of men and nations, and . . . of rapid industrial and commercial expansion. In such a world all modes of energy came to seem continuous, either in fact or in significance, at least when contrasted with the fixed forms of authority and feudal privilege which seemed opposed to them all. Anyone brought up in the idiom of Biblical prophecy now had little trouble thinking mythically about the continuity of "power": under the one "idea of power" Hazlitt included, not only the idea of cause, but "all that relates to force, energy, weakness, effort, ease, difficulty, impossibility". . . . In [Wordsworth's] poems . . . the political overtones of the word mingle strangely with the scientific, religious, and literary (or, more specifically, neo-Longinian) associations. . . . With one myth or another of Apocalypse floating in their heads, it is not surprising that the English Romantic theorists uniformly failed to provide lucid explanations of why "power" should tend to form one "idea" (or one polarity of ideas) in the mind. Hazlitt backed out of the difficulty by saying that there could be no "formal definition" of the idea, and the best that De Quincey could do was to suggest . . . that the continuity of all genuine "power" in the mind is "deep sympathy with truth."[18]

We could map the entire century along these central, if always elusive, lines: in terms of the search for that Protean essence Emerson celebrated as "elemental power." Poe's quest for a universal *prima mobilia* (initial force) should be included in that map, as should Melville's heaven-defying vision of a buried human power to be regained. No less relevant are Margaret Fuller's hope to "rouse the latent powers" of women and Whitman's persona as the bardic incarnation of American energy. Or we could jump forward to the end of the century. We must include Henry Adams's lifelong search for "the sequence of force," his wish to encourage new "mental powers" able to cope with an industrialized age, and William James's like-minded call for a new "topography of the limits of human power," his commitment to unlocking "the energies of men." And sufficient space must be left for all those various naturalistic, "universe of force theories" that became so prominent in America after the Civil War. Such theories were, Ronald Martin writes, able to be expanded, popularized, "glorified into cosmic philosophy" precisely because terms like force or energy were so inclusive, so "semantically imprecise" to begin with.[19]

We may conclude—hasty though this survey has been—that, if the century began with power as an indefinite, infinitely suggestive term, attracting a wide spectrum of minds (philosophers, poets, and scientists who never really agreed on what it meant), then it ended in a no less ambiguous way. "Force" and "energy" continued to draw large numbers of writers (and readers) despite the vagueness, the confusion of figurative and literal language, they encouraged. From its opening to its closing decades, from the Romantic emphasis on "interior force" to the deterministic vision of the self as merely one more point of energy in a hostile universe, power managed to retain its currency as one of the century's all-purpose master tropes. It enjoyed what Martin calls "an amazing career in nineteenth-century thought."[20] An always mutable idea, it was adapted to so many different uses that all modes of energy—even the most hypothetical of configurations—began to seem, as Kinnaird puts it, "continuous" and equally viable.

This will barely do, of course, even as a prefatory, thumbnail sketch of so large and recalcitrant a topic. But it is sufficient for our purposes. For if we focus on Emerson's persistent hunt for the elusory "motive power" propelling a dynamic world, it becomes clear that he hardly deserves the kind of indignant portrait Perry Miller and so many others have painted of Emerson the eccentric, the "utterly fantastic" Idealist, sequestered on the genteel sands of Boston, safely above the main currents of his time. His search after power marks him, rather, as a mind at the center of the nineteenth century's intellectual mainstream, a mind quintessentially of its time.

The assumption of my book is that Emerson is best understood when we begin to see him in this context. We gain a better grasp on a writer often pronounced ungraspable if we approach him as one of the nineteenth century's primary "philosophers of power" (a description that implies writers like Carlyle, Emerson, or Marx but is usually reserved solely for Nietzsche). Emerson's work needs to be seen as representative of a century's preoccupation with power, a preoccupation with force in all its myriad forms, that seems to remain constant (though ever shifting in emphasis) through what are usually regarded as distinct periods, from the age of Hazlitt to the age of Nietzsche.

One of the most significant and confusing aspects of Emerson's continuing reliance on power as a master term is that it occurs through the century's middle decades. Emersonian power occupies a pivotal position historically and thus seems to look both forward and backward in time, resonating with Wordsworthian as well as Nietzschean connotations. Sometimes it suggests purely spiritual or imaginative power, sometimes psychological (or unconscious) power, sometimes a Victorian enthusiasm for the force of will and character. Sometimes it aligns itself with the Darwinian, even the Marxist, notions of force. Or it denotes, in a way that makes Emerson the major precursor of Henry Adams, the great subterranean forces of culture, race, and sex and the potentially overwhelming forces of technology, economy, government, or war. Often the literal and figurative, the "hard" and "soft," connotations of power are conflated. Yet, for all of its overlapping implications, it seems to me that Emerson's attraction to power remains a fundamentally "Romantic" preoccupation (one inherited by Adams, James, and Nietzsche). It is, in other words, a preoccupation that originates in the mind's desire to test its own energies, to define its own will and capacities, by measuring them against some force other than its own.

Howard Mumford Jones summarized that endeavor as the Romantic attempt "to reach the utmost bounds of human life, to examine the human potential, and to judge it against the energy, incessant and inexplicable, of the universe. . . . Either the human personality would so expand itself that it could confront and perhaps control a dynamic universe or it must retreat before the demons of electricity, of steam, of earthquake, of tidal wave, or some other vast manifestation of cosmic power."[21] That description fits Emerson, and the vocation he chose for himself, perfectly. It would be difficult to come up with a better introduction to the drama, the large antagonism, that unfolds through the major essays.

This overview also suggests an important point that must be made regarding the particular approach I have taken. Like power itself, *Emerson and Power* is not one subject but many. Such a title implies a diverse array of potential topics and methodologies other than those I have chosen to pursue here. Power as a subject ramifies endlessly and so do the possible perspectives from which it might be studied. One could take up Emerson's theories of power from the perspective of the natural or physical sciences, political theory, theology, sociology, history, gender studies, or American studies—to name just a few alternatives. All are approaches that would undoubtedly yield valuable results.

My title, however, suggests one perspective in particular, an approach that has remained at the forefront of critical theory during the years in which this book was written and which therefore deserves some comment. I refer, of course, to the expectation now raised by any book or article with the word "power" in it: the expectation that it will be a Foucauldian interpretation, one premised on the currently fashionable, quasi-Nietzschean assumption (an assumption I do not share) that every text, every truth, can be reduced to a question of power (or an "ideology of power").

I do believe that setting a writer like Michel Foucault next to a writer like Emerson can be productive. The Foucauldian attempt to reach some critical vantage point free of the post-Enlightenment idea of "man" can be a valuable emetic for Emerson's relentless vindications of the human. (Santayana's Catholic skepticism about an anthropocentric Protestant-Romantic tradition serves a similar purpose.) And I have found Foucault and his speculations about an eighteenth- and nineteenth-century "military dream of society" useful in my attempt to explain Emerson's enthusiasm for the energies and creative discipline of war. But anyone who expects a Foucauldian reading (or a new historical deconstruction) of Emerson will be disappointed.

Someone else may wish to write such a book. My own concerns have led me, for the most part, to more traditional methods: close attention to Emerson's texts and a concurrent attempt to place them in the context of what used to be called "intellectual history." To some readers this may seem so rudimentary a procedure that it is not worth mentioning. To others it will seem theoretically regressive. I have taken, in other words, an approach that places me in a precarious middle ground. Those Emersonians who are not willing to accept the "Nietzschean" Emerson for which I argue will find that I have gone too far. Those who anticipate a Foucauldian excavation will conclude that I have not gone far enough.

I can only respond, to either objection, that "close reading" and "the history of ideas" are approaches that remain, in Emerson's case, unusually warranted. Those who are not familiar with Emerson criticism might assume that his essays have by now been read and reread as exhaustively as, say, *Moby-Dick* or *The Scarlet Letter*. Library shelves certainly appear to sag under an equivalent amount of commentary. But the commentary on Emerson is really not so equivalent. Nor can the history of his critical reception simply be described as yet another example of "the usual cycles of inflation and crash."[22] Emerson's reception history is, on the contrary, unique. The scholarship that surrounds him has (at least until his current revival) approached his work in a thoroughly equivocal spirit. It has always been unsure about the value of his actual writing and ideas, unsure about the degree of critical seriousness they merit. The study of Emerson seems, as a result, always to begin skeptically: there is always doubt about the degree of scrutiny or serious thought his texts should receive. This has meant that even those major essays routinely anthologized and dutifully assigned have remained largely, as Gertrude Hughes puts it, "underread." If the prose itself has been neglected, the ideas have often been similarly avoided or downplayed. Or they have been explained in terms of every intellectual context but that of their own immediate decades—upheld as beautiful examples of eternal wisdom or of a timeless God-intoxication or accounted for in terms of Berkeleian Idealism, Edwardsean enthusiasm, Cambridge Platonism, Vedantism, medieval mysticism, Spinozistic pantheism, or first-century Christianity.

This equivocal nature of Emerson's reception—the curious anti-Emerson bias of the traditional approach—has, it seems to me, placed current scholarship in an awkward situation. It means, to state it bluntly, that anyone who assumes that there is a trustworthy, standard reading of him (some generally agreed-on interpretation that will allow further historical, biographical, or theoretical work to proceed) will be risking his or her labor on a figure who is really not so clear, a figure who is, perhaps, only half there. Scholarship on any author always faces a similar obstacle, of course (it is a kind of scholarly "catch-22"), but in Emerson's case it exists in the extreme. It cannot be assumed that Emerson has received anything like the primary textual interpretation that Hawthorne or Melville has—or that such readings have now paved the way for newer or more elaborate methodologies. For Emerson has, in a crucial sense, just begun to be read. A quarter-century ago it might have been possible to discern the outlines of a standard or canonical reading, possible to rely on some generally agreed-on party line. Increasingly, however, any party-line understanding of Emerson seems to be disappearing. It is being replaced by a widening diversity of approaches, some of them not at all complementary.

My own reading of Emerson has convinced me that there are, for all the various and contradictory connotations of "power" that may crop up, fundamental patterns of empowerment in his essays, recurring patterns that give his work a singular unity. My principal goal has simply been to try to recover those patterns. I shall have succeeded if their existence has, by the book's end, been persuasively established. For the recognition of those deep structures of Emerson's thought has, I think, quite significant ramifications for any interpretation of his work—certainly for any of those various other approaches to Emersonian power that might be taken.

In its organization, this attempt to recover those patterns reflects Emerson's own tendency to return, tirelessly, to a central, abiding theme: to some vision of force, some form of use or work, some celebration of the "absorbing" or "assimilating power." What follows are variations on that single theme: a series of essays that keep circling back to the same topic. Each chapter comes back to the same idea (or family of ideas) but attempts to offer a slightly different perspective. Each tries to isolate and clarify fundamental, related patterns of thought. And each makes some attempt to place those patterns in what have seemed to me their appropriate contexts.

I have tried to suggest, as well, the difficulties—moral, philosophical, and stylistic—this kind of thinking presents.

I did not begin this study with any intention of making it a synthesis of critical opinion or a continuing dialogue with that opinion—not, at least, to any degree greater than what is usual in a work of interpretation. But it became increasingly clear to me that that is what it would have to be. My focus has therefore really been dual: both on Emerson and on the commentary that surrounds him. My reasons for allotting more space than is usual to other interpretations (interpretations with which I both agree and disagree) has, finally, little to do with the academic rituals that make attention to reception history mandatory. They lie, rather, in the peculiar situation of Emerson's reception. The "Emerson Image," as Lawrence Buell calls it, simply looms so large and has so effectively limited our understanding of him that it has been necessary to confront it head on and to make my frequent disagreement with that tradition, at the very least, my secondary theme.

One more point needs to be stressed at the outset. The argument I make is intended to apply primarily to Emerson's essays. This is not to imply that the patterns of empowerment prevailing in the essays are absent from those other genres in which he labored so prolifically. But it is the essays that have remained, always, the focus of my attention. Even when I have shifted that focus to the journals, the letters, the early lectures, or the late, generally neglected, essays, my aim has been to shed additional light on the surprisingly consistent imaginative patterns underlying those works for which he is best known.

I realize that there are many who believe Emerson's greatest accomplishment lies not in the essays but in his collected journals, even in his poetry. Such claims may be correct: the sixteen volumes of the *Journals and Miscellaneous Notebooks* may truly be Emerson's final masterpiece. Yet this kind of revisionary estimation of his worth raises a host of subtle problems. They are wholly unobjectionable, indeed commendable, claims in theory, but they are problematic given the history of Emerson's reception. For there is, in the tradition of Emerson criticism, an extraordinarily stubborn tendency to look away from, to look at everything but, the major texts themselves. There is a persistent impatience with his texts, an anxious readiness to believe that there is some essential deficiency at the heart of his reputation—an incoherence, a naïveté, which demands that his real significance be sought elsewhere. That elsewhere may reside in the nobilities of his personal character, in his sheer historical importance, his varied influence, his usefulness as a barometer or encyclopedia for the ideas and prejudices of his time, or in the actual story of loss and overcoming to be found in his biography. There is hardly, of course, in principle, anything at all problematic about the pursuit of such necessary lines of inquiry. But Emerson's case creates its own sui generis problems. Time and again the attempt to go outside the text, or around, over, or beneath it, has been premised on an assumption that has only hindered understanding—the assumption that something is fundamentally lacking in those major essays themselves.

Thus Lawrence Rosenwald's valuable attempt to argue for the journals as Emerson's masterwork begins in the conviction that the essays lack "an organizing poetic power," that their "notorious critical abstractions" can be forgiven if we shift our attention to the unexpurgated journals. Or Evelyn Barish's illuminating reconstruction of Emerson's youth begins in the belief that there is an "unfathomable serenity," an "impenetrable" manner, an alien surface to his prose that can be breached only by recovering the full complexity of his life. It is grotesque, yet entirely typical of Emerson scholarship, that one of his most recent biographers should regard his poem on the death of his son—not any one of his books, not any one of the essays—as his most successful and enduring work of art.[23]

There exists, in short, ample reason for simply reaffirming, particularly at this moment in Emerson's resurrection, the achievement and centrality of the essays. They seem to me to require no apology. They contain, in ways we have only just begun to appreciate, sufficient tension, coherence, expressive skill—sufficient humanity and psychological insight—to make them an unequaled achievement in and of themselves.

CHAPTER

1

The Anti-Emerson Tradition

> Melville and Whitman persuasively strive to give us the substance promised by their titles: grass and a whale, earth and the sea are delivered. . . . But Emerson? Is there not something cloudy at the center of his reputation, something fatally faded about the works he has left us? When, I ask myself, did I last read one of his celebrated essays? How much, indeed, are Emerson's works even assigned in literary courses where the emphasis is not firmly historical?
>
> —*John Updike, "Emersonianism" (1984)*

In 1982 Alfred Kazin worried that criticism had for too long underestimated or overlooked entirely Ralph Waldo Emerson's "central concern with power": "There is no book that truly does justice to Emerson's sense of power"; "[T]here is no satisfactory book on Emerson's mind itself and his relation to the romantic, bourgeois, 'progressive' sense of individual power that became the stock gospel of the nineteenth century." A scant five years later, in a reinterpretation of Emerson, Richard Poirier complained that the study of "power"—indeed, the word itself—had become a cliché: "Thanks mostly to Foucault and his followers, the word 'power' has become tiresomely recurrent in discussions of cultural forms or the order of things." But, Poirier hastened to add—and his own "Emersonian reflections" are cogent testimony—power is "nonetheless unavoidable in any consideration of Emerson."[1]

Such diverse progress reports indicate how much has been happening inside the "Emerson industry" in the past decade and a half. The 1980s mark a definite turning point for Emerson criticism. The changes that have taken place in our understanding and valuation of his work might well, as Lawrence Buell has noted, astonish even those who would once have considered themselves Emerson's defenders.

Salutation and Dismissal

The revived emphasis on "Emerson's stature as a pivotal American cultural hero" is one manifestation of that transformation. For Kazin, Emerson

is "the father of us all"—the "teacher of the American tribe." For Harold
Bloom, Emerson is "the mind of our climate; he is the principal source of
the American difference in poetry and criticism and in pragmatic post-
philosophy. . . . [He] is the inescapable theorist of virtually all subsequent
American writing. From his moment to ours, American authors either are
in his tradition, or else in a countertradition originating in opposition to
him." Emerson's influence has been so extensive, Poirier argues, "that his
works now constitute a compendium of iconographies that have gotten
into American writers who may never have liked or even read him." For
Denis Donoghue and Joel Porte, Emerson remains "the founding father of
nearly everything we think of as American in the modern world": "To the
extent to which the sentiments of power, self-reliance, subjectivity, and independence attract to themselves a distinctly American nuance, its source
is Emerson." For Stanley Cavell, Emerson is, along with Thoreau, the ("repressed") "founder" of American thinking. "When we trace the history of
American literature or of American ideas," John Michael writes, "we re-
trace the influence of Emerson." He was, David Bromwich suggests, simply one of history's great men who irrevocably altered American culture.[2]

Such testimonials may sound, Buell writes, "pushed to an extreme." But
they are not new. Emerson was only thirty-five years old and the author of
one slim book when Harriet Martineau reported back to her English and
European readers that it was not "too much to say that the United States
cannot be fully known" without knowing Emerson. In 1850 Theodore
Parker dubbed him "the most American of our writers" and the one with
the greatest reputation. Walt Whitman called him "the actual beginner of
the whole procession," the writer who would always be "nearest" to his
country. "Mr. Emerson always draws," James Russell Lowell remarked of
his popularity as a lecturer; "Few men have been so much to so many." In
the 1880s Matthew Arnold surveyed the century that was drawing to a
close and pronounced Wordsworth's "the most important work done in
verse" and Emerson's *Essays* "the most important work done in prose."[3]

Emerson is, John Dewey said at the turn of the century, "the prophet
and herald of any system which democracy may henceforth construct . . .
when democracy has articulated itself, it will have no difficulty in finding
itself already proposed in Emerson." To John Jay Chapman, Emerson
seemed "the first modern man," looming "above his age like a colossus . . .
towering like Atlas over the culture of the United States." Henry James
would speak of him as "the first, and the one really rare, American spirit
in letters." He is, George Woodberry claimed in 1907, "the only great
mind that America has produced in literature." Even during the Modernist
decades, when T. S. Eliot proposed that Emerson be "carved joint from
joint," it was still not difficult to argue that he had "obtained a recognition
such as no other of his countrymen can claim." "It becomes more and
more apparent," Paul Elmer More wrote in 1921, "that Emerson, judged
by an international or even by a true national standard, is the outstandin~

figure of American literature." "The leader of these minds," Lewis Mumford said five years later—referring to the writers of that epoch that F. O. Matthiessen would call "the American Renaissance"—"the central figure of them all, was Ralph Waldo Emerson."[4]

From the late 1830s on, Emerson has always been perceived as an American cultural hero, although our willingness to accept such putative heroes has varied dramatically. (Heroes, Emerson was well aware, are destined to become bores.) But there seems never to have been a time when Emerson's critics have questioned for very long his historical importance or have forgotten his significance as either a benign or a destructive influence on other American writers. ("America produced him," Barrett Wendell wrote in 1900, "and whether you like him or not, he is bound to live." "We must take Emerson into the bargain," Charles Feidelson conceded in 1953, "whether we like it or not.") Emerson has always been accorded what D. H. Lawrence called "museum-interest."[5]

What has changed over the years is, quite simply, the complexity that critics have been willing to ascribe to Emerson's writing and ideas. If, a quarter-century ago, the contours of Emerson scholarship were "reassuringly clear" (even, as Buell puts it, "cozy," like a Brahmin parlor), then those contours have been and continue to be radically stretched and refashioned or abandoned altogether. The boundaries that seemed, in the mid-1960s, firmly to prescribe both the value accorded his work and the historical context in which he was to be comprehended have been so expanded that it is now possible to say, as Emerson scholars do increasingly, that there appears to be much in Emerson that has been blunted, much that has still to surface, much that we have not been able or willing to see. Emerson is, Cavell writes, still far from "settled." Or, as David Marr puts it, "it is at least possible that much of Emerson's significance has eluded us, that there is [still] a literary-philosophical narrative of Emersonianism to be written." We need, Peter Carafiol writes, to find "other terms" and "a new place for Transcendentalism, or a new notion of Transcendentalism to go in the old place."[6]

The transformations that have occurred in Emerson criticism can all be described, it seems to me, as playing some part in that broad movement that Buell has christened the "de-Transcendentalizing" of Emerson. That Emerson's detranscendentalizing has gone hand in hand with an increasing respect for his work is no accident, for the perception of Emerson as essentially "Transcendentalist"—always the predominant public image of him, an image still stubbornly embedded in much Emerson scholarship—has always been what Porte calls "a positive hindrance" to the appreciation of his writing. Porte put it this way, in a remarkable admission, in 1973:

> What I am prepared to state categorically is that the familiar rubrics of
> Emersonian thought, the stock in trade of most Emerson criticism, though
> undeniably there, are a positive hindrance to the enjoyment of Emerson's

writing. Though some Emersonians will undoubtedly continue until the end of time to chew over such concepts as Compensation, the Over-Soul, Correspondence, Self-Reliance, Spiritual Laws, et id genus omne, the trouble with such things is that they are not very interesting. They make Emerson seem awfully remote, abstract, and—yes—academic. My experience has been that when these topics are mentioned the mind closes, one's attention wanders.[7]

That one of Transcendentalism's preeminent scholars never doubted, some twenty years ago, that such dullness does indeed lie at the heart of Emerson's thought says much about our main tradition of Emerson scholarship. Even more telling is the failure of Porte's critique to elicit, as far as I am aware, even a single direct response or rejoinder from Emerson scholars. It could still simply be taken for granted, in 1973, that much of Emerson's thought was a closed book—essentially "transcendental" (easily classifiable under the familiar Transcendentalist catchwords) and too tedious to merit any serious reflection (though continuing to supply the material for an endless succession of scholarship).

"As any candid teacher of American literature can report," Porte concluded, "[Emerson] has manifestly *not* made his way 'on the strength of his message.' He has become the least appreciated, least enjoyed, least understood—indeed, least read—of America's unarguably major writers." (Emerson is, William Dean Howells concluded in 1900, "the most misunderstood man in America.") In other words, a great deal is still to be done in arguing for Emerson's inherent worth. In these "new historical" days such "recanonizing," as Cavell speaks of it, may appear distinctly old-fashioned, but the ambivalent way in which Emerson has been canonized makes it necessary.[8]

My point is not that Porte was imperceptive or even wrong, for he actually records a valuable perception about the way our major tradition of Emerson criticism has dehistoricized, simplified, and devalued Emerson and has made him seem dull, much more parochial, and much less complicated than he is. The same tradition that has ensured Emerson's continuing canonization, while never failing to uphold his historical importance, has, when it turned to his work itself, generally found little reason for *any longer* taking Emerson seriously as a writer or a thinker. There exists, David Robinson notes, "the uneasy feeling among historians of American thought and literature that Emerson's influence outdistances his achievement." Porte puts succinctly the value most critics have accorded Emerson "the Transcendentalist": worthy of preservation as the source of historical attention, but inherently objectionable or uninteresting. This attitude underlies most Emerson criticism, whether it is the outright condemnation by his enemies or the patronizing or vague disapproval of his friends. ("We turn to him," one Emerson scholar writes, "as to an amiable lunatic who seems to tell us whatever it is we think we want to hear.")[9]

In his canonization, as in so many things, Emerson presents a productive test case for the various theory and culture wars now being waged. Emerson is indeed a well-canonized American writer. But what does that mean? Is there a difference between canonization in one's own lifetime (early in it) and canonization after one's death? What are the ramifications of a canonization that is also, as it undoubtedly has been in Emerson's case, a "sanctification" as "the unshakably serene and satisfied," the "bloodless or nebulous" Sage of Concord?[10] Is there a difference between literary reputation in America and canonization in, say, England or France? Does canonization imply appreciation or condescension, or both? Does it impede or quicken public and academic understanding?

Emerson is, O. W. Firkins concluded in 1915, "at the same time honored and forsaken." Or, as he dryly restated it in 1933: "[Emerson] is certain of the due toll of inscriptions, invocations, appraisements, and obeisances—of that form of greeting from posterity which combines salutation with dismissal." Peter Carafiol reaches the same conclusion in a more recent backward glance at Emerson scholarship. The ambivalent terms in which Emerson's so-called Transcendentalism has been received may, Carafiol goes on to suggest, lie more "in the peculiarities of scholarship about Transcendentalism . . . than in Transcendentalism itself."[11]

> Assertions of Emerson's centrality and discomfort with it have gone hand in hand in Transcendentalist scholarship from the start. In 1876, O. B. Frothingham argued that "by sheer force of genius Emerson anticipated the results of the transcendental philosophy, defined its axioms and ran out their inferences to the end." But he complained that "Mr. Emerson's place is among poetic, not among philosophic minds." In one of the first "academic" studies, H. C. Goddard found Emerson's writing marred by absurd and unpoetic figures, and subsequent scholars have seen him as too abstract, too detached, or lacking in philosophical rigor. Even the most respected of Transcendentalism's modern commentators sometimes seem to hold the subject in something not far short of contempt. Lawrence Buell, for example, chastises the Transcendentalists for their "awkward and inchoate style" and "half-baked content," and the editors of Emerson's Works seem uncertain about how to evaluate him. They praise his earlier writing for its "absolute literary merit" but seem uncomfortable with the "excesses" of its "irrational eloquence." They apparently prefer the "dispassionate depth and balance" of the later work.[12]

According him equal parts reverence and contempt was a well-established convention in Emerson's own time, and it has continued, through a long line of distinguished scholars, to the present. "*Almost* everyone," as Cavell remarks, "gets around to condescending to Emerson." Orestes Brownson's 1838 defense of Emerson's controversial "Divinity School Address" is a notable, early example of that traditional condescension:

Brownson defended Emerson's good intentions and benevolent influence but apologized for "the puerility of his concepts," "the affectations of his style," and "the unphilosophical character of his speculations." Such backhanded compliments continued in John Morley's conclusion, in 1881, that "Emersonian transcendentalism" must be regarded as "gospel" rather than "philosophy proper" and in W. C. Brownell's concession that Emerson had no artistry, "no sense of composition."[13]

T. S. Eliot launched a forthright attack on Transcendentalist foolishness, but there was no less disdain in Perry Miller's remark, in 1940, that Emerson's ideas were "too utterly fantastic to be any longer taken seriously." In the 1950s, Leslie Fiedler characterized Emerson as a writer of considerable historical "though not often sympathetic interest, who erected a notable monument to an insufficient view of life." More recently, Lawrence Buell has concluded that "Emerson and his circle *are* more important for historical reasons than for the quality of their achievements in art, philosophy, and theology." "It is hard to suppose," Irving Howe remarked in 1986, "that anyone could now take Emerson as a sufficient moral or philosophical guide—and impossible to suppose that anyone could find him very helpful in understanding the span of Western history between the time of his death and the present."[14]

Emerson's canonization has been, then, double-edged. Always granted museum-interest, he has in the same ambivalent motion been raised to the pedestal as a Transcendentalist-idealist saint and put down as, in William Dean Howells's phrase, "a national joke" ("all that was most hopelessly impossible, . . . the type of the incomprehensible, the byword of the poor paragrapher"). This is not only, as Howells saw it, Emerson's image in "the popular mind" but also the foundation for most Emerson criticism. It has resulted in what Cavell justly identifies as that still "fixated critical gesture toward Emerson both on the part of his friends and of his enemies."[15]

That gesture is twofold. It consists of "denying to Emerson the title of philosopher" (even, in most cases, the title of serious or morally complex thinker) and of describing Emerson's prose as, on the whole, a second- or third-rate failure, "a kind of mist or fog." In 1903 Dewey was already impatient with this "old story" that "puts away" Emerson as neither an artist nor a philosopher. That fixated critical gesture has been repeated so often by so many of Emerson's "friends" that it is not too much to say that Emerson's canonization has been a curse as well as a blessing and not an exaggeration to characterize the dominant tradition of Emerson criticism as also an anti-Emerson tradition. It is as if Emerson scholarship has thoroughly internalized, consciously or unconsciously, T. S. Eliot's caveat that Emerson was not "individually," or intrinsically, "very important" and "ought to be made to look very foolish."[16]

A long, venerable, and continuing critical tradition has decided that

Emerson is primarily not a philosopher, thinker, or writer but the preacher of a New England gospel (a semimystical figure steeped in the atmosphere of religion). This idealizing, moralizing, transcendentalizing Emerson is the patron saint of those who seek to retire upward to a life of the spirit—to a "spiritual transcendence," as Philip Gura puts it, that takes us away from our "surroundings," away from "the things of this world." ("Transcendentalism" has, of course, always been a highly problematic description. In chapter 6 I shall have more to say about it and about the "Transcendentalist Image" of Emerson to which I refer here.) It is important to demarcate clearly and keep in mind this interpretation of Emerson, for it would seem, as Cavell notes, that "[i]f you insist on this view you will seem to find a world of evidence to support it." (And if you have settled on this definition of Emerson, then it is no longer necessary, or even very interesting, to ask again what Emerson thought. More important, then, are biographical questions, questions of textual history, questions about the immediate theological or social history that surrounds him.)[17]

But a crucial question needs to be raised. Can we say that a scholarly tradition has given an author a fair hearing, a hearing fair enough to establish what can be called a standard or canonical evaluation, if the interpretation it offers habitually denies the intrinsic value of his work? Does a critical tradition that has, for more than a century and a half, relegated "the quality of [Emerson's] achievement in art, philosophy, or theology" to secondary importance deserve to remain the dominant approach? Did it ever?

For there have been important counterstrains in the history of Emerson's reception, responses to what Porte calls "the problem of Emerson" that represent major alternatives. These approaches have judged Emerson's writing to have the highest intrinsic value aesthetically, philosophically, culturally, even politically, and have stressed an Emerson far different from the idealist-organicist-Transcendentalist preacher. The past quarter-century of the Emerson "revival" has witnessed the rapid expansion of those countertraditions, and it is now clear that a new canonization of Emerson is under way, that a new narrative of his importance as an artist and thinker is being written. The goal is still to answer the prolix, Emerson sphinx: Emerson as ungraspable (Henry James Sr.), as "elusive, irreducible" (Henry James Jr.), as a writer "who retains so much secrecy" (Cavell). The goal is still, as Jonathan Bishop phrased it in 1964, to identify "a central core of imaginative activity that will throw into intelligible relief the multitudinous details of doctrine and rhetoric" among "the broken sequences of essays, the scattered poems, the large numbers of letters and journals, the overlapping continuities of published and manuscript material."[18]

What has changed is what criticism has taken as that central core. Emerson the Transcendentalist prophet of the (young, history-evading,

American) soul increasingly gives way to Emerson the redoubtable writer, Emerson the mainstream nineteenth-century (and pre-twentieth-century) thinker, Emerson the philosopher, Emerson the theorist of power, Emerson the pragmatist (an allusion often made but infrequently explored), Emerson the "cultural critic," Emerson the (still-timely) literary theorist ("essentially a philosopher of language and literature"), Emerson the still-vital defender of the "theory of free being" (an achievement that is still underestimated, overshadowed as it has been by the perception of Emerson as an idealizing escapist), Emerson the vitally historical thinker who views experience not in terms of the individual's "transcendent relation to his surroundings" (Gura) but "in terms of [the] relations and interactions" of this world (Cornel West).[19]

Porte, for example, helped to redirect that major tradition of Emerson criticism that finds insufficient artistic sense in his work by emphasizing Emerson's brilliant "manipulations of language and figure." Emerson's "interest and appeal," Porte argued, "reside in the imaginative materials and structure of his writing—in his tropes and topoi, his metaphors and verbal wit, in the remarkable consistencies of his conceiving mind and executing hand."[20] Porte's *Representative Man: Ralph Waldo Emerson in His Time* (1979) was followed closely by Barbara Packer's *Emerson's Fall: A New Interpretation of the Major Essays* (1982) and by the works of a number of critics who have returned successfully to the intricacies of Emerson's writing with the kind of sensitivity to metaphor and language that would once have been considered irrelevant in the face of Emerson's allegedly inartistic style.

"Why has America never expressed itself philosophically? Or has it—in the metaphysical riot of its greatest literature?" That was the groundbreaking question first posed by Stanley Cavell in *The Senses of Walden* (originally published in 1972). Thoreau's masterpiece was, Cavell suggested, "a book of sufficient intellectual scope and consistency to have established or inspired a tradition of thinking." At first put off by Emerson in the way most twentieth-century critics have been ("[Emerson] kept sounding to me like a second-hand Thoreau"), Cavell soon renounced his original bias and turned his attention to recovering Emerson as a "founding" American thinker and a central nineteenth-century mind. Cavell's commitment to putting Emerson into the company of Wittgenstein, Heidegger, Spengler, Freud, Descartes, Kant, or Nietzsche represents a notable breakthrough—not because Emerson has never been paired with most of these writers but because Cavell's powerful essays have none of the condescension toward Emerson that heretofore characterized such comparisons.[21]

Generally, the dominant (and anti-Emerson) critical tradition, as I have characterized it, has felt comfortable chiding Emerson for misinterpreting Kant or for temperamentally lacking the profundity of a Coleridge or Nietzsche. Even more predictable is the still almost inevitable comparison that finds Emerson incapable of the moral complexity of a Melville, Hawthorne, or Henry James. Emerson scholarship has traditionally looked skeptically on the importation of foreign names onto New England soil. (It still comes as a surprise to many Americanists that Nietzsche ever admired or even read Emerson.) But, as Cavell reminds us, Nietzsche's lifelong engagement with Emerson's essays may well be considered a conduit for Emerson's influence on later European intellectual tradition (Heidegger especially), just as Coleridge's or Carlyle's engagement with German writing was originally a conduit for Kant or Fichte into England and America.[22] Since his first essay on Emerson in 1978, Cavell has made it possible to approach the question, "What did Emerson think?" with a seriousness never before maintained. He has pushed the issue of Emerson as a philosopher (and the requestioning of what philosophy is or can be) to the forefront of Emerson criticism, and he has argued that the tone and terms of the discussion will need to be more sophisticated than ever before.

In the wake of Cavell's work there have appeared several studies, most notably by Poirier, that, if not directly indebted to Cavell, have avoided the patronizing tone of most previous criticism and, without apology, have taken Emerson as a central resource in what Giles Gunn calls our current "culture of criticism." Several complex social, literary, and academic factors have contributed to this revival. If the reediting of Emerson's journals, essays, lectures, letters, and sermons that began in 1959 constitutes its foundation, then the widespread revaluation of Romantic thought and writing (exemplified in the work of Northrop Frye, M. H. Abrams, Paul de Man, Geoffrey Hartman, Harold Bloom, and, most recently, Cavell) has provided an atmosphere in which Emerson can be reaffirmed (in what Hartman calls a counter-"emigration of ideas from within") as a key American answer to the massive influence of Continental and post-Modernist theory. European and deconstructive theorists, situated within the context of an American, Emersonian tradition, can appear as "belatedly catching up with the illuminating discoveries of our great creative writers."[23]

The most vulnerable side to the dominant tradition of Emerson criticism has always been its provincialism. "Emerson scholarship," Kazin writes, "is fiercely local. . . . [It] is intense and minuscule." Emerson's stolid Transcendentalist image and our underestimation of American culture generally have made us reluctant to count him among those "North Atlantic cultural critics who set the agenda and terms for understanding the modern world." The commitment to recovering Emerson's place in American tradition has too often merged confusedly with the misperception of Emerson as a timeless "mystagogue" (James Russell Lowell's word) and has denied his work a place in the mainstream of nineteenth-century thought. That denial has exerted such a tenacious hold that even some of our most formidable critics continue to see Emerson as at heart a displaced, first-century Christian or as a New England anachronism with little or nothing to tell us about the larger course of post-Enlightenment thought or history.[24] Cornel West puts well the point I wish to make. Those approaches, he writes, that have stressed Emerson's American context (and have emphasized Emerson's "flight from history, his rejection of the past, his refusal of authority") have, however valuable in themselves, helped to blind us to Emerson's broader significance.

> Unfortunately, these influential . . . readings of Emerson hide the degree to which Emerson's perspective is infused with historical consciousness; they also conceal his seminal reflections on power. These interpretive blindnesses result, in part, from situating Emerson in the age of the American literary renaissance (along with Hawthorne, Melville, Thoreau, and Whitman) rather than relating him to the European explosions (both intellectual and social) that produced Karl Marx, John Stuart Mill, Thomas Carlyle, and Friedrich Nietzsche. We can no longer afford or justify confining Emerson to the American terrain. He belongs to that highbrow cast of North Atlantic cultural critics who set the agenda and the terms for understanding the modern world.[25]

At the same time that Emerson the "representative American" comes to seem "acutely marginal" from the polemical perspective of the new historicism, he is being recanonized as an inexpendable participant in that mid- and late-nineteenth-century debate over power, culture, and history waged by writers like Carlyle, Marx, Nietzsche, or Henry Adams. It is a detranscendentalizing, a redemption from an insular Transcendentalist image that has for too long postponed our appreciation of Emerson's significance and artistry. West postulates an Emerson important for his "seminal reflections on power," an Emerson important for his preoccupation with determining "the scope of human powers and the contingency of human societies," an Emerson who struggled (exactly as Carlyle had) to find his vocation as a new kind of "cultural critic" or "theorist of power" (an intellectual vocation unprecedented before the nineteenth century) and then attempted to formulate "a conception of power" that could enable "himself and others to respond to the crises of his day."[26]

Emerson is significant, West argues, for his influential, pragmatic evasion of a transcendental/epistemology-centered philosophy as "antiquated, anachronistic, and outdated" in a century that needed a new kind of "philosopher of power."[27] West is thus the latest in a series of critics who have de-emphasized Emerson as a seeker of a transcendent truth or cosmic unity and stressed instead the essentially agonistic nature of his thought. Emerson was committed, Carolyn Porter writes, "not [to] a soaring transcendence, but a perpetual resistance." "The Emersonian quest," Gertrude Hughes concludes, is "after power, not after truth"; "Emerson's essays are designed to empower rather than to instruct." Charles Feidelson believed that Emerson's "characteristic form" was "an autonomous series of visionary events." But the Emersonian "self," as Poirier contends, does not come about in an autonomous or visionary act of "reflection" or transcendence. It is pressured into existence as a reaction to something else: "The self can . . . be located here and now, not by reflection but, so far as Emerson and William James are concerned, by virtue of 'acts.' These acts are variously named—'resistance,' 'antagonism,' 'transition,' 'abandonment.' None has to do with compliance. They are *reactive*." Or, as Donoghue puts it, writing of *Nature*: "Not knowledge but power is its aim; not truth but command." Emerson is, Eric Cheyfitz observes, our "devout psychologist of power": "throughout his work the term ['power'] is as omnipresent as the Deity itself." "Power," Bloom writes, is "Emerson's key term."[28]

This mid-nineteenth-century "theoretician of power" (as Bloom calls him) is my subject. Clearly the time has been right for several years now for the collective reinterpretation of Emerson committed to clarifying that synthesis of disparate, often warring, elements that accounts for what Edmund Wilson called the "dynamic" nature of Emerson's thought. The time is propitious for a rereading of Emerson's work in light of his unchanging conviction that "Power is the first good" (W, 8:272)—and for a recovery of what Richard Grusin calls "the structure of Emersonian action."[29]

The poststructuralist obsession with demystification and deidealizing has, to be sure, helped to make possible Emerson's detranscendentalization. The post-Foucauldian obsession with the study of history and texts as scenes of power struggles has made power the latest ("tiresomely recurrent") catchword. The present moment might, in fact, be defined by its "disenchantment with transcendental conceptions of philosophy"—a skepticism that "has led to a preoccupation with the relation of knowledge and power" and a "small-scale intellectual renascence . . . under the broad banner of pragmatism."[30] Because such transformations have done much to generate a renewed concern for Emerson the pragmatic philosopher of power, it is important to make clear—without denying the influence of poststructuralist thought—that I believe the detranscendentalizing of Emerson I advocate is an act of historical recovery. I do not regard it as merely a social construction of the late twentieth century, as the product of the latest-model deidealizing in order to squeeze out one more in an infinite number of possible Emersons. My approach, in short, though it will explore central strains in Emerson's thought that may be called antitranscendental or deconstructive or antifoundationalist, is in itself quite foundationalist. I believe, in other words, that there really exists a primary and definitive aspect of Emerson's thought that has been, as Cavell and Poirier put it, "repressed" by the critical-philosophical establishment.

Equally foundationalist is my assumption that there was such a thing as "Romanticism" and that there is a family of intellectual problems and tendencies which define a distinctively nineteenth-century (more accurately, a post-Kantian) tradition. It is a presupposition of this study that "there arose significantly new forms of thought and standards for evaluation in the post-Enlightenment period, and that these not only marked a radically new epoch in intellectual history but came to dominate almost all schools of European thought for something over one hundred years."[31] It is necessary to insist on such a context because Emerson has so often been left out of it.

Henry James, Santayana, Dewey

Interpretations of Emerson as most vitally a theorist of action or power have existed since the nineteenth century, though they have always been kept in check as critical countertraditions by the weight of the Transcendentalist image or that Modernist/New Critical, anti-Romantic prejudice that has only given way, as far as Emerson is concerned, in the last twenty-five years. Surely there is some significance in the ability of Nietzsche, William James, and Dewey (major proponents or inheritors of that nineteenth-century transnational tradition that produced philosophies of will) to place a far greater value on both Emerson's art and thought than has that line of scholars who have accepted Emerson as a Transcendentalist.

Nietzsche saluted Emerson as one of the century's "masters of prose" (GS, 92) and regretted that America lacked an academic culture capable of providing "some strict discipline, a really scientific education" in philosophy. Nietzsche's lament—"As it is, in Emerson, we have *lost a philosopher*"—is quite the opposite of the common scholarly conclusion that finds Emerson temperamentally or intellectually incapable of philosophical thought. Indeed, for Nietzsche, Emerson was a "brother soul," an intellectual twin. "Never have I felt so much at home in a book," he wrote of Emerson's essays, "and in *my* home, as—I may not praise it, it is too close to me." Emerson was, he declared, "the author who has been richest in ideas in this century so far."[32]

For Matthew Arnold, Emerson's prose was, as it has been for so many critics since, an embarrassment: "Unsound it is, indeed, and in a style almost impossible to a born man of letters." Henry James returned a similar verdict: Emerson never found his proper "form"; his writings "were not composed at all." But for William James, Emerson was, above all, a consummate *writer:* "[I]f we must define him in one word, we have to call him Artist"—"[his] mission culminated in his style." "No previous literary artist," James claimed, had achieved "such penetratingly persuasive tones." Even the essence of Emerson's message (that "the point of any pen can be an epitome of reality") was best captured, for James, in a writer's metaphor.[33]

Dewey, too, championed Emerson's "concentration of form and effect." Dewey's brief, but astute, 1903 defense of Emerson has remained, until

Emerson's recent revival, the most serious argument for Emerson's continuing importance.[34] It is today remembered primarily for its description of Emerson as "the Philosopher of Democracy" (the whole phrase is "not only a philosopher, but . . . the Philosopher of Democracy"), but it merits far closer attention than it has received. It is particularly relevant for my own argument because Dewey begins in the recognition that Emerson is, first of all, in need of defense from both literary critics and philosophers. Any appreciation of Emerson, Dewey insists, must begin with a clear sense of the false limitations imposed by Emerson's reception-history. Anticipating Cavell's hypothesis of a twofold "fixated critical gesture toward Emerson," Dewey suggests that we must first avoid "the condescending patronage by literary critics"—the usual, easy accusations of incoherence—as well as the habitual rejection of the possibility that Emerson's writing could constitute philosophy. The problem, Dewey argues, lies not in any "lack of method" or artistry on Emerson's part but in the stupidity of critics and professors of philosophy.[35]

Dewey continues his defense by dissociating Emerson from the "remotenesses" of "the transcendentalists." Emerson only borrows from them, Dewey says, certain idioms, "certain pigments and delineations." Emerson was not a "Platonist" or "idealist" but achieved a new kind of synthesis that "reduced" the names and ideas associated with those movements to a new philosophy—he put them to use in the service of his own experiential, pragmatic interests, put them to "the test of trial by the service rendered the present and immediate experience." Plato and Platonism may appear as elements in Emerson's writing, but it would be wrong to take Emerson's thought as, therefore, immaculately or chiefly Platonic or transcendental: Emerson was not interested in "the immanence of absolute ideas in the world," in "any Reality that is beyond or behind or in any way apart," or in "the reputed transcendental worth of an overweening Beyond and Away."[36]

To claim him for the Transcendentalist-Idealist party amounts, in Dewey's eyes, to Emerson's unjustified appropriation by a conservative, Brahmin class: it means "embezzling" him away from the democratic and pragmatic tradition ("the common man" and "the common store") to which he properly belongs. The misrepresentation of Emerson's thought as transcendentalism not only robs his work of sustaining interest and artistic credibility but also leaves him vulnerable to unfair moral and political attack. Emerson, Dewey insists, "drew the line which marks him off from transcendentalism—which is the idealism of a Class."[37]

Dewey's vision of an ongoing battle between a democratic and an elite, "embezzling" class—with Emerson's reputation at stake—undoubtedly reflects his own commitment to civic activism. Dewey opposed any philosophy or intellectual tradition that could deteriorate into "an esthetic appreciation carried on by a refined class or a capitalistic possession of a few learned specialists."[38] Clearly much could be gained if Dewey, still early in his career, could demonstrate that Emerson was not the fastidious idealist—as Emerson's critics were painting him—but Dewey's true pragmatic and "instrumentalist" precursor. It would be wrong, however, to construe his essay as merely "a creative misreading of Emerson," an attempt to dress Emerson "in Deweyan garb."[39] For Dewey's portrait of Emerson (first delivered in the same month as William James's speech at Concord and as Santayana's Harvard address on "Emerson the Poet") needs to be set in the context of that pivotal, still influential, reassessment of Emerson's legacy that was being waged throughout the three or four decades after his death. That "second stage" of Emerson studies, which began in 1882, had already witnessed an even more intense apotheosization of an otherworldly Emerson than had occurred in his own lifetime; it would culminate in 1911, when Santayana eloquently banished Emerson's memory to the pale regions of "the genteel tradition"—an association that has stuck securely to the Emerson image.[40]

Dewey was, in 1903, waging a rear-guard but necessary battle. He was attempting to counter the burgeoning mystical-transcendental image of Emerson, attempting to rescue and articulate for the twentieth century an Emerson who was disappearing behind the relentless characterizations of him as provincial, clerical, Brahminical, the declaimer of a fragile or empty idealism.

Empty, vacant—the image is invoked repeatedly in Henry James's and Santayana's portrayals of Emerson. For James, Emerson's memory evoked an unforgettable series of "impressions" of New England's cultural barrenness. "Emerson's personal history," he recalled, could be "condensed into the single word Concord, and all the condensation in the world will not make it look rich." He continued, in his 1888 essay, to associate Emerson with the "terrible paucity of alternatives," the "achromatic picture" his environment presented him. As far as James was concerned, the whole "Concord school" had, as Matthiessen notes, "enacted a series of experiments in the void." Emerson's "special capacity for moral experience"—which for James meant Emerson's "ripe unconsciousness of evil," his inability "to look at anything but the soul"—was the result of his coming to maturity in a community that "had to seek its entertainment, its rewards and consolations, almost exclusively in the moral world." The "decidedly lean Boston" of Emerson's day was self-enclosed, an island above the extremes of common human experience.[41]

Emerson's limited moral world was, like the "New England [of] fifty years ago," sealed off, perpetually untested by the "beguilements and prizes" of experience. Boston existed serenely, James writes (and he means Boston to stand for Emerson), "like a ministry without an opposition." It was no surprise, then, that his eyes were "thickly bandaged" to all "sense of the dark, the foul, the base," no surprise that there was "a certain inadequacy and thinness in [Emerson's] enumerations" and "quaint animad-version[s]." "We get the impression," James concludes, "of a conscience gasping in the void, panting for sensations, with something of the movement of the gills of a landed fish."[42]

Santayana was even more explicit about the hermetic nature of Emerson's life and thought. He had "a certain starved and abstract quality . . . ; [he] fed on books. . . . And to feed on books, for a philosopher or poet, is . . . to starve. . . . [Emerson] was employed in a sort of inner play, or digestion of vacancy." Once again Emerson was depicted as a mind weakened and starved by its narrow circumstances. (T. S. Eliot would use the same imagery a few years later, associating Emerson's outdated volumes with gentility, Boston aunts, and "the barren New England hills" in his early satire, "Cousin Nancy.") By the end of the nineteenth century Emersonian Transcendentalism had indeed come to seem, as Irving Howe puts it, "toothless, a genteel evasion." The document that best expressed and further propagated that version of Emerson was Santayana's hugely influential critique of "the genteel tradition." Santayana reintroduced Emerson to the twentieth century as the "detached, unworldly, contemplative" spokesman for a moribund nonphilosophy that subsisted in the modern world as a "sacred mystery only."[43]

Santayana hoped that America's "genteel tradition" would one day give way to a new, more "naturalistic" morality. "Only a morality frankly relative to man's nature," he warned, "is worthy of man, being at once vital and rational, martial and generous; whereas absolutism smells of fustiness." Its debilitating "moral absolutism"—the same untested "conception of the moral life" James had cited as Emerson's (dubious) "great distinction"—was, Santayana charged, the very "essence" of the genteel tradition. (The year after Santayana's famous address, Irving Babbitt would again employ Emerson as the great "absolutist" counterweight to the relativism of Sainte-Beuve. Emerson had "lost himself," Babbitt would later conclude, "in a mystical-transcendental mist, where it was impossible to follow him." That Emerson embodied a misty absolutism, as opposed to the naturalist-experiential thought of a Melville or a Twain, would remain, until recent years, one of the axioms of Emerson scholarship.)[44]

Santayana's conception of Emerson may well have evolved as he considered and reconsidered him in his 1886 essay on "The Optimism of Ralph Waldo Emerson," the chapter on Emerson in *Interpretations of Poetry and Religion* (1900); his 1903 address on "Emerson the Poet;" and the extended meditation on Emerson's legacy offered in his 1936 novel, *The Last Puritan.* But in each work Emerson is once again invoked as a genteel, distant cleric, a mystic rather than a philosopher, a chilly pantheist whose beloved nature was a convenient escape from "human life." "He is never a philosopher," Santayana contended in 1886, "but always Emerson philosophizing." He preached "the lesson of indifference to circumstances." He

"walked this earth with a bland and persistent smile." He was "in no sense
a prophet or herald for his age or country," Santayana wrote in 1900 (in
an essay with which Dewey must surely have been familiar)—he "was not
primarily a philosopher, but a Puritan mystic." (And even in this, as Santayana noted in 1886, he was often "the mystic turned dilettante.") "Reality eluded him." Unequivocally an "idealist," Emerson stood "aside from
the life of the world" in the quasi-Platonic, quasi-Oriental, "abstract
sphere" of mysticism. His "single theme" was "imagination." He was "a
poet whose only pleasure was thought," and "he showed in his life and
personality the meagerness, the constraint, the frigid and conscious conse-
cration which belonged to his clerical ancestors."[45]

"He's simply a distinguished-looking old cleric with a sweet smile and a
white tie," Jim Darnley remarks in *The Last Puritan,* "he's just honourable
and bland and as cold as ice." As one minor character states it earlier in
the novel: "Emerson served up Goethe's philosophy in ice-water." Santayana's later, no less sardonic description of Oliver Alden and Mario Van
de Weyer's pilgrimage to Concord comes as no surprise: "They looked at
the dreadful little house in which Emerson lived, and at his cold little
sitting-room; and then they looked at each other. Could such great things
leave such mean traces?" (Emerson appears to have permanently lowered
the temperature everywhere he went. Oliver remembers his room at the
Harvard Divinity School—the room once occupied by Emerson—as "a
beastly hole: impossibly far from everywhere, and impossibly cold.")[46]

In 1903 Santayana spoke of the "political thinker" ("a moralist interested in institutions and manners, a democrat and Puritan") that lay behind the pantheist. But, Santayana continued, "chiefly what lay there was
a mystic, a moralist athirst for some superhuman and absolute good."
Emerson's glance "sometimes . . . rested on human life, but more often
and far more lovingly on Nature. . . . The love of nature was Emerson's
strongest passion."[47]

Now Santayana was keenly aware that "transcendentalism"—in either
its German or American variety—was but an outgrowth of the Protestant
spirit and that however mystical or Neoplatonic its rhetoric, it fundamentally shunned "the endless battle of metaphysics" (what Dewey called the
"overweening Beyond and Away") for a more pragmatic "philosophy of
enterprise." Santayana was well aware that Emerson had at least one foot
in this tradition—well aware that Emerson was, like William James, like
Dewey, radically concerned with "the Here and Now" of common experience and committed to the use and testing of the life one confronts "on the
highway." In a review of Dewey's *Experience and Nature* (1925), Santayana suggested that Emerson, William James, and Dewey all asked the
same pragmatic question. "In order to get to the bottom and to the substance of anything," Santayana phrased it, describing Dewey's pragmatism, "we must still ask with Emerson, What is this *to me?* or with

William James, What is this *experienced as?*" Pragmatism shared with transcendentalism and empiricism the conceit that the universe exists "to subserve the interests of mankind," the conviction that mankind has "a right to treat the world as its field of action." American pragmatism was, Santayana said, "the most close-reefed of philosophical craft[s], most tightly hugging appearance, use, and relevance to practice today and here."[48] But it is precisely the pragmatic, experiential thinker—the Emerson who proposed "the great doctrine of Use" (CW, 1:26), defined "wisdom" as the "return" for "fit actions" (CW, 1:60), spurned "inaction" as "cowardice," and condemned "every opportunity of action past by, as a loss of power" (CW, 1:59)—it is this confrontational theoretician of human power who all but vanishes in James's or Santayana's accounts.

There are, finally, scattered through Santayana's books and essays, two quite distinct Emersons (and two Transcendentalisms); their coexistence he never adequately explained. The dominant Emerson—the figure depicted in those essays in which Santayana considered Emerson specifically—is the genteel Transcendentalist, disincarnate and naive, removed from the real forces at work in nineteenth-century America. But in Santayana's asides on Emerson, in his perceptive comments on the Promethean/Faustian nature of Romantic literature as a whole, a different figure emerges. When Santayana turned his attention to the Romantic movement in general, he had no difficulty situating Emerson in a German-Anglo-American, Protestant tradition that enshrined the exercise of the human will and perpetually ached for new trials of its strength. Transcendence in the context of this tradition meant not Buddhistic withdrawal but what Emerson—and, later, Nietzsche—called the "incorporation" or "assimilation" of the world. This Protestant "appetite for action" (Hegel called it the "appetitive relation to the external world") devoted its energies not to pantheism or the life of the spirit but to "world-building."[49] It was mystical only in its "faith in will and action." Ironically, it was in his appraisal of European tradition, in the introductory comments to *Three Philosophical Poets,* that Santayana offered his most astute summation of Emerson's thought. His remarks, though brief, cover a great deal of territory in capturing what Kazin calls the neglected "romantic, bourgeois, 'progressive,' sense of individual power" underlying Emerson's work. The "Teutonic races," Santayana wrote in 1910,

> turn successively to the Bible, to learning, to patriotism, to industry, for new objects to love and fresh worlds to conquer; but they have too much vitality, or too little maturity, to rest in any of these things. A demon drives them on; and this demon, divine and immortal in its apparent waywardness, is their inmost self. It is their insatiable will, their radical courage. Nay, though this be a hard saying to the uninitiated, their will is the creator of all those objects by which it is sometimes amused, and sometimes baffled, but never tamed. Their will summons all opportunities and dangers out of nothing to

feed its appetite for action; and in that ideal function lies their sole reality. Once attained, things are transcended. Like the episodes of a spent dream, they are to be smiled at and forgotten; the spirit that feigned and discarded them remains always strong and undefiled; it aches for new conquests over new fictions. This is romanticism. . . . It was adapted by Emerson and ought to be sympathetic to Americans; for it expresses the self-trust of the world-building youth, and mystical faith in will and action.[50]

The Conduct of Life

In his earliest essay on Emerson, Santayana had raised the specter of this Faustian thinker, an Emerson who hardly sounded "detached, unworldly, contemplative," when he quoted one of Emerson's many passages welcoming war, temptation, and antagonism as heroic forms of self-overcoming—as the very foundation of nature, the cosmos, culture, art, religion, and history.[51] Santayana quotes three sentences from the following paragraph in "Considerations By the Way," one of the many meditations on power that make up *The Conduct of Life* (1860). But the paragraph is worth citing in its entirety. It is surely one of the many Emersonian precursors of Nietzsche's doctrine that culture and selfhood are born not in the escape from time and history but in "creative tension and fruitful struggle."[52] It makes conspicuous the Emerson suppressed in James's and Santayana's rendering of a ministerial mystic, quaintly unconscious of evil or conflict. (This is an objection that would be repeated endlessly in the twentieth century and still stands as one of the clichés of Emerson criticism.)

> In front of these sinister facts, the first lesson of history is the good of evil. Good is a good doctor but Bad is sometimes a better. The oppressions of William the Norman, savage forest laws and crushing despotism made possible the inspirations of Magna Charta under John. Edward I. wanted money, armies, castles, and as much as he could get. It was necessary to call the people together by shorter, swifter ways,—and the House of Commons arose. To obtain subsidies, he paid in privileges. In the twenty-fourth year of his reign he decreed "that no tax should be levied without consent of Lords and Commons;"—which is the basis of the English Constitution. Plutarch affirms that the cruel wars which followed the march of Alexander introduced the civility, language and arts of Greece into the savage East; introduced marriage; built seventy cities, and united hostile nations under one government. The barbarians who broke up the Roman Empire did not arrive a day too soon. Schiller says the Thirty Years' War made Germany a nation. Rough, selfish despots serve men immensely, as Henry VIII. in the contest with the Pope; as the infatuations no less than the wisdom of Cromwell; as the ferocity of the Russian czars; as the fanaticism of the French regicides of 1789. The frost which kills the harvest of a year saves the harvests of a century, by destroying the weevil or the locust. Wars, fires, plagues, break up immovable routine, clear the ground of rotten races and dens of distemper, and open a fair field to new men. There is a tendency in things to right themselves, and

the war or revolution or bankruptcy that shatters a rotten system, allows things to take a new and natural order. The sharpest evils are bent into that periodicity which makes the errors of planets and the fevers and distempers of men, self-limiting. Nature is upheld by antagonism. Passions, resistance, danger, are educators. We acquire the strength we have overcome. Without war, no soldiers; without enemies, no hero. The sun were insipid if the universe were not opaque. And the glory of character is in affronting the horrors of depravity to draw thence new nobilities of power; as Art lives and thrills in new use and combining of contrasts, and mining into the dark evermore for blacker pits of night. What would painter do, or what would poet or saint, but for crucifixions and hells? And evermore in the world is this marvellous balance of beauty and disgust, magnificence and rats. Not Antoninus, but a poor washer-woman said, "The more trouble, the more lion; that's my principle." (W, 6:253–55)

It is difficult not to remain silent in the face of such an astonishing passage—especially astonishing if one comes to it after James's and Santayana's judgment that Emerson, either through provincialism or through mystic withdrawal, managed to avoid the nineteenth century. It is even more difficult to hold off citing all those equivalent passages in Emerson that deserve to be placed beside it. (The conception of culture Emerson presents here is—to cite just one example—condensed into one extraordinary line, a line worthy of Nietzsche at his best, in the aphoristic theory of Christianity's evolution Emerson advances in *English Traits*. "The violence of the northern savages," he writes, "exasperated Christianity into power" [ET, 139].) Santayana, however, passed quickly over such characteristically Emersonian thinking about the place of evil and the power of blackness, about the origin of culture and morality, about the physical laws of polarity. He dismissed such moments as digressions, unrepresentative of Emerson's main concerns: "The title under which these remarks appear ["Considerations By the Way"] is for once appropriate. . . . To give these views a fundamental importance would be to misunderstand Emerson."[53]

Yet there is sufficient evidence in this paragraph alone to suggest the extreme partiality and inadequacy of the James/Santayana image of Emerson. There is, for one thing, nothing provincial about it. The thick package of allusions—to Greece, Rome, and "the Savage East"; to English law and history; to the Cromwellian and French Revolutions; to the Thirty Years' War; to contemporary Russia—suggests that Emerson did not stand outside time and that he had not left history behind him. Nor is there anything to suggest that Emerson ignores evil. One can hear the relish with which he plunges into the dark, foul, and base; the prose is as tautly balanced as Nietzsche's aphoristic "dynamite."

It was Emerson's verse Santayana had in mind when he concluded that Emerson's passion for nature "was sincere adoration, self-surrendering devotion . . . not qualified or taken back by any subsumption of nature under human categories"; but there are no grounds in this passage, in all of *The Conduct of Life,* and in most of Emerson's prose, for ascribing to him so self-effacing a form of pantheism.[54] The "subsumption of nature under human categories" is precisely what *Nature,* what *The Conduct of Life,* champions. It was not nature's "inhuman perfection" Emerson adored (as Santayana claims) but nature's ultimate usefulness as a "tool chest," a "field of action," for human "appetites" (W, 6:88–90, 246). The "deferential," "universal passive hospitality" that James found in Emerson's personality (and that, James seems to imply, is also the hallmark of his thought) is manifestly not the point in this exhortation to self-strengthening.[55]

The question of whether Emerson was a mystic hinges, of course, on the definition of mysticism one accepts. But clearly the ascetic withdrawal Santayana imputes to Emerson fails to account for so fervent an invocation of "resistance." And it is at least an open question whether this vision of the terrible process by which "things right themselves" is merely another instance of that blandly optimistic and familiar Emersonian rubric, "Compensation," or something more akin to Nietzsche's definition of "the sublime" as "the artistic taming of the horrible" (BT, 7) or to the Nietzschean conception of civilization as the beautiful balance of brutally warring oppositions. Is such a passage evidence of Emerson's naïveté, his "cheerful Monism" (as Robert Frost called it)?[56] Or does it suggest an "optimism" closer to Nietzsche's ideal: the Hellenic capacity for looking "boldly right into the terrible destructiveness of . . . world history as well as the cruelty of nature" and, in the face of such suffering, for overcoming the mystic's "longing for a Buddhistic negation of the will" in order to achieve the "blissful affirmation of existence that seeks to discharge itself in actions" (BT, 7, 15). "The blossom of the Apollonian culture," Nietzsche writes, sprang "from a dark abyss, as the victory which the Hellenic will . . . obtains over suffering" (BT, 17). "What terrible questions are we learning to ask!" (W, 6:318) Emerson says: "Let us replace sentimentalism by realism, and dare to uncover those simple and terrible laws which, be they seen or unseen, pervade and govern" (W, 6:215). However one chooses to approach this passage, it is no longer possible to ignore or dismiss it in the way James or Santayana did.

Nor is it possible to argue that such moments are atypical of Emerson. It is baffling and, finally, testament to the pernicious way in which Emerson's ministerial image has blinded us to his words themselves, that Santayana could ever have thought so. Santayana's equation of transcendentalism and idealism with Emersonianism—and those chestnuts that have been taken as the too familiar rubrics of Emersonian thought (Compensation, the Over-Soul, Organicism, Pantheism, Absolutism, Monism, Passivity)—need to be balanced, ultimately reconceived, and redefined, in light of the tendencies (call them Nietzschean) that are so overt in the above paragraph.

We might label these, using only Emerson's own language, "the good of evil," the good of war, antagonism, resistance, education, the search for strength, overcoming, affronting, the search for power (the "combining of contrasts" in the search for new power), the use of darkness. We might expand this list, still confining our terminology to the language of *The Conduct of Life,* to include the command to "know the realities of human life" (p. 261), to "taste the real quality of existence" (p. 323), and to "try the rough water" (p. 162). "Nature," Emerson writes, "forever puts a premium on reality" (p. 189). And we might continue this list with the addition of the Emersonian terms and concepts emphasized in the following passages from the same book (further evidence that the Nietzschean strain beneath Emersonian "optimism" is anything but a digressive anomaly). These concepts are the ever-present imperatives of power, use (using what is near), resistance, testing, and overcoming (and confronting temptation—like the possibility of suicide), the perpetual friction ("perpetual tilt and balance") between man and nature, giving "form and actuality" to thought (p. 93), execution, instrumentation (tools), knowing, command ("command of nature" [p. 95]), "taking things up" into one's self/conversion/absorption/incorporation/transmutation ("the assimilating power" [p. 142]), conquest, vigor, action, will, "working up," "the extension of man" (p. 284), building, taking advantage, the charm and power of practicality (p. 317).

> [Man's] instincts must be met, and he has predisposing power that bends and fits what is near him to his use. . . . As soon as there is life, there is self-direction and absorbing and using of material. (p. 38)
>
> Everything is pusher or pushed; and matter and mind are in perpetual tilt and balance. (p. 43)
>
> The friction in nature is so enormous that we cannot spare any power. It is not question to express our thought, to elect our way, but to overcome resistances of the medium and material in everything we do. (p. 79)
>
> [Man] is tempted out by his appetites and fancies to the conquest of this and that piece of nature, until he finds his well-being in the use of his planet, and of more planets than his own. . . . [T]he elements offer their service to him. . . . The world is his tool-chest, and he is successful, or his education is carried on just so far, as is the marriage of his faculties with nature, or the degree in which he takes up things into himself. (pp. 88–90)
>
> Kings are said to have long arms, but every man should have long arms, and should pluck his living, his instruments, his power and his knowing, from the sun, moon and stars. (p. 95)
>
> Man was born to be rich, or inevitably grows rich by the use of his faculties. (p. 99)

[T]he student we speak to must have a mother-wit invincible by his culture,—which uses all books, arts, facilities, and elegancies of intercourse, but is never subdued or lost in them. . . . And the end of culture is not to destroy this, God forbid! but to train away all impediment and mixture and leave nothing but pure power. (p. 134)

Man's culture can spare nothing, wants all the material. He is to convert all impediments into instruments, all enemies into power. The formidable mischief will only make the more useful slave. . . . [W]e shall dare affirm that there is nothing he will not overcome and convert, until at last culture shall absorb the chaos and gehenna. He will convert the Furies into Muses, and the hells into benefit. (p. 166)

I have no sympathy with a poor man I knew, who, when suicides abounded, told me he dare not look at his razor. (p. 201)

Yet vigor is contagious, and whatever makes us either think or feel strongly, adds to our power and enlarges our field of action. (p. 246)

We learn geology the morning after the earthquake. . . . In our life everything is worked up and comes in use,—passion, war, revolt, bankruptcy, and not less, folly and blunders, insult, ennui and bad company. (p. 262)

Alchemy, which sought to transmute one element into another, to prolong life, to arm with power,—that was in the right direction. . . . [A] man is a fagot of thunderbolts. All the elements pour through his system; he is the flood of the flood and fire of the fire; he feels the antipodes and the pole as drops of his blood; they are the extension of his personality. His duties are measured by that instrument he is. (pp. 282–83)

[I]f a man can build a plain cottage with such symmetry as to make all the fine palaces look cheap and vulgar; can take such advantages of nature that all her powers serve him; making use of geometry, instead of expense; tapping a mountain for his water-jet; causing the sun and moon to seem only the decorations of his estate;—this is still the legitimate dominion of beauty. (p. 302)

The Conduct of Life, Emerson's last great book, may well be the work in which his speculations on the search for power, the antagonism of fate, the service of culture, the force of behavior, worship, and wealth are most explicit. *The Conduct of Life* is, as Porte suggests, obsessed with power.[57] It is obsessed with "the sovereignty of power" (p. 63), with "coarse energy" (p. 64), with "the excess of virility" (p. 69) and the "man of force" (p. 58), "the charm of practical men" (p. 317) and men of superior will (p. 248), with health, "recuperative force" (p. 61), and "the advantage of a strong pulse" (p. 56), with "personal power" and "the enormous elements of strength which . . . make our politics unimportant" (p. 61), with "aboriginal might," "hairy Pelasgic strength," "*plus* or positive power" (pp. 71–73) and "beast-force" (p. 252). But it must be emphasized (because the common perception of distinct early and late periods in Emerson's thought would seem to deny it) that the concern for power, for use and command, and the predominance of the Emersonian pattern of overcoming are not at all new.

Although *The Conduct of Life* was not published until 1860, the lectures that form its basis were first delivered in 1851. The anxiety over the ebb of vital force, the compensating obsession with power, the "underlying psycho-physiological anxiety" over the proper expending and conservation of energy, and the attendant "fantasies of size, power, violence, debauchery, and fertility"—all, as Porte argues, can be traced back to the journal entries of the 1840s.[58] But one needs only to return to Emerson's first book, in 1836, to find exactly the same founding patterns reexpressed so vehemently in *The Conduct of Life*. There is, in *Nature,* the same call for "the kingdom" (or "dominion") of "man over nature" (CW, 1:45), the same stress on the "endless exercise" of all human "faculties" (CW, 1:37), the same affirmation of "new activity" (CW, 1:41), "new creation" (CW, 1:16) (as opposed to "barren contemplation"), the same "doctrine of Use" (CW, 1:26), the same concern for "self-command" and "the varying phenomenon of Health" (CW, 1:27), the same push to grasp "the keys of power" (CW, 1:21), to transmute "unconscious truth" into "the domain of knowledge" where it may become "a new weapon in the magazine of power" (CW, 1:23). There is the same emphasis on "heroic action," "the energy of [man's] thought and will" (CW, 1:15), and the necessity of work (CW, 1:12).

"At present," Emerson complains, "man applies to nature but half his force" (CW, 1:42). *Nature* is the prophecy of man's "resumption of power," his taking advantage of nature "with his entire force" and building his world (CW, 1:43). "By the time he composed *Nature,*" Leo Marx notes, "Emerson had adapted the rhetoric of the technological sublime to his purposes." The "submerged metaphor" in *Nature,* Marx suggests, was technology; it is submerged—rendered obscure or ambiguous—in the heavy counterpresence of traditional idealist terminology and Christian imagery:[59]

> The exercise of the Will or the lesson of power is taught in every event. From the child's successive possession of his several senses up to the hour when he saith, "thy will be done!" he is learning the secret, that he can reduce under his will, not only particular events, but great classes, nay the whole series of events, and so conform all facts to his character. Nature is thoroughly mediate. It is made to serve. It receives the dominion of man as meekly as the ass on which the Saviour rode. It offers all its kingdoms to man as the raw material which he may mould into what is useful. Man is never weary of working it up. He forges the subtile and delicate air into wise and melodious words, and gives them wing as angels of persuasion and

command. More and more, with every thought, does his kingdom stretch over things, until the world becomes, at last, only a realized will,—the double of the man. (CW, 1:25)

This is the vision of the world as tool chest and field of action for the extension of man that would inform all of Emerson's subsequent work. (This passage, like many of those I have cited from *The Conduct of Life,* is also a good example of a point I shall stress in chapter 2. Emerson is, for all the emphasis that has been placed on his faith in intuition, a philosopher of tuition. He generally defines man in precisely the same terms he uses in the above passage—as a perpetual student in a universal school of power.) Marx is undoubtedly correct in noting the allusion to technological power in this passage, but it might be more accurate to include technology as part of a broader Emersonian project that anticipates Dewey's rejection of "the spectator theory of knowledge." That project is the attempt to approach the world not as a spectator who knows things at a distance but as a worker or user for whom nature and materials are known only as they become "*tools* and *instruments,* with which we can do things and satisfy our desires."[60]

Maurice Mandelbaum identifies such an approach as the "pragmatic-economical view of the human mind" that first became prominent in the latter decades of the nineteenth century.[61] But that pragmatic perspective is certainly apparent, in greater and lesser degrees, throughout the post-Kantian era: in Fichte and the German tradition; in Carlyle; and, most centrally, in Emerson.[62] "Our nineteenth century," Emerson said—summing up his fundamental point of view as aptly as any single sentence could—"is the age of tools" (W, 7:157). "Without tools," Carlyle had earlier insisted, in *Sartor Resartus,* "[man] is nothing, with Tools he is all."[63]

Johann Gottlieb Fichte, the German philosopher who may well have had an important, if indirect, hand in shaping Emerson's thought, proposed, in 1800, that man's vocation was "Not merely TO KNOW but . . . TO DO." "Not for idle contemplation of thyself," Fichte argued, "not for brooding over devout sensations;—no, for action art thou here; thine action, and thine action alone, determines thy worth."[64] In his own Fichtean defense of the scholar class, Emerson upheld a similar ideal: "The preamble of thought, the transition through which it passes from the unconscious to the conscious, is action. Only so much do I know, as I have lived. . . . [H]e who has put forth his total strength in fit actions, has the richest return of wisdom" (CW, 1:59–60). The problem of the times, as he diagnosed it in 1841, was that men were inclined not "to a deed, but to a beholding. . . . [They] are paralyzed by the uncertainty what they should do" (CW, 1:179). "Metaphysics," as he later restated it, "is dangerous as a single pursuit. . . . The inward analysis must be corrected by rough experience. Metaphysics must be perpetually reinforced by life;

must be the observations of a working man on working men . . . the record of some law whose working was surprised by the observer in natural action" (W, 12:13).

The remarkable image in that last phrase, difficult to forget once it has been noticed, suggests that metaphysical truth, or knowledge, can only be grasped at, captured, or surprised—like an animal observed or hunted—in the midst of some active pursuit, an action that must be natural. Emerson's ambiguous syntax suggests that both the observer and the law or truth that is surprised are in states of action. Knowledge, in other words, begins in reciprocal action or what Emerson elsewhere calls friction. "By how much we know, so much we are," Emerson says a few pages earlier (W, 12:10): and what we know, what we are, comes about only in antagonism or *re*action. Our knowledge, our identity, must be "corrected" and "perpetually reinforced" by a life and experience that are *rough*—that push back. "Intelligence," as Dewey put it, "must throw its fund out again into the stress of life; it must venture its savings against the pressure of facts."[65]

We are now better prepared to appreciate Dewey's crucial, turn-of-the-century defense of Emerson. Dewey was, as I have said, endeavoring to refute those interpretations that relegated Emerson to the transcendentalist-genteel camp. Upholding Emerson as the prophet and herald of modern democracy appears to be a direct rebuttal of Santayana's belief that Emerson was "in no sense a prophet for his age or country"; Dewey's insistence that Emerson's philosophy not be misunderstood as the nostalgic "idealism of a Class" even anticipates Santayana's charge that Emerson was anachronistically "genteel." But Dewey was trying to suggest something even more significant than this. His famous praise for Emerson as "the philosopher of Democracy," the philosopher of "any system which democracy may *henceforth* construct" (my italics), was the attempt to recover Emerson (at a time when he was entering the twentieth century in the white smile and tie of the New England saint) as a distinctively modern mind—a mind whose strikingly original contribution (clouded as it was behind its surface, absolutist pigments) was still not fully apparent, was "just now dawning" and still difficult to classify. Its validity as a "new type of literary art" and "method of knowledge," its relevance to the modern world, would, Dewey argued, become clearer—like the significance of Platonic thought for the Old World—in retrospect.[66]

Cornel West suggests that it is precisely Emerson's swerve away from metaphysical idealism to a new kind of "cultural criticism" that defines Emerson's modernity; it was precisely this pragmatic and pioneering "evasion of philosophy" that Dewey inherited from Emerson—and it was this central, still underappreciated Emersonian legacy that Dewey was attempting to pull from beneath Emerson's confusing, Platonic language and his Transcendentalist image. Emerson's claim that "philosophy is still rude and elementary . . . [and] will one day be taught by poets" (generally taken by scholars as further evidence of Emerson's desire to escape into poetry's idealisms) was welcomed by Dewey as a path-breaking "more-than-philosophy," commendable precisely because it preferred to work "by art, not by metaphysics." As West puts it: "Dewey understands Emerson's evasion of modern [metaphysical, epistemology-centered] philosophy . . . as a situating of philosophical reflection and poetic creation in the midst of quotidian human struggles for meaning, status, power, wealth, and selfhood."[67] Emerson, "the philosopher of democracy," was—to put it another way— not transcendental "man in the open air" (that "pure, will-less, painless, timeless knowing subject" Nietzsche hoped to abolish [GM, 3:12]) but a mind committed above all to reaction—committed to finding ways of coping with those natural and cultural forces that made life in mid-nineteenth-century America (and in any future democratic society) a "quotidian struggle."

West is, I think, right. Emerson is "like Friedrich Nietzsche . . . , first and foremost a cultural critic obsessed with ways to generate forms of power." "Cultural critic," however (and Stanley Cavell has recently made a similar claim), is, like power, problematic. Its meaning and nineteenth-century context can be further clarified. We can note, first of all, that Emerson anticipated Dewey's pragmatic insistence that philosophical debate (the discourse, as Emerson portrayed it, of "four or five noted men") resolve itself "into a practical question of the conduct of life. How shall I live?" (W, 6:3). Dewey reinstated Emerson's priorities in 1917 in his key essay, "The Need for a Recovery of Philosophy"; he condemned any philosophical tradition that existed as "an ingenious dialectic exercised in professorial corners by a few who have retained ancient premises, while rejecting their application to the conduct of life." Dewey wanted philosophy to be the democratic medium for "releas[ing] the powers of individuals for cultural expression"—a philosophy premised on the necessity of "an active coping with conditions," committed to "the possibilities of action."[68]

He was not the only one to feel that the modern mind required a new kind of education in the possibilities of human power. In his popular 1917 essay, "The Energies of Men," William James called for a new theory of human power as a basis for reconstructing the system of "individual and national education" in the twentieth century:

> The two questions, first, that of the possible extent of our powers; and, second, that of the various avenues of approach to them, the various keys for unlocking them in diverse individuals, dominate the whole problem of individual and national education. We need a topography of the limits of human power. . . . We need also a study of the various types of human being with reference to the different ways in which their energy-reserves may be appealed to and set loose.[69]

The history of Henry Adams's struggle to measure "man as a force" would finally be published a year later. Modern education, Adams theorized, "should try to lessen the obstacles, diminish the friction, invigorate the energy, and should train minds to react, not at haphazard, but by choice, on the lines of force that attract their world." Adams claimed that his vocation had been the attempt of the mind "to invent scales of force" for all those nonhuman powers that surround and threaten it. "A new avalanche of unknown forces," he warned, had fallen upon the mind and "required new mental powers to control."[70] But Adams's vocation as a "student of force" was not new—though his example as a mind lost in the attempt to find new scales for new forces and viable scales for old ones may stand as a paradigm by which we can measure the aims and achievements of minds like Emerson, Nietzsche, or Carlyle (or for that matter, Marx, Darwin, and Freud, who were similarly committed to finding the "scale of force" that could best explain to an energy-obsessed age the fundamental forces that set individuals and societies in motion).

Adams may not have sensed it in the way Dewey, William James, or Nietzsche did. But the nineteenth-century penchant for seeing the world *sub specie vis* had already found its first American spokesman in Emerson. It was Emerson who first spoke of himself as the "geometer of [human] forces" (EJ, 507). "There is not yet," he announced in the opening sentence of his essay on "Power," "any inventory of a man's faculties" (W, 6:53). We lack, as he put it in his lecture, "Aristocracy," an "anthropometer"—a quintessentially Emersonian coinage to describe his vision of a machine that would improve society by providing every man with a true appraisal of the degree of power he could be trusted to "carry and use" (W, 10:49). It was Emerson who first saw himself (as Nietzsche would later see himself) as a source of cultural strength—the hero who could restore the balance of power between man and his environment, the modern prophet who could "enumerate the resources we can command," "reinforce [man's] self-respect, show him his means, his arsenal of forces, physical, metaphysical, immortal" (W, 10:69).

Emerson was, as West puts it, one of the century's first "grand valorizer[s] of human power."[71] Culture, Emerson said, must replenish that "pure power" and "mother-wit" that allows the student to use "all books, arts, facilities, and elegancies of intercourse" without becoming "subdued" by them or "lost in them" (W, 6:134). Our current "habit of thought" is "poor and squalid"; our "common experience" a (genteel) "egg-shell existence" (W, 6:271). What was needed "to add somewhat to the well-being of men" (and give us "the courage to be what we are") (W, 6:278) was a teacher who could remind his readers of their "magical powers over nature and man" and inspire "new ways of living, new books, new men" (W, 6:271).

Emerson's last important book ends, like his first, with the prophecy that man will one day liberate himself from those illusions that blind him to his "elemental power" (CW, 1:42). Emerson's vision of a teacher who can awaken in his audience new energies, energies capable of "renovat[ing] life and our social state" (CW, 2:43), capable of rising to the resistances and impediments offered by nature and history, stakes out a new kind of intellectual or cultural vocation. It is one of many similar self-portraits.

We may call this new vocation a kind of "cultural criticism" concerned with securing the balance of human and nonhuman powers. Or we may define it as pragmatism—devoted to "the Here and Now," to the testing of truth by immediate experience, to promoting (in Alexander Bain's phrase) "an attitude or disposition of preparedness to act."[72] Or we may feel that pragmatism is too limiting a label (for it localizes Emerson within American tradition) and stress its broader connections to concurrent European philosophies of will. Whatever we may decide to call this new way of thinking, this new vocation, it was largely neglected by Emerson scholarship until the middle of this century.

Not that Emerson's devotion to will and action went unnoticed. It was noted repeatedly: in a series of articles on Emerson and pragmatism, or Emerson and Nietzsche, in Kenneth Burke's perception that "Emerson's brand of transcendentalism was but a short step ahead of out-and-out pragmatism," in Eduard Baumgarten's prescient linking of Emerson, James, Dewey, and Nietzsche as founders of a pragmatic *Philosophie der Macht*," in Matthiessen's comparison of Emerson's ideal individual and "the hard-willed [Nietzschean] *Übermensch*," in Perry Miller's remarks on the Napoleonic propensities beneath Emerson's worship of genius, in Daniel Aaron's discussion of Emerson as "the seer of *laisser-faire* capitalism and the rampant individual."[73]

But "theoretician of power" was always seen as one of Emerson's "lesser roles."[74] Emerson remained chiefly what he had been in Santayana's portrait of "the Genteel Tradition": fundamentally a literary anachronism, whose ideas were for the most part sufficiently distant that they could be easily classified as Platonic or Neoplatonic, as transcendental organicism or pantheism, as Puritan (or Oriental) mysticism. In the works of Matthiessen, Hopkins, Paul, Miller, Feidelson, and others, Emerson remained primarily the influential expounder of a transcendental (often mystical) aesthetic. If that aesthetic seemed anachronous, it was because Emerson continued to be perceived as awkwardly attempting "to describe an ancient way of seeing [a nonrational, organic vision] by means of a modern vocabulary which had been designed to repress it."[75]

That aspect of Emerson's thought that seemed more intrinsically (and troublesomely) modern—his "attraction . . . toward every form of power"[76]—the critical establishment of the time could only begin to identify as the most drastic form of Nietzscheanism. Emerson's "Nietzschean strain" existed, when it surfaced, as the disturbing underside of the Transcendentalist image—and almost always it was defused by that very image. Emerson's fascination with power was treated as anomalous, a temporary extravagance amid his overall moral mildness, the exception that proved the Transcendentalist rule. Thus Matthiessen noted the connection between Emerson's "ideal man of self-reliant energy" and "the brutal man of Fascism." "It is no long step," Matthiessen wrote, "from [Emerson's] indiscriminate glorification of power to the predatory career of Henry Ford." But Emerson's temperate monistic image could finally not be reconciled with what appeared to be a Nietzschean vision of *Machtpolitik;* the potential link had to be acknowledged but defined as simply the denaturing or degradation of true ("unworldly") Emersonianism. "The sentiments of such essays as those on 'Wealth' and 'Power,'" Matthiessen said, "working on temperaments less unworldly than their author's, have provided a vicious reinforcement to the most ruthless elements in our economic life."[77]

What was lost between the extremes of these two perspectives—Emerson as upholder of an ancient holism, Emerson as harbinger of an all-too-modern fascism—was the much more prominent middle ground recent criticism has sought to recover: Emerson as Nietzschean (and quintessentially of his time) in his omnipresent rhetoric of "power" (one of the central, ambiguous tropes or "master signs" of the nineteenth century generally);[78] Emerson as Nietzschean in his persistent patterns of resistance, overcoming, and incorporation; Emerson as pragmatic in his commitment to testing and use; Emerson as Nietzschean "geometer of force," committed to the generation and extension of human energies.

Stephen Whicher's *Freedom and Fate*

Stephen Whicher's *Freedom and Fate: An Inner Life of Ralph Waldo Emerson,* first published in 1953 and still considered by many the single most important and revolutionary critical work on Emerson, changed the course of scholarship in several ways. For one thing, it redirected critical attention to Emerson's startlingly original reflections on power; that emphasis would have important consequences for the criticism of the next forty years. Unfortunately, Whicher also did much to keep alive many of the central tenets of the anti-Emerson tradition. Because his ideas and, even more significantly, his methodology have exerted so controlling an influence on later scholarship, they are worth considering here.

Freedom and Fate is a masterful job of summary and synthesis. It remains one of the most sensitive studies of an American writer ever written. Out of what had always been "a distressingly sprawling topic," Whicher presented, more forcefully than had any previous critic, the portrait of a dramatic evolution: Emerson moved from an early, apocalyptic rebellion in the name of an emancipated individualism to a chastened acquiescence before fate and experience.[79] But Whicher's evolutionary paradigm—his very insistence that Emerson had a dramatic development—though intended to rescue Emerson from an even shallower, hagiographic image, has resulted in an overly schematic and still pejorative perception of his thought. That perception has made it possible to continue speaking of Emerson in simplistic either-or terms: Emerson as either optimistic or pessimistic, revolutionary or acquiescent, idealistic or skeptical, nonconformist or conservative, and so forth.

Such overschematizing is the major difficulty inherent in any attempt to impose on Emerson anything like the usual evolutionary thesis that finds distinct early and late periods in a writer's career. It is all too likely that the standard biographical rubrics of youth and age (and the built-in value judgments they impose) will only perpetuate the traditional prejudices against Emerson as intellectually and artistically naive and underdeveloped. An evolutionary paradigm that posits an artist's growth from youthful illusion to mature disillusionment is implicitly anti-Romantic; the earlier idealistic, revolutionary, or Romantic period will, in the framework of such a scheme, always be associated with immaturity. Such an approach, in other words, seems predisposed to repeat, consciously or not, the Arnoldian or Eliotic bias that finds Romantic literature inherently immature, blind to experience or evil, and in need of some further growth or knowledge before it can be, morally and artistically, of the highest seriousness. Whicher's thesis of a drastic development in Emerson's thought has thus, as Poirier remarks, "helped perpetuate the view that when [Emerson] is not naively wide-eyed he is only reluctantly sensible." It has helped preserve, Hughes notes, "the chiding solicitousness with which readers [have] regarded the unfolding of Emerson's work." Julie Ellison justly speaks of it as "the hypothetical divide in Emerson's career that has plagued us for decades."[80]

The temptation to simplify Emerson's thought in this way remains a potential obstacle for any chronological interpretation of his work; and until recently criticism has been reluctant to consider Emerson's ideas in any context *but* a chronological one. No one, of course, can or would want to argue with a biographical approach to a writer's thought. But Emerson's case is more complicated than it might appear. When the critical tradition has been largely antipathetic to a writer's work, as I have tried to suggest it has been in Emerson's case, one has reason to be suspicious of criticism that seems ever anxious to balance (or shore up) one strain (or phase) of thought with another, as if the ideas or style of a single essay or book were somehow not enough in themselves or were intellectually embarrassing taken on their own. At what point does an insistently chronological perspective on Emerson become something other than just respectable scholarship—become, rather, another reflex action in that fixated, critical need to highlight, apologize, and account for Emerson's failings? At what point does chronology become yet another aspect of Emerson scholarship to act as a positive hindrance to appreciation?

Whicher's method—the employment of a broad, biographical framework for assessing not just Emerson's life but his *ideas*—has been repeated so often now, over several decades, that it has become virtually de rigueur. This method—committed to getting at Emerson through the identification of phases and periods—has been the explicit or implicit foundation for most criticism of the last forty years. It has dictated, in large measure, the shape of most book-length studies, which generally move from early to late stages, mapping out transitions and crisis points, identifying the various degrees of Emersonian "optimism." Even books like Bishop's, which have tried to focus on a single topic and have attempted to abstract "the essence of the Emersonian achievement . . . from the whole body of his work," have based their interpretations on some version of development, and have defined Emerson in terms of immature or mature degrees of idealism.[81]

The Whicherian method is, as Ellison has argued, disposed to finding growth (or surrender) and attempts at resolution rather than repetition or complex, persisting tensions. Its origin, as a method, lies in a perception of Emerson that is basically impatient with his actual work; it therefore lends itself most readily to overviews, to biography, not to thorough explorations of ideas or to the kind of intensive pressing or leaning on lines and passages that recent critics have practiced. Whicher's method does not encourage attempts to recover or argue for, in any extensive or systematic way, an Emersonian philosophy. It depends on the assumption that "optimism" (loaded term that it is) and "idealism"—or the lack of them—are adequate parameters for fixing and defining Emerson's thought. Whicher, Bishop, and Emerson's readers generally have assumed that they were; but recent scholarship has not.[82] These limitations are part of the general and, finally, crippling weakness underlying Whicher's entire approach—that is, the basically deprecatory or apologetic attitude that Whicher, in 1953, was obliged to take toward his subject or, more specifically, to his subject's ideas.

"It is only," Whicher claimed, "as we see [Emerson] *sub specie temporis* that we can justly estimate his quality as a writer." That central statement of method may sound unobjectionable. Who would not wish to understand an author *sub specie temporis*? But the operative word (as the context of Whicher's argument makes clear) is that qualifying *only*. So we need to ask, "Why won't 'Self-Reliance' or 'Experience' in and of itself vouch for Emerson's 'quality as a writer'?" Or, to push the point, what negative presumptions are at work if we insist that the only way for estimating, say, Nietzsche's or Shakespeare's quality is in the context of comprehensive appraisals of evolution over a lifetime of work? Can't the examination of a single play or, say, Nietzsche's publications in 1886 and

1887 provide sufficient evidence of the intrinsic merit of their author's achievement? Whicher assumes that in any other approach Emerson will not come off well, that his ideas are intrinsically moribund, and that only a procedure that can bring to life again the large, chronological outline of Emerson the man can make his readers overcome their aversion to his work itself. "Increasing numbers of critics and readers," Whicher remarks, "conclude that [Emerson] is, in Eliot's phrase, 'already an encumbrance.'"[83]

The conclusion of *Freedom and Fate,* while upholding Emerson's "craftsman's skill," reasserts the traditional charges. Emerson's optimistic faith is irritating in a modern age; his ideas are irrevocably anachronistic ("the story of his thought seems an episode from a vanished past"); and— the central charge leveled by Santayana, John Morley, and so many others—they are essentially a form of gospel thinly disguised as "modern philosophy."[84]

One could garner several such disparaging remarks from Whicher, from Bishop's *Emerson on the Soul* (1964), and especially from Feidelson's *Symbolism and American Literature* (published in the same year as *Freedom and Fate*). (Feidelson's influential study is, like others that followed it, a sustained use of Emerson as a bad example, a foil to the more complex modernity of Melville.) These books have routinely been considered key contributions to a midcentury resurrection of Emerson. They might, with equal reason, be described as central works in the last important generation of criticism to replicate, in various degrees, the negative presuppositions of the James/Santayana version of Emerson.

But if *Freedom and Fate* retained much that was characteristic of the anti-Emerson tradition, it also broke new ground. Most significant, at least in terms of the influence Whicher would have on Emerson's current revival, is the renewed emphasis placed on the centrality of power in Emerson's thought. No topic receives greater space in Whicher's index than power, and there is an additional lengthy entry under "vital force." (It should be noted, for purposes of comparison, that the subject is not even indexed in Feidelson, in Vivian Hopkins's *Spires of Form* [1951], Sherman Paul's *Emerson's Angle of Vision* [1952], Ralph Rusk's *The Life of Ralph Waldo Emerson* [1949], or F. I. Carpenter's *Emerson Handbook* [1953].) What is most striking, however, about *Freedom and Fate*'s discussion of Emerson's "radically anarchic" devotion "not [to] virtue, but freedom and mastery" is that it reasserts not the James or Santayana version of Emerson but a response that recalls Dewey's.[85]

Whicher does, in closing, characterize the Nietzschean strain in Emerson as merely the obsolescent, "final eruption of protestant perfectionism." But his main discussion of Emerson's philosophy of power or action otherwise resembles Dewey's. The way Whicher presents this genuinely revolutionary aspect of Emerson's thought—and the same thing can be said of Dewey's essay—recalls Ezra Pound's remark that "Artists are the antennae of the race." For this new and surprising commitment to an agonistic vision of human power and the total "emancipation of man" seems to emerge in Emerson's thinking semiconsciously, obliquely, in response to pressures of which Emerson is himself only half aware. Like Dewey, Whicher sees this concern for action, for mastery or use as the source of Emerson's true originality.[86]

It is, Whicher writes, "one of the most startlingly new notes . . . ever to be struck in American literature." Whicher finds traces of this new strain in Emerson in an inherited, Edwardsean vitalism, in an even older tradition of Antinomianism (the "discovery of the God within"), in the Ideal theories of Platonic tradition as well as "the Locke-Berkeley-Hume tradition." But he associates it most closely with what was still the major philosophical tradition of its time: the German conception of philosophy (or the Romantic union of philosophy and poetry) as the revolutionary medium for *Selbsttätigkeit* (self-activity) and freedom ("the liberation of humanity," as Matthew Arnold called it). And it is his commitment to this tradition—not his conventional ethical thought or moralistic language, not the vestiges of mysticism or Platonic idealism—that makes Emerson, Whicher suggests, still significant, still impressive.[87]

Whicher's discussion of this radical, still half-emergent core of Emerson's thought has had a central and continuing influence on Emerson scholarship. His emphasis on Emerson's concern with mastery and power was reapplied, repeatedly and variously, through the 1970s: in Bloom's essays on Emerson's assertions of "the autonomy of the imagination" (1971), in Quentin Anderson's attack on Emerson's "pseudopodial" self (1971), in Lewis Simpson's analysis of Emerson's discovery of "the Archimedean Self" (1971), in Laurence Holland's suggestion that Emerson's writings constitute "a hymn to power" (1978), in Porte's examination of the broad significance of vital force in Emerson's thought (1979).[88] By the end of the decade, the ground had been securely laid for Emerson's "detranscendentalizing," for that renewed emphasis on a pragmatic, agonistic (not a monistic, organicist) Emerson that would mark the criticism of the 1980s.

Like Dewey, Whicher is certain that there is something new and unique in Emerson's emphasis on power but is uncertain what to call it. We are faced with the same problem. Whicher speaks of Emerson's Nietzschean side; yet—although the Emerson-Nietzsche connection is undoubtedly more significant than criticism has generally recognized—Nietzschean is an unsatisfactory description (though I shall continue to use it), if only because Emerson came first. Dewey identifies this side of Emerson as the precursor of an American "new individualism," the preeminent herald of pragmatism and Deweyan "instrumentalism." Whicher associates it with a Germanic "transcendental egoism" or "self-centeredness" that is part of

Romantic philosophy's longing for "the emancipation of man."[89]

But Whicher also speaks of Emersonian power as "the Power present and agent in the soul"—a description that leaves open another, very different possibility. It suggests that such power may ultimately be divine in origin, that Emerson is really only giving fresh expression to a God-intoxication older than Christendom. Firkins long ago summed up this theocentric view of Emersonian power when he proposed that Emerson's claim on posterity, his "whole secret," could be defined as the ubiquitous "experience of God"—"the successful practice," as Firkins phrased it, "of unbroken commerce with omnipresent deity." The essentially anachronistic nature of such conviction Firkins made clear in a memorable image. "Emerson in the history of religion," he concluded, "was a guest of honor who reached a party at the moment when its members were dispersing. His arrival evoked a brief sensation—on the doorstep, as it were—but did not finally reconstitute the party."[90]

If this view of Emerson is correct—and it is certainly part of Emerson's commonly accepted Transcendentalist image—then there is, in substance, really little that is new about Emerson's adoration of a power that is essentially divine or spiritual. Firkins finds "the notion of unbroken spiritual commerce" an audacious and "a novel thing"; but such fundamentally pantheistic and mystical God-intoxication (Firkins hails Emerson as "the first of mystics") can be traced back to, among others, Spinoza, Plotinus, and the English Christian Platonists. Thus Henry Bamford Parks reasoned that Emerson was a "pseudo-mystic," a throwback to the middle ages without "any unusually deep insight into reality."[91]

We have arrived, however, at a fundamental paradox: Emerson provides, apparently, sufficient evidence for reading him as both a late-arriving Plotinus and an early Nietzsche or William James. It is a paradox familiar to students of Emerson, one of which Dewey and Whicher were keenly aware. "Emerson was," Denis Donoghue remarks, "just as readily available to Pragmatism as to Transcendentalism." Or, as Gay Wilson Allen observes: "One of the paradoxes in Emerson's Idealism is that he grounds it on empiricism." "What is puzzling about Emerson's writing," Anthony Cascardi notes, "is his simultaneous attraction to and repulsion from idealism." We shall return to this paradox again. What I wish to emphasize here is that it is Emerson's startlingly new, not easily identifiable ruminations on power and action in "the Here and the Now" that draws both Dewey and Whicher. Emerson's "voluntarism" and "vocabulary of Will," as Donoghue has more recently concluded, founded "a pragmatics of the future."[92]

2

The Doctrine of Use

Use, labor of each for all, is the health and virtue of all beings.
—*Ralph Waldo Emerson, "American Civilization" (1862)*

John Jay Chapman concluded that "if an inhabitant of another planet should visit the earth, he would receive, on the whole, a truer notion of human life by attending an Italian opera than he would by reading Emerson's volumes."[1] The problem for the critic of Emerson, however, lies not in confronting a mind that is limited in its perspective on human life but in attempting to understand systematically a mind extravagantly open to all experience, an intellect rigorous and aggressive in its determination to confront reality directly and to make use of it for its own increased power.

The Use of Everything

"Used faculties strong" (TN, 1:175)—that is probably the most succinct formulation Emerson ever gave to the psychological/philosophical principle that forms the unvarying bedrock of his thought. He called it, in *Nature*, "the great doctrine of Use, namely, that a thing is good only so far as it serves; that a conspiring of parts and efforts to the production of an end, is essential to any being" (CW, 1:26). As he restates this doctrine elsewhere in the same book: "The imagination may be defined to be, the use which the Reason makes of the material world" (CW, 1:31); "All the uses of nature admit of being summed in one, which yields the activity of man an infinite scope" (CW, 1:37). "There are innocent men," he laments at *Nature*'s close, "who worship God after the tradition of their fathers, but their sense of duty has not yet extended to the use of all their faculties" (CW, 1:43–44).

If the mass of men lead lives of quiet desperation, then it is, as Emerson observed repeatedly, because they exist untested, unused. Only in the exercise of using, only through the concerted effort of all our capacities in the production of some end, can we learn the extent of our "infinite scope" and acquire, as Emerson puts it, the "power of self-protection" (W, 7:257). The terrified infant studies every moment "the use of his eyes, ears, hands, and feet, learning how to meet and avoid his dangers." The real problem begins when this education "stops too soon" and the adult falls into "some routine of safe industry" away from the "rough experiences," like those faced by the soldier or frontiersman, that instill courage and self-subsistence (W, 7:257). Tough reality—war, evil, terror, danger, pain, want, the harsh necessity of "initiated action" to impress one's own form on a hostile environment—compels men to self-actualization, to subduing and utilizing the world.

> Men live on the defensive, and go through life without an action, without one overt act, one initiated action. They buy stock, because others do, and stave off want & pain the best they can, defending themselves; but to carry the war into the enemy's country; to live from life within & impress on the world their own form, they dare not. Thousands & thousands vegetate in this way, streets full, towns full, and never an action in them all. (EJ, 400)

Carlyle had, in his youth, been particularly drawn to Goethe's definition of the unhappy man as one "who is possessed by some *idea* which he cannot convert into an *action,* or still more which restrains and withdraws him from action."[2] A similar fear, the fear of living in a world that could not be used or mastered, a world where "the production of an end" was not possible, always haunted Emerson. It crops up repeatedly, for example, in his 1841–1842 "Lectures on the Times." Emerson had, in 1836, defined nature as a discipline whose end was "to form the Hand of the mind;—to instruct us that 'good thoughts are no better than good dreams unless they be executed'" (CW, 1:24).[3] This idea is reasserted as Emerson turns his attention to contemporary reform movements in his "Introductory Lecture." "The new voices in the wilderness crying 'Repent,'" he writes, "have revived a hope, which had wellnigh perished out of the world, that the thoughts of the mind may yet, in some distant age, in some happy hour, be executed by the hands. That is the hope, of which all other hopes are parts" (CW, 1:174).

The tentative manner in which this hope is expressed suggests, of course, that it may well result in disillusionment. (Emerson's highest hopes rarely lead him into triumphant celebrations of an ideal achieved. They are often the prelude to further self-doubt when the initial moment of faith lets him down. Despair or loss then provokes a renewed emphasis on the overcoming, or the use, of that very doubt or failure.) Throughout the series of lectures, Emerson voices just such misgivings about his own capacity to produce or serve, to use, or to be useful. In his portrait of "the conservative," he worries that his ownership of his house and field depend not on "the knowledge of my countrymen that I am useful" but on the social machinery that upholds law and order (CW, 1:199). The conservative's property and full pantry are a "costly culture" in more ways than one: they rob him of the necessity of labor and the opportunity for self-subsistence. "I want," Emerson complains (speaking for the property owner), "the necessity of supplying my own wants" (CW, 1:195).

The sense of alienation Emerson is attempting to describe here—alienation from the empowering effects of labor—can sound very much like Hegel's famous analysis of the paradox underlying the master-worker relationship, a fundamental paradox of capitalist society that was not lost on Marx. But such alienation is not reserved for the property-owning conservative alone. In the lowest moment in "The Transcendentalist" (the companion lecture to "The Conservative"), Emerson records the same sense that "the doctrine of Use" has been violated: "My life is superficial, takes no root in the deep world; I ask, When shall I die, and be relieved of the responsibility of seeing an Universe which I do not use?" (CW, 1:213).

The "deep world" to which Emerson refers may be taken by some readers to mean an idealist world, a Neoplatonist, spiritual world or Kant's noumenal world. But the sentence suggests that, whatever "the deep world" is, it is, above all, created for and available to human use. There is good reason to suspect that "the deep world" is nothing less than what Emerson, in "The Conservative," calls "the existing world," "the Actual order of things," which man is obliged both to use and resist. "For the existing world is not a dream," he insists, "and cannot with impunity be treated as a dream; neither is it a disease; but it is the ground on which you stand, it is the mother of whom you were born" (CW, 1:188). ("The master," as Emerson phrases it in "Works and Days," is he who puts to use "the deep to-day which all [other] men scorn": "In daily life, what distinguishes the master is the using those materials he has, instead of looking about for what are more renowned, or what others have used well" [W, 7:175–76].)

There follows a shrewd rejoinder, delivered from the perspective of "the conservative," to those idealists and reformers who hope to disburden themselves of "the past" and "the existing social system." It is worth quoting if only to answer those frequent allegations that Emerson possesses no historical sense, no sense of the constraints and complications of social life. The problem with such criticisms is that they misconstrue the fundamentally antithetical nature of Emerson's imagination. They ignore his theories of power and their crucial reliance on the concepts of use, mastery, work, resistance—all activities that involve not the transcendence of experience, society, or conflict but action (which is, of necessity, always *re*action), production, antagonism. We are all conservatives, Emerson suggests, because any action, any attempt at self-definition or change, must be a reaction against something that was there before. We "cannot jump from the ground without using the resistance of the ground." Life simply is the use of things, whether it is the transformation or the rejection of what is being used. (Emerson defines even the rejection of something as "using it to dis-use it.") "We live & grow by use" (TN, 1:159). "What is useful will last" (TN, 1:68). Life is not transcendence. The "superficial" man, the man who "takes no root" in this world, is the man who fails to use the world.

> Moreover, so deep is the foundation of the existing social system, that it leaves no one out of it. We may be partial, but Fate is not. All men have their root in it. You who quarrel with the arrangements of society, and are willing to embroil all, and risk the indisputable good that exists, for the chance of better, live, move, and have your being in this, and your deeds contradict your words every day. For as you cannot jump from the ground without using the resistance of the ground, nor put out the boat to sea, without shoving from the shore, nor attain liberty without rejecting obligation, so you are under the necessity of using the Actual order of things, in order to disuse it; to live by it, whilst you wish to take away its life. The past has baked your loaf, and in the strength of its bread you would break up the oven. . . . (CW, 1:189)

The doctrine of use—the conviction that the world was made to be used, that men are obliged to "put their gifts to use" (as Emerson often states it), obliged to exercise their "infinite productiveness" (CW, 2:84)—encompasses that family of linked terms we have already encountered. They represent concepts with notable affinities to Nietzschean philosophy: incorporation, conversion, appropriation, education, the use of evil, over-coming, mastery. Emerson's essays may be read, individually and collec-tively, as so many variations on this single, ample, yet reductive theme of use. (The use of something is an inherently reductive—not a transcenden-tal—act: Emerson's prescription for the "use of truth" is the "reduction" of learning to practice [CW, 1:136]. He alternately speaks of use as a "melting down" or "degrading.") In essay after essay Emerson further elaborates and refines his fundamental perception of a universe in which all varieties of relationships—relationships between people, between mind and nature, human will and history, individuals and institutions—may be defined in terms of our capacity to use or be used. "The rule is, we are used as brute atoms until we think: then we use all the rest" (W, 6:252). He stated it with even greater candor in his notebooks: "We are used as brute atoms until we think. Then we instantly use self control & control others" (TN, 1:78).

The examples Emerson offers of this universal process may range, in any single essay, from the mundane to the sublime. "Nominalist and Real-ist," for example, begins with an extended, disillusioned meditation on one of Emerson's favorite themes: "the uses of great men." ("The whole value of history, of biography," as he states it early in his career, "is to increase my self-trust, by demonstrating what man can be and do" [CW, 1:102].

"Hermes, Cadmus, Columbus, Newton, Bonaparte, are the mind's ministers" [CW, 3:46].) The problem is that heroes seldom prove useful to the extent that we anticipate. "The least hint," Emerson writes, "sets us on the pursuit of a character, which no man realizes": "But there are no such men as we fable; no Jesus, nor Pericles, nor Caesar, nor Angelo, nor Washington, such as we have made. . . . It is bad enough, that our geniuses cannot do anything useful, but it is worse that no man is fit for society, who has fine traits" (CW, 3:133–34). The doctrine of use that forms the basis of this introductory lament is summed up more concisely later in the essay, as Emerson turns from the uses of great men to the uses of good authors: "I think I have done well, if I have acquired a new word from a good author; and my business with him is to find my own, though it were only to melt him down into an epithet or an image for daily use" (CW, 3:141).

Earlier in this same paragraph, Emerson lets drop an even more striking remark, one that likewise exemplifies that principle that decrees that we either use (something or someone else, or our own powers) or submit to being used. The metaphors he employs here are not of use, precisely, but of the related concepts of "imposition" and "absorption." The passage makes dramatically clear what is always implicit in the law of use: that the universe is, like man himself, a "stupendous antagonism" (W, 6:22)—that identity, health, and life itself depend on the successful counterbalancing of contending powers. "Each man," Emerson writes, "is a tyrant in tendency, because he would impose his idea on others; and their trick is their natural defence. Jesus would absorb the race; but Tom Paine or the coarsest blasphemer helps humanity by resisting this exuberance of power" (CW, 3:140–41). This balancing act of perpetual "duality" is "necessary to the existence of the World" (JMN, 5:30).

As he brings the essay to a close, Emerson restates what may be the most extreme ramification of the doctrine of use. It may well be the most perverse aspect of his thought, or at least the most difficult for us to comprehend or accept. The subject is death, specifically the death of those close to us. Divine Providence, Emerson writes, stating the general principle, conceals from each man all persons and objects "that do not concern" him; yet, when he "needs a new object" or a new road, that object or road suddenly is made visible to him. Similarly,

> When he has exhausted for the time the nourishment to be drawn from any one person or thing, that object is withdrawn from his observation, and though still in his immediate neighborhood, he does not suspect its presence. Nothing is dead: men feign themselves dead, and endure mock funerals and mournful obituaries, and there they stand looking out of the window, sound and well, in some new and strange disguise. (CW, 3:143)

There is certainly much to comment on in this passage, one that sounds so curious at first reading. There is the strange imagery of transparency

and the weirdly humorous tone Emerson seems to adopt toward so sacro-
sanct a topic. (How do men "feign themselves dead, and endure mock fu-
nerals"?)[4] There is the bizarrely solipsistic tendency of the whole description: Emerson seems to suggest that friends and relations will die—or, as
he archly phrases it, be "withdrawn from the immediate neighborhood"—
not because of anything that has happened to *them* but because *we* have
used them up. ("Men cease to interest us," he writes in "Circles," "when
we find their limitations. . . . As soon as you once come up with a man's
limitation, it is all over with him" [CW, 2:182].) How are we supposed to
respond to this disturbing, quasi-oral imagery of assimilation through
nourishment? In later, no less eccentric-sounding passages, Emerson will
call this process "suction" or "vampyrizing."[5] Such a passage may sound
extreme—yet it deserves our closest attention. For it is, despite its apparent
oddity, a thoroughly characteristic example of Emersonian psychology.

As criticism has come to emphasize Emerson as an antithetical and
Nietzschean thinker, one who sees things in terms of empowerment, opposition, and relation, increasing attention has been given to what James Cox
calls the "enormous psychological cost" such a philosophy may involve.
What Cox has in mind is the psychology at work in passages like the one
just cited—a psychology John McAleer calls "psychic vampirism." Emerson can, in moments like these, seem positively to require pain, loss, even
the death of those closest to him, as catalysts to his greatest, rebounding
assertions of power. "There is a sense," Cox remarks, "in which Emerson
literally feeds off the death of those around him. . . . For if Emerson was
austerely coming out of evil, he was at the same time asking for more. It
would be the fuel for his flame."[6]

This distinctive aspect of Emersonian psychology can indeed seem
harsh. Harold Bloom is quite right to suggest that Emersonian "compensation" is not the comforting platitude it is usually taken to be but the much
more exacting doctrine that "nothing is got for nothing." The audacious
pun (or puns) he seems to make in the middle of his essay on the loss of his
son to scarlet fever *is* shocking. "The mind goes antagonizing on," he
writes, "and never prospers but by fits. We thrive by casualties" (CW,
3:39). Emerson appears in lines like these, and in the many equally blunt
lines in "Experience," to have sunk, as Barbara Packer puts it, "to brood-
ings that at times border on the psychotic."[7]

Such sentiments, cruel as they may sound, are, however, wholly consistent with Emerson's doctrine of use, his confidence that we can confront
nothing that is not potentially in some way usable and his faith that the
universe exists as the embodiment of this principle. "Nothing in nature,"
he writes, "is exhausted in its first use. When a thing has served an end to
the uttermost, it is wholly new for an ulterior service. In God every end is
converted into a new means" (CW, 1:26). (Or, as he states it earlier in *Nature:* "nature's dice are always loaded . . . ; in her heaps and rubbish are

concealed sure and useful results" [CW, 1:25].) This belief in the malleability of the universe and in our consequent obligation to put all nature (even its "heaps and rubbish") and all experience (even pain and evil) to use—this is the basis of Emerson's severest lesson: his belief that suffering and defeat are somehow ultimately determined by what we need, what we can use, and that they can therefore be accepted (can even, in a sense, be welcomed) as both necessary and useful.

There are several passages in *Nature* where Emerson voices this belief directly or where it is expressed implicitly. Emerson's pragmatic commitment to "the Hand of the mind" comes, for example, at the conclusion of a long description of nature as a discipline—a call for the human "use of the world." Emerson is commonly thought of (and commonly written off) as "the philosopher of intuition"—a writer whose ultimate reliance on spontaneous or ecstatic insight makes him a poetic, antinomian, or mystical, rather than a philosophical (or even a morally tolerable) mind. This way of defining what Emerson means by intuition may well deserve, as Stanley Cavell suggests, to be redefined precisely in philosophical terms. But what is even clearer, in passages like those I quote, is that whatever else Emerson is, he remains, in an even more fundamental and consistent way, one of our central philosophers of *tuition*. I mean "tuition" in the Nietzschean sense: the education, resistance, discipline—the slavery, the tyranny, the imposition of a goal—we require in order to attain the power necessary to impose a shape on our own lives and on the world we inhabit.

Emerson returned often to the subject and imagery of tuition to reconfirm his belief that "The world exists for the education of each man" (CW, 2:5), that "The world is a system of mutual instruction" (EL, 3:42). "Whatever one act we do, whatever one thing we learn, we are doing and learning all things,—marching in the direction of universal power" (W, 8:23). He asserted unstintingly that the universe is "a school of power" (W, 10:128) to be used in the endless process of empowerment or self-creation—then simply left behind when its usefulness has ceased and the desired end has been attained. "Can I doubt that the facts & events & persons & personal relations . . . that now appertain to me will perish . . . utterly when the soul shall have exhausted their meaning and use? The world is the gymnasium on which the youth of the Universe are trained to strength & skill. When they have become masters of strength & skill, who cares what becomes of the masts & bars & ropes on which they strained their muscle?" (JMN, 5:229).

Emerson criticized Goethe for his devotion to pragmatic truth ("truth for the sake of culture") over "pure truth." But Goethe's failure to surrender himself to the universal "moral sentiment" did not make his philosophy of tuition—his dedication to putting all creation to the pragmatic question, *"What can you teach me?"*—any less attractive (CW, 4:163). Emerson was no less committed to "truth for the sake of culture," no less committed to the pragmatic belief "that knowledge is an instrument for doing work in this world."[8] The very structure of *Representative Men* (the book from which this passage comes) is an example of that philosophy at work. If it ends with Emerson's new gospel of pragmatism (we must "first, last, midst, and without end . . . honour every truth by use") it begins with the irreverent question Emerson ascribes to Goethe: what are—as Emerson titles his introductory chapter—"the *uses* of great men"? What can the past, what can genius, still *teach me*? The book's working title had been "Tests of Great Men," and each chapter is just such a pragmatic test. Each is an appreciation, but each is also an interrogation, a trying out of figures from Plato to Napoleon. *What can you teach me? Of what use is it?* Those were always the primary questions Emerson himself directed to nature, books, history, fate, to other people—to all being itself.

The most immovable and insurmountable facts ought all to be put to use as the pressure (the "tuition") necessary for the unlocking and empowerment of the human faculties. "Space, time, society, labor, climate, food, locomotion, the animals, the mechanical forces, give us sincerest lessons, day by day. . . . Every property of matter is a school for the understanding,—its solidity or resistance, its inertia, its extension, its figure, its divisibility" (CW, 1:23). The more important the faculty to be cultivated—the greater "the importance of the organ to be formed," as Emerson phrases it—the more extreme and intense will be the tuition necessary to shape it. The development of common sense, the knowledge that there is no substitute for executing a thought—these lessons must be learned (they may be, Emerson says, "pretermitted in no single case"), and they may require a lifetime of petty or harsh experience. "What tedious training, day after day, year after year, never ending, to form the common sense; what continual reproduction of annoyances, inconveniences, dilemmas; what rejoicing over us of little men; what disputing of prices, what reckonings of interest,—and all to form the Hand of the mind" (CW, 1:24). Or, as he restates this doctrine in "The American Scholar": "Drudgery, calamity, exasperation, want, are instructors in eloquence and wisdom" (CW, 1:59).

Emerson's further illustration of this principle, in *Nature,* is even more telling. He first suggests that the tuition our faculties receive is somehow ultimately "proportioned" to what they need and can bear. He goes on to state quite bluntly that adversity (poverty, the death of a husband or a father) is "needed most by those who suffer from it most." "Great spirits," "the sons of genius," are not merely the products of spontaneous vision: the greater the spirit, Emerson seems to suggest, then the longer and more acute will be the history of suffering and privation. This is one of Emerson's many parables on the use of failure—the imperative process he will call, in a later journal entry, "harvesting our losses." Here he calls it the "good office [in other words, the ultimately benevolent lessons] performed by Property [that is, the woeful lack of it] and its filial systems of debt and credit."

> The same good office is performed by Property and its filial systems of debt and credit. Debt, grinding debt, whose iron face the widow, the orphan, and the sons of genius fear and hate;—debt, which consumes so much time, which so cripples and disheartens a great spirit with cares that seem so base, is a preceptor whose lessons cannot be foregone, and is needed most by those who suffer from it most. (CW, 1:24)

Emerson ends his chapter on "Discipline" with a further, equally audacious, illustration of the same principle. He suggests, exactly as he will again in the above passage from "Nominalist and Realist," that the lives and deaths of those closest to us must ultimately be put to use. They must be made to serve, like the ravages of debt and the deaths of fathers, as the necessary preceptors in our own education. They must be welcomed, finally, Emerson implies, as what we most need. They must be accepted as the necessary foundation for the development of "great spirit" and "genius." They are the necessary price for our own "solid and sweet wisdom."

> It were a pleasant inquiry to follow into detail their ministry to our education, but where would it stop? [Emerson has been speaking of "these forms, male and female."] We are associated in adolescent and adult life with some friends, who, like skies and waters, are coextensive with our idea; who, answering each to a certain affection of the soul, satisfy our desire on that side. . . . We cannot chuse [sic] but love them. When much intercourse with a friend has supplied us with a standard of excellence, and has increased our respect for the resources of God who thus sends a real person to outgo our ideal; when he has moreover become an object of thought, and, whilst his character retains all its unconscious effect, is converted in the mind into solid and sweet wisdom,—it is a sign to us that his office is closing, and he is commonly withdrawn from our sight in a short time. (CW, 1:28–29)

A variety of responses might be made to such passages. One might choose to reject them as morally repellent. The reduction of the world, of other people, to convenient tools, "ministers to our education," opportune forms who seem to appear ("coextensive with our idea" of them) in order to satisfy our needs and desires, only to disappear again when those needs are answered—such a philosophy seems the crass embodiment of that "Golden Rule for Solipsists" (as Packer calls it) Emerson tosses off in "Experience": "Let us treat the men and women well: treat them as if they were real: perhaps they are" (CW, 3:35). His disgust with such a philosophy lies behind Quentin Anderson's famous accusation that Emerson was utterly unable "to imagine a world in which other persons really counted."[9]

One might, however, choose to temper one's immediate recoil from such sentiments with the knowledge that Emerson is recommending something that is really not so perverse as it sounds, a kind of psychology that actually has quite old and pious roots. For Emerson had, even in his youthful years as a minister, assured his parishioners that affliction could "be made to redound to your good"—and such readiness to "turn . . . every experience to good use" is, as Gay Wilson Allen notes, quite typical of a Puritan-derived belief in Providence: the faith that there is no happiness and no affliction, however severe, that is not God's specific punishment or reward. One of Emerson's 1827 sermons was devoted specifically to "The Uses of Unhappiness." The doctrine of use is indeed, as I shall suggest, indebted to a long tradition of Protestant perfectionism and to Unitarianism's signal devotion to self-culture.[10]

Yet there is a sense in which Emerson's unyielding determination to make all experience useful may be taken as something more than the reassertion of an inherited belief in moral perfectionism and as something other than, something more interesting than, solipsism. There is a sense in which the psychology being worked out in such eccentric-sounding passages is something more, even, than the expression of the quite understandable defense mechanisms Emerson needed in order to survive the loss of his father, his wife, his brothers, and a son.

Emerson is, in passages like this—in his suggestion that people (and adversity) will appear to us, then disappear, "coextensive with our idea" of them, "proportioned" to our need for them—trying out extreme claims, claims that invite equally extreme responses. Such extravagance positively asks for misreading. Yet, like many of his audacities, these claims are put forth simply, with an apparent serenity, without much in the way of fanfare or afterthought, so that it is easy to read them without really noticing them or easy to overlook them as the vague clichés of a genteel idealism. Getting at the peculiar quality and the implications of such passages will mean, therefore, recognizing just how strained and unnatural they do sound. Emerson's need, in passages like this, to flaunt or overturn conventional logic is itself highly significant. (His improbable logic seems to be that the calamities we suffer are somehow proportioned precisely to what we need; the deaths of others are therefore somehow determined by our use for them; there is therefore really no such thing as death—only use and the transformation of what is suffered or lost into what is used.) For it is in passages like this that Emerson comes closest to the kind of rhetorical and logical perversity Nietzsche practiced—and it may be that his inversion of conventional logic arises out of a similar attempt to experiment with novel and extreme ideas.

By perversity I mean Nietzsche's willingness to say, in the attempt to formulate a radically new perspective or a transvaluation of values, things that sound shockingly illogical. One thinks, for example, of a number of Nietzschean pronouncements: that we have "killed God"; that we "are not rid of God because we still have faith in grammar"; that there are no facts, only interpretations; that evil is the basis of good; that altruism is only a species of egoism; that the gods did not create evil but that evil created them (so no suffering would have to go unwitnessed); and so on. Such statements may sound to us less wrenched than they did originally, so prophetic have some of Nietzsche's ideas proven and so deeply have Nietzsche and a form of Nietzschean cant taken root in contemporary critical theory. But Nietzsche's reliance on overstatement, or what appears to be egregious misstatement, has traditionally left him uniquely vulnerable to misreading and to the charge that he cannot be taken seriously.

Emerson's explorations of the most extreme ramifications of the doctrine of use run that same risk. Emerson seems, in passages like these, to be experimenting with ideas that prefigure Nietzsche's. They are the very ideas that define the backbone of Nietzschean psychology—yet, when Nietzsche pushes them to their limits, they have resulted in some of the most confusing, controversial aspects of his thought. I refer to that central principle of Nietzschean philosophy Alexander Nehamas has emphasized: the commitment "to make a perfectly unified character out of all that one has done"—the Nietzschean doctrine of use that decrees that "[I shall] become flexible enough to use whatever I have done, do, or will do as elements within a constantly changing, never finally completed whole."[11]

Arthur Danto calls this the Nietzschean insistence that "we must affirm ourselves in our fate." Karl Jaspers calls it the aspiration to a "freedom without transcendence"—the only kind of freedom that can make a "life of authentic creation" possible. It is one of Nietzsche's "most central views": the desire to make "everything one does [everything that happens to one] equally essential to who one is." At the furthest boundaries of such a philosophy loom those doctrines that have seemed so baffling or even nonsensical—the doctrine of eternal recurrence, the rhapsodic declarations of *"amor fati."* Such, however, is Nietzsche's Dionysian "formula for greatness": do not "merely bear"—*learn to love* "what is necessary" (EH, 2:10)—live ready to say "Yes to opposition and war" (EH, 3:on BT, 3), ready to make "a Dionysian affirmation of the world as it is" (WP, 1041).[12]

Emerson was, of course, no less affected by the Romantic cult of self-cultivation than was Nietzsche. And it would be possible to take this idea that we treat our lives like unified or coherent works of art—that we become, as Nietzsche says, "poets of our life" (GS, 9)—as a form of self-culture already quite familiar to anyone who has studied the Transcendentalists. (Thoreau, for instance, voices this Romantic confusion of life and art when he writes in his journal: "Not how is the idea expressed in the stone or on canvas, is the question, but how far it has obtained form and expression in the life of the artist.") But what is insufficiently appreciated, it seems to me, is the extent to which Emerson's commitment to the use of things (always his guiding principle) marks his self-creation philosophy as something far closer to the kind of elaborate "self-actualizing" philosophy we recognize readily (and take more seriously) in Nietzsche. The hardness toward oneself that becoming an individual requires, the recognition that calamity is necessary for genius, that good is inseparable from evil ("good actions are sublimated evil ones" [HH, 1:107]), that failure is inseparable from success, suffering from life or form, pain from power, that death is a source of life, that poverty is a source of richness, that war is the source of creativity—we acknowledge and argue about such concepts as they are elaborated in Nietzsche, in his theories of the *Übermensch,* the will to power, the "eternal recurrence." But we are reluctant to give Emerson much credit for them.[13]

Yet Emerson is no less insistent that we must affirm ourselves in our fate, no less insistent that adversity "is needed most by those who suffer from it most." He unfailingly asserts that we are obliged to "make ourselves over in an image of our own," that the vocation of the scholar is henceforth "to make of mankind something more than it [has] been."[14] He embraces, no less enthusiastically than does Nietzsche, any "rough-plastic, abstergent force" (W, 6:172) that can push us from one state of humanity to another. Like Nietzsche, Emerson speaks of this as the overcoming of one kind of culture, or morality, or humanness, and the creation of a new kind of "superhumanity" (W, 10:214). It is a keystone of his thought that everything we do, everything that befalls us, ought to be put to use in what Nietzsche would call some "healthy" or "life-affirming" way.

He favors, no less than does Nietzsche, not the avoidance of evil and pain, not "an excision of ills from life," but "the conquering of defects by their inclusion in a richer life."[15] This distinction between denying evil and insisting that it be transfigured or incorporated so as to enrich, in some way, one's own life and philosophy is—as Josiah Royce suggests in a prescient, posthumously published defense of Nietzsche—absolutely crucial. Yet it is a distinction lost on most of Emerson's critics. We generally ignore or tone down such ideas when they appear in Emerson, or we misclassify them as cosmic optimism. Or we condemn them as the simplistic solipsism that is merely the flip side of that brand of idealism we usually ascribe to him. We generally fail to appreciate the Nietzschean and confrontational nature of such thinking and, instead, categorize it as "escaping from history" or "retreating from the actual to the ideal."

Jaspers notes the way in which necessity (that is, the acceptance or affirmation of necessity, accident, inner impulses—what Emerson calls fate or casualties) takes the place of transcendence in Nietzsche's philosophy. His description is just as applicable to Emerson. Before Nietzsche, it was Emerson who tried to teach us that "The material of freedom consists of necessities" (TN, 1:80). "In the place of transcendence," Jaspers writes, "Nietzsche puts 'necessity' metaphysically so conceived that every accident that happens to me and every impulse that stirs within me appears as meaningful in relation to the totality of my development as a *creator.*"[16]

Jaspers calls this a Nietzschean *"mode of existential actualization."*

Nietzsche advances such conceptions repeatedly, of course—as in Zarathustra's advice that "instead of seeking revenge for a wrong, it is better to show that an enemy has done one some good. Instead of resenting a harm, it is better to use it as material for further development and so to prevent it from constituting a harm at all."[17] The Dionysian man, Nietzsche writes, can balance any form of negation with his excess of "fertilizing energies that can still turn any desert into lush farmland" (GS, 370). We ought, as Nietzsche puts it, to find motives for the accidents in our lives, not sulk at fate and poverty but make them into needful, productive parts of our lives: "*Finding motives for our poverty.*—There is no trick that enables us to turn a poor virtue into a rich and overflowing one; but we can reinterpret its poverty into a necessity so that it no longer offends us when we see it and we no longer sulk at fate on its account" (GS, 17).

Emerson invokes a similar type of *Übermensch* when he speaks of the God (the potential power) that can be found in the bleakest rocks. Like Nietzsche, he calls this the need for "poverty" in our search for self-recovery, action, a firmer mastery of ourselves: "And yet is the God the native of these bleak rocks. That need makes in morals the capital virtue of self-trust. We must hold hard to this poverty, however scandalous, and by more vigorous self-recoveries, after the sallies of action, possess our axis more firmly" (CW, 3:46). The truest symbols—all "success, reality, joy and power"—reside precisely in this "rich poverty" of "the deep to-day." It is a poverty most men scorn and hate but one a master will put to use (W, 7:175–76).

However indebted such a philosophy of use and self-actualization may be to the familiar Romantic ideal of self-culture, it is certainly something other than idealism as Emerson scholarship usually defines it. It seems to lean more in the direction of Nietzschean pragmatism, toward what Nietzsche scholarship calls a "creative nihilism." It might be more accurately identified as what Allan Megill calls the "aestheticist ontology": the controversial attempt, undertaken by Nietzsche and his twentieth-century descendants, "to expand the aesthetic to embrace the whole of reality."[18] Nietzsche, for instance, speaks of his philosophy as "an anti-metaphysical view of the world—yes, but an artistic one" (WP, 1048).

Emerson makes a similar turn toward an aestheticist ontology and away from the epistemological concerns of a Kantian or post-Kantian idealism. He passes quickly over the whole problem of the "noble doubt . . . whether nature [and other people] outwardly exist" by simply suggesting that the question itself (the question of whether nature is "ideal" or verifiable by "the accuracy of my senses") is not very important or worth much further dispute. What *is* important is whether nature, men and women, all our experience, can be put to use—whether it can be treated, in other words, like an artist's materials in an act of creation—to minister to our education and to supply us with standards of excellence, with forms of thought, with matter for our own "solid and sweet wisdom," with material for the endless production that Emerson and Nietzsche both uphold as the purpose of human life and culture. "Whether nature enjoy a substantial existence without, or is only in the apocalypse of the mind," Emerson abruptly concludes (as if the whole prodigious issue could really be resolved in a sentence), "it is alike useful and alike venerable to me" (CW, 1:29). His wording allows us at least to raise the question: is it venerable precisely because it is useful?

"The test of a religion or philosophy," Emerson writes, "is, the number of things it will explain" (TN, 1:132). And how are we to read that? (Interpreting Emerson is, as I have suggested, often like trying to scan a line of verse in which the emphasis may fall in ways that imply quite contradictory meanings.) One may wish to take such a claim as the expression of a correspondence theory of truth; it is, after all, with theories of "correspondence" that we usually associate Emerson. One may take him to mean that the business of a religion or philosophy is, as comprehensively as possible, to explain—or correspond with—the truth that is really out there. But there is certainly equal reason for interpreting such a claim as the expression of a pragmatic theory of truth. What is finally most important about a religion or a philosophy, Emerson seems to imply, is not what it is—or the accuracy of its correspondence to an absolute God or an absolute truth—but what it does, how consistently it may be put to human use. "We live day by day under the illusion that it is the fact or event that imports, whilst really it is not that which signifies, but the use we put it to, or what we think of it" (W, 8:293–94).

. . .

The doctrine of use looks forward to a kind of pragmatism or creative nihilism we associate with Nietzsche or William James. But it also looks back toward a long Protestant tradition. Emerson's New England forebears lived with the stringent demands of a theology that asked them to "thwart the . . . elemental impulse [of protest or despair] for the sake of the higher unity of experience; as when we rejoice in the endurance of the tragedies of life." It is, as Royce phrased it in "The Problem of Job," a commitment not to the "abolishment" but to the "overcoming," the "subordination," of evil—a commitment to the "strenuous whole of life": "It is not those innocent of evil who are fullest of the life of God, but those who in their own case have experienced the triumph over evil. . . . You can never clean the world of evil: but you can subordinate evil."[19]

A psychology of overcoming and creative sublimation is, precisely, Nietzsche's and Emerson's. But it was a staple of Puritan writing as well. (As Andrew Delbanco suggests, it even goes back to the Aristotelian notion that "virtue, like a muscle or a limb, requires continual strengthening through exercise.") The Puritans understood the uses of adversity, the danger of gainsaying Providence, and the need for "gracious afflictions." They understood that "all ordeals are tests to be met with delight." John Cotton advised his congregation to remember the "joy & consolation" to be found in accepting afflictions as God's "speciall favour." "Adversity," Cotton Mather proclaimed, "makes the best Christians." One of the justifications for the appropriation of North America was the Protestant faith in sheer use—the conviction that a land unworked remained a void awaiting its rightful owners: "It is a principle in nature, that in a vacant soil he that taketh possession of it, and bestoweth culture and husbandry upon it, his right it is." Jonathan Edwards's *Dissertation Concerning the End for which God Created the World* unrolls a majestic vision of God's absolute self-sufficiency. Yet undergirding even that description of omnipotence is the urgent emphasis on the "proper exercise and expression" of divine power. God's sovereignty, Edwards insists, was not meant to remain "dormant and useless."[20]

A self, a world, existed to be used. It was there to be cultivated, exercised, disciplined, made productive. If we wish to look only at the native tradition of self-perfection in which Emerson grew up, we can cite a long list of representative figures from Franklin to Gatsby who have made "the promise of America" the promise "of power over all experience, and ultimately sole authorship of one's very being." But closest to Emerson's native grounds is the Boston Unitarianism that prized "self-development and self-fulfillment" as "the essence of religion and the chief end of man." Daniel Walker Howe has amply documented Unitarianism's extraordinary commitment to what William Ellery Channing called "self-culture." Liberal Christianity would, Joseph Tuckerman promised, "remove, or enable every individual to surmount, every obstacle in the way to the highest moral completeness within his attainment."[21] Unitarianism taught that "every man had within his soul a microcosmos of faculties, which, if properly developed, would enable him to rule himself." The new American deserved, Orestes Brownson declared, a new philosophy that would grant him the freedom to develop "by practical demonstration" "all the faculties of the human soul."[22]

Behind Channing's claim that "no right is so . . . necessary . . . as the right of exerting the powers which nature has given us" lies, of course, the Christian humanism of the Renaissance, with its exalted view of human potential. It was a claim intensified by the endeavor of the Scottish common sense philosophers—Dugald Stewart in his *Philosophy of the Active and Moral Powers of Man* or Thomas Reid in *The Active Powers of the Mind*—to prove, in refuting Hobbes, or Hume, Locke, and Bentham, that men were moved to action by an innate moral or benevolent power or faculty. Thus James Walker, Harvard's Alford Professor of Moral Philosophy and later president of the university, preached that "the mysterious omnipotence of which Christ spoke was nothing other than the exercise of one's own 'latent powers.'"[23]

"Perfect"—as a noun, verb, and adjective—is one of the key words in Emerson's vocabulary. Much will, once again, depend on whether we choose to stress Emerson's conception of perfect as a *noun*—as alluding to a Platonic "Perfect"—or as a *verb,* in the sense of making or perfecting a self. Local sources for this latter sense of perfection may be found in the self-perfection the Unitarians revered, as well as in the hunger for Christian perfectionism marking the persistent series of religious revivals in antebellum America. Revivalism, as it is now clear, was the "dominant theme in America from 1800 to 1860," and at its high tide "perfectionism was the crest of the wave."[24] The self-culture of the Unitarian aristocracy and the evangelical zeal for personal holiness were not, of course, the same thing. Yet by the 1850s it was becoming apparent to many that revivalism, Unitarianism, Quaker doctrine, and Transcendentalism were all part of a larger movement that cherished the belief that the world was the proscenium before which men could attain an ideal self.[25] "Columbus," as Emerson phrased it, "needs a planet to shape his course upon" (EL, 2:18). "The WORLD is a theatre on which you are to prove yourself a Christian," Henry Ware Jr. wrote in his classic exposition of Unitarian principles, *Formation of the Christian Character.* He went on to espouse the quest for perfection ("Never be satisfied while short of it and then you will always be improving") and to define the proper conduct of life as "an exercise of perpetual self-discipline."[26]

One fundamental link between Unitarianism, Emersonian Transcendentalism, and the pragmatism of William James and John Dewey is precisely this notion that one uses the world as the means of self-improvement. And Sampson Reed—who left the Harvard Divinity School after his conversion to Swedenborgianism and whose writings found an avid audience in Emerson—should not be left out here as a key early influence on Emerson's thought. Reed's prescription for the cultivation of "the powers of the mind" fits well into the tradition of Protestant perfectionism I have been sketching. Beneath the muddiness of Reed's rhetoric is a transparent call for "a life of active usefulness" ("the end of all education"). Society, the word of God, the natural world—each was intended "to draw forth the latent energies of the soul." Each creature in "the animal world" will one day, Reed prophesies, "seem to be conscious of its use . . . and man will become conscious of the use of everything."[27]

"Draw" or "call forth" are the verbs Reed employs most often to describe the relationship between the world and human power. For Channing and Emerson, the more common image is the "unfolding" of human potential. Man's "spiritual nature," Channing writes, is "unfolded by right and vigorous exertion."[28] Society for the Unitarians was necessary, if only, as one contemporary observer remarked, as "a mere discipline for the nourishment of individual character." Yet social life posed an equal dan-

ger, threatening the loss of the "moral judgment, and of power over ourselves."[29] Emerson toed the same fine line when it came to social existence.
Connection with the wrong society scattered your force, yet the Me always
demanded other men "to act upon" and a complex, resisting Not Me on
which to unfold its faculties:

> Insulate a man and you annihilate him. He cannot unfold—he cannot live
> without a world. Put Napoleon into an island prison and let the great facul-
> ties of that man find no men to act upon, no Alps to climb . . . and he would
> beat the air and appear stupid. Then transfer him to large countries, dense
> population, complex interests, and antagonist power and you shall see him
> unfold his masterful energies. (EL, 2:17)

. . .

A philosophy of use invites an array of objections subtler than the accusations of solipsism we have already encountered. Use and action may, for
instance, become, according to the logic of such a philosophy, ends in
themselves. The whole idea of moral values is then rendered crucially ambiguous. This was Randolph Bourne's criticism of Deweyan instrumentalism: it assumed "that just any growth was justified and almost any activity
valuable so long as it achieved ends." Americans have, Bourne added, habitually "been content with getting somewhere without asking too closely
whether it was the desirable place to get."[30]

George Santayana had a similar objection in mind when he accused
William James of mistaking a *psychology* of self-realization for a philosophy. Jamesian pragmatism was not a *philosophy,* in any true sense of the
word: it was merely a "local and temporary grammar of action." This was
Santayana's definition of barbarism: "the admiration for mere force," the
belief "that the exercise of energy is the absolute good, irrespective of motives or of consequences."[31] Nehamas notes the related moral confusion in
Nietzsche: "Nietzsche is clearly much more concerned with the question of
how one's actions are to fit together into a coherent, self-sustaining, well-
motivated whole than he is with the quality of those actions themselves."[32]

At this point, most Emersonians would probably respond that moral
value is precisely what is least ambiguous in Emerson's thought. His well-
known faith in "the moral law" is routinely accepted as the superego to all
of his ideas: it seems to function as the moral guardian, ready always to
qualify even his most extravagant assertions. "The moral law," Alan Hodder writes, "was Emerson's bulwark against doubt. . . . [E]arly and late it
remained the ground of an unshakable faith."[33] Yet, despite all of his de-
ferrals to the moral law, the actual role of moral value in Emerson's work
seems to me something that is, at most, arguable, not something to be
taken for granted. It occupies a far more fragile position in his thought
than is generally recognized. I shall return, in chapter 5, to the way in
which Emerson's emphasis on use and "will" throws into question that

notion of an absolute moral law we usually ascribe to him.

Santayana raises a further, perhaps an even more serious, objection to this tradition of Protestant perfectionism. A reasonable morality, Santayana argues, a morality frankly relative to man's *im*perfect nature, will achieve some sort of harmony between an imperfect self and a world man can never perfectly comprehend. It will terminate not in endless strife but in philosophy and the arts. But an "anthropocentric" morality, the morality that takes "the apotheosis of the human spirit" as the end of creation, will undertake the never-ending process of surrounding the self "with objects and points of resistance, so as to become aware of its own stress and vocation." For the egotist the world is so much content for his mind to envelop, piece by piece, to prove itself the larger thing. (German idealism, transcendentalism, liberal Christianity, even Christianity in general—each is, according to Santayana, egoistic to the degree that it relies on an anthropocentric God.) "To despise the world and withdraw into the realm of mind, as to a subtler and more congenial sphere, is quite contrary to [the transcendentalist's] idealism. Such a retreat might bring him peace, and he wants war. His idealism teaches him that strife and contradiction, as Heraclitus said, are the parents of all things." A philosophy of self-culture and self-testing will ultimately—so Santayana predicts—find its "most adequate and soul-satisfying expression" in "universal battle."[34]

For Emerson, war *was* "the Father of all things" (W, 11:341). War and endless strife were within "the highest right" because they mimicked nature's tendency to "break up the old adhesions" and allow "the atoms of society to take a new order" (W, 11:341–42). The history of the soul's enlargement was—inevitably—also "the natural history of calamity." Growth "comes by shocks." The "outward biography of man," Emerson said, must be "a putting off of dead circumstances day by day" (CW, 2:72).

We are back, in other words, at that most paradoxical aspect of Emersonian psychology: destruction—the relinquishment of dead circumstances— is the necessary foundation for expansion, the necessary starting point for a "self" in any sense. It is the failure that is necessary for victory, the overcoming necessary for power, the calamity necessary for creation. A philosophy of use seems to require some "stupendous antagonism": it seems to require a loss for every gain, some form of death or dying "out of nature" (CW, 3:41) for every moment of regeneration. It decrees that the history of the self's expansion must be concurrently the history of its defeat. It implies that beneath the humanistic affirmations of self there will always remain some trace of the antihumanistic urge to "write off the self."[35] This will to overcome the "merely human" in the very gesture of asserting its capacities—to imagine nonhuman interpretations of the world in the human act of interpreting it (WP, 616)—is most familiar to us as a characteristic of Nietzschean philosophy. But it is characteristic of Emerson's as well.

We shall return again to the necessary role that failure, negative power, and war play in Emerson's imagination. It will be helpful at this point, however, to look closely at his doctrine of use as it takes shape in some representative texts, early and late.

The Early Lectures, 1833–1836

Emerson's 1833–1834 lectures on natural science, delivered after his resignation from the Second Church ministry and his first trip to Europe, make clear his commitment to a newly emerging intellectual vocation. That vocation—the forerunner of William James's call for a "topography of the limits of human power" or Nietzsche's attempt to discover what "might yet *be made of man*" (BGE, 203)—was to chart the unrealized boundaries of human potential. The lectures on natural science put forth a conception of "the relation of man to the globe" (as Emerson titled the second lecture) that he would uphold for the rest of his life. They confirm not Whicher's notion of Emerson's evolution through different stages but Thomas McFarland's hypothesis that individual philosophical development is most typically "an unwrapping of something already there," "the unfolding of a single, constant orientation to life."[36]

For the early lectures stress the same imperatives, the same commitment to approaching the world as a "field of action" (or, as Emerson elsewhere called it, "a theatre for action" [CW, 3:57]) that we have seen in *Nature* and *The Conduct of Life*. Maurice Gonnaud is right to note the "appetite for experience and . . . striving to push human faculties to their limit" revealed in these early lectures.[37] As much as anything in Emerson, they document what I have called (borrowing Hegel's terms) the Emersonian "appetitive relation to the external world": the central Emersonian conception of a perpetual, universal dualism in which "the relation of man to the globe" is a "relation of use" (EL, 1:48); in which natural energies exist as a challenge and stimulus, "provok[ing]" and "invit[ing] man . . . to activity and commerce" (EL, 1:74, 48); in which human and nonhuman forces are kept in proportion (EL, 1:34, 35, 49), adjustment (EL, 1:37–39, 48), symmetry (EL, 1:49), balance (EL, 1:38), or counterbalance (EL, 1:68). The third lecture, "Water," ends with the image of the hydrostatic paradox ("we learn that in a bucket of water resides a latent force sufficient to counterbalance mountains" [EL, 1:68]), one of Emerson's favorite metaphors for the universal necessity of resistance, or balancing of powers. It is an image Emerson was fond of reworking. Years later he would restate it in his notebooks: "We should be crushed by the atmosphere but for the reaction of the air within the body" (TN, 1:84).

Firmly in place in the early lectures are the central Emersonian ideas of use, testing (or experimenting), practical power, the use of evil, danger or privation, education, resistance, war (all antagonisms that can provoke or invigorate), overcoming, and mastery. The concept of conversion or assimilating power is here most frequently represented as "possession." There is, as Gonnaud comments, "an almost barbaric primitivism" in Emerson's calculated invocations of hazard and self-testing.[38] "Let a man keep his presence of mind," Emerson writes, "and there is scarcely any danger so desperate from which he cannot deliver himself" (EL, 1:38). "The adjustment of [man's] forces to the forces of nature from which he would be in danger, is very nice, and if it had been a little less, would have been insufficient" (EL, 1:35). The history of navigation illustrates "the nearness with which [man] comes to the edge of destruction and yet has powers just sufficient to bring him off in total safety" (EL, 1:35).

Natural history is, above all—like nature itself—a tool, a source of power. (To farmers, "these strong masters," Emerson writes in *Society and Solitude,* "the landscape is an armory of powers / Which, one by one, they know to draw and use / They harness beast, bird, and insect, to their work" [W, 7:135].) It is not knowledge or natural beauty for its own sake that Emerson admires but the "practical naturalist" (EL, 1:6), "the uses of natural history" (the title of the first lecture), the "salutary effect upon the mind and character" (EL, 1:19) scientific study confers.

Like Antaeus, man is a "broken giant" whose "conversation with nature" restrengthens and "invigorates" him (EL, 1:11). Man's central position in the universe "has been prophesied in nature for a thousand thousand years before he appeared" (EL, 1:29). (The globe, Emerson writes, "was given to [man] to possess" [EL, 1:48]. "Ages ago it was settled that man should be master" [EL, 1:42].) And natural force is the necessary antagonist that can provoke him to discover and develop his own counterforce as he resists, overcomes, and takes possession. Scientific knowledge and the powers inherent in the "symmetry of [human] parts" are the requisite tools, man's "equipment for the conquest of nature" (EL, 1:41). "The fact which commands our attention," Emerson declares, "is the manner in which man is led on by his wants to the development of his powers and so to the possession of the globe" (EL, 1:41). (Emerson, famously, restates this vision in the first paragraph of *Nature* when he challenges his readers "to action proportioned to nature"—"proportioned" suggesting, as it usually does in Emerson, the *resisting* or *counterbalancing* of nature. Such action or world building, if rightly undertaken, will, Emerson once again prophesies, end with "the kingdom of man over nature.") What is finally of greatest value is not knowledge or the scientific process but the new stores of strength—the "accumulated force," "the prospective power," "the armed hand"—that process imparts to the naturalist himself (EL, 1:13).

"The highest state of man, physical, intellectual, and moral," Emerson concludes, "can only coexist with a perfect Theory of Animated Nature" (EL, 1:83). Natural history, in other words, makes possible man's highest state. As always, it is the reaffirmation and strengthening of "the constitution of man" (the image suggests sheer vital force) that is Emerson's true concern—and, because the universe is anthropocentric, all nature can richly serve that cause. Man is centrally connected to all the kingdoms of life and able to put "all beings" to use (EL, 1:71).

One could go on through all eighty-some pages of the natural science lectures, cataloguing the many small tales of power that make up Emerson's great, abiding theme. Every page offers new anecdotes or fables of empowerment and use—"illustrations," as Emerson would later call them, "of human power in every department" (CW, 2:179). (This practice of collecting illustrations of power, action, or contests of will is so characteristic of all Emerson's essays that it may be considered one of his principal methods of composition.) A visit to the Jardin des Plantes in Paris enlarges "the limits of the possible." The "main advantage" of natural history is "the direct service which it renders to the cultivator and the world, the amount of useful economical information which it communicates" (EL, 1:10–11). "Mountain minerals," Emerson promises, "will pay their searcher with active limbs and refreshed spirits. And he who wanders along the margin of the sounding sea for shellfish or marine plants, will find strength of limb and sharpness of sight and bounding blood in the same places. . . . [The Naturalist] discovers the virtues of these bodies and the mode of converting them to use" (EL, 1:11–12).

Man's "knowledge and use" of coal "contribute to our pleasure and prosperity at this hour"—and, more important, illustrate the principle that "there is not an object in nature so mean or loathsome, not a weed, not a toad, not an earwig, but a knowledge of its habits would lessen our disgust and convert it into an object of worth" ("every thing," Emerson says, "is a monster till we know what it is for") (EL, 1:17). The sense of sight—which is to play so prominent a role in *Nature*—is here celebrated for its practical power. To the average eye the world may appear dull and unprofitable, but let a Galileo regard the same landscape and it becomes no longer alien to us but genial and usable. It becomes, as Emerson would later express it, "domesticated." (A painful, "alien world," Emerson would remark in "Literary Ethics," is "a world not yet subdued by the thought" [CW, 1:106].) A world scanned and identified is a world converted to human use. No longer dumb or threatening, it now sings to us. It has been rendered user-friendly:

> A dull dumb unprofitable world is this to many a man that has all his senses in health. But bring under the same arch of day, upon the same green sod, under the shadow of the same hills Linnaeus or Buffon or Cuvier or Humboldt and the sea and the land will break forth into singing, and all the trees of the field will clap their hands. (EL, 1:18)

This celebration of "the kingdom of man over nature" looks forward to

Nature and back to Sampson Reed's *Observations on the Growth of the Mind*. The day must come, Reed had promised, when "Everything will seem to be conscious of its use; and man will become conscious of the use of everything." On that day even "brutes may add to their instinct submission to human reason," subjecting their will "to the will of the rider" as graciously as did "the animal on which the King of Zion rode into Jerusalem."[39]

. . .

Francis Bacon, the most famous of English natural scientists, was, quite appropriately, on Emerson's mind in these years, as he struggled to put together his own "first philosophy" (JMN, 3:360). His description of Bacon's achievement is equally a description of the new vocation on which he himself had embarked. Emerson finds much to censure in Bacon's notorious duplicity, but for "the exalted side of [Bacon's] character"—Bacon's dedication to making all human faculties "productive"—he has only praise (EL, 1:326). Bacon was, Emerson announces in an 1835 lecture, "the first conspicuous example of modern times of the philosopher in action" (EL, 1:187). Bacon had demonstrated that "the literary man" could "know the whole theory of all that was done in the world" and still be "master of the practice also" (EL, 1:328–29).

There was for Bacon nothing "in being and action" that could not be mastered, nothing that could not be "drawn and collected into contemplation and doctrine" (EL, 1:328). Bacon was venerable as "the profound and vigorous thinker who has enlarged our knowledge in the powers of man, and so our confidence in them" (EL, 1:325–26). Bacon had, in short, transformed the speculative man into a new kind of "pragmatical" man. He left behind him books "designed to invigorate the power of the mind," books whose "new logic" was not intended for idle "dispute" but as "arts for the use of mankind . . . to subdue nature by experiment and inquiry" (EL, 1:330–31). The very history of Bacon's hard-won achievement was itself another lesson in power and resistance. Carried out in the face of all manner of adversity, it gave "new courage and confidence in the powers of man" (EL, 1:335).

Such an accomplishment made Emerson think immediately of Goethe, the contemporary poet/scholar who had continued to uphold Bacon's belief in human potential. It was Goethe, Emerson writes, who "in our age . . . has summed up . . . the powers of man." He goes on to cite the extended survey of mankind's diverse faculties from Carlyle's translation of *Wilhelm Meisters Lehrjahre* (EL, 1:326). It is one antecedent for the many catalogues of human power Emerson himself would compile—most notably, perhaps, the "occasional examples of the action of man upon nature with his entire force" (CW, 1:43) adduced at the conclusion of *Nature*. Goethe had called for the cultivation of all human faculties, "from the first bickerings of boys, up to the vast equipments by which countries are conquered and retained." It is the same vision of all natural powers made productive, under the dominion of "man's kingdom," that Bacon had embraced (EL, 1:326).

Emerson was, in these early years of self-definition, clearly searching for predecessors for his own vocation—for the project that would give him "room and verge enough," as a modern-day prophet of power, to survey and expand the possibilities for human action. Bacon and Goethe may have been the preeminent examples of this modern "priest" (or "perfect man"), this new "interpreter of Nature" capable of reenvisioning the world as the arena for human exertion and expansion (EL, 1:326). But they were not the only ones. All of the lectures on great men Emerson delivered in the years prior to the publication of *Nature* emphasize the ways in which the great figures of the past extended the limits of human power. And in each biographical case study Emerson is intent on extracting the "lesson of power" or the parable of mastery and resistance that an exemplary life can offer.

Michelangelo is thus enlisted as one whose stubborn overcoming of impossible odds "enlarge[d] . . . the known powers of man." A paragon of self-reliance (Emerson compares him with George Washington), Michelangelo possessed "unexpected dexterity in practical and even small contrivances": he ground his own paint and made his own files, chisels, and scaffolds. The sublime beauty of his art had pragmatic roots. It was nourished by the "severe laws" of opposition and adversity, grounded and tested in "action and practice" (EL, 1:106–7). Like Bacon or Goethe, Michelangelo was a teacher who preached the full extent of human potential. His genius was not merely a matter of intuition or spontaneous vision. It required the harshest discipline, the trial and practice in which the faculties could be provoked and developed. It required the disciplined—not the indolent—eye. "Here was a man who lived to show his fellow men that to the human faculties on every hand worlds of grandeur and grace are opened which no profane eye and no indolent eye can behold but which to see and to enjoy demands a severest discipline of all the physical, intellectual, and moral faculties of the individual" (EL, 1:116).

This Emersonian insistence on self-cultivation through severe laws and severe discipline is, it should be noted, also fundamental in Nietzsche's theory of creation. The anarchist's notion of immediate or complete freedom never, according to Nietzsche, produced anything of value or anything that made existence worth affirming. Virtue, art, culture, government ("all that there is or has been on earth of freedom, subtlety, boldness, dance, and masterly sureness") required the tyranny—the "slavery"—of laws and discipline. "The long unfreedom of the spirit . . . the discipline thinkers imposed on themselves to think" were, Nietzsche claimed, "the means through which the European spirit has been trained to strength" (BGE, 188). Every expansion of the human spirit requires "a new kind of enslavement" (GS, 377). As Nehamas states it, "The assumption that human nature is best expressed in perfect freedom . . . , [Nietzsche] insists, is unjustified"; "freedom does not consist in leaving rules and principles behind but in their appropriate internalization."[40]

It is still common for scholars to speak offhandedly of Emerson's "strategic retreat from the actual to the ideal, the specific to the universal." There is no weight of the real in Emerson, Quentin Anderson argues, no "heavy givenness which we must encounter." The Emersonian self is an abstraction "which creates its world instead of acting in it." "Missing from Emerson's . . . early work," Jeffrey Steele writes, "is any fully realized sense of centripetal force, pushing inward, restraining the onrush of power." According to David Simpson, Emerson simply "project[s] a world that is all ego, all self." He was, John Updike remarks, an early proponent of that Yippie rallying cry: "If it feels good, it's moral."[41]

But there is nothing more characteristic of Emerson's thought (early and late) than the conviction that the individual must seek empowerment through the disciplined confrontation of the painful "actual." "It is only on reality," Emerson insists time and again, "that any power of action can be based" (CW, 3:59). The Emersonian self is not an ideal (or universal) abstraction but something that can only take form and reality within the context of a resisting reality. Identity can only be established within "the reality of relation" (CW, 3:78). Emerson "rarely thought of things in calm isolation," as William Gass observes, "but in angry and anxious juxtaposition."[42] "More are made good by exercitation," Emerson writes, quoting Democritus, "than by nature" (W, 6:79). "The toughness of the actual world is the measure of our weakness. . . . [I]t is needful that the soul should come out to the external world. It is imperfect until it does" (EL, 2:310–11). "Every man's character depends in great part upon the scope & occasions that have been afforded him for its development. . . . [T]he Mind is something to be unfolded & will disclose some faculties more & some less just in proportion to the room & excitements for action that are furnished it" (L, 1:220). "The fact of two poles, of two forces, centripetal and centrifugal, is universal, and each force by its own activity develops the other" (CW, 3:124).

Nietzsche believed there can be no "asocial or presocial self," that no self can exist "independently of some sort of relation to other selves" or exist prior to being shaped by some form of resistance or will to power.[43] So did Emerson. Though we should recognize our social selves as "contingent and rather showy possessions," they remain the necessary foundation for our identity and for our capacities for action. "I must have children," he insists, "I must have events, I must have a social state and history, or my thinking and speaking want body or basis" (W, 6:158). The fronting—Emerson called it "the old game, the habit of fronting the fact"

(CW, 3:55)—the overcoming, the "appropriate internalization" of opposition we usually think of as a distinctively Nietzschean idea. But it is also distinctively Emersonian: before Nietzsche made it a founding principle in his vivisection of European value systems, Emerson had worked and reworked it as the keystone of his own philosophy. An anarchic, perfect freedom or perfect self, innocent of the discipline imposed by the hard facts of experience, was never Emerson's goal. "No house," as he put it in "Manners," "though it were the Tuileries, or the Escurial, is good for anything without a master" (CW, 3:79).

Just as Nietzsche believed that the most powerful and life-affirming art came out of the most severe imposition of spiritual "tyranny," so Emerson held that the most eloquent speaker "learned his lessons in a bitter school," honed his "aboriginal strength" in particular and direct acts of resistance (W, 7:95–96). "Wherever the polarities meet," Emerson said, "wherever the fresh moral sentiment, the instinct of freedom and duty, come in direct opposition to fossil conservatism and the thirst of gain, the spark will pass. The resistance to slavery in this country has been a fruitful nursery of orators" (W, 7:95). Only friction, exercitation, and the toughness of the actual world can create the spark of power.

In his searching, still largely unappreciated lecture on "The Conservative," Emerson criticizes both the conservative and radical parties for advocating social systems that legislate away the very "friction" that makes "self-help" necessary. The conservative "makes so many additions and supplements to the machine of society, that it will play smoothly and softly, but will no longer grind any grist." The idealistic radical, legislating "for man as he ought to be," makes "no allowance for friction" at all— "and this omission makes his whole doctrine false" (CW, 1:196–97).

Everything of value comes not in retreat or in utopian isolation but in specific moments of conflict or war: "There is nothing real or useful that is not a seat of war" (CW, 3:59). Every nation begins in a particular act of strong will. Every tradition may be traced back to a particular moment of reaction, a successful instance of usage or mastery: "every [state] was once the act of a single man; every law and usage was a man's expedient to meet a particular case" (CW, 3:117). True eloquence was "not differenced from action"; it was the conversion of "opposition" into "opportunity" (W, 7:97).

Milton was one of Emerson's lifelong heroes. Samuel Johnson he was prone to calling "mutton-head." Yet it was entirely characteristic of Emerson that he saw fit to condemn Milton for an easy idealism (an unrealistic and peremptory manner of arguing a point) and to praise Johnson precisely for his dogged willingness to confront obstacles and objections head-on. Emerson never wavered in his reverence for such demonstrations of the force of character. Like William James, he believed that a man should earn his assertions instead of helping himself to them.[44] Milton's prose tracts

were "earnest, spiritual, rich with allusion" but failed "as writings designed to gain a practical point" because they demanded "on the instant,
an ideal justice," rarely deigning to admit the possible objections (EL,
1:146). Johnson's "fine essay on Perseverance" was, on the other hand, an
invaluable study in power and the necessity of overcoming resistance (EL,
1:369).

Martin Luther's life presented yet another fable of perseverance. Like
Johnson or Michelangelo, Luther was "a fountain of strength" (EL,
1:141), an exemplar of "indomitable Will" (EL, 1:136) and "prodigious
efficiency" (EL, 1:141). Unlike those well-meaning men who "wanted a re-
serve of power to make good their enterprise," Luther delighted in the opposition that required "the exercise of his warlike genius" (EL, 1:140–41).
Great men, as Emerson never tired of repeating, will rise to the demands of
the occasion ("men of valor and reality are known, and rise to their natural place" [CW, 3:73]). Luther was the perfect example of this law of personal force. Great opposition—Satan, the Pope, paper wars, real battles—
only quickened all his faculties and set in motion an equal, resisting force
(EL, 1:140–41). ("A good indignation," as Emerson would later state it,
"brings out all one's powers" [JMN, 8:134].)

The psychological portrait of Luther that Emerson draws is the embodiment of his own central principle of equipoise: his controlling belief that a
healthy personality is the function of radical oppositions, the counterbalancing of opposing powers. If Luther's warlike talents were catalyzed in
great conflicts, they were also kept in check by the counter-"discipline of
the affections" (EL, 1:140). Luther's innate good humor, his marriage to
Catharine of Born, the exercise of his "domestical" nature, tempered "the
religious reformer so prone to fanaticism" (EL, 1:138–39). "The healing
principle," Emerson writes, "the balance-wheel that kept these dangerous
powers from extravagant motions was his warm social affections" (EL,
1:138).

Shakespeare was another example of a great man whose poetic powers
were kept in equipoise by "the natural check of a clear Reason" and "in
quite equal energy, that of Common Sense" (EL, 1:305). (The two 1835
lectures on Shakespeare are studies in the way genius can maintain itself in
a "healthful mind" through a complex balancing of contrary energies: if
Shakespeare's imagination ran to morbid excess, it was tempered by his
"self-recovering, self collecting force" and his "reflective powers" [EL,
1:297].) If Luther's prodigious will revealed itself in his "warlike genius,"
Shakespeare's personal force lay in the "despotism of the imagination"
(EL, 1:292). Shakespeare possessed "the assimilating power of passion that
turns all things to its own nature" (JMN, 3:299). In imagery that would
shortly find its way into *Nature*, Emerson describes poetry as that form of
tyranny in which the mind can most freely exercise its "overmastering"
power (EL, 1:293, 295). (The poet must have, as Emerson would later

phrase it, a "tyrannous eye" [CW, 3:21].) Above all else, Shakespeare was to be celebrated for putting nature to use. The imagery of incorporation and conversion, the conception of human power as generated only in the context of resistance, in particular acts of appropriation, should by now be familiar.

> All reflexion goes to teach us the strictly emblematic character of the material world. Especially is it the office of the poet to perceive and use these analogies. He converts the solid globe, the land, the sea, the sun, the animals into symbols of thought: he makes the outward creation subordinate and merely a convenient alphabet to express thoughts and emotions. This act or vision of the mind is called Imagination. It is that active state of the mind in which it forces things to obey the laws of thought; takes up all present objects in a despotic manner into its own image and likeness and makes the thought which occupies it the center of the world. (EL, 1:224)

Nature

We shall probably never be rid of that cliché in undergraduate bluebooks: "Emerson wants to become one with nature." Indeed, Emerson often seems to encourage such comments. If he celebrates his readiness to "die out of nature," he speaks no less rhapsodically of his emancipation from "human relations." His sympathies seem to lie, instead, with the primordial elements. "I become a moist, cold element. 'Nature grows over me'. . . . I have died out of the human world & come to feel a strange, cold, aqueous, terraqueous, aerial, ethereal sympathy & existence" (JMN, 5:496–97). He even speaks of nature's "serene superiority to man & his art": in the thought of its capacious "excellence . . . man dwindles to pigmy proportions" (L, 1:133–34). His most famous epiphany proclaims that on an unpeopled common the "lover of nature" loses his routine identity and becomes "always a child." Often forgotten, however, are the concluding lines of that "transparent eye-ball" passage; they remind us that in the moment of transcendence only "*mean* egotism" vanishes and that the landscape is only "*somewhat* as beautiful" as the man who beholds it (CW, 1:10; my emphasis).

Such qualifications, ever present in Emerson, suggest something more complicated than a self lost, like Melville's drowning masthead stander, amid the natural sublimity. But it is not difficult to see why descriptions like this lend themselves to the common, bluebook reduction of Emerson to a nature-loving pantheist. Teachers continue to teach him this way. Critics and poets continue to write of his "magnificent defense of nature," of his yearning to become "one with" or "'part and parcel' of Nature."[45] It is all the more important, therefore—without wishing to underrate the very real inspiration that Emerson did find in nature—to stress how wrong this all-too-common interpretation is.

It is, for one thing, a way of reading him that seems to end up, time and again, as the foundation for much wider-ranging critiques. The pantheist interpretation, though it may nod approvingly at Emerson's sensitivity to natural beauty (who could not but approve of the nature lover?), seems invariably to find such sentiments without much sustaining interest—or it finds them morally and aesthetically discreditable. Thus David Marr's belief that "Emersonian man remains fixated in a posture of total wonderment before nature" leads to an extensive criticism of Emerson (and his tradition) as profoundly antipolitical. Emerson, Marr argues, implicitly denies the need for the "human community"; he hovers, instead, "spellbound in his private, blissful, enchanted moment." (According to Stephen Whicher, this Buddhistic "awe and entranced surrender at the spectacle of nature's vast creative power" is mainly characteristic of Emerson's later work.) Charles Simic offers a like-minded reading. *Nature* is simply "an instruction manual for visionaries." Its lesson: "One is . . . part of everything." This leads to the inevitable complaint: our central, poetic influence, by condoning the "escape from here and now," left American poetry adrift in immaterial space. "The American poet [since Emerson] is the high trapeze artist in a visionary circus where the lights have been turned off."[46]

But Emerson's conception of nature reveals him to be, once again, primarily a philosopher of tuition, a philosopher of use. Nature was, like everything else, "only a teacher" and never an end in itself. Natural beauty was, like the universe itself, a school of power valuable only because it could be used. What made it genial and beautiful was its unfallen state ("Man is fallen; nature is erect" [CW, 3:104]). And that unfallen state was venerable not because of any intrinsic merit it possessed but because it was so crucially useful to man. Nature was important not for its own sake but because it could be made to "serve," as Emerson phrases it, "as a differential thermometer, detecting the presence or absence of the divine sentiment in man" (CW, 3:104).

Nature should be regarded, always, as a mere tool, an awesomely beautiful but ultimately dispensable tool. It is only a reminder, for man in his "fallen" or "pygmy" state, of humankind's own original and potential power. At times Emerson advocates what he calls "union" with nature (EL, 3:188), but his emphasis is always on the use of nature by the mind. The "modern tendency," he writes, "is to marry mind to nature, to put nature under the mind" (JMN, 11:201). This may sound, if one catches only half the sentence, like a relationship of harmony, equality, atonement—but it is not. If it is a "marriage" Emerson celebrates, it is a marriage followed by nature's subordination and man's "dominion" (CW, 1:25)—by what he calls a "degrading [of] nature," a "put[ting] nature under foot" (CW, 1:35). Man will stand in his proper, "primary relation . . . with the work of the world" only when he is ready and sufficiently "cunning," to "become a master" and "extort . . . from nature its sceptre"

(CW, 1:152). The relationship between mind and nature is ultimately antagonistic and necessarily reductive. Between man and things there will always exist, Emerson says, a state of war and insult—an opposition that can terminate only in the victory of one or the other. Mind and Nature are like "two boys pushing each other on the curbstone of the pavement"; history is the story of that contending "action and reaction of . . . Nature and Thought" (W, 6:43).

The state of purely static or mystic wonderment before nature that so many readers ascribe to him is precisely what Emerson condemned as the "great danger": the "noxious" possibility that man would become so enamored of nature's sirenlike beauty that he would forget that "sun and moon, plant and animal," have no value except as catalysts to his own innate energies. Nature, Emerson warns, must remain only a means to a greater end, "a means of arousing [man's] interior activity." This is how Emerson summed it up in the 1860s. The description is perfectly consonant with his portrayal of nature a quarter-century earlier.

> Victory over things is the office of man. Of course, until it is accomplished it is the war and insult of things over him. His continual tendency, his great danger, is to overlook the fact that the world is only his teacher, and the nature of sun and moon, plant and animal, only means of arousing his interior activity. Enamored of their beauty, comforted by their convenience, he seeks them as ends and fast loses sight of the fact that they have worse than no values, that they become noxious, when he becomes their slave. (W, 10:127)

I do not mean to suggest that a work like *Nature* does not contain unforgettable paeans to nature's beauty. There are, to be sure, passages in which Emerson captures the certain slant of light, as it floods the American landscape (CW, 1:13–14), with an exactness and evocativeness impossible to surpass. But what is most significant about such descriptions, at least in the context of the entirety of *Nature,* is how few and far between they actually are. For *Nature* is not about natural beauty or nature itself: it is about the human use of nature. "Nature" is merely, as Alan Hodder comments, *Nature*'s "pretext": "In actuality, nature is substantially absent from *Nature.* . . . [I]n a characteristically Emersonian turn, nature provides only the starting point for a meditation that gravitates back toward the self." "But beauty in nature is not ultimate," Emerson writes, "It is the herald of inward and eternal beauty, and is not alone a solid and satisfactory good" (CW, 1:17). The very title of Emerson's first book is, Harold Bloom notes, another of his central misnomers, another of his blandly delivered and easily overlooked self-deconstructions. For its real subject is nature's subservient place in "the kingdom of man." *Man* would have been a more appropriate title.[47]

Nature is important to Emerson not for what it is but for what it does—for the exalted function it can be made to serve. And the function nature serves, the ways in which it can be put to use, are really not so different from the uses of poverty, failure, adversity—or, for that matter, the uses of history, authors, friends, and the deaths of sons and lovers. Nature, friends, books: the three often form a subtly linked trio of topics and interwoven allusions in Emerson's imagination. Each functions as an object (an "other," a Fichtean nonego, or NOT ME) that the mind can love and emulate—a nonself in which the self can find, as Emerson terms it, the deepest, most "occult" sympathies (CW, 1:10) and most profound inspiration. Yet that same nonself—however exhilarating it may be—constitutes, in each case, a threat. Friendship, for instance, always brings with it a potential loss of identity: "Then, though I prize my friends, I cannot afford to talk with them and study their visions, lest I lose my own" (CW, 2:126). The past genius recorded in books poses an equivalent threat: it may harden into an oppressive "over-influence" on the present. "The poet chanting, was felt to be a divine man. Henceforth the chant is divine also. The writer was a just and wise spirit. Henceforward it is settled, the book is perfect; as love of the hero corrupts into worship of his statue. Instantly, the book becomes noxious. The guide is a tyrant" (CW, 1:56).

Natural energies (the sublime energies of American nature, particularly) are no less dangerous. For they always threaten to overwhelm human force and instate themselves as similarly "noxious" tyrants. Thus Emerson worried that "the most extraordinary powers that ever were given to a human being would lose themselves in this vast [American] sphere" (JMN, 2:115). "Does great territory," he wondered, "make men diminutive?" (TN, 1:206). The sprawling American continent filled him with "a certain *tristesse*" because "man seems not able to make much impression" on it (ET, 186–87). "My own quarrel with America," as he once expressed it, "was, that the geography is sublime, but the men are not" (JMN, 11:284).

Every kind of relationship—whether it was the relationship between mind and nature, between present and past, or between friend and friend—was a matter of balanced powers. "I ought," as Emerson puts it in "Friendship," "to be equal to every relation" (CW, 2:118). True friendship demanded the counterpoise of "two large formidable natures, mutually beheld, mutually feared" (CW, 2:123). Literary tradition demanded an equally adversarial balancing act. True genius must, Emerson insists, always be "sufficiently the enemy of genius by over-influence" (CW, 1:57). Nature's ever-renewing momentum demanded a similar counterforce from man. Yet it met (this was Emerson's chronic complaint) only man's "inertia": "This exuberance of nature requiring a correspondent receptiveness and ardor of obedience in man to carry out her great tendencies meets on the contrary in him a dulness and inertia, a disposition to stop and recede" (EL, 3:376). It was this—not surrender to nature but the correction of that fallen state in which "man applies to nature but half his force" (CW,

1:42)—that was the goal of Emerson's first book. "Nature stretcheth out her arms to embrace man," he writes, "only let his thoughts be of equal greatness" (CW, 1:16).

Nature, friends, books—they all fulfill their highest potential not when they merge with the "ME" but when they can be made to function as "beautiful enemies," as the source of productive antagonism. The more unyielding the resistance, the better. The "society of my friend," Emerson says, should be "as great as nature itself" (CW, 2:123). Friendship should, in other words, provide—like nature—an honorable, always energizing opposition: "Let [your friend] be to thee forever a sort of beautiful enemy, untamable, devoutly revered, and not a trivial conveniency to be soon outgrown and cast aside" (CW, 2:124). The psychology at work here we have come to identify as Nietzschean: to the strong nature, to the personality capable of absorbing it and putting it to use, poison can be a source of health. Pain and evil can be a source of virtue. The mightiest enemy can be the truest friend. "Henceforth," as Emerson states it, "I will call my enemy by my own name, for he is serving me with his might, exposing my errors, stigmatising my faults" (JMN, 5:494).

Nature was, for Emerson, another "beautiful enemy." There is, Hodder perceptively notes, "nothing particularly trusting in Emerson's attitude toward nature. On the contrary, there is a certain wariness . . . even perhaps a little cynicism." Such a statement comes as a welcome corrective to the now well-ensconced "caricature of Emerson as one of America's original Nature-worshippers, an armchair advocate of the great out-of-doors." But it still understates the case. For if there is reason to consider Emerson one of our central nature writers, there is even greater reason to consider him our preeminent antinature writer. Emerson is the primary American exponent of that antinatural tradition of Romantic thought that begins in Kant's notion that it is the perceiving mind, not the perceived objects of nature, that is sublime.[48]

That antinature tradition can be traced from Wordsworth's "Nutting," to Whitman's fear that he might lack creative powers equal to nature's ("Dazzling and tremendous how quick the sun-rise would kill me / If I could not now and always send sun-rise out of me"), to Zarathustra's boast to the sun, "You great star, what would your happiness be had you not those for whom you shine?" (Z, 1:Pref.). Bloom's admonition regarding this point bears repeating, for Emerson's prominent place in the tradition of antinature "nature writing" remains insufficiently appreciated: "Romantic nature poetry, despite a long critical history of misrepresentation, was an antinature poetry. . . . [Romantic poetry] tends to see the context of nature as a trap for the mature imagination. This point requires much laboring, as the influence of older views of Romanticism is very hard to slough off."[49] The mixed tone Bloom finds in Romantic poems, the conflicting sense of envy and wariness toward nature—one might call it a

reverential hostility—surfaces early in *Nature* and builds steadily to the climactic prophecy of that longed-for day when man will at last be capable
of countering nature "with his entire force."

That school of criticism that associates Romantic literature with a retreat into nature has traditionally assumed that Emerson advocates some
form of pantheistic leveling or atonement with nature. Emerson's "Harmonism," E. R. Curtius writes, aims at "the reimmersion of the mind in
nature, the redemptive harmony with the stars, the clouds, and the winds."
According to Sherman Paul, Emerson's Transcendentalist vocation hinged
precisely on such fundamental "harmonizing with nature." It is this desire
for cosmic unity that "destroys"—as Charles Feidelson phrases it—"the
concept of fixity and with it the concept of hierarchy." In Emerson's visionary moments the "mind is fused with the world in a flux of wavelike
forms; the identity of the self is lost in a pantheistic sea." "To submerge in
[that] sea," Feidelson reminds us, "is to drown; the self and the world are
two, not one."[50]

But such readings neglect the quite explicitly hierarchical—the tri-
umphantly dualistic—relationship Emerson hopes to establish between nature and mind. If one diagrammed the plot of *Nature,* using two separate
lines to represent nature and man, they would not cross or form parallel
lines but would, instead, describe a triangle rising at something like a 45°
angle, with man in the ascendant. Natural beauty is extolled in the book's
first part, and harmony between man and nature is invoked (CW, 1:10).
But man's tendency to forget that nature is only a tool, his fatal eagerness
to lose himself in the shimmering unreality of nature's splendor, is consistently stressed and cautioned against. It was not nature but, as Barbara
Packer remarks, power that was always "Emerson's True Grail."[51] Natural beauty, "if too eagerly hunted," can be, Emerson reminds us, a trap, a
tinsel "show" or "mirage" that mocks those attempting to clutch it (CW,
1:14). The ultimate goal is not nature but the full recovery of mankind's
lost "elemental power" (CW, 1:42).

As *Nature* proceeds, the idealistic emphasis on the necessity of degrading nature becomes more and more pronounced. "Thus even in physics,"
Emerson observes, "the material is ever degraded before the spiritual. . . .
The sublime remark of Euler on his law of arches, 'This will be found contrary to all experience, yet is true;' had already transferred nature into the
mind, and left matter like an outcast corpse" (CW, 1:34). Emerson finally
feels obliged to interrupt his ascent to "the kingdom of man over nature"
in order to reassure the reader that he is not proposing a literal attack on
nature, only attempting "to indicate the true position of nature in regard
to man." (That true position is, of course, "to establish man" as preeminent.) "I have no hostility to nature," he insists, "I do not wish to fling
stones at my beautiful mother" (CW, 1:35–36).

These lines, and the revealing paragraph from which they come, are frequently adduced as merely further evidence of Emerson's nature worship. They are actually further evidence of the pattern Kenneth Burke first discerned nearly three decades ago, in an astute, though generally overlooked, analogy. It is an analogy whose ramifications have still to be fully recognized. Like many of Burke's best insights, it is introduced parenthetically, as an aside in an argument with somewhat different priorities. It deserves, therefore, to be explored in some detail.

Nature's function for Emerson is—so Burke proposes—analogous to the role of the bourgeoisie for Marx: it is necessary but ultimately expendable. It is a necessary step—but only a step, only a tool to be used for a higher goal—in the movement toward the restoration of mankind's proper "relation to the universe." For Marx, the emergence of the bourgeoisie, and of the capitalist system on which it depended, was a welcome sign of progress. It was the means by which feudalism could be left behind. But capitalism itself would be eventually degraded, or put under foot, by the arrival of the final socialist state. The class heralded as "the bearer of the future" was, like Emerson's celebrated nature, thoroughly mediate: it was also "the class that is to be buried by the future."[52]

The parallel mechanics of Marxian dialectics and Emersonian transcendence of nature are, after all—as it is all too easy to forget—the hallmarks of two quite contemporary visions of human development. Both are products of a nineteenth-century "historicism"—that prevailing philosophical tendency "to view all of reality, all of man's achievements, in terms of the category of development."[53] Emerson, of course, had little real interest in any kind of socialist state. But the pattern of human development *Nature* describes is, in its outline, comparable to Marx's. Marx sought to establish the central place of one particular social order and thereby chart the proper relationship between classes, periods, and economic systems; Emerson hoped to establish man in his central place and thereby clarify "the true position of nature in regard to man." Both projects are prophecies of Promethean growth, predictions of mankind's progression to its rightful state of power. Both projects imply that that progression will begin in the state of "war and insult" between man and things. Both imply that that progression will involve some amount of struggle, will require obstacles to be overcome, pitfalls to be avoided, and some synthesis or assimilation of antagonistic energies. Emerson's scheme of relentless development cannot, therefore, be adequately understood as simply a grand, pantheistic, or Buddhistic system of "Harmonism." It is, no less than Marx's vision, a thoroughly nineteenth-century phenomenon and the exemplification of a historicist ethos of conflict and transformation.

Ultimately Emerson's metaphors imply not atonement but—as his second essay on nature once again makes clear—a system of use, a system of balances and counterbalances, and the inevitable hierarchy of man over nature. Nature is, in the 1844 "Nature," once again depicted as a potential trap, "unreal and mocking" until it finds men "as good as itself." It serves, once again, a purely mediatory function, one that will be rendered obsolete once the right human energy has been recovered. When the king has been restored to his palace, Emerson says, no one will admire the walls: "If there were good men there would never be this rapture in nature." Human power must be fully reinstated, and nature returned to its proper and subordinate station. It must one day "look up to us." Emerson's images are not, as in Marxist theory, of one class burying another. But they are comparable images of elemental competition. They describe one element— man or nature—shaming, mocking, equaling, transcending, outshining, one-upping, or discrediting the other.

> Nature is loved by what is best in us. It is loved as the city of God, although, or rather because there is no citizen. The sunset is unlike anything that is underneath it: it wants men. And the beauty of nature must always seem unreal and mocking, until the landscape has human figures, that are as good as itself. If there were good men, there would never be this rapture in nature. If the king is in the palace, nobody looks at the walls. It is when he is gone, and the house is filled with grooms and gazers, that we turn from the people, to find relief in the majestic men that are suggested by the pictures and the architecture. The critics who complain of the sickly separation of the beauty of nature from the thing to be done, must consider that our hunting of the picturesque is inseparable from our protest against false society. Man is fallen; nature is erect, and serves as a differential thermometer, detecting the presence or absence of the divine sentiment in man. By fault of our dulness and selfishness, we are looking up to nature, but when we are convalescent, nature will look up to us. We see the foaming brook with compunction: if our own life flowed with the right energy, we should shame the brook. The stream of zeal sparkles with real fire, and not with reflex rays of sun and moon. (CW, 3:104)

Symbolic Action

The strong antinatural tendency in Emerson's thought has hardly gone unnoticed. Criticism has frequently documented the alienation Emerson is capable of feeling toward his "beautiful mother." His idealism, as Packer puts it, often takes the form of a "scorched earth policy . . . devastat[ing] the countries it passes through." His "will to power over nature," Julie Ellison writes, "leaves him free from nature, not in it."[54]

Yet the point seems perennially to need stressing. For the reduction of Emerson's complex conception of the mutual rivalry between mind and nature to what Perry Miller once described as primarily a question of "mysticism and pantheism"—such reduction has continued, from Santayana's day to the present, to undermine his reputation. Most recently, for instance, David Simpson has attacked "Emerson and his kind" for being politically incorrect in all the ways that a writer like Fenimore Cooper is not. Cooper possesses, Simpson argues, something Emerson sorely lacks: a disdain for universalizing, a consciousness ready to acknowledge conflict and unwilling to retreat into a false sense of cosmic harmony. It is a consciousness alive to conflict, an imagination prepared to make the "Hobbesian state of nature and the war of every man against every man" the basis for its art. Emerson's imagination, on the other hand, insistently "dissolves . . . any observed or theorized tension between man and nature." All conflict—the entire conception of life as struggle, life as *bellum omnium,* that defines so much of the historicist nineteenth century—all this, in Emerson's hands, disappears into that serene system of atonement Curtius labeled as Emerson's "Totalism." All conflicts are, Simpson writes—so far as Emerson is concerned—"brought into harmony under the benign gaze of an Omnipotent God."[55]

Simpson's accusation that his "organicist fantasies" allowed Emerson to ignore the political realities of his time may be new historical revisionism. But there is nothing at all new about using Emerson as a straw man in order to boost another writer's reputation. Miller leveled similar charges several decades ago. The story of the really vital issues that engaged the nineteenth-century mind could be told, Miller claimed, with little attention to an already obsolescent "Emersonian nonsense." (Modern readers, Miller concluded, could not help but be put off by such foolishness. The "utterly fantastic" philosophy Emerson and Thoreau represented was "but a sort of midsummer madness that overtook a few intellectuals in or around Boston about the year 1840.") The central struggle of the nineteenth century was, Miller postulated, the struggle between mind and nature, the mind's endeavor to "cope with [the] infinite expanse of Nature" and "keep pace with further and further discoveries." And the history of that struggle could be told "with no reference whatsoever to Emerson's *Nature* or to any Transcendental wrestling with duality." Emerson's "mysticism and pantheism" were, in short, profound anachronisms. Fortunately, as Miller hastened to reassure his readers, no one was any longer obliged to take them, or Emerson's philosophy, seriously.[56]

We return, then, in Miller's reading, or in Simpson's more recent one, to the Henry James/Santayana portrait of the reality-eluding cleric—a hermetic figure, undisturbed by the actual forces that surround him. Most interpretations that believe Emerson's thought can be understood as monistic—concerned primarily with some form of atonement—seem to reach that point. Yet the blind spots in that interpretation remain the same. It sees the organicist strain, the Transcendentalist rhetoric, the absolutist proclivities. It does not see the extensive outlines of quite contrary patterns in Emerson's thought or the quite alternative projects in which he is engaged. It does not see that behind Emerson's professed love for Unity there lies an imagination drawn, as much as any other mind in the nineteenth century, to the idea of the balance and power achievable only in conflict.

It does not see the Emerson who believed "The world is a battle-ground" (W, 10:87) and "a series of balanced . . . antagonisms" (JMN, 11:371). It does not see that a work like *Nature* is—Miller's judgment notwithstanding—actually a central text in the history of that escalating rivalry that preoccupied so much of the nineteenth century: the struggle between human and natural powers.

One needs, in the face of such approaches, to repeat Dewey's answer to those ready to close the book on Emerson's philosophy as the genteel "idealism of a Class." Beneath the attraction to an "overweening Beyond and Away" and the outworn, transcendental pigments, there lies—in Cornel West's phrase—a pragmatic "future-oriented instrumentalism, that tries to deploy thought as a weapon to enable more effective action." It is a philosophy that may long for atonement. But it is founded on the idea of resistance. It anticipates those later attempts by William James and Henry Adams (those other philosophers of tuition) to establish "man as a [counter]force" capable of coping with, balancing, the century's "new avalanches of forces" that "require . . . new mental powers to control." Nietzsche had similar priorities in mind when he spoke, in one of his most Emersonian works, of our modern need to "educate ourselves *against* our age" (UM, 3:4). In this new premium placed on the "opposing self"—this new stress on the need to balance outward force with an equivalent form of inward, human force—Emerson is himself crucially anticipated by Carlyle. "There has," as Carlyle reassured his readers in 1831, "been an inward force vouchsafed [man], whereby the pressure of things outward might be withstood."[57]

Nature, and the lifelong project of symbol making it initiates, cannot be explained, as they usually are, solely in terms of idealism, organicism, or Swedenborgian correspondence. The received, scholarly wisdom may continue to read *Nature* as the Transcendentalist attempt to find "moral truth in the benevolent plan of nature." And scholarship may continue to dismiss such an attempt as "no longer . . . useful or viable."[58] But that is simply not an adequate description to begin with. For Emerson's first book is conceived not only out of love of nature but also out of fear of it. It is, like all of the essays that follow, about finding a way to convert a threatening power (a power that could be, variously, the power of nature, genius, books, death, sex, history, war, technology, society, other people, or simply all the proliferating energies of the nineteenth century) into what Emerson calls "wholesome" (which means humanized or usable) force.

"Every jet of chaos which threatens to exterminate us," he remained convinced, "is convertible by intellect into wholesome force" (W, 6:32). Nature, genius—every anarchic or potentially destructive force—could be "put under the mind," made symbolical, representative, or subordinate to man. Emerson's famous doctrine that "The world is emblematic" (CW, 1:21), that "Nature is the symbol of spirit" (CW, 1:17), is not a defense of

nature but a defense from it—a means of believing that nature can ultimately be put under the power of the mind and put to use. Because the
world is "thoroughly anthropomorphized," because there is "nothing to
which man is not related," everything is available to him: "every thing is
convertible into every other" (W, 8:23).

This is the great theme of Henry Adams's late career: the search for adequate symbols, the search for an effective form of symbolic action by
which the imagination might resist and cope with a materialistic age.
Works like *Mont-Saint-Michel and Chartres* or *The Education* attempt, R.
P. Blackmur suggests, to reaffirm and reimpose "the human significance"
on the age's "vast stores of new energies." Adams's last books enact that
"struggle for images—for symbols—in which to create the human significance, the significance to humans, out of the energies which moved him
and which, as he aspired to affirm himself, he must move." Finding adequate symbols meant finding a counterforce, a way of confronting, converting, coping with every jet of chaotic force that threatens to exterminate
us. For symbols were, Adams believed, forces themselves. "The symbol
was force, as a compass-needle or a triangle was force." This was Emerson's theme as well: the force of the symbol, symbol making as a way of
using or converting, "troping" as a form of mastery.[59]

> We are such imaginative creatures that nothing so works on the human
> mind, barbarous or civil, as a trope. Condense some daily experience into a
> glowing symbol, and an audience is electrified. They feel as if they already
> possessed some new right and power over a fact which they can detach, and
> so completely master in thought. (W, 7:90)

If we reduce Emerson to a visionary isolationist, we overlook the extent
to which he presents ways of thinking that became more and more prominent, more necessary, as the nineteenth century wore on. We lose touch as
well with the important connections Emerson has with a critic like Kenneth Burke and his "dramatistic" conception of art as always a form of
"symbolic action" or reaction. For the philosophy of use articulated in
Emerson's essays remains a valuable, if still underappreciated, example of
Burke's principle that every imaginative act originates *"in terms of a situation and [as] a strategy for confronting and encompassing that situation."*[60] The principle for reading Emerson I am suggesting is perhaps best
summarized in Burkean terms: Emerson's affirmations of power are never
simply one-dimensional projections of the ego or easy retreats into the
ideal. Every Emersonian claim to power arises out of a situation—some
perceived threat to human force—and represents some strategy for confronting and encompassing that situation. The human situation, as Emerson conceived it—whether it was the relationship between man and nature, life and death, the mind and the technologies it had created, the
private self and the masses, or the energies of genius and the burden of the

past—always came down to the imagination's need to find such strategies for coping. It came down to the need to find ways of maintaining a universe of securely balanced antagonisms.

Emerson does indeed speak of turning the energies of nature, the energies of the times, into "universal symbols." But adequate symbols were not easily found (ascertaining the true creative forces of the nineteenth century required "subtile and commanding thought" [W, 8:34]), and when they were found they represented a means of effectively countervailing some antagonistic force. The symbol making Emerson envisions was intended to be, in short, confrontational, not escapist. Emerson's language may be, in part at least, Platonic; the impulse behind it is pragmatic.[61]

If there is this irreducible antinatural thrust to Emerson's thought, it is not the same thing, I want to emphasize, as the industrialist's desire to "Birminghamize" (ET, 63) the world or the capitalist's simple hunger for the profits such industrialization brings. It arises, rather, out of the same fear that moved Carlyle, William James, Henry Adams, Dewey, or Nietzsche to the attempt to find ways of generating an adequate human response to a threatening environment, an environment on the point of overtaking "the energies of men." The difference between Emerson and a writer like Adams is the confidence each was capable of bringing to that attempt. For Adams, coping with the century's "great rampages of energies" was an always precarious, probably doomed, task.[62] Emerson's faith that the mind could prevail, that one man could offset a city, was always tested, but it never seemed to flag for very long.

Whitman had thoroughly absorbed this aspect of Emerson's thought by the time he willed himself into the role of the nation's strongest imagination in 1855. He described precisely the kind of healthy, adversarial imagination and the kind of imaginative "affluence," or symbol-making power, Emerson had been calling for. "The most affluent man," as Whitman boasts in the preface to *Leaves of Grass*, "is he that confronts all the shows he sees by equivalents out of the stronger wealth of himself." Seventeen years later, in *Democratic Vistas*, he was still upholding (though not without some new note of equivocation) the capacity of "the esthetic worker in any field" to seize, put to use, and thereby counterbalance and cope with "the shows and forms presented by Nature" and all "the actual play of passions, in history and life." Symbols were still a form of force. Art—indeed, "aesthetic work" in its broadest sense—was still "the image-making faculty, coping with material creation, and rivaling, almost triumphing over it."[63]

The Late Emerson: "Fate"

Emerson's ideas on specific issues, on abolition, for example, or race, nationalism, England, industrialization, marriage, or his opinions on figures like Wordsworth, Byron, or Webster, all of these developed, or waffled perpetually back and forth, through the course of his career. But the premium Emerson placed on use, on empowerment, on the counterbalancing that creates identity—and the attendant psychology of resistance, assimilation, mastering—these severe laws and disciplines constitute a distinctly Emersonian way of thinking that never changed. It exists as the intellectual and psychological substratum under all his major essays, or—to change the metaphor slightly—what a sculptor would call the single, common armature employed as the foundation for a series of varying, diversely molded and accentuated, but fundamentally similar, sculptures.

"His philosophical biography," Thomas McFarland writes of Coleridge, "records not an access of wisdom, but a continuing process of elucidation of primary orientations." The same thing can be said of Emerson's philosophical biography: his philosophy of use, psychology of empowerment, and rhetoric of power—these define the primary orientation, or complex of orientations, that is elucidated in essay after essay. To trace this primary orientation as it unfolds through each of Emerson's essays or collections of essays (as I have been stressing it in *The Conduct of Life, Nature,* or the early lectures) would be, in large measure, an exercise in repetition—repetitive simply because it is such an enduring attitude or predisposition on Emerson's part. "Emerson is," as James Cox observes, "an alarmingly repetitive writer."[64]

Emerson did not move from idealism to a new maturity, from a virginal or "once-born" innocence to an access of new wisdom, or even, as Emerson's own phrasing might suggest, from the naive delusion that "positive power" is "all" to the final recognition that "negative power, or circumstance, is half" (W, 6:15).[65] His essays rehearse, rather, an abiding drama of empowerment—which means antagonism. And antagonism always requires, by definition, the continual interplay of both positive and negative powers, human power and recalcitrant fate, human identity and tough circumstances. Human power may ebb or flow in this Emersonian drama, but Emerson's own primary orientation always remains an unswerving readiness to put to use. It is, as Emerson says, a cunning readiness to become master—through the disciplined process of learning and in the act of labor—over what one opposes or confronts (CW, 1:152).

Even in the late essay, "Fate"—usually regarded as a vivid example of Emerson's mature "acquiescence" to fate's omnipotence—the fundamental orientation remains the same. Emerson concludes the essay hymning "the Beautiful Necessity" that counteracts human power and "dissolves persons." But his primary concern, his instinctive stance, throughout the essay is, as always, to insist on the "lesson" the "odious facts" (W, 6:19) can teach, to demonstrate the ways in which those facts can be fronted, or the myriad ways in which man can learn from, absorb, shape, tame, or put to use (and thereby achieve a form of mastery over or counterbalancing of) such omnipotence. "'T is the *best use of Fate,*" Emerson writes, "to teach a fatal courage" (W, 6:24; my emphasis). Man's "instincts must be met, and he has predisposing power that bends and fits what is near him to his use. . . . As soon as there is life, there is self-direction and absorbing and using of material" (W, 6:38).

"Fate" is usually read as a late illustration of "a more 'holistic' or organic" relationship between man and nature, in which "the balance clearly tilts in the direction of Nature (or Fate)." It is usually perceived as further admission, on the part of an aging Emerson, that "energy and rigor themselves may not be all they are cracked up to be."[66] But "Fate" can, with equal if not greater reason, be considered one of his most graphic lessons in human power, one of his most finely detailed sermons on the old Emersonian theme: "the great doctrine of Use," or "the assimilating power," the faith that "limitation is power that shall be" (W, 6:35).

Whicher's description of the early Emerson as a "naïve rhapsodist" (SE, 253) is all too typical of a well-established, all-too-simple perception. But his influential opinion that the later Emerson should be approached under the rubric of "acquiescence"—his famous conclusion that the two poles of Emerson's mature thought are "submission to law and benevolent tendency" and "entranced surrender at the spectacle of nature's vast creative power"—is difficult to accept as anything other than an egregiously wrong call.[67] For Emerson, though he may appear to surrender to the necessary calamities of our natural life, never remains submissive for long. "Fate," far from teaching acquiescence, is a particularly good example of the contrary principle: the Emersonian doctrine that "Every thing good is the result of antagonisms" (JMN, 15:237).

The late Emerson emphasizes what he always has: use, lordship, action, balance. As the following passage from the middle of the essay makes clear, the point is, once again, not surrender to nature but resistance: our need "to bring up our conduct" to nature's loftiness, our need to assert ourselves with "deeds on the scale of nature." We must, he insists, counter "a river, an oak, or a mountain"—we must resist, indeed, the very "atmosphere"—with a comparable energy, a comparable "rudeness and invincibility," a human power equal to gravity. Man must remain equal to nature, one omnipotence counterbalancing the other. Once again, the hydrostatic paradox is invoked as the perfect symbol of an antagonistic universe.

> The right use of Fate is to bring up our conduct to the loftiness of nature. Rude and invincible except by themselves are the elements. So let man be. Let him empty his breast of his windy conceits, and show his lordship by manners and deeds on the scale of nature. Let him hold his purpose as with the tug of gravitation. No power, no persuasion, no bribe shall make him give up his point. A man ought to compare advantageously with a river, an oak, or a mountain. He shall have not less the flow, the expansion, and the resistance of these.
>
> 'T is the best use of Fate to teach a fatal courage. Go face the fire at sea,

or the cholera in your friend's house, or the burglar in your own, or what
danger lies in the way of duty,—knowing that you are guarded by the cheru-
bim of Destiny. If you believe in Fate to your harm, believe it at least for
your good.

For if Fate is so prevailing, man also is part of it, and can confront fate
with fate. If the Universe have these savage accidents, our atoms are as savage in resistance. We should be crushed by the atmosphere, but for the reaction of the air within the body. A tube made of a film of glass can resist the
shock of the ocean if filled with the same water. If there be omnipotence in
the stroke, there is omnipotence of recoil. (W, 6:24–25)

There are, to be sure, throughout "Fate," passages that suggest that
Emerson is advocating surrender to an omnipresent law larger than man
and indifferent to him. That fatal power, Emerson says, "is not in us, but
we are in it" (W, 6:26). The essay's famous final paragraph does present
an Emerson apparently ready to bow before fate's inviolable decree, an
Emerson who no longer speaks (as Nietzsche would) of man's need to
transform himself from creature to creator. No essay by Emerson lingers
so long, with such deliberate detail, on man's naked vulnerability and the
ferocious, hostile force of nature. It is a nature apparently designed, from
the "infusory biters" of the intestinal parasite to the crushing jaws of the
sea-wolf, for the swift, efficient destruction of humanity.

The way of Providence is a little rude. The habit of snake and spider, the
snap of the tiger and other leapers and bloody jumpers, the crackle of the
bones of his prey in the coil of the anaconda. . . . The planet is liable to
shocks from comets, perturbations from planets, rendings from earthquake
and volcano, alterations of climate, precessions of equinoxes. Rivers dry up
by opening of the forest. The sea changes its bed. Towns and countries fall
into it. At Lisbon an earthquake killed men like flies. At Naples three years
ago ten thousand persons were crushed in a few minutes. The scurvy at sea,
the sword of the climate in the west of Africa, at Cayenne, at Panama, at
New Orleans, cut off men like a massacre. Our western prairie shakes with
fever and ague. The cholera, the small-pox, have proved as mortal to some
tribes as a frost to the crickets, which, having filled the summer with noise,
are silenced by a fall of the temperature of one night. Without uncovering
what does not concern us, or counting how many species of parasites hang
on a bombyx, or groping after intestinal parasites or infusory biters, or the
obscurities of alternate generation,—the forms of the shark, the labrus, the
jaw of the sea-wolf paved with crushing teeth, the weapons of the grampus,
and other warriors hidden in the sea, are hints of ferocity in the interiors of
nature. Let us not deny it up and down. Providence has a wild, rough, incal-
culable road to its end, and it is of no use to try to whitewash its huge,
mixed instrumentalities, or to dress up that terrific benefactor in a clean shirt
and white neckcloth of a student in divinity. (W, 6:7–8)

Fate's "Law," this later Emerson concludes, "rules throughout existence; a Law which is not intelligent but intelligence;—not personal nor

impersonal . . . it dissolves persons; it vivifies nature" (W, 6:49). Nature is, indeed, "the tyrannous circumstance, the thick skull, the sheathed snake, the ponderous, rock-like jaw" (W, 6:15). One of Emerson's central metaphors—the image of ingestion, incorporation—has apparently been reversed. Man is no longer, as Emerson once dreamed, eating the world like an apple. The world is eating man.

Yet it hardly seems accurate to describe a passage like this, so calculated a tour de force of imagery, sound, and allusion—with its all-important, ironic beginning and end—as lachrymose or resigned. Even "stoicism" is a barely adequate description. One suspects that if a Schopenhauer were to rewrite this account, we would be left with an entirely different vision. In the hands of a Schopenhauer, things *would* begin to seem utterly hopeless, human action *would* begin to seem wholly, maddeningly, futile. Buddhistic acquiescence *would* seem like our only viable response. But this is not the case with Emerson. There is, on the contrary, something cavalier, even playful, about the entire passage—from that wonderfully dry, prefatory admission that Providence can be "a little rude," to the closing remark that it is no use trying to dress up bloodthirsty nature in a clean shirt.

Emerson seems to be enjoying the rhetorical exercise the occasion has provided him—enjoying the understatement, the snap and crackle of the language (its exotic roll call of labrus, bombyx, and grampus), enjoying his chance to shock us with that staccato catalogue of sudden massacres. There remains, after all, at the conclusion of this long set piece, the kind of reassurance one would never find in a truly acquiescent writer like Schopenhauer. There remains the doctrine of use: Emerson's confidence that nature, however violent, is still a tool, with its "mixed instrumentalities." There remains the belief that it is still, for all its terrific power, a potential benefactor. "So long," he continues, "as these strokes are not to be parried by us they must be feared" (W, 6:8). The point, of course, is—once again—our need and ability to parry them. "We see the causes of evil," as he states it elsewhere, "and learn to parry them and use them as instruments" (W, 10:73).

Whicher's description of Emerson's drift into a late naturalism in which the self merges with nature is, in short, a singularly one-sided and misleading way to account for the essay as a whole.[68] It leaves out the continuing emphasis on resistance, tuition, and use. If Emerson's essays are dialectical—contrapuntal explorations of contradictory viewpoints or states of mind—then their perorations and concluding images are usually good indicators of the direction in which the rhetorical balance tilts, indicators of just where Emerson's final sympathies lie. And "Fate" closes, like *Nature,* like "Experience," like *Representative Men,* not with a passive image of surrender or motionless wonderment but with an image of use. If *Nature* concludes with the invitation to a restored, human dominion, if "Experience" closes with the promise of practical power—and *Representative Men* with the gospel of use—"Fate" ends with the assurance of fate's willingness to serve, its gracious solicitation of man to "draw on all its omnipotence" (W, 6:49).

Alfred Kazin restates Whicher's thesis in his portrait of an older but wiser Emerson, an Emerson compelled at the last to concede that "the infinite universe cannot be domesticated to man's religious needs."[69] But "Fate" suggests precisely the opposite. There is always, Emerson continues to argue, a way for man to *domesticate* the world (precisely the metaphor Emerson employs) to his myriad needs. There is always a way to find victory in defeat, a way to make use of whatever limitations fate presents.

"Every spirit makes its house," he writes early in the essay, "but afterwards the house confines the spirit" (W, 6:9). This remark has, as Gertrude Hughes notes, "persistently been seen in terms of decline."[70] But by the essay's close, that image of spiritual defeat has been revised to fit a conception of ultimate human mastery. The idea of fatal "limitation" has been redefined as the foundation for further growth—an unending process not unlike that unstoppable expansive force he had described nineteen years before in "Circles." In an earlier essay, Emerson had defined nature as man's "differential thermometer," the tool for measuring human power. Here nature is once again degraded and put under foot. The limits of our natural existence are once again reduced, redefined as limits no longer, but as human tools—"the meter of the growing man." Nature's contingencies are the dragonlike, yet necessary, "retarding forces" we learn to "ride and rule." Such lordship, Emerson promises, is inevitable:

> We can afford to allow the limitation, if we know it is the meter of the growing man. We stand against Fate, as children stand up against the wall in their father's house and notch their height from year to year. But when the boy grows to a man, and is master of the house, he pulls down that wall and builds a new and bigger. 'T is only a question of time. Every brave youth is in training to ride and rule this dragon. His science is to make weapons and wings of these passions and retarding forces. (W, 6:30)

The point is made repeatedly: we must learn life's "odious facts," learn to turn them to our benefit. Our "sound relation to these facts," Emerson says, "is to use and command, not to cringe to them." "Intellect annuls Fate" (W, 6:23). "A man's power is hooped in by a necessity which, by many experiments, he touches on every side until he learns its arc" (W, 6:19–20). All facts, all apparent constrictions, however immovable they may seem, can be saddled and made to serve. All power, however threatening to man, can be converted to his good use.

Emerson's ironic description of the potentially destructive torrent as "mischievous" has the same effect as his earlier quips about "the odious facts" or rude Providence. It suggests the kind of coolly skeptical attitude we need to maintain toward negative power in even its most daunting form. For the torrent too is at last "taught to drudge for man." The wild beasts man "makes useful." Chemical explosions he learns to control "like his watch." Man masters all modes of energy: legs, horses, wind, steam, gas, electricity. "There's nothing he will not make his carrier" (W, 6:33). The once diabolic force of steam becomes the perfect "workman." The anarchic force of the mob becomes, through the transformations of democracy, "the most harmless and energetic form of a State." The Watts and Fultons, the great statesmen of the world, have all grasped the same principle: "where was power was not devil, but was God"—if only properly put to use (W, 6:33–34).

"The horseman serves his horse," Emerson complained in 1846, in one of his best-known poems: "Things are in the saddle, / And ride mankind" (W, 9:77–78). But he made a career telling a different story, a continuing story of human overcoming. Our ultimate capacity to bridle the beast, channel the destructive force, outmaneuver the hoops, the structures, the "adamantine bandages" (W, 6:17) imprisoning us—these remain his main theme, his controlling metaphors.

Society and Solitude

Numerous modifications of Whicher's thesis have been suggested over the last forty years. The most valuable has been the direct counterthesis offered by Hughes. Emerson's career represents, Hughes argues, not an intellectual development (or decline) but a movement from "certainty to exemplification." "Emerson moves neither toward nor away from [his] initial conception. He moves within it." "Thus the supposed capitulations of later works like 'Experience' and *The Conduct of Life* do not recant the bold faith of earlier works . . . ; rather the later essays articulate those earlier affirmations more fully."[71]

Ample evidence for Hughes's paradigm can be found not only in "Experience" and *The Conduct of Life* but in that even later volume, *Society and Solitude* (1870). (This generally neglected revision of lectures from the late 1850s and early 1860s was the last book Emerson published before lapsing into the chronic aphasia that marked the remaining dozen years of his life.) If any genuinely new note is sounded in these last essays it is not acquiescence but the remarkable expression of forthright satisfaction with what has been achieved: the recognition that the doctrines of use and labor have been right all along, that they have accomplished what they were meant to accomplish, that they have granted what Emerson calls "cumulative power." I am speaking here specifically of the conclusion Emerson reaches in "Old Age," the closing essay of *Society and Solitude*. It represents an admission not of defeat but of gradual success. And it must come, for any reader who has followed him this far, as one of the most moving moments in the entire Emerson canon.

One reason it seems so is purely biographical. "Old Age" (like *Society and Solitude* as a whole) is clearly intended as a final taking stock; with Emerson's mental deterioration close at hand, that is indeed what it turned out to be. There is, consequently, something altogether right and fitting in watching so prolific, so introspective a career draw to its close on a well-deserved major chord. Can any reader not take heart at Emerson's acknowledgment, at the last, that the effort and perseverance have been worth it? Age, he has learned, grants what youth cannot: the fulfillment of initial promise, the eventual finding of the proper expression, the necessary trying out of all the latent faculties.

Emerson gets around to the advantages of age slowly, first taking the opportunity to joke about its disadvantages. "We do not count a man's years until he has nothing else to count" (W, 7:320). But *Society and Solitude* has, from its early emphasis on "the secret of cumulative power" (W, 7:20), been leading up to Emerson's final acknowledgment that "Life and art are cumulative" (W, 7:320)—the recognition that "The best things are of secular growth" (W, 7:329), that "Every one is sensible of this cumulative advantage in living" (W, 7:326). Old age is finally redefined not as a period of decrepitude but as the true occasion for what Hughes calls "confirmation." It is only at the end of a long life that the laws of use and action can be fully appreciated—vindicated, as Emerson says—for the culminating power they bestow. "Where there is power," he writes, "there is age" (W, 7:317). Those prodigies who succeed in youth are nature's exceptions; her rule is on the side of experience. "Skill to do comes of doing," knowledge comes with experience, "and there is no knowledge that is not power." The longest-lived workmen are the best (W, 7:321).

I have said that this retrospective sense of accomplishment is a genuinely new note for Emerson. That claim needs some additional explanation, for it is still often taken for granted that his essays are little more than easy projections of an unrestrained ego or cheerful bundles of self-congratulations. Emerson's visions of empowerment are generally predictions of what should be or will be, however, not records of what is. "Every touch *should* thrill," he declares in "The Poet" (my italics)—making it clear that in our present state "there is some obstruction, or some excess of phlegm in our constitution."[72] The "impressions of nature" we receive are "too feeble . . to make us artists." We remain "partial men," expressing ourselves "dwarfishly and fragmentarily." "I look in vain," he concedes, "for the poet whom I describe" (CW, 3:4, 21–22).

Lawrence Buell identifies this as Emerson's double-edged sense of "prospectiveness." Fulfillment always hovers on the horizon, but it is not here now and may never arrive at all. "Emerson's stance in the essays," as one recent commentator puts it, "is one of waiting and desiring": he finds his "true form . . . in not finding."[73] Throughout even the most affirmative essays there runs this strong sense of dissatisfaction with the shortcomings of the country, a consistent regret over our lack of creative power and the routine failures of friends, hopes, and projects.

This sensitivity to all manner of unrealized potential is still very much alive in *Society and Solitude*. The book begins with another of Emerson's many portraits of failed young men (W, 7:3–5). "Our perception," he remarks at one point, "far outruns our talent" (W, 7:301). It comes as a surprise, therefore, for any reader aware of this persistent elegiac strain beneath his affirmations, when Emerson moves, in "Old Age," away from the familiar remorse over power unused—when he goes beyond even the characteristic prospective vision of the great work we may perform some day—and proceeds to make the frank and unequivocal declaration that the work has been completed, the "personal power" attained, the "ripeness" utilized. The youth, Emerson writes, suffers from "powers untried": "Every faculty new to each man thus goads him and drives him . . . into doleful deserts until it finds proper vent." But with age, he has learned, one by one, day by day, "to coin his wishes into facts." This is the "supreme pleasure" that comes with age. "[A]ge sets its house in order, and finishes its works." In age, a man's proper "expression" *is* found (W, 7:326–29).

Society and Solitude may, in its prose, lack the intensity of the earlier essays. Its simpler style may make it the most accessible of Emerson's books. But the "digestive" imagery of man's "assimilating power," the emphasis on man's "appetitive" relationship to the world, his readiness to work up and put to use—these Emersonian principles remain as conspicuous as ever. Age, Emerson suggests, actually brings with it greater powers of incorporation than does youth: "What to the youth is only a guess or a hope, is in the veteran a digested statute. . . . The Indian Red Jacket, when the young braves were boasting their deeds, said, 'But the sixties have all the twenties and forties in them'" (W, 7:328). Youthful hopes, with nothing better to show than their glittering "heap of beginnings," can, with age, at last be "refined" into "results and morals" (W, 7:328).

Emerson is, as always, committed to finding the way in which all threatening power can be made to serve. Time, for instance, that omniscient enemy of age, that thread on which are strung all the restrictive lords of life, is here revealed to be the foundation for cumulative power. Poisonous as it may be, time is also one of the great benefactors that come with age. In a long passage of examples (W, 7:329–30), Emerson illustrates the way "patience and time" help us to possess a new kind of power, the way they help us to the completion of our work. Linnaeus awaits specimens to justify his botanical system, the conchologist builds his cabinet expecting to fill it with new shells, the scholar waits to match a citation with its source, the poet waits for the right line—and in each case time, that tireless "finder," provides, at last, the missing materials, the longed-for insight.

Walden is a book about the finding of true speech, the driving home of one true nail. But the house Thoreau envisions exists in the dawn still to come: man has not yet succeeded in reducing "a fact of the imagination to . . . a fact of his understanding."[74] Not only does Emerson assert that a correspondence between our wish and our possession must be found, he attests that it can be. We *can* learn to express ourselves fully, not just fragmentarily. We can domesticate our world. We can not only begin to build our houses, we can finish them. We can take a final satisfaction in having found an adequate counterpoise or proportion—some adequate balance of antagonisms—in our lives. Old men can take pleasure in "finishing their houses," in "reducing tangled interests to order, reconciling enmities." "It must be believed that there is a proportion between the designs of a man and the length of his life: there is a calendar of his years, so of his performances" (W, 7:331).

One would be hard-pressed to find sentiments quite like these in the rest of Emerson. It is even difficult to think of similar moments of such unalloyed completion and satisfaction in most of American literature. For if there exists any common thread that defines a singularly American literary tradition, it would have to be the familiar tale that keeps being retold: the witnessing of great promise unfulfilled, the story of possibilities lost.

The other essays in *Society and Solitude* return to characteristic Emersonian themes. "Civilization" suggests that it is not only great individuals, like Shakespeare or Michelangelo, whose genius depends on the right balance of contrary powers. The "tendency to combine antagonisms and utilize evil" is the foundation of high civilization as well. Man can control forces far greater than himself. Salt water can be turned to freshwater. Prisons can be made to yield a revenue. Negative force must not be shunned but put to use. The desired end product is, as always, the "manufactory" of human force, the liberation of man into "joyful action." Human power, self-reliance, human "skill" (one of the most frequently used words in this late book)—all are born in this balancing of "complex details" (W, 7:25).

From the progressive "unswaddling" of man into joyful action, Emerson moves, in "Domestic Life," to yet another illustration of his doctrines of tuition and use. In 1836 he had proposed that "The exercise of the Will or the lesson of power is taught in every event. From the child's successive possession of his several senses up to the hour when he saith, 'thy will be done!' he is learning the secret, that he can reduce under his will, not only particular events, but great classes, nay the whole series of events, and so conform all facts to his character" (CW, 1:25). That image is amplified, albeit in the more sentimental language characteristic of *Society and Solitude,* in his portrait of the infant "strong in his weakness" (W, 7:103). The child is at first, Emerson says, "overpowered by the [sun]light and by the extent of natural objects, and is silent." But he "studies power" and quickly learns the use of things. He learns the use of tools, learns to domesticate his world, learns to ride on the shoulders of those stronger than himself, learns to take up and subdue whatever natural limitations surround him and to utilize them as means for his own ends (W, 7:104–5).

Like each of the previous collections of essays, *Society and Solitude* is a string of exhortations to use. In the introductory essay, the problems of both private and public life are resolved in the closing lesson on "the use of society" (W, 7:11). Our need for solitude, our opposing social obligations, place us "between extreme antagonisms": yet both are "wonderful horses" we can learn to ride (W, 7:15).

The essay on "Clubs" begins with the pledge to use the world ("I will use the world and sift it, / To a thousand humors shift it") and reasserts our need to use society ("The lover of letters loves power too. . . . What new powers, what mines of wealth! . . . He uses his occasions; he seeks the company of those who have convivial talent" (W, 7:231). The opening paragraph is an extended conceit that redefines *Homo sapiens* as a living force pump, a power machine that must always be properly used ("We are delicate machines, and require nice treatment to get from us the maximum of power and pleasure" [W, 7:225]).

Emerson's emphasis through the entire book is on power, tools, skill, mastery, "the useful arts of life" (W, 7:228). "These arts open great gates of a future, promising to make the world plastic and to lift human life out of its beggary to a godlike ease and power" (W, 7:158). We must learn to use adversity (the beneficial "hoop" and "iron band of poverty, of necessity, of austerity" [W, 7:121]), to use our days and time ("The use of history is to give value to the present hours and its duty" [W, 7:177]). We must use books, society, our own bodies. We must use conversation ("Conversation is the laboratory and workshop of the student. . . . I prize the mechanics of conversations" [W, 7:227–28]). Like the farmer, we must use the air, the earth, until the world has become our "machine . . . of colossal proportions" (W, 7:142). Emerson's mission, once again, is "to help the young soul, add energy, inspire hope and blow the coals into a useful flame; to redeem defeat by new thought, by firm action" (W, 7:311).

"Works and Days" states concisely *Society and Solitude*'s central theme. Modern man, "the patent office" of all things, has transformed the world into his tool:

> Our nineteenth century is the age of tools. They grew out of our structure. "Man is the meter of all things," said Aristotle; "the hand is the instrument of instruments, and the mind is the form of forms." The human body is the magazine of inventions, the patent office, where are the models from which every hint was taken. All the tools and engines on earth are only extensions of its limbs and senses. One definition of man is "an intelligence served by organs." Machines can only second, not supply, his unaided senses. The body is a meter. (W, 7:157)

This can hardly, of course, be considered a new phase in Emerson's thought. The insistence that things are only the extensions or "boundaries of man" (as Nietzsche would phrase it) is also the central theme of *Nature,* with its emphasis on "the Hand of the mind," its conviction that nature must yield to "the activity of man an infinite scope," its belief in the unappreciated consanguinity of nature and man (CW, 1:24, 37, 38). Late essays like "Fate" or "Works and Days" are not retrenchments. They restate, in imagery that is usually more specific, the point that *Nature* makes in the abstract: the abiding doctrine that "Nature is so pervaded with human life, that there is something of humanity in all, and in every particular" (CW, 1:38).

If there is anything new, it is the sense that Emerson is no longer speaking prophetically, no longer merely painting an apocalyptic vision of man one day regaining the lost reins of power. The earlier emphasis on our present, fallen state has been replaced (partially, never wholly) by a new sense of self-congratulation. Emerson now reports on what has been attained. He alludes to the performance that has already taken place, the use of things that has already been learned.

A younger Emerson habitually denounced America's tendency toward inaction and the national want of "animal spirits." Ennui, he complained in 1841, was one of the signs of the times (CW, 1:180). "True success is the doing," he argued—but "As yet we have nothing but tendency and indication" (CW, 1:113, 107). By 1870, however, American "Success" has become a reality and, finally, a topic worthy of an entire essay. American power and performance have at last outstripped their promise. "The earth is shaken by our engineries. . . . We have the power of territory and seacoast, and know the use of them." "'T is the way of the world," Emerson concludes, after cataloguing American expansion, "'t is the law . . . of unfolding strength" (W, 7:283).

The late essays exhibit no lack of faith in strength. Emerson's confidence in the capacity of man to possess his world has not changed. There is only a renewed stress on the power to be found in what Emerson, like Nietzsche, calls our quotidian "poverty." There is a renewed stress on the power that awaits us in "the common . . . the familiar, the low" (CW, 1:67). "We are not strong," he writes, "by our power to penetrate, but by our relatedness. The world is enlarged for us, not by new objects, but by finding more affinities and potencies in those we have" (W, 7:302). Nietzsche's Zarathustra encourages his listeners to *"remain faithful to the earth."* He bids them find their redemption in the present moment, and the immediate use of loss, not in "otherworldly hopes" or in a brooding *ressentiment* (Z, Pref.:3).[75] Emerson offers a similar doctrine of "the deep to-day": faith in the power that always lurks in "the rich poverty" of the present. "No man," he writes, "has learned anything rightly until he knows that every day is Doomsday" (W, 7:175). The true scholar uses ("fills") the present hour: he can "unfold the theory of this particular Wednesday." The true master utilizes the materials of daily life to become a day himself (W, 7:175–81).

It is difficult to detect any new note of acquiescence amid the relentless imagery of use. If anything, the world depicted in *Society and Solitude* is a world in which the earlier stress on conflict—conflict as a benevolent and daily part of all human life—is even more intense. All productive human activity, as Emerson pictures it, involves what he calls "friction": it requires some contest of wills, some testing out of human powers, high or low. "Conversation," he writes, "is the Olympic games whither every superior gift resorts to assert and approve itself" (W, 7:241). The world simply *is* the theater for constant human competition in one form or another. "However courteously we conceal it, it is social rank and spiritual power that are compared; whether in the parlor, the courts, the caucus, the senate, or the chamber of science,—which are only less or larger theatres for this competition" (W, 7:235). "All that man can do for man" is to be found in this "market" of competition (W, 7:234).

It is an old Emersonian doctrine (sometimes referred to as his "leader principle"). Men will "take each other's measure, when they meet for the first time,—and every time they meet" (W, 6:190). The selection of a natural aristocracy, as he described it in 1844, is an inevitable human preoccupation. Some "new class" will always find "itself at the top, as certainly as cream rises in a bowl of milk": "if the people should destroy class after class, until two men only were left, one of these would be the leader, and would be involuntarily served and copied by the other" (CW, 3:76).

Why, then, have scholars so persistently read these late essays as Emerson's valedictory surrender to the nonhuman forces in the universe? One way to answer that question is to look closely at one of those late passages Jonathan Bishop adduces as evidence of "Emerson's newly sharpened sense that nature rather than the Soul is the true agent in the realm of commodity."[76] The "hitch your wagon" section from "Civilization," one passage Bishop has in mind, is too long to be quoted in full. I cite just enough to suggest the way in which such passages remain problematic and open to opposite interpretations.

> Everything good in man leans on what is higher. This rule holds in small as in great. Thus all our strength and success in the work of our hands depend on our borrowing the aid of the elements. You have seen a carpenter on a ladder with a broadaxe chopping upward chips from a beam. How awkward! at what disadvantage he works! But see him on the ground, dressing his timber under him. Now, not his feeble muscles but the force of gravity brings down the axe; that is to say, the planet itself splits his stick. The farmer had much ill temper, laziness and shirking to endure from his hand-sawyers, until one day he bethought him to put his saw-mill on the edge of a waterfall; and the river never tires of turning his wheel; the river

is good-natured, and never hints an objection.

We had letters to send: couriers could not go fast enough nor far enough; broke their wagons, foundered their horses; bad roads in spring, snowdrifts in winter, heats in summer; could not get the horses out of a walk. But we found out that the air and earth were full of Electricity, and always going our way,—just the way we wanted to send. . . .

I admire still more than the saw-mill the skill which, on the seashore, makes the tides drive the wheels and grind corn, and which thus engages the assistance of the moon, like a hired hand, to grind, and wind, and pump, and saw, and split stone, and roll iron.

Now that is the wisdom of a man, in every instance of his labor, to hitch his wagon to a star, and see his chore done by the gods themselves. That is the way we are strong, by borrowing the might of the elements. The forces of steam, gravity, galvanism, light, magnets, wind, fire, serve us day by day and cost us nothing.

Our astronomy is full of examples of calling in the aid of these magnificent helpers. . . . All our arts aim to win this vantage. We cannot bring the heavenly powers to us, but if we will only choose our jobs in directions in which they travel, they will undertake them with the greatest pleasure. (W, 7:27–29)

The ideas in this passage are, for one thing, not at all new. The passage originates in an 1836 journal entry that predates the publication of *Nature.* "All powerful action," the young Emerson there insists, "is by bringing the forces of nature to bear upon our objects. . . . [W]e do few things by muscular force but we place ourselves in such attitudes as to bring the force of gravity . . . to bear upon the <shovel>." We do not grind corn or wield axe without bringing not our own, but "a quite infinite force to bear." The same principle holds for our "intellectual works" (JMN, 5:166).

Whicher and those critics, like Bishop, who have accepted his thesis only claim that the later Emerson acquires a newly *sharpened* sense of natural power. The tendency has existed all along as one strain in his thought; its predominance in the later essays is simply a matter of shifting emphasis. But we need to ask if this tendency can justifiably be categorized as acquiescence at all. Is Emerson advocating, as Bishop goes on to suggest, passivity before "Ideal Nature"? Is he, in passages like these, describing a pantheistic or deterministic merging of man and nature? Can we read such passages as evidence of Emerson's movement away from an anthropomorphic deity toward a Buddhistic submission to "an unknown, unnamable" Fate, an "Oriental" Oneness "indifferent to all human values"?[77]

One answer is yes. Emerson certainly speaks of man's ubiquitous dependence on a higher power. In the essay on "Art," which immediately follows "Civilization" in *Society and Solitude,* he writes of the necessary *"abandonment,"* the "self-surrender," the shoving aside of "egotism" and "will" that any great artist must accept (W, 7:49). This line of thought has always played a major part in his work. It is, in fact, one pole of his thought that would appear to contradict the interpretation I have been arguing. It represents a philosophy of "abandonment"—not, it would seem, a will to power, or a proto-Nietzschean philosophy of resistance, tuition, and unceasing use. It is a philosophy that urges man not to work but to be worked on. The "prominent fact" in any work of art, as Emerson put it in 1836, is not human power but the "subordination of man" to nature and "the universal mind": "The omnipotent agent is Nature; all human acts are satellites to her orb" (EL, 2:44–45). I have been stressing Emerson's enduring emphasis on the use, the possession, the degrading of nature. But Emerson also speaks of the necessity of human submission—that universal law that decrees that man must approach nature like a child, practicing a "patient, docile observation" (EL, 1:20).

We are back, in short, at the paradox we reached at the end of chapter 1. Emerson seems to be a Neoplatonist, a mystic, an absolutist, and a precursor of Nietzsche and William James. He advocates both the exercise of the will and its abandonment. I know of no writer who is a more stubborn believer in tuition; but he may also be read as the philosopher of intuition. He is a pragmatist and a Transcendentalist. I shall return to this paradox, and the problems it creates for Emerson's readers, in chapter 5.

We must not leave behind the passages I have just cited, however, without taking a closer look at the questions they raise. Are such passages really examples of an acquiescent Emerson? Do categories like pantheism, transcendentalism, abandonment, mysticism, and submission adequately describe what Emerson is talking about? There is, as I have suggested, reason to conclude that they do. But there is at last equal—I would argue, a great deal more—reason to conclude that they do not. For whenever Emerson speaks of "abandonment" (he employs the word repeatedly) the discussion inevitably leads not to a loss of self in any Buddhistic or mystical sense but to some new form of empowerment, some new practical action, some new tool or advantage. Abandonment only begets some firmer stroke of the axe, some more expedient means for domesticating the elements, some more effective form of human manipulation. There is never, for Emerson (for the Emerson of the essays, at least), self-surrender without self-strengthening, never submission that does not lead to mastery. The artist must practice abandonment and self-surrender; but they always lead him to greater "triumphs of the art" (W, 7:49).

If this is abandonment, it is misleadingly named, for it is an abandonment that never leads to what the word itself would suggest: to passivity or self-annihilation. It leads instead to the production of something, to works of art, to new human skills, to the catalogue of useful arts Emerson celebrates in the above passage: to improved mills and instruments, better pumps, crowbars, and couriers. And it is at this point that we must ask if there is, then, ultimately any difference between Emersonian abandonment (which is always defined in the context of the strength it bestows, the "magnificent helpers" it brings to man) and a Nietzschean philosophy of conflict and use (which similarly values the inner life only insofar as it issues in "cultural products" and renewed human force). A spiritual life has, for Nietzsche, little intrinsic value; it has only "instrumental value."[78] It is never an end in itself. It is valuable not for its own sake but for the pragmatic result, the human power, the cultural products it helps create. Precisely the same thing can be said of Emerson. Abandonment is never an end in itself. The inwardness and spiritual life of which Emerson speaks is, likewise, never an end in itself. It has only instrumental value. It is mediate: it leads always to power, to work, to the production of some benefactor that can improve human culture.

Emerson indeed speaks of submission—but we need always to ask in which direction his rhetorical balance tilts. "Whosoever would gain anything of [nature]," he writes, "must submit to the essential condition of all learning, must go in the spirit of a little child. The naturalist commands nature by obeying her" (EL, 1:20). But how should we read that? Does the emphasis fall on the initial, necessary obedience to nature or on the eventual command of nature such submission will bring?

Whicher noted what critics who repeat his thesis often forget—the special quality of Emerson's putative acquiescence: "It is not a simple submission, but also a positive assertion of power."[79] Is it not, then, something other than acquiescence? Would it not be more accurate to take the process of hitching, borrowing, and leaning on described in the above passages as a late variation on—final confirmation of—the doctrine that remains ever present in Emerson's essays, "the great doctrine of Use"? Enlisting the assistance of the moon to grind your corn, allowing the weight of the planet to guide your axe—only in a very limited sense can these be considered types of surrender. For they represent no ultimate loss of human control. They are, rather, acts of use, acts in which intelligence learns to counter potentially threatening energies. They are all anthropocentric: they only extend the capacities of civilization.

Early or late, Emerson's essays offer nothing equivalent to the kind of truly acquiescent conclusion Walt Whitman reaches in his late poem "Twilight." Whitman's brief "song of parting" offers a good point of comparison: it is all willing surrender to the "soft voluptuous opiate shades." Its elliptical closing line disappears into wordlessness: the poet drifts into "haze—nirwana—rest and night—oblivion."[80] Emerson, on the contrary, always returns to reassert the *use* of the powers of night. Any claim to abandonment, any apparent impulse to rest in oblivion, is superseded by some action, some new vision of human dominion. "[W]e can," he declares (later in the "hitch your wagon" passage), "thus ride in Olympian chariots by putting our works in the path of the celestial circuits, we can harness also evil agents, the powers of darkness, and force them to serve against their will the ends of wisdom and virtue" (W, 7:30). Man, as Emerson paints him, remains in the saddle—the user, not the used.

3

The Uses of Failure

[M]y entire success, such as it were, is composed wholly of particular failures,—every public work of mine of the least importance, having been (probably without exception) noted at the
time as a failure. . . . I will take Miss Barbauld's line for my
motto "And the more falls I get, move faster on."

—*Ralph Waldo Emerson, "Journals" (1834)*

In the same late work in which he praised Emerson, Nietzsche
turned to Goethe as the century's greatest example of the Dionysian self-
creator capable of "a joyful . . . acceptance of fate" (TI, 9:49). This Nietzschean conception of the affirmation of all life is, Erich Heller cautions,
easily misread: "we should lose track of [this central Nietzschean theme] if
we allowed ourselves to be persuaded that it was . . . Apollo's child's play
for Goethe to persevere in affirmation, or simply due to his superbly fortu-
nate temperament and genius."[1] Heller's caveat for Nietzsche's readers is
entirely appropriate for Emerson's as well. For Emerson's greatest theme—
the brand of affirmation he alluded to as "the Good of Evil," the "harvesting of losses," "finding a resource in every moment," or the "use of failure"—has been quite regularly ignored. It has been misconstrued, for more
than a century and a half now, as mere child's play.

Emerson's contemporaries (Hawthorne, Melville, Carlyle, Fuller,
Brownson, Henry James Sr.) believed that he spouted beautiful moonshine,
that he was one of those rare "once-born" souls whose indifference to suffering was simply the accident of his "altogether personal" moral "virgin-
ity." Santayana portrayed him as "a cheery, child-like soul, impervious to
the evidence of evil." George Woodberry concluded that he could "find no
room for evil in the universe." Sidney Hook took it for granted that he was
a naively "cheerful affirmer." Russell Kirk judged him the chief apologist
for the American public's "ostrich-tendency" to turn its back on evil. This
interpretation of Emerson as an idealist in the popular and most damning
sense of the word has been repeated for so long, by so many, that it may
be futile to try to replace it with something more just. Even Nietzsche

pictured him as "nourish[ing] himself only on ambrosia, leaving behind what is indigestible in things" (TI, 9:13).[2]

"[Emerson's] metier was singing of victories, not defeats," John McAleer has more recently stated it: "he was the poet of the positive."[3] That puts concisely what has now become the standard line. Yet it represents an astonishing simplification of Emerson's actual thought. It seems necessary, therefore, to reemphasize what has been all along an underlying point of my argument: Emerson was never the exasperatingly invulnerable poet of the positive.

Positive power was inconceivable for Emerson without negative power—so much so that it would be equally accurate to say that his genuine métier was really failure and weakness. If he was the poet of the positive, he was no less profoundly the poet of the negative. This is so basic a feature of Emerson's psychology that his search after power can at times resemble Poe's fascination with self-destruction and "the imp of the perverse." Victory required defeat. True success was impossible without failure. Health was the overcoming, not the avoidance, of disease. Power lay in the use, not the transcending, of loss and weakness.

The Emersonian quest for power often reveals itself as a Nietzschean craving for suffering, a hunger for "authentic distress." "*Not ist nötig!* [Neediness is needed!]," Nietzsche insists (GS, 56). "The best and most fruitful people" will, like the tallest trees, find their truest nourishment in "bad weather and storms," in "misfortune and external resistance" (GS, 19). "The highest type of free man should be sought where the highest resistance is constantly overcome" (TI, 9:38). "Every calamity," Emerson likewise insists, "is a spur" (W, 6:36): "He has not learned the lesson of life who does not every day surmount a fear" (W, 7:276). "Acknowledge your weakness," he urged his New England audiences, "as eagerly as you use your strength" (EL, 2:259): "[N]o man had ever a defect that was not somehow made useful to him" (EL, 2:153).

The typical image O. B. Frothingham presented in 1876 ("[Emerson] lives in the region of serene ideas. . . . [His] characteristic trait is serenity. He is faithful to his own counsel, 'Shun the negative side'. . . . He seems to be perpetually saying 'Good Morning'") has, it is true, been steadily dislodged by Emerson's biographers. "His achievement," Evelyn Barish concludes, "began when he recognized that something or some things essential to life were missing, accepted this as his starting point, and made of his isolation a usable freedom." "The growth of unique strength out of insuperable defects was," she notes, "a process he knew well." "Just as Hawthorne's scarlet letter stands out vividly against a background of black," Alan Hodder writes, "so Emerson's magisterial productions emerge from a predominant background of loss and repeated death. . . . [A] careful reading of Emerson's life suggests not that he created in spite of his losses but that he created in consequence of them."[4]

But one hardly needs to fall back on the often tragic facts of Emerson's life to appreciate the indispensable role that negative power plays in his writing. Its centrality is evident on nearly every page of his prose. Take, for example, "Aristocracy," one of his key essays on the heroic action necessary for true self-reliance. Emerson does indeed proclaim that the "self-dependent mind" acts always out of the conviction "that it is impossible to fail" (W, 10:57). Such remarks—like his definition of evil as "merely privative, not absolute" (CW, 1:78) or his private confession that he "could never give much reality to evil & pain" (JMN, 14:355)—have helped to earn him his dubious reputation as the poet of the positive. But it is clear, as Emerson goes on to describe the actual process of success, that strength begins in weakness, in pain. Man cannot achieve "the erect position," as Emerson christened it, without a history of falls. "The noble mind is here to teach us that failure is a part of success. . . . [A] man's success is made up of failures, because he experiments and ventures every day." The good horseman is not the rider who has never been thrown. Rather, Emerson says, "a man never will be a good rider until he is thrown; then he will not be haunted any longer by the terror that he shall tumble, and will ride" (W, 10:58).

Compare the same sentiment in "Perpetual Forces." Once again, Emerson admires not the man who safely avoids a fall but the tenacious continuer who has endured defeat and learned to use resistance.

> I delight in tracing these wonderful powers, the electricity and gravity of the human world. The power of persistence, of enduring defeat and of gaining victory by defeats, is one of these forces which never loses its charm. The power of a man increases steadily by continuance in one direction. He becomes acquainted with the resistances, and with his own tools; increases his skill and strength and learns the favorable moments and favorable accidents. He is his own apprentice, and more time gives a great addition of power, just as a falling body acquires momentum with every foot of the fall. How we prize a good continuer! (W, 10:78–79)

One of the most intriguing passages in the essays is Emerson's description, in "Spiritual Laws," of the principle we might term his own, revisionary doctrine of the fall (or, more exactly, doctrine of falling). It comes just a few pages after his better-known remark that "the theological problems of original sin, origin of evil, predestination, and the like" are merely "the soul's mumps and measles, and whooping-coughs" (CW, 2:77–78). (That perennial question of philosophy—*unde malorum*—is, Emerson seems all too cavalierly to suggest, an inevitable cause of anxiety, but one easy enough to outgrow.) But this apparent rejection of the whole problem of evil is followed by the new spiritual—and natural—law he would put in its place:

> Let us draw a lesson from nature, which always works by short ways. When the fruit is ripe, it falls. When the fruit is despatched, the leaf falls. The

circuit of the waters is mere falling. The walking of man and all animals is a falling forward. All our manual labor and works of strength, as prying, splitting, digging, rowing, and so forth, are done by dint of continual falling, and the globe, earth, moon, comet, sun, star, fall forever and ever. (CW, 2:80)

"This is certainly a curious passage," Joel Porte comments, "for though it is ostensibly intended to assure us that all's right with the world, its effect is quite different. It sounds as if Emerson were trying to exemplify the Second Law of Thermodynamics [Entropy]." Emerson's recurrent meditations on depravity and "the Fall" must, Porte proceeds to argue, "be accounted as much a part of Emerson as his 'affirmative philosophy.' Though he might come to conceive of evil as being merely privative—the absence of good—that absence, or emptiness, would always yawn somewhere at the bottom of Emerson's consciousness."[5]

But Emerson's quite unconventional speculations on the Fall suggest that evil and sin occupy a place in his thought that is significantly more complicated and comprehensive. For so richly allusive a passage implies an acceptance of evil that is a good deal more drastic than even Porte's interpretation suggests—if we read it in light of the dual connotations the Fall always had for Emerson, as both original sin and failure. The passage suggests that evil (and all the suffering, weakness, and imperfection associated with our fallen nature) is not simply a reality that will always lurk somewhere at the bottom of things, deny it how we may. It suggests, rather, that the reality of our fallen state is an absolutely natural and inevitable part of all experience—that it is a fundamental part of all activity in the universe. It suggests that if the world is, as Emerson claimed, "saturated with the moral sentiment," then it is also saturated with all the failings and negative powers that characterize our fallen (and ever-falling) state. Those victories we usually regard as testament to our affirmative or positive philosophy can hardly be divorced from the universal reality of failure. For victory (positive power, affirmation, self-reliance) originates in defeat.

The key lies, as always, in the doctrine of use. The trick lies in our readiness to use, not deny, the universal realities of failure, death, gravity, entropy. Neither positive nor negative power is absolute or privative for Emerson, despite his oft-quoted claim to the contrary. The actual psychology at work in essay after essay rejects the idea that either positive or negative force can exist in the absence of the other. Positive energy simply is the use of—the acceptance and assimilation, incorporation, or conversion of—negative energy. Power is the use of powerlessness. "We see the causes of evils," Emerson says, "and learn to parry them and use them as instruments" (W, 10:73). We must find a resource in every moment—in every moment of defeat. Power lies not in assertions in the void but in constant acts of recovery, in bending forward with the causes of evil to make them work for us: "Heroes do not fix, but flow, bend forward ever and invent a resource for every moment" (SE, 146).

In his influential series of lectures, *The Varieties of Religious Experience,* William James classified writers like Emerson or Whitman as once-born, healthy-minded souls—examples of that type of character who will, regardless of the circumstances, remain forever untainted by the consciousness of sin. "This childlike quality of their nature"—so James put it— "makes the opening of religion very happy to them. . . . [I]n fact, they have no vivid conception of *any* of the qualities in which the severer Majesty of God consists. . . . Of human sin they know perhaps little in their hearts and not very much in the world; and human suffering does but melt them to tenderness."[6] Thus have most of Emerson's critics defined and underestimated him.

But of the contrasting personality types James postulated in 1902 (once-born versus twice-born souls, healthy-minded versus morbid characters) it is actually the latter type—the more complete, more synthetic type—that is most applicable in Emerson's case. And it is in his characterization of the more complex, twice-born personality that James comes closest to describing the doctrine of use, the principle of "sublation" or synthesis, that defines the true Emersonian psychology:

> It is indeed true that the outlook upon life of the twice-born—holding as it does more of the element of evil in solution—is the wider and completer. The "heroic" or "solemn" way in which life comes to them is a "higher synthesis" into which healthy-mindedness and morbidness both enter and combine. Evil is not evaded, but sublated in the higher religious cheer of these persons.[7]

It is, of course, not Emerson's name that comes to mind when we think of those nineteenth-century writers who took failure as their theme or embraced it as the organizing principle of their art, even their lives. It is to Henry Adams, to Emerson's contemporaries Hawthorne, Poe, Dickinson, perhaps to Melville, above all, whom we turn as examples of writers who explored the artistic and psychological possibilities of failure. "The necessity of voyaging and the equal necessity of failure" is, Charles Feidelson notes, a central theme and the "largest paradox" of *Moby-Dick.* As Melville himself put it: "It is better to fail in originality than to succeed in imitation. He who has never failed somewhere, that man can not be great." "To scale great heights," he wrote in *Mardi,* "we must come out of lowermost depths. The way to heaven is through hell."[8]

But schematizing the writers of Emerson's era into opposing Transcendentalist and anti-Transcendentalist camps has blinded us to failure as a major theme in the psychology of Melville's allegedly transcendental contemporaries. We forget that the risk, even the necessity, of failure was as important to Thoreau as it was to Melville. ("Defeat is heaven's success," Thoreau proclaimed in 1840, "He cannot be said to succeed to whom the world shows any favor. In fact it is the hero's point d'appui, which by offering resistance to his action enables him to act at all. . . . He vaults the higher in proportion as he employs the greater resistance of the earth.")[9] Most significantly, we overlook—when we forget that his essays accept failure as their donnée—one of the ways in which Emerson was truly a mirror of his times.

Emerson's understanding of the ambiguous nature of success, his devotion to wringing victory from defeat, provided, as is now clear in retrospect, the complementary philosophy for the Jacksonian years—that era defined by its currency wars, economic unpredictability, and high incidence of rapid financial failures and new starts. The representative American democrat of the antebellum years found himself, according to Marvin Meyers, in an economic universe with "no secure resting place." The typical "nervous striver" of the 1830s and 1840s developed, Meyers writes, "an acute awareness of loss and failure": "If failure was not final, neither was success definitive." The democrat-capitalist of the Jackson years was compelled to embrace "a highly elastic notion of achievement": bankruptcy did not necessarily mean defeat, yet success could never be trusted.[10]

Emerson's doctrine of use—his persistent acceptance of failure as an "inlet . . . to higher advantages" (CW, 1:99)—is, as I have been suggesting, a crucial precedent for Nietzsche's idea of conversion. Nietzschean conversion is, as Stephen Donadio phrases it, "that process of transformation . . . by which one state of feeling reverses itself and becomes its opposite." That process of transformation is one of the underlying concerns of Donadio's study, *Nietzsche, Henry James, and the Artistic Will,* and he traces its progress in the protagonists of the major-phase novels who move "from self-denial and renunciation to an undivided affirmation of the will."[11] Such conversion is central to Emerson's psychology—and philosophy—of confrontation and resistance. Use and conversion are the mechanisms by which any force greater or potentially greater than one's own can be absorbed and transmuted into strength. Emerson summarizes the idea well when he writes in his journal that the secret of self-reliance is "to make your supposed deficiency redundancy. If I am true, the theory is, my very want of action, my very impotency, shall become a greater excellency than all skill & toil" (JMN, 7:521).

Art was, for both Nietzsche and Emerson, one principal means of conversion. Art, Emerson suggests, provides a means of compensation for the weakness or imbalance in the character of the artist. It is because the poet "is not well mixt that he needs to do some feat by way of fine or expiation" (JMN, 11:226). "A man's 'sin,'" as Kenneth Burke puts it, "can drive him into great piety of style." Art can become the altar of atonement, on which personal failure is converted into expressive force, "the sense of guilt" quickening "the sense of style."[12]

For Nietzsche, all greatness in art or culture began in the greatest reversal or overcoming of suffering or disease. True health was never merely the accidental lack of infection—it was, rather, the ability to overcome disease. "It seems impossible," he theorized, "to be an artist and not to be sick" (WP, 811). It is not difficult to discern beneath such a psychology an "unresolved conflict . . . between vital instinct and death urge."[13] Just such an unresolved antithesis, in whatever varying degrees, seems to define a common psychological landscape for Nietzsche, Carlyle, and Emerson and for their theories of power.

If Carlyle's search for power ultimately found its resolution in the political world, *Sartor Resartus* testifies to the profound confusion in his mind between work as an expression of the vital instinct and work as the means for the "Annihilation of Self" for which Carlyle-Teufelsdröckh longs. If Nietzsche could accept "the bad conscience" as "an illness as pregnancy is a illness" (GM, 2:19), Carlyle could assure himself that the disease of self-consciousness was really "the beginning of Inquiry."[14] Emerson is usually thought of as a salubrious contrast to the tragic struggle in Thoreau's career between instincts of life and death. But Emerson could welcome disease, as Nietzsche did, as the opportunity for "the strength of the constitution" to prove itself: "I delight that we can never be utterly demented[,] that the very rancor of the disease denotes the strength of the constitution" (JMN, 8:137).

"The province of art" for Henry James was "all life, all feeling, all observation, all vision." Emerson would have agreed. The age was defined by its proliferating energies, both natural and human, and it demanded of culture an equal inclusion of the powers of blackness and the powers of good. "For that culture then which every noble mind in these times needs and should seek," Emerson declared in 1842, "should be built on the broadest base of experience, and open to every influence of pain and pleasure, of science, and of speculation" (EL, 3:376). "No theory of life can have any solidity which leaves out of account the value of Vice, Pain, Disease, Poverty, Insecurity, Disunion, Affection, Fear, and Death" (EL, 3:104). The value of pain, of all forms of negative power, was—once again—its ultimate usefulness. Emerson was committed, no less than was Hawthorne, to assimilating and converting the powers of blackness—the humanizing sins and energies of the unconscious that make art possible. "The poet," he claimed, "cannot spare any grief or pain or terror in his experience; he wants every rude stroke that has been dealt on his irritable texture[.] I need my fear & my superstition as much as my purity & courage to construct the glossary which opens the Sanscrit of the world" (JMN, 7:390).

Nietzsche scorned anyone who desired to abolish suffering. Suffering was the indispensable stimulus to perfection: "The discipline of suffering, of *great* suffering—do you not know that only *this* discipline has created all enhancements of man so far?" (BGE, 225). Emerson similarly held that life was a capacious and beautiful museum whose "smart" must be known with its "sweet" if we are to master its "serene and beautiful laws" (CW, 1:111). Heroism, for Emerson, demanded the "exercising of the soul" in suffering. Power lay in "fronting" the objects of our "worst apprehension" (CW, 2:139). Familiarity with the "rarer dangers which sometimes invade men"—with that reality that comes only in strokes of pain—conferred the strength of immunity. "And not only need we breathe and exercise the soul by assuming the penalties of abstinence, of debt, of solitude, of unpopularity, but it behoves the wise man to look with a bold eye into those rarer dangers which sometimes invade men, and to familiarize himself with disgusting forms of disease, with sounds of execration, and the vision of violent death" (CW, 2:154).

Power could be gained only if one shuddered—in Nietzsche's phrase, "face to face with great ruin"—with weakness, temptation, evil (BGE, 225). "He is a strong man who can look them in the eye," Emerson wrote, "see through this juggle, feel their identity, and keep his own" (W, 7:174). Untested virtue was not strength but "canting impotence" (JMN, 7:239), for it had not undergone what Nietzsche called "the tension of the soul in unhappiness," in which true strength is cultivated—that process of conversion by which personal and artistic weakness becomes moral and expressive force.

A long tradition of critics has found in Emerson that "peculiar moral passiveness," as Newton Arvin labeled it, born of an indifference to evil and pain. Yvor Winters attacked Emerson for believing that "the passive mind" is "the best medium for reaching truth."[15] But such criticisms ignore the patterns of his metaphors and the workings of a mind that is, more than any other American writer's, characterized by its restless need for an antagonism by which to define itself, grow stronger, and create its art. Emerson would have agreed with Melville that "he knows himself and all that's in him who knows adversity."[16] "The natural measure" of the power of character lay, as he often restated it, in the "resistance of circumstance" (CW, 3:57). "We must have an antagonism in the tough world for all the variety of our spiritual faculties, or they will not be born" (CW, 1:150). This was, in conjunction with his doctrine of use and work, the root premise of his thought.

"The first thing man requires of man, is reality," Emerson writes in *Essays: Second Series* (CW, 3:79). Indeed, in the second book of essays, from the painful "Experience" to the final, chastened "New England Reformers," he seeks, at times in desperation, to ground, anchor, or center himself. He longs to penetrate the counterfeit surface of things, longs to find some immovable reality whose "sharp peaks and edges" will allow the "crescive self" to measure, define itself, and begin again the process of gaining power. The second volume of essays records Emerson's search for an antagonistic reality that will, as he put it in an 1841 letter, save him from the "lassitude" and "metaphysical flux" of "perpetual observation, perpetual acquiescence" (SE, 184). "Always a referred existence, an absence, never a presence and satisfaction," he complains in the middle of the volume. "Must we not suppose somewhere in the universe a slight treachery and derision?" (CW, 3:112). The true catastrophe is not that evil is a palpable entity but that it is not real enough:

> There are moods in which we court suffering, in the hope that here, at least, we shall find reality, sharp peaks and edges of truth. But it turns out to be scene-painting and counterfeit. The only thing grief has taught me is to know how shallow it is. That, like all the rest, plays about the surface, and never introduces me into the reality, for contact with which we would even pay the costly price of sons and lovers. . . . Nothing is left us now but death. We look to that with a grim satisfaction, saying, there at least is reality that will not dodge us. (CW, 3:29)

"We are weary of gliding ghostlike through the world, which is itself so slight and unreal," Emerson cries out in his final pages, "We crave a sense of reality, though it comes in strokes of pain" (CW, 3:161).

Those are some of Emerson's most bitterly dramatic lines. But the oppositional psychology behind them was, as I have attempted to argue, a fundamental Emersonian principle long before the death of his son. In a remarkable letter to Samuel Gray Ward, written in the July before Waldo's sudden death, Emerson asks for the same rigorous, pragmatic reality—and all its invigorating reinforcement—that he seeks in *Essays: Second Series*. The endless beach at Nantasket and "this Syrian summer," Emerson begins, have drawn "the cords of the Will out of my thought," leaving him "nothing but perpetual observation, perpetual acquiescence." "Can you not save me," he asks Ward, "find me some girding belt, that I glide not away into a stream or a gas, and decease in infinite diffusion? Reinforce me, I entreat you, with showing me some man, work, aim or fact under the *angle of practice,* that I may see you as an elector and rejector, an agent, an antagonist and a commander." Noah's flood was "a calamity less universal than this metaphysical flux which threatens every enterprise, every thought and every thinker." Even the life of pantheistic abandonment to the blueberry pastures at home, Emerson complains, was weakening his will (SE, 184). (And will, as he would later say in "Natural History of Intellect," "is the measure of power" [W, 12:46].) To live without the "girding belt" of a work or an antagonist is to drown in that sea of ennui and "metaphysical flux" that threatens every enterprise, every thinker. The real calamity is not calamity itself but the absence of resistance.

Emerson's journal entry of 17 October 1840 is an equally suggestive example of the way in which he found reality's resistances energizing. When the Transcendental Club met in the fall of 1840 to discuss its plans for a socialist community at Brook Farm, Emerson found the venture a self-delusive retreat from reality. It was all "an anchor to leeward against a change of weather," a denial of the storms of real experience. The mere thought of the idealistic community robbed him of power: "And not once could I be inflamed, but sat aloof and thoughtless; my voice faltered and fell. It was not the cave of persecution which is the palace of spiritual power, but only a room in the Astor Hotel hired for the Transcendentalists" (JMN, 7:408).

For Nietzsche and Henry James, art (and life) was, Donadio suggests, the continual struggle to master and reshape a hostile or ugly reality. The role of the real in that process is so similar to the use Emerson makes of it in his search for power—the process so close to his doctrine that "in proportion to the energy of his thought and will [man] takes up the world into himself" (CW, 1:15)—that Donadio's summary is worth quoting at length:

> [A]rt thrives by feeding on all that opposes it: it is strengthened by the op-position of the actual, and indeed it requires that continual opposition to provide it with living material to be transformed. It therefore works its will by converting to its own advantage whatever is formless, painful and chaotic; as a result, the more intractable experience it succeeds in assimilating and transmuting, the more actuality it is able to appropriate and make over in its own ideal image, the more powerful it becomes.[17]

The "antagonizing mind" (CW, 3:39), as Emerson called it, thrives by feeding on all that opposes it. The image of eating or taking up is central. For Emerson's imagination, his posture toward the world, is omnivorous. "I dreamed," he wrote in his journal in 1840, "that I floated at will in the great Ether, and I saw this world floating also not far off, but diminished to the size of an apple. Then an angel took it in his hand & brought it to me and said 'This must thou eat.' And I ate the world" (JMN, 7:525). Whatever reference this dream may have to Adam, to the Book of Revelation, or the straitened dietary habits of Emerson's own youth, the imagery can certainly be interpreted according to the contrary terms of floating powerless versus controlling or mastering circumstances by incorporating "the world."[18]

In what has come to be his most famous journal entry, written in the months after his son's death, Emerson recorded his consciousness of immense helplessness at the hands of fate and the coexistent certainty that "all Power" was yet "practicable" and within his grasp: "I am *Defeated* all the time; yet to Victory I am born" (JMN, 8:228). Critics have always questioned the audacity that allows Emerson to profess simultaneous victory and defeat, to acknowledge within himself "latent omniscience coexistent with omni-ignorance" (ibid.) or claim, in one breath, "I am God in nature; I am a weed by the wall" (CW, 2:182). But such victories were, by Emerson's own dictate, hard won. They crystallized under the pressure of an imagination always aware of its own weakness. They took shape in the defensive war against "the encroaching All" (EL, 3:104) that included "Pain . . . Insecurity, Disunion," fear of the ennui of one's own will. They imply the failure, or latent failure, in which they begin.

Like Henry Adams's education, the essays were experiments in which failure could be courted for the knowledge and power it conferred. His sentences were the medium for containing, in a single line, the conversion of powerlessness into power—contradictory moods that hold together uneasily, like "infinitely repellent particles" (CEC, 185). The essays provided the arena in which Emerson's search for power could take place, where "the antagonizing mind" could discover and admit its fears and casualties and could turn them into the expressive force that was his art.

4

Extravagance

> Yet can Emerson really believe what he says in these essays: that "With consistency a great soul has simply nothing to do," for instance, or "I think nothing is of any value in books excepting the transcendental and extraordinary"; since we see him regularly exaggerate his case? He becomes hyperbolic the way others grow hysterical. Overstatement creates the Oversoul, and Emerson's tight lapidary style contributes to it, for it is a style intolerant of qualification, reservation, convolution. Nothing is less Jamesian than the hard precise bites of his mind.
>
> —*William Gass, "Emerson and the Essay" (1982)*

Any interpretation of Emerson must, sooner or later, address the problem William Gass raises in the passage I have used as an epigraph: the problem of tone. This is, of course, true of any writer. But in Emerson's case, the "hard precise bites of his mind"—the willful avoidance of connections, qualifications, explanations—and the frequent reliance on some manner of hyperbole have made his tone and intentions, his sincerity (or lack of it), seem difficult, even impossible, to pin down. Gass is unusual but, I would argue, quite correct in stressing the essentially hyperbolic nature of Emerson's writing. For it can seem at times that his ideas are primarily examples of the trope of hyperbole, by-products of his overstated rhetoric. He is, Harold Bloom remarks, "a writer who, like his admirer Nietzsche, would dare to say anything."[1]

Nietzsche—who believed that "Nothing succeeds if prankishness has no part in it" (TI, Pref.)—recognized the essential wit, the excess, underlying his essays. "Emerson," he said, "has that gracious and clever cheerfulness which discourages all seriousness" (TI, 9:13). Emerson's friend Oliver Wendell Holmes long ago emphasized his "exquisite sense of the ridiculous," his "splendid hyperbole" and *"felix audacia."* "Without a certain sensibility to the humorous," he warned, "no one should venture upon Emerson." Those readers unused to his "over-statement, extravagance, paradox, eccentricity" might otherwise be tempted to "shut [Emerson's] book up as wanting in sanity."[2]

Holmes's insight into the often-overlooked subtleties of Emerson's rhetoric needs always to be borne in mind by Emerson's readers. No one who attempts to pass judgment on him can afford to forget the image Holmes leaves us of Emerson's always potentially irreverent, half-facetious tone. A smile, he reminds us, was wont to cross Emerson's face "as he delivered one of his playful statements of a runaway truth, fact unhorsed by imagination." Walt Whitman was yet another writer alert to Emerson's Yankee prankishness. Emerson possessed, Whitman said, a pure and sweet, but consummately canny, talent for keeping himself just on the edge: "The most exquisite taste and caution are in him always saving his feet from passing beyond the limits, for he is transcendental of limits." That practical, Emersonian respect for limits, conjoined with a properly transcendental indifference to them, has, Whitman concluded, inspired in his literary descendants "a secret proclivity, American maybe, to dare and violate and make escapades."[3]

Like Barbara Packer a century later, Holmes attributed the apparent juxtaposition of mutually contradictory tones and authorial motives, and the confusion and ambiguity this can create, to the discrepancy between an orally delivered text and a printed one. Without the presence of the author/lecturer himself, we can miss Emerson's irony or self-deprecation and can be uncertain about how literally we are to take him. Warner Berthoff suggests that it is Emerson's essentially self-projective manner of writing that creates ambiguity. Self-dramatization implies both revelation and falsification: it can make it difficult to tell when Emerson is aiming for honesty and when he is being "artful, sly, disingenuous."[4]

For other readers, Emerson's audacities have seemed hidden by what Stanley Cavell calls "the genteel surface" of his prose. "An essay such as 'Fate,'" Cavell writes, "seems to me excruciatingly difficult to come to terms with, presenting writing that is as indirect and devious as, say, Thoreau's is, but more treacherous because of its care to maintain a more genteel surface." "The texture of the prose," as Quentin Anderson puts it, "operated to conceal the extravagance," even the "blasphemous character," of Emerson's ideas. O. W. Firkins refers to this as the tendency of Emerson's usually well-mannered style to overshadow his boldest, most aggressive essays. Emerson's most shocking assertions can be delivered, Firkins notes, with "an almost casual air, as if a man should blow up a minster [that is, a cathedral] by way of correction to the monotony of an evening walk."[5]

The genteel Emerson image has not made it any easier to come to terms with him. It has allowed readers, for a century and a half now, to tone down, ignore, or explain away the hard edges and extremes of Emerson's thought. Critics have repeatedly stopped themselves in the middle of their double takes (one of the classic, initial reactions to Emerson) to ask themselves if the distinguished-looking cleric with the white smile and tie could really intend all that he seems to say, all that he may imply. More often than not (it is further evidence of the prevalence of the anti-Emerson tradition) they have concluded that he cannot. "No one who reads much of the critical literature about Emerson," Barbara Packer writes, "can fail to be struck by the number of critics who assert that Emerson *was unconscious of* some significant implications contained in, or response likely to be provoked by, his own texts."[6] As a result, much of the sharp edge (CW, 2:30) that Emerson insisted one's prose and one's affirmations of goodness must have has been blunted.

We need to confront the formidable problem of Emerson's "extravagance"—as he called it, and as I shall call it—before proceeding any further. The way in which we resolve, or fail to resolve, the problem of Emerson's tone will play an important part in determining the way we respond to his work as a whole. It is probably already apparent why consideration of the spirit, and not just the letter, of his writing is particularly crucial in an examination of his theories of power and use. But I should state, at the outset of this chapter, that I intend neither to resolve the moral problems his speculations on power present nor to apologize for what may appear to be the objectionable ramifications of those speculations. How one chooses to take Emerson's language of power or his assertions that "There is always room for a man of force" (W, 6:58), that "There is nothing real or useful that is not a seat of war" (CW, 3:59), that "Power is in nature the essential measure of right" (CW, 2:40) will be up to the individual reader.

I can imagine a variety of defensible responses, just as there are a variety of possible reactions to the power philosophies and accompanying extravagant rhetoric of Nietzsche or Carlyle. I do argue, however, that there can be uninformed and irresponsible interpretations, readings that stand in need of important qualifications and are therefore misreadings of Emerson. And I shall try to suggest the several complicating factors that need to be taken into account before any final evaluation, moral or aesthetic, can be made. I refer, specifically, to that rather confusing array of diverse, nineteenth-century rhetorical traditions that define the context for Emerson's own work and vocation. Those traditions include American humor and oratory, Romantic irony, the nineteenth-century notion of the prophet, sage, or edifying philosopher, and the German ideal of a propaedeutic poetry-philosophy. Each helps to underwrite a conception of literature and philosophy, of writing and thinking, as hyperbolic, educative, unsettling, difficult, provocative, indirect, masked, dangerous—extravagant.

By extravagance I mean, on the one hand, simply the hyperbole that is so constant and unforgettable a feature of Emerson's writing. I mean, for example, Emerson's well-known fondness for such jolting declarations as "Good nature is stronger than tomahawks" (W, 7:233), "New York is a sucked orange" (W, 6:136), "The young men were born with knives in their brain" (W, 10:329), or "Man is the dwarf of himself" (CW, 1:42). But I refer also to something that is much broader: the essential spirit in which Emerson's essays are offered. I mean to suggest much the same thing as Alexander Nehamas does when he prefaces his study of Nietzsche with the warning that "Nietzsche's writing, and his thinking, is *essentially* hyperbolic." Hyperbole means, as Nehamas defines it, the habit of saying something unpredictable, something "more than is strictly speaking appropriate"; but it also means, in Nietzsche's case at least, what we might call a perversity of spirit, a willingness to violate what appears to be good sense, a readiness to overstate or defy conventional logic or decorum in a way that invites—sometimes whimsically, sometimes defiantly—outright rejection or misreading.[7]

"Time after time," Nehamas writes, "Nietzsche tears at the fabric of common sense, at the sense of ordinary language, at the language of reasonable thought." Nietzsche may have "done himself a great disservice" by adopting so extreme an authorial tone and by relying so extensively on a hyperbolic style. It has made him elusive and hard to take, fascinating some readers and alienating others. It has thrown into question his seriousness as a philosopher, has left open to doubt whether he should be considered a philosopher at all. It has "made it easier to attribute to him views that are often impossible to accept," has made it easier to dismiss his work "as the thoughts of someone more interested in shocking than in teaching." (Nietzsche, Nehamas adds, "never considered shocking incompatible with teaching"; we shall come to this crucial, underlying goal of his extravagant style shortly.)[8]

I do not wish to claim that Emerson exemplifies such fundamental perversity. Nietzsche himself *did* claim Emerson as the American precursor of his own "dangerous," apocalyptic manner of philosophizing, philosophizing that is not afraid to hurt somebody, not afraid to set "all things at risk." And it cannot be denied that Emerson, in an essay like "Circles"— his most experimental and most perverse essay—can indeed sound as if he has in mind something very much like Nietzsche's doctrine of perpetual self-creation and self-overcoming, his transvaluation of all values, and deconstructive ("hammering") role as a philosopher. A man, Emerson writes in "Circles," can only gain "the power of self-recovery" by "preferring truth to his past apprehension of truth." He must be ready to believe that new truth may come "from whatever quarter." He must be ready to accept "the intrepid conviction that his laws, his relations to society, his christianity, his world, may at any time be superseded and decease" (CW, 2:183). Emerson called this revolutionary (and Nietzschean) process the "revising and condemning" of what is accepted as "science," "literary reputation," "the so-called eternal names" (CW, 2:183).

The degree to which Emerson does indeed seem to anticipate Nietzsche's

antihumanism and transgressive role as annihilator of established philosophies is too complicated to take up here. (Richard Poirier has recently considered the ways in which Emerson anticipates writers like Nietzsche or
Foucault in his attempt to release us "from any settled, coherent idea of the
human, from the conceptual systems and arrangements of knowledge by
which man has so far defined himself." Such marked similarities between
Emerson and Nietzsche, coexisting as they do alongside so many apparent
differences in tone, background, or intent, can make Emerson, as Poirier
remarks, "extraordinarily hard to know how to take.")[9] What I do wish to
argue, however, is that the essential spirit of Emerson's philosophizing may
be considered, like Nietzsche's, irreducibly hyperbolic—and that this creates definite problems for Emerson's readers, just as Nietzsche's hyperbole
creates what have now become quite notorious problems for his readers.

Barbara Packer has examined closely Emerson's extravagant figurative
language, his readiness to test—or, to use Emerson's own favorite expressions—unsettle, agitate, provoke, and even offend his readers. (Cavell
speaks of Emerson's "developed taste for linguistic oddity," his eagerness,
as a prose writer, "to court the derangement of intellect.") Emerson's
rhetoric, Packer argues, was shaped by his belief in "the merit of not explaining," the merit of dropped "connections," and the ultimate advantages of "aim[ing] above the mark to hit the mark." "In the end," she concludes, "he came to suspect that a text's susceptibility to misinterpretation
was itself a mark of greatness. . . . It must be admitted that Emerson did
everything he could to make the reader's task difficult"; "Emerson's tendency from the first is to efface himself, to leave the reader no clues as to
how his text is to be privately performed. If his reticence leaves room for
the freedom of the reader, it also invites his distortions and mistakes."
Most discomforting, perhaps, are those moments when Emerson appears
to retreat from responsibility for his boldest claims. After one of his most
"violent and disturbing" paragraphs, as Packer calls it—a passage "that
seems to have been designed to contain something to offend everyone"—
Emerson can, with what appears to be an altogether inappropriate and
capricious blandness, refuse to explain himself and simply move on to his
next point: "I would write on the lintels of the door-post *Whim*. I hope it
is somewhat better than whim at last, but we cannot spend the day in explanation" (CW, 2:30). Emerson's critics have traditionally found it difficult to credit him with much consciousness of what he was doing and have
thus been reluctant to ascribe to him anything like the rhetorical strategies
of a Blake or Nietzsche. But "we can conjecture," Packer suggests, "that
[Emerson] had formulated some version of Nietzsche's warning to
philosophers. . . . 'Flee into concealment. And have your masks and subtlety, that you may be mistaken for what you are not, or feared a little'"
(BGE, 25).[10]

Emerson, in other words, presents us with many of the same interpretive problems that Nietzsche does. My concern here is, specifically, with the dilemmas we face in attempting to come to terms with Emerson's rhetoric of force and his theories of power—dilemmas that are, of course, also central to our reading of Nietzsche. There is something about Nietzsche's prose, something about his philosophy of power, that makes him available to quite contradictory programs. He can be enlisted as a sponsor of Nazism or defended as proponent of the benevolent notion of "the good European." He can be read as one of the most eloquent spokesmen for a nineteenth-century humanism or as the progenitor of deconstruction, as the guardian of an aristocratic individualism or as the prophet of human self-annihilation. The very extremism of his authorial pose, his reliance on *"the magic of the extreme"* (WP, 749), seems to insure that his writing will be misinterpreted, abused, or claimed by opposing communities of readers.

Something similar can be said about Emerson. I cite, as examples, two recent, contradictory readings. Both are alert to important strains in Emerson's thought, yet both represent, if taken by themselves, an inadequate understanding of his thought as a whole. The first quotation is from the resounding denunciation of Emerson that Bartlett Giamatti delivered to Yale University seniors in 1981. The second, published five years later, is by Emerson scholar Robert Richardson.

> Where did it all start in our culture, this worship of power as force, this contempt for restraining or complex connections, and the consequent devaluation of political life? . . . With extraordinary literary skills at a crucial moment in our nation's life, it is Emerson who freed our politics and our politicians from any sense of restraint by extolling self-generated, unaffiliated power as the best foot to place in the small of the back of the man in front of you, and who promoted shoving as the highest calling abolitionist, moral New England could conceive.
>
> Emerson was a potent figure in his time, and his influence on our culture is powerful to this day. You do not have to read the prophet to realize his ideas are all around us. Strangely enough, he lives in the popular imagination as the Lover of Nature, a sweet, sentimental, Yankee Kahlil Gibran. In fact, Emerson is as sweet as barbed wire, and his sentimentality as accommodating as a brick. . . . [He] found in our independent character xenophobia, and he made it into a gospel. . . . [H]e infected American culture with a scorn of the past. . . . Emerson licensed our violent swings from extreme to extreme by insisting that whatever willful impulse sat in the throne of the heart holds legitimate sway. In another creed, his self-reliance would be the sin of pride.
>
> Rootless save for immersion in the rich soil of the endlessly admiring self, glowing with animal energy, completely devoid of any sense of our common past, a new technocrat of force, Emerson's figure of power formed more than the nineteenth and much of the twentieth centuries' view of the politician. It formed what became an acceptable public personality, and that view

of power and its uses is still with us; and it still calls forth reactions to itself as extreme as it is. . . . Emerson's views are those of a brazen adolescent and we ought to be rid of them.[11]

Emersonian individualism is neither antisocial nor imperial; it does not advocate withdrawal from society, nor does it seek to rule others. It is overwhelmingly concerned with the self-education and development of the individual, and convinced that there can be neither love nor society unless one first has a group of autonomous individuals. Emersonian self-reliance is, like the Stoic's self-respect, the necessary means to self-culture, to the development of the self. Insofar as it is a means to power it is only power over the self, not over others.[12]

Much in Giamatti's address seems simplistic. His "brazen adolescent" Emerson may be a slightly more mature, more interesting figure than Santayana's "childlike soul." Yet the image seems to be based on the same misperception of Emerson as a hermetic mind. It pictures him as attempting to remain arrogantly aloof from society, from history, from Europe, rather than as engaged in the attempt to resist and cope with those forces that antagonize (but also define) a self. It reduces the whole Germanic and Romantic commitment to self-realization, and the complex tensions that commitment created, to a sophomoric narcissism. It is almost as reductive an understanding of Emerson as those clumsy readings that still construe Nietzsche's writing as a handbook for fascism. And it goes demonstrably wrong in aligning Emersonian individualism with the very reformist fanaticism (Emerson dubbed it "ultraism") whose hypocrisy he so regularly caricatured.

Richardson's remarks represent an altogether more balanced, more informed understanding. They provide a necessary response to those readers who confuse Emerson's commitment to the German ideal of self-culture (*"Bildung des Menschen"*)—to "Self-Knowledge and Self-Mastery," as Emerson preached it—with imperial egotism.[13] But Giamatti is sensitive to something in Emerson that Richardson's fair-minded resolution neglects: his extravagance, his willingness to risk misunderstanding, "to have masks and subtlety" and "be feared a little." Richardson overlooks, as Giamatti does not, the imaginative and rhetorical excess in Emerson's writing, an excess that "still calls forth reactions to itself as extreme as it is."

I mean to suggest the same point that Stephen Donadio makes in regard to Nietzsche. The most extreme readings (or even misreadings) a text or writer has inspired, particularly those texts that claim to impart prophecy or wisdom (texts like those of Rousseau, Marx, or Freud), can sometimes tell us something that more defensible readings cannot. "The abuses apparently invited by a particular body of ideas," Donadio notes,

are often highly revealing; indeed, careful consideration of such abuses may be as essential to a complete understanding of the significance of a specific line of thought as is a detailed analysis of those texts in which the line of thought is first presented and developed. There is . . . no doubt that Nietzsche was well aware of the potentially dangerous character of his ideas from very early on: indeed, he took pride in their threatening aspect.[14]

Like Nietzsche, Emerson must be read with an awareness of those various rhetorical traditions that imply that the potential for such dangerous misinterpretation is one criterion of serious thinking. Emerson's essays show the influence of a number of aesthetic traditions (some of them apparent in Nietzsche's prose as well, others peculiar to America) that emphasize the act of reading as creative—a noble exercise, as Thoreau called it, requiring the shared labor of writer *and* reader. ("One must be an inventor," Emerson said, "to read well. . . . There is then creative reading, as well as creative writing" [CW, 1:58]. "The reader and the book,—either without the other is naught" [W, 7:187]. "Reading must not be passive. The pupil must conspire with the Teachers" [EL, 1:214].) These traditions take hyperbole, intentional difficulty, the deliberate provocation of the reader, and the susceptibility to misinterpretation as rhetorical goals.

William Ellery Channing warned Emerson's generation against all such extravagant behavior. But extravagance, excess, paradox, experiment, surprise, Thoreau's "obscurity," and Whitman's "indirection" became keystones of Transcendentalist aesthetics. They may even be considered virtual synonyms for American Transcendentalism itself. "There is hope in extravagance," Emerson proclaimed in 1839, "there is none in Routine" (EL, 3:90). "Congratulate yourself," he advised his readers, "if you have done something strange and extravagant and broken the monotony of a decorous age" (CW, 2:154). Transcendentalism was, by Emerson's own definition, "the Saturnalia or excess of Faith" (CW, 1:206): "It is faith run mad" (JMN, 8:313). "Exaggeration," he said, "is in the course of things. . . . Every act hath some falsehood of exaggeration in it" (CW, 3:107). Nature itself worked by surprise and "excess of direction" (CW, 3:108): "Nature delights in breaking all bounds in her creation of men. She indulges herself in every extravagance and disappoints every expectation" (EL, 3:372). Thoreau made *"extra vagance"* (the going beyond boundaries) a rhetorical goal as well as a spiritual one. "It is a ridiculous demand which England and America make," he complained, "that you shall speak so that they can understand you." "We live by exaggeration," Thoreau insisted, defending Carlyle's Titanic style: "He who cannot exaggerate is not qualified to utter truth. . . . [Y]ou must speak loud to those who are hard of hearing, and so you acquire a habit of shouting to those who are not."[15]

Margaret Fuller similarly longed for some "larger [rhetorical] scope." If it made her writing "not sufficiently easy to be understood," then it might at least "prepare the reader," as she put it, "to meet me on my own ground."[16] Orestes Brownson, looking back on his tumultuous years as a Transcendentalist, recalled that one of the movement's underlying goals was to shock the American public into mental activity:

> Whether I preached or wrote, I aimed simply at exciting thought and direct-ing it to the problems to be solved, not to satisfy the mind or furnish it with dogmatic solutions of its difficulties. I was often rash in my statements, be-cause I regarded myself not as putting forth doctrines that must be believed, but as throwing out provocatives to thought and investigation. . . .
>
> My aim was not dogmatism, but inquiry; and my more immediate pur-pose was to excite thought, to quicken the mental activity of my country-men, and force them to think freely and independently on the gravest and most delicate subjects. I aimed to startle, and made it a point to be as para-doxical and as extravagant as I could without doing violence to my reason and conscience.[17]

The Transcendentalists were not the only writers of the period to adopt an aesthetic of creative reading. "The masked and difficult works of Amer-ican romanticism," as Michael Gilmore calls them—works like *Moby-Dick, The Confidence-Man, The Narrative of Arthur Gordon Pym,* Hawthorne's romances, *Leaves of Grass,* Dickinson's poems—all seem de-signed to test their readers. "First-class works," Whitman said, should "free, arouse, dilate": "the process of reading is not a half-sleep, but . . . an exercise, a gymnast's struggle. . . . [T]he reader is to do something for himself, must be alert, must himself or herself construct indeed the poem, the argument, history, metaphysical essay—the text furnishing the hints, the clue, the start, or framework." Thoreau called such interpretive labor heroic reading—"a noble exercise" that "requires a training such as the athletes underwent, the steady intention almost of the whole life to this ob-ject": "we must laboriously seek the meaning of each word and line, con-jecturing a larger sense than common use permits out of what wisdom and valor and generosity we have." Emerson's practice of an unsystematic, aphoristic prose and Dickinson's gnomic verse and devotion to telling the truth slantwise place similar demands on the reader. The intense self-con-sciousness, failed quests, and unending ambiguity of a Poe, Hawthorne, or Melville make their texts no less cryptic or problematic.[18]

Americans, D. H. Lawrence once remarked, "refuse everything explicit and always put up a sort of double meaning. They revel in subterfuge." Like most of Lawrence's criticism, this is an unwieldy generalization that manages to contain an important insight. For the classic writers (as Lawrence called them) of the antebellum period do seem to voice, at one time or another, a conception of reading as a form of creative action in its own right. They speak of reading as a higher mode of cryptography or as preparation to meet the writer on his or her own ground. Reading is de-picted as a kind of work or deciphering that can be as arduous as writing.

It is presented as a form of apprenticeship in which the reader must learn to be both sympathetic and antagonistic, engaged but skeptical toward writing that relies extensively on hyperbole or subterfuge. Behind that notion of a literature whose intentional difficulty and ambiguity require the colabor of reader and writer lie cultural traditions that may indeed be categorized as distinctly American. Most centrally, there is what Constance Rourke, in her classic *American Humor: A Study of the National Character*, defines as the "archetypal largeness" of a national, comic tradition.[19]

Rourke's groundbreaking study stresses a fundamentally theatrical tradition of tall tales and confidence games: a native tradition of storytelling that deliberately blurs the line between burlesque and serious intention, where the very purpose is often the deadpan duping of the listener. Barbara Packer and Joel Porte have both employed Rourke's analysis to emphasize Emerson's tonal complexity or the spirit of revel and comic extravagance the Transcendentalist ferment shared with the revivalism and cultism of the antebellum decades. The movement's major literary works were born, Porte suggests, in the "fruitful interplay between extravagant action or thought to which one is committed and a simultaneous awareness of comedy." Emerson's affirmations (and negations) need to be read as products of that complicated juxtaposition of overreaching and ironic self-awareness. For Emerson is, as Porte writes, "one of the great American masters of combining participation with ironic detachment."[20]

An aesthetic of ironic participation was, however, hardly unique to America. It defines one rhetorical tradition that Emerson, Carlyle, and Nietzsche have in common: the German tradition of Romantic irony. Nineteenth-century reviewers often blamed "Carlyleese" and "the school of Jean Paul" for the excesses of Transcendentalist writing or the extravagancies of Melville, Whitman, or Poe. Thoreau equated Carlyle's style ("the richest prose style we know of") with Jean Paul's, but he admired the way it startled, provoked, and placed demands on its readers: "he who runs may read [Carlyle's prose]; indeed, only he who runs *can* read, and keep up with the meaning."[21] The goal of Romantic irony, as it was delineated in the work of the Schlegel brothers, Tieck, Novalis, Solger, Jean Paul Richter, and others, was precisely this cultivation of an active readership. Romantic irony aimed, above all, to draw the reader, through art, into self-activity *(Selbsttätigkeit)* and self-discovery. "An imaginative book," as Emerson stated it, "renders us much more service at first, by stimulating us through its tropes, than afterward, when we arrive at the precise sense of the author" (CW, 3:18). Books "are for nothing but to inspire" (CW, 1:56). They have only one right use: to cultivate "the active soul" (CW, 1:56) and communicate "new activity to the torpid spirit" (CW, 1:41). "Truly speaking," he insists, "it is not instruction, but provocation, that I can receive from another soul" (CW, 1:80). "I read Proclus, and sometimes Plato, as I might read a dictionary, for a mechanical help to the fancy and the imagination" (CW, 3:137).

This conception of art as preparative or propaedeutic to philosophy or creative thinking, the paradigm of the reader as fellow laborer, and the aesthetic of incomprehensibility were hallmarks of Romantic irony. The use of paradox, wit, parody, overstatement, deliberate obscurity, incompleteness, indirection, the reliance on the fragment, the aphorism, the dialogue, convolution, and the breaking of unity and decorum were all intended to tease, goad, and entice the reader out of literal-mindedness and passivity into the process of self-cultivation and truth-seeking. Truth was not, as Hegel would later put it, "a minted coin that can be given and pocketed ready made."[22] It was a labor, a process, that demanded the reader's participation. The "true reader," Novalis claimed, "must be an expanded author." Art's apparent difficulty or inscrutability functioned as a puzzle, hieroglyph, or mental exercise—"the activity of decipherment"—deliberately challenging the reader. "What we love most," Friedrich Schlegel concluded, "is to seek out what [the author] has hidden from our gaze." The notion that art could deliver "complete comprehensibility" or do more than set the reader in the direction of truth was, for the Romantic ironists, "a false expectation of what art or philosophy could offer." An author could only give his readers an opportunity to cultivate their imaginations—"but to the Romantics this was the greatest gift possible."[23]

Emerson and Nietzsche also hold in common those various, exalted nineteenth-century conceptions of the seer—the artist-philosopher or poet-thinker capable of initiating profound transfigurations in culture and humanity. Poet-bards, Emerson said, "are liberating gods. . . . They are free, and they make free" (CW, 3:18). Nietzsche believed that the true philosopher should be allowed "the uncanny privileges of the great educator": he should be beyond good and evil, indifferent, as true sages always are, to any conventional standards of accountability. He should be free to employ any duplicity, any rhetorical trick, in his endeavor to lure and push his readers up to his lonely height (WP, 980). Such "revisors" of inherited mythologies, as Cavell identifies them, "can seem to make themselves willfully difficult to understand." Biblical rhetoric can be similarly opaque, consisting largely of "a discontinuous prose of aphorisms or oracles in which every sentence is surrounded by a silence." Calculated obscurity has, in short, always been one tool of the prophet's trade.[24]

But we might also approach this tradition of willfully difficult, literary-philosophical prose in terms of the distinction Richard Rorty draws between systematic-programmatic-constructive and edifying-therapeutic-provocative philosophers. Nietzsche's philosophy or the later work of Dewey, Wittgenstein, and Heidegger are, Rorty writes, "therapeutic rather than constructive, edifying rather than systematic, designed to make the reader question his own motives for philosophizing rather than to supply him with a new philosophical program." "Great systematic philosophers are constructive and offer arguments. Great edifying philosophers are reactive and offer satires, parodies, aphorisms. . . . Great systematic philosophers, like great scientists, build for eternity. Great edifying philosophers destroy for the sake of their own generation." Edifying philosophers "dread the thought that their vocabulary should ever be institutionalized." They therefore seek the kind of writing that will seem, as Emerson says, "fluxional"—"vehicular and transitive" (CW, 3:20)—which can mean the kind of writing that is most self-contesting and difficult to pin down. It is a kind of writing that, though it may passionately wish to teach, may also deliberately frustrate the reader's attempt to find a clear distinction between the literal and the metaphorical. ("Emerson's 'circle,'" Porte writes, "is essentially hermeneutic—an invitation to interpretation that has no real beginning or ending, and that equally offers no clear demarcation between the literal and figurative.") Like the literature of the German ironists, it sees the reader's desire for unequivocal, unmediated truth and complete comprehensibility as a delusion—"a major misconception of the nature of truth and communication, and a false expectation of what art or philosophy [can] offer." Such indirection can indeed seem devious or dangerous. It will undoubtedly strike some readers as simply moral equivocation and a poor excuse for foggy or fraudulent thinking. Thus Yvor Winters criticized Emerson as a morally bankrupt hypocrite—a teacher, but a teacher whose lessons were specious and pernicious.[25]

The possibility of just such denunciation, the possibility of hostile or harmful misinterpretation, were risks Emerson was willing to accept. "Hard words," words that have some edge to them, always run that risk. The most famous passage in "Self-Reliance" is not just an apology for self-contradiction; it is also a defense of the right of "great souls" to say what is difficult, oblique, painful, extreme, unpopular, polemical, revolutionary.

> A foolish consistency is the hobgoblin of little minds, adored by little statesmen and philosophers and divines. With consistency a great soul has simply nothing to do. He may as well concern himself with his shadow on the wall. Speak what you think now in hard words, and to-morrow speak what to-morrow thinks in hard words again, though it contradict every thing you said to-day.—"Ah, so you shall be sure to be misunderstood."—Is it so bad then to be misunderstood? Pythagoras was misunderstood, and Socrates, and Jesus, and Luther, and Copernicus, and Galileo, and Newton, and every pure and wise spirit that ever took flesh. To be great is to be misunderstood. (CW, 2:33–34)

Passages like this make one wonder how much Emerson Nietzsche may have absorbed without even realizing it. For the more one reads Nietzsche with Emerson in mind, the more one finds not just similar sentiments or ways of thinking but also specific verbal echoes, parallel lines and images. Was Nietzsche thinking of Emerson when he said, in *Beyond Good and*

Evil, "Every profound thinker is more afraid of being understood than of being misunderstood" (BGE, 290)? Nietzsche's early record of his "innermost history" (EH, 3:on UM, 3) is a meditation on "Schopenhauer as Educator." But what lessons he learned may owe as much, most likely a great deal more, to Emerson.[26]

"Schopenhauer as Educator" is a sustained attack on all those "weak phantoms" (Emerson calls them "little statesmen, philosophers, and divines" and "shadows on the wall") who avoid hard words and hide under the mantles of philosophy and professorial wisdom. Nietzsche defines "the secret of all culture" as "liberation," as the revelation of "the fundamental law of your own true self." Only this constitutes true, as opposed to sham, education (UM, 3:1). (Emerson claimed that he had no wish "to bring men to me, but to themselves. . . . This is my boast that I have no school . . . & no follower" [JMN, 14:258].) Culture's "supreme goal," Nietzsche contends, is "the production of the genius": "the goal of culture is to promote the production of true *human beings* and nothing else" (UM, 3:6). ("The main interest of history," Emerson writes, is "the discovering of human power": "Culture in the high sense does not consist in polishing or varnishing but in so presenting the attractions of Nature that the slumbering attributes of man may burst their iron sleep & rush full grown into day" [JMN, 5:410–11].)

The beginning of "Schopenhauer as Educator"—with its demand that we "live precisely today"—reads like a conscious imitation of "Self-Reliance," though Nietzsche does not seem quite aware that he is also citing directly the last paragraph of "Circles." The essay's fourth paragraph ("But how can we find ourselves again?") seems, once again, to echo Emerson (this time the opening of "Experience")—and Nietzsche's conclusion is finally explicit in its citation from "Circles" and its homage to Emerson as the guide for all men called to "the search for power." Nietzsche quotes Emerson's dramatic prophecy of the apocalypse that arrives "when the great God lets loose a thinker on this planet." A true thinker, Emerson promises, will "instantly revolutionize the entire system of human pursuits": "It is as when a conflagration has broken out in a great city, and no man knows what is safe, or where it will end" (CW, 2:183–84). This is precisely the kind of danger Nietzsche wants philosophy to pose: it should shock, disturb, and "remove things from their hinges" (UM, 3:8).

What is clear in passages like these is that Nietzsche and Emerson were, whatever their differences, both prepared to accept the dangers of unsettling and its potential for what we might call psychic or intellectual violence—drastic philosophical change, the destruction of the old, the established—as part of the price one pays for great thinking. ("People wish to be settled," Emerson says, "only as far as they are unsettled, is there any hope for them" [CW, 2:189].) Both were prepared to accept danger as part of the risk one takes, part of the price one pays, to earn the authority necessary to think or speak in a way that is genuinely revolutionary or philosophical (capable of affecting "the entire system of human pursuits") as opposed to merely professorial. "Each claim to speak for philosophy," as Cavell puts it, "has to earn the authority for itself."[27] To put this another way: Nietzsche and Emerson were, differences notwithstanding, both well aware of the danger, the extravagance, of thought and language and of the potential for misunderstanding inherent in the vocation of any thinker who aspires to more than lecture-hall wisdom. Both speak of the hyperbolic and apocalyptic nature of their own profession; both recognize the potential destructiveness involved in the transformations great thinkers can initiate. "Genius," Emerson said, "may be dangerous" (EL, 3:354). "Genius even, as it is the greatest good, is the greatest harm. . . . [I]t needs a perpetual tempering, a phlegm, a sleep, atmospheres of azote, deluges of water, to check the fury of the conflagration; a hoarding to check the spending, a centripetence equal to the centrifugence" (W, 7:145–46).

How are we to read such writers? The problem with such "prophets of extremity" as Nietzsche, Allan Megill notes, is that they often become hyperbolic in order to achieve a particular rhetorical effect. One would be foolish or mad to take them literally. "Yet . . . the rhetorical effectiveness of these [same] assertions very much depends on their being taken literally." Perhaps, then, we should read Emerson in the way his own imagery suggests and in the way Megill suggests we read Nietzsche: with some measure of tempering, counterbalancing resistance, "in a spirit of sympathetic skepticism." We ought to take such extravagant thinkers "not as guides but as opponents. We ought to view their writing, as we view the work of the artist, as existing in a state of tension with the given." Emerson, who always abhorred discipleship and generally spoke of literary influence in antagonistic terms, would probably approve.[28]

The point is worth stressing. One of Emerson's great strengths, one of the things that makes prolonged scrutiny of his writing not only possible but also rewarding, is what Albert Camus once called his astonishing "tonic" power. At one time criticism was unprepared to say much about this other than to classify it prematurely as the cosmic optimism that makes his essays "happiness pills."[29] Recent criticism has begun to appreciate it as something far more profound and valuable, something that confronts the question "How shall I live?" in a manner that is shrewder, more capacious, tougher—and far more useful for the way we do live—than has been recognized. The current emphasis on *Emerson's Demanding Optimism* (surely one of the aptest titles any book on Emerson has ever had) and on the confrontational nature of his imagination—or the increasing recognition that whatever Emerson's idealism may be, it is not a denial or transcendence of skepticism but a continuing engagement with skepticism's claims, a form of skepticism itself—exemplify a new respect for Emerson's achievement.

But taking Emerson with a new seriousness also requires the acknowledgement that there is much in his thought that is self-consciously and pointedly extreme, experimental, polemical, dubitable. While there is, in other words, much in Emerson that is affirmative and pragmatic in the sense that it is applicable, in both direct and complex ways, to the conduct of life, his work also encompasses much that is purely negative in a Nietzschean sense. I mean by this that there is an important strain in Emerson's thought that constitutes—like much of Nietzsche's work or the work of his many descendants in the twentieth century—a rhetorical tool that may be uniquely powerful as a vehicle for critical thought, as a basis for unsettling and critiquing orthodoxies, but is notoriously ineffective as anything else. Much in Emerson marks him as, in Cavell's words, an "orienter," a "philosopher of direction," a philosopher who returns us to the ordinary and asks us where we stand, what it is we face, where we want to live, and what we want to live in us.[30] But it can be difficult to tell when Emerson needs to be read ironically—as something more extravagant, less creditable, less humanistic, less imitable, a thinker inapplicable in anything like a literal or practical way. Emerson is, in short, both a philosopher of direction, a philosopher of the ordinary, and a prophet of extremity, a rhetorical provocateur. There is still much to be done in our recovery of both aspects of his work and of the way in which they play against and/or sustain one another.

5

Working and Being Worked Upon

And labor is every where welcome; always we are invited to work. . . .

—*Ralph Waldo Emerson, "The American Scholar" (1837)*

Let me move to an example, taken almost at random, of the kind of overstated, highly vulnerable rhetoric on which Emerson habitually relies. Unpacking the ramifications of even the following brief passage will take us further into Emerson's persistent themes. But the whole issue of his tone and intentions, and just how literally we are to take him, will never be far away. This is from the closing pages of "Compensation": "It is the nature of the soul to appropriate all things. Jesus and Shakespeare are fragments of the soul, and by love I conquer and incorporate them in my own conscious domain. His virtue,—is not that mine? His wit,—if it cannot be made mine, it is not wit" (CW, 2:72).

How are we to read this? As anyone who has ever taught Emerson knows, it is quite possible to read over such passages without reading them at all. Students expecting to find in Emerson only the naive cleric usually remember such sentences as little more than his usual preaching about virtue and the soul. Yet these closing remarks from an essay that has come to stand for the dullest of Transcendentalist dogmas present us with a problem that is central to Emerson's work as a whole. We might phrase the problem this way: is Emerson talking about—glorifying—soft power or hard power?

Emerson, it seems clear, is referring, literally, to soft power, to power over one's self or what he calls on the following page "the growth of character." But one of the things that makes Emerson's lines, his portrayal of moral development, so vivid (intriguingly so for some readers, repellently so for others) is the military rhetoric, the language of conquest and dominion. (Such rhetoric has certainly been one distinguishing feature of much of the prose I have cited so far, in the imagery of overpowering and in Emerson's references to "the armed hand," the "weapons in the armoury of universal genius," or "new weapons in the magazine of power.")

To say that Emerson means only soft power—that he is simply referring to the quite benign, Transcendentalist notion of the Over-Soul—may be correct, or may at least suffice, as a strictly literal interpretation. But it will not suffice as a description of Emerson's imagery. Nor does it very accurately suggest the defiant, willful tone of the passage. One may say that to appropriate all things, to incorporate—by love—such figures as Jesus or Shakespeare means merely to learn from them or to imitate them. (As Benjamin Franklin came to realize, this is a sufficiently audacious goal in and of itself.) Why, then, didn't Emerson simply say that? Why does he employ a rhetoric of force that so strikingly suggests a Nietzschean process of mastery? ("Appropriate," "incorporate," and [self-]"conquest" are central terms for both Nietzsche and Emerson. "Life itself," Nietzsche concludes, in one of his most notorious passages, "is *essentially* appropriation, injury, overpowering of what is alien and weaker; suppression, hardness, imposition of one's own forms, incorporation and at least, at its mildest, exploitation. . . . [I]t is the consequence of the will to power, which is after all the will of life" [BGE, 259].) Why does Emerson use the rhetoric of hard power (brute force) to describe the experience of soft power (spiritual development)? Could he not have stated things differently, in a way that would never have created any ambiguity in the first place?

"Virtue," remember, is the English descendent of the Latin words for man, valor, and power. To appropriate another's strength or virtue has military (perhaps even cannibalistic) connotations—and Emerson is well aware of them. This is made emphatically clear earlier in "Compensation," when Emerson anticipates Nietzsche's definition of strength ("*Out of life's school of war:* What does not destroy me makes me stronger" [TI, 2:8]). "In general," Emerson writes, "every evil to which we do not succumb, is a benefactor. As the Sandwich Islander believes that the strength and valor of the enemy he kills, passes into himself, so we gain the strength of the temptation we resist" (CW, 2:69). (As he would restate this in *The Conduct of Life:* "We acquire the strength we have overcome" [W, 6:255]. It is one of his fundamental doctrines, repeated countless times throughout his career.) Although Emerson is talking about self-improvement and a pious resistance to temptation, he uses the rhetoric of war, in this case an "aboriginal" war in which enemies are literally assimilated.

"Metaphors of oral aggression," as Barbara Packer notes, "are always a sign of recovered self-confidence in Emerson"—signs, that is, of power gained or of power to come.[1] "Power," Emerson declares, "is ever eating up the limitation" (TN, 1:89). We should be wary, however, of reducing this cornerstone of his philosophy to a psychological tic on Emerson's part. The "appetitive relation to the world" ("the bourgeois tradition of the 'I' as 'consumer,'" as Eugene Goodheart labels it) is one characteristic of the nineteenth century. It defines, as much as Emerson's often-analyzed imagery of the soul, the eye, or the Fall, the primary nature of Emersonian thought. Criticism has emphasized his moments of Transcendentalist epiphany; but the celebration of what Nietzsche called the primeval joy we derive in "acquiring the power to shape things according to our wish"— the pleasure we take in contemplating a "world that we ourselves have made" (WP, 495)—is the far more persistent pattern in Emerson's thought.

Recall, for instance, the passage cited previously in which Emerson suggests that each man is "a tyrant in tendency," ready to impose his ideas and absorb the world. Such appropriation is only prevented, he claims, because men also possess an inborn resisting force: "Each man, too, is a tyrant in tendency, because he would impose his idea on others; and their trick is their natural defence. Jesus would absorb the race; but Tom Paine or the coarsest blasphemer helps humanity by resisting this exuberance of power" (CW, 3:140–41). Or consider this passage from "Works and Days," in which "the assimilating power"—the power of ingestion, of conversion, or working up (variants of the doctrine of use or mastery)—is described as the principal activity of all creatures, from reptiles to Apostles:

> [T]hough many creatures eat from one dish, each, according to its constitution, assimilates from the elements what belongs to it, whether time, or space, or light, or water, or food. A snake converts whatever prey the meadow yields him into snake; a fox, into fox; and Peter and John are working up all existence into Peter and John. (W, 7:178)

Rhetoric of this kind reverberates through "Compensation" (as it reverberates through Emerson's essays as a whole) and gives a particular coloring to Emerson's praise for virtuous action. Virtue begins to sound desirable not for its intrinsic moral worth but because of the godlike or Caesar-like power it confers. "In a virtuous action, I properly *am*," Emerson writes near the essay's close, "in a virtuous act, I add to the world; I plant into deserts conquered from Chaos and Nothing, and see the darkness receding on the limits of the horizon" (CW, 2:71).

It can indeed be difficult to know what significance we should ascribe to rhetoric like this. What are we to make of Emerson's wish to assimilate the virtues of both Jesus and Shakespeare? It is surprising to find the two linked, for they would appear to be antithetical figures. One is sacred, one secular; one is divine, one human; one symbolizes the renunciation of carnal ambition, the other has come to epitomize fame and achievement. Yet both are habitually associated in Emerson's writing with supreme forms of power, in this case spiritual and imaginative power. Emerson repeatedly invokes such couplings of biblical and historical figures, figures in many ways antithetical yet alike in their power or influence—Caesar and Adam, Caesar and Christ, Columbus and Jesus—when he prophesies power to come. Emerson's descriptions of "the central man," or our potential for self-creation, usually involve this synthesis of diverse, powerful figures (EJ, 354–55, 430–31).

It is difficult to believe that Nietzsche did not have this Emersonian conception of empowerment in mind when he postulated his own version of the highest form of self-creation, the supreme example of counterbalancing energies, as a "Caesar—with Christ's soul." This ideal, synthetic figure was, Walter Kaufmann writes, "the very heart of Nietzsche's vision of the overman." Nietzsche's conception of the ideal self as "a large number of powerful and conflicting tendencies that are controlled and harmonized" is surely forecast, as I have suggested in chapter 2, in Emerson's notion of a healthy personality as the perfect counterpoise of contradictory powers.[2]

Emerson and Nietzsche both revered Shakespeare and Goethe as supreme examples of self-creators able to hold "the greatest multiplicity of drives" in productive equipoise (WP, 966). Such complexity, and such control, were, for both Emerson and Nietzsche, further examples of the doctrine of use. Nietzsche's overman incorporated all kinds of energy—both good and evil—growing, like a great tree, in trunk, branch, and root simultaneously (GS, 370, 371). Emerson's "complete man" similarly traversed "the whole scale," entertaining "all travellers, tongues, kindreds, . . . all eccentricities, all crimes even, in its vast charity and overcoming hope" (EL, 3:356). Shakespeare was such a "generic catholic genius," "able to use whatever he found" (CW, 4:112, 115). Goethe was likewise able to take in his hands all the weapons "in the armoury of universal genius" (CW, 4:163), able to grasp all the multiplicities of his age "and dispose of them with ease" (CW, 4:156). The "end of life," as Emerson once put it, "is, that the man should take up the universe into himself, or, out of that quarry leave nothing unrepresented, and he is to create himself (JMN, 11:440–41).

One could continue the comparison I have been making at much greater length. The philosophy of the "always becoming" superman, the individual who is self-creator rather than creature, is one of the central paradigms for the self in the nineteenth century. Margaret Fuller spoke prophetically of such a figure as the "self-centered woman," able to live "a beautiful, powerful . . . complete life."[3] That vision is founded on the century's conception of identity as coming into being primarily through some form of action, its conception of self-creation as taking place only in the work of using or remaking the world one confronts. It is the outgrowth of the reverence for what Hegel, at the beginning of the century, anatomized as the human capacity for action or "work" in the creation or humanization of the world.

The Doctrine of Labor

"Activity," "doing," and "work" are, to be sure, often very general concepts in Hegel's own philosophy. They refer, as Robert Solomon writes, to an "active grasping" notion of consciousness, as opposed to the "passive-receptive model of empiricism or intuitionism." Hegelian "action" thus needs to be "construed in the general sense, not necessarily [as] a full-blooded action or even activity in the usual sense." But Hegel certainly could, just as much as Carlyle, extol action and work in the form of sheer physical labor—as he does in his pivotal discussion of the development of self-consciousness through labor and use. (It is this section of *Phenomenology of Spirit,* the chapter on "Lordship and Bondage," that would, in the 1840s and 1850s, exert so great an influence on Marx's theories of alienated labor.) Hegel was himself, it should not be forgotten, deeply influenced by the Protestant work ethic. He was well aware of Adam Smith's labor-theory of value and famous thesis "that only labor has intrinsic value."[4]

This underlying commitment to activity, the necessity Hegel ascribes to the "articulation" or "externalization" of consciousness, defines one of the century's most influential philosophies of action. Consciousness, as Hegel put it in the *Phenomenology,* seeks the "unity of action and being": "An individual cannot know what he [really] is until he has made himself a reality through action"; "In work . . . consciousness becomes what it is in truth"; "The *true being* of a man is . . . his deed." This philosophy reappears (in however debased a form) in what one scholar has called "the *raison d'être* of the [nineteenth-century] bourgeois (and the proletarian)"— the belief in "the capacity to create value through labor." The classic philosophical precept, "Know thyself," had become, as Carlyle warned in *Sartor Resartus,* unattainable "folly." It urgently needed translation into the only philosophy that was any longer feasible in the nineteenth century: *"Know what thou canst work at."* "Produce! Produce!" Carlyle thundered, "Work while it is called Today; for the Night cometh, wherein no man can work."[5]

Emerson repeated that imperative endlessly. Like Carlyle, he formulated his own doctrine of labor, which upheld the appropriation and reformation of the world as an inalienable human right. As he put it in a lecture to the Mechanics' Apprentices' Library Association in 1841, every man, rich or poor, should have the right to make "his march to the dominion of the world": "Every man ought to have this opportunity to conquer the world for himself" (CW, 1:152). It was government's fundamental duty to promote and protect each man's right to labor, for all forms of labor were, in essence, types of self-creation, the "actualizing" (as Hegel would have put it) of all the self's latent powers: "Labor: a man coins himself into his labor; turns his day, his strength, his thought, his affection into some product which remains as the visible sign of his power; and to protect that, to secure that . . . is the object of all government" (W, 11:297). Labor was the means through which society fulfilled its true function: the production of human power, the pure power of the individual.

"But do your work," Emerson insists, "and I shall know you. Do your work, and you shall reinforce yourself" (CW, 2:32). This conception of labor as inherently empowering, the primary means for discovering one's personal force, defined Emerson's own vocation as well: "By doing his work [the public speaker] makes the need felt which he can supply, and creates the taste by which he is enjoyed. By doing his own work he unfolds himself. . . . Somewhere, not only every orator but every man should let out all the length of his reins; should find or make a frank and hearty expression of what force and meaning is in him" (CW, 2:83).

"Feudalism and Orientalism," Emerson argued, "had long enough thought it majestic to do nothing; the modern majesty consists in work" (CW, 1:112). Civilized societies could be distinguished from "ignorant and semibarbarous communities" by the premium they placed on individual productivity. "In every society of right-minded men" the question is not "How can [a man] fight?" or "Has he money?" but "What can he do?" (EL, 2:244). New England was superior to the Southern, slave-owning, "planting states" ("a nation of served") because, as Emerson put it, "We have not the fatal pride of idleness. . . . There is a great deal of work in our men" (EL, 2:244). "A man is fed," he claimed repeatedly, "not that he may be fed, but that he may work" (CW, 1:12). "The sum of wisdom is, that the time is never lost that is devoted to work" (W, 7:294). The trouble with reformers was that they "were not equal to the work they pretend" (CW, 3:154). American scholars were likewise culpable: "Our anniversary is one of hope," he reminded his Harvard audience in 1837, "and, perhaps, not enough of labor" (CW, 1:52). The "creative reading" Emerson urged them to pursue required a "mind braced by labor and invention" (CW, 1:58).

Humankind will forgive much—"everything short of infamous crime will pass"—to those men of will who "pay substantial service and work energetically after their kind; but they do not extend the same indulgence to those who . . . render no returns. . . . To live without duties is obscene" (W, 10:51–52). The radical reformer Emerson describes in "The Conservative" may object to the entire social system, with its laws of property and ownership; but even he reveres the hard labor of the capitalist establishment (CW, 1:190–91). Popular education had failed in failing to teach the doctrine of labor: "We cannot use our hands, or our legs, or our eyes, or our arms"—"Am I not defrauded of my best culture in the loss of those gymnastics which manual labor and the emergencies of poverty constitute?" (CW, 3:152). "That book is good," Emerson insisted, "Which puts me in a working mood. / Unless to Thought be added Will / Apollo is an imbecile" (W, 7:188). "Working heroes" are "the class of power" (CW, 3:76). "The true romance, not which will be written but which the progress of life & thought will realize, will be the transformation of genius into practical power. The symbol of this is the *working king* like Ulysses, Alfred, Czar Peter" (JMN, 9:53).

The working leader and a community of fellow workers is one of the great Carlylean themes—one of the great themes of the century—that Thoreau singled out in his 1847 essay on Carlyle. The new "Man of the Age," Thoreau observed, was "working-man." (Thoreau would introduce his own masterpiece by reminding his readers that he too earned his living by "the labor of [his] hands only.") As Elizabeth Peabody emphasized it, defending the Brook Farm experiment: *labor is the germ of all good.*[6] Ultimately work was, for Emerson—like nature, discipline, virtue, and "the moral sentiment" itself—desirable not for its results, not for what it produced, but because one could always rely on it as a source of individual power. The argument he offered in "Man the Reformer" for the fundamental necessity of labor was wholly typical: "No separation from labor can be without some loss of power" (CW, 1:153). The "beauty of Use," the beauty of labor, was that it was so certain a source of power. "Fidelity to a humble work," Emerson was assured, gives us access to "new regions of action and thought" (EL, 2:245). Labor's real value lies not in what is made but in the improvement it makes in the worker: "For every man is possessed by the idea that infinitely more important than any outward ends which his work is to answer, abides the permanent and supreme end of the amelioration of the workman himself" (EL, 2:234).

In "The American Scholar" Emerson championed "drudgery, calamity, exasperation, want" as "instructors in eloquence and wisdom" (CW, 1:59). In the late essay, "Power," he was still asserting the superiority of "practitioners"—with their long hours of drill—to idle "amateurs" (W, 6:79). Work is once again defined as that exercise that grounds us in reality ("necessity") and helps us to equal and offset whatever we resist or whatever resists us. Work is that essential activity in which mankind, "by thousands of manipulations," masters "the use of the tools" and learns "to overcome resistances of the medium and material in everything we do" (ibid.).

It is the disciplined labor of meeting and triumphing over necessity—not spontaneous, ecstatic, Platonic or Neoplatonic inspiration—that makes the artist. An artist becomes a master through "the use of drill," through the "vital act" of taking "command of the instrument" and hewing his art out of "the odious materials" (ibid.). "You must elect your work," Emerson says, "and drop all the rest." "Everything is good which takes away one plaything and delusion more and drives us home to add one stroke of faithful work." Only the proper concentration of "vital force" can "make the step from knowing to doing"—and lacking that, the artist "lacks all." Work is more valuable to the muse than is inspiration (W, 6:74).

The doctrine of work or use, apparent in all of Emerson, defines much of nineteenth-century thought: Carlyle worshipped it, Whitman apostrophized it, Stowe domesticated it, Thoreau apotheosized it in his fable of the artist of Kouroo, Melville made it the ambiguous foundation of his American epic, Emerson made it the pragmatic backbone of his "Transcendentalism" and in doing so helped lay the ground for William James. Emerson and Nietzsche may well be the century's two most famous spokesmen for this doctrine of work, as it applies to the work of self-mastery and self-perfection—though the latter's indebtedness to the former is still insufficiently appreciated. Perhaps, to bring this point to some conclusion, it is only necessary to note that the underlying model for this process of self-cultivation, for both Nietzsche and Emerson, is aesthetic: the work of making art, most specifically, the making of literature itself. Both men, whose lives were both so profoundly, if not obsessively, literary, habitually returned to the poet, the writer, the literary revisor and reinterpreter as the primary model of self-creation.[7]

Emerson on the Will

We have arrived once again at the central, inescapable, interpretive crux in Emerson. What I have been emphasizing in the previous chapters and in glossing some few lines from "Compensation" is the Emerson committed to self-creation as empowerment: the Promethean, Faustian, Archimedean, or Nietzschean Emerson. This Emerson is fiercely committed to an agonistic view of life and identity. He is committed to the Nietzschean idea that strength, health, and self-knowledge are attainable only in "life's school of war," not in a presocial, Platonic, or transcendental realm of eternal Oneness or a monistic Unity of Being. Like Nietzsche, Emerson believes there is no happiness without struggle.[8] He looks for obstacles; he requires something to overcome.

Emerson's thought, to state this another way, can be defined as exemplary of that post-Hegelian philosophical tradition that postulated what one critic has called "the metaphysics of will." For Hegel, self-consciousness could not exist in the "pure abstraction of being-for-self." It could exist only in that *activity* that could be acknowledged (or mediated) by other people. Individual self-consciousness was not, as Solomon notes, "an already established matter," not a mystical Oneness, not an "immediate intuition" (concepts Hegel found repugnant), but something that demanded what he called "struggle" (which could even entail "trial by death"), some activity that demanded the staking of one's life. "The general context for formation of self," in this tradition is, Solomon writes, "*conflict* and *opposition*": "the assertion of self is a *react*ion, not an 'immediate intuition.'"[9]

I have, in other words, located Emerson's ideas in a large tradition of nineteenth-century thought that views the world as the balancing and conflict of powers—spiritual or intellectual capacities as well as brute force. It is a tradition preoccupied with will, with action, and, ultimately, with what William James hailed as "the martial virtues." This tradition is inherently controversial and (especially from the all-too-comfortable vantage point of retrospection) open to moral and ethical objection. I have, in stressing Emerson's philosophy of power, focused on what is perhaps the most dangerous aspect of his thought. Power is, in itself, an inherently ambiguous concept, and it is rendered no less ambiguous by Emerson's handling of it. The rhetorical and psychological patterns that define the Emersonian search after power—the centrality of antagonism, the rhetoric of force and war—are no less open to potential moral objection. (Though interpretation of this aspect of Emerson's thought will, as I have suggested, be a particularly complicated matter, for it must take into account the fundamentally extravagant nature of his rhetoric.)

As any student of Emerson is aware, however, there is much in his writing that would appear to contradict the emphasis I have been making. If "Compensation" contains lines that suggest the Nietzschean view that the will to life is always manifest in some demonstration of appropriation and overpowering, then it also contains a great deal of the kind of language and ideas that can be found nowhere in Nietzsche. Emerson's discussion of force and action seems to be, as critics have traditionally almost always concluded, kept firmly in check by his belief in the "moral law" or "moral sentiment."[10]

Thus if Emerson seems on one page to celebrate appropriation and mastery, on another he regrets our urge "to sunder, to appropriate" as part of our unfortunate propensity "to act partially." The will to power, Emerson makes quite clear, must have a moral aim: "The soul says, Have dominion over all things to the end of virtue; the body would have the power over things to its own ends" (CW, 2:61). The monistic Over-Soul, "the inworking of the All," Emerson is assured, has a moral purpose (CW, 2:62): "God re-appears with all his parts in every moss and cobweb. . . . All things are moral. . . . Every secret is told, every crime is punished, every virtue rewarded" (CW, 2:60). Emerson's love of heroic action decreed that "the education of the will is the object of our existence," that a man "will venture all to put in act the invisible thought in his mind." But even our most antagonistic acts of will must be rooted in our "faith in the beneficent power above." The man of educated will "is free to speak truth," Emerson says, "he is not free to lie" (W, 7:274–77). "Great action must draw on the spiritual nature. The measure of action is, the sentiment from which it proceeds" (CW, 4:154–55). The pursuit of practical power in and for itself becomes at last "carrion and an offence to the nostril" (CW, 1:133). "Only a virtuous will is omnipotent" (JMN, 4:257).

Yet Emerson also seems to suggest—on the one hand, at least—a voluntarism sufficiently radical that it demands to be considered primarily in the context of such fellow nineteenth-century philosophers of will as Schopenhauer, Kierkegaard, and Nietzsche. Voluntarism, that enormously influential but still controversial philosophical tradition, can be defined, Maurice Mandelbaum argues, by its common belief—a belief Mandelbaum finds quite misguided—"that our thought is always to be interpreted in terms of its relation to the goals of the will."[11] It is precisely in this problematic, nineteenth-century tradition that Denis Donoghue has recently placed Emerson (a judgment that is increasingly visible in Emerson criticism). Emerson's work, Donoghue writes, can be explicated "only by recourse to the vocabulary of Will":

> [T]he site of his poetry and his sageness is the history of voluntarism. The more we read *Nature,* the more clearly it appears that the whole essay is predicated upon the capacity of Will. Not knowledge but power is its aim; not truth but command. Human will is deemed to participate in the vitality of natural forms. Mind is a chosen direction of Will.[12]

Failing to find "any passage [in *Nature*] in which Emerson refers to the mind as separable from the will," Donoghue concludes by reminding us of "the misgivings that should attend the claims Emerson makes for [the Will] as nothing less than a moral principle."[13]

There is evidence on virtually every page of Emerson to suggest that Donoghue is right. Emerson's well-known Transcendentalist belief in (an absolute) Truth, in the Universal Mind, even—as I would argue—in the Soul or the Moral Law, is associated so repeatedly by Emerson with the empowering, the enlarging, or the energizing of the human will that important distinctions begin to blur: the empowered Will comes to seem, even in spite of Emerson's apparent professions to the contrary, the fundamental and, finally, the only real moral principle. And, as Donoghue's discussion suggests, it is difficult to consider Will a moral principle at all; a philosophy that confuses will and morality, that seems to celebrate one while it is speaking of the other, should inspire our misgivings. However we may finally judge such a philosophy, it certainly presents us with an extraordinarily difficult problem in interpretation. It is a far more difficult problem than that scholarship that has taken Emerson as a purely transcendental thinker has allowed.

From his earliest lectures to his last essays, Emerson can sound so radically voluntaristic that it can be difficult to distinguish him from Nietzsche. It is even, at times, difficult to distinguish him from his contemporary, Schopenhauer, whose relentless theme was that there was no "thing in itself" but "the will." (Philosophy, according to Schopenhauer, had erred in failing to recognize the will as the original force behind all phenomena, "the *prius* of [all] knowledge," of all we have come to think of as metaphysical truth, culture, or morality.) Emerson can, as one critic puts it, make the will "seem almost palpable."[14]

He can make it sound as if action, as if acts of will, proceed not from some preexistent, disinterested, or objective moral law but vice versa—that action creates value, that morality is a function of will, that what we consider to be morality, theology, civilization are born only through willpower, that they are history's "triumphs of will" (CW, 2:5). Moral values, and culture in general, Emerson can seem to suggest, are the transparent surface beneath which we can always glimpse the strong, human will and the over-men responsible for them in the first place. "Arts, Letters, States, Religion, Customs," Emerson writes in 1837, "are only signs more or less near of the human will" (EL, 2:143). "The character, the will . . . is the ultimate object of history" (EL, 2:129). "A strong person makes the law and custom null before his own will" (CW, 1:194). "Strong will is always in fashion" (CW, 3:78). "The exercise of the Will or the lesson of power is taught in every event" (CW, 1:25). "The one serious and formidable thing in nature is a will. Society is servile from want of will, and therefore the world wants saviours and religions" (W, 6:30). "Nothing," Emerson assures us, "is impossible to the man who can will" (W, 6:248).

In the posthumously published *Natural History of Intellect,* there is this striking anticipation of the distinction Nietzsche would draw between the aristocracy of self-creators (users) and the herd (the used) who lack the will to be anything but creatures:

> Will is the measure of power. To a great genius there must be a great will. If the thought is not a lamp to the will, does not proceed to an act, the wise are imbecile. He alone is strong and happy who has a will. The rest are herds. He uses; they are used. He is of the Maker; they are of the Made. (W, 12:46)

"The law of nature," Emerson says in "Compensation," "is, Do the thing, and you shall have the power: but they who do not the thing have not the power" (CW, 2:67)—or, as he puts it in one of the essay's intro-ductory poems, "power to him who power exerts" (CW, 2:54). "The thing done avails," he writes in *English Traits,* "and not what is said about it" (ET, 5).

Just how close are such remarks to Nietzsche? "It is not *what* a man ac-complishes or does or creates that finally interests Nietzsche," as Good-heart puts it, "but the *feeling* of power that attends the accomplish-ment."[15] "How is truth proved?" Nietzsche asks: "By the feeling of enhanced power" (WP, 455). "The criterion of truth resides in the en-hancement of the feeling of power" (WP, 534). "Knowledge works as a tool of power. Hence it is plain that it increases with every increase of power" (WP, 480). "The overcoming of metaphysics," with its pretensions to truth and knowledge, was precisely Nietzsche's goal. There were, for Nietzsche, no preexisting ideas. What was important was not whether a particular idea was true or false, good or evil per se—logically or morally irrefutable in and of itself—but whether it was species-preserving, life-affirming, "calculable and usable to us." "The [Kantian] categories" were, for instance, "'truths' only in the sense that they are conditions of life for us" (WP, 515).

Can we say the same of Emerson—of the Emerson, at least, who champions the exercise of the Will and the consequent feeling of empowerment, the Emerson for whom Will appears to be the ultimate, working principle of the universe? (I pass over here those other manifestations of Will Emerson so persistently celebrates: the creative power of thought or imagination.) How close does Emerson come, in passages like those I have been quoting, to Nietzsche's voluntaristic thesis that what we call truth, knowledge, or identity are definable, ultimately, by no other criteria than the feeling of power they instill in the individual who has sufficient will to life to be a doer, actor, and creator? How close does he come to Schopenhauer's acceptance of the "metaphysics of a life force"? How close to Schopenhauer's principle, "that which does not *act* likewise does not *exist*," or his conception of "the will to live" as "the kernel of reality itself"—"that which is incapable of further explanation"?[16]

To this question, as I have raised it, there are a number of possible responses. One can, for example, argue that if Emerson does, in discrete passages, seem to come close to this extreme and "immoralist" position of Nietzsche, it is only fleetingly, in his most overbold and experimental moments. To stop at such extreme formulations, however, would be a serious mistake, for these are exactly the kinds of Emersonian audacities that we should be wary about taking too literally: they require careful explication and qualification by his critics.

More significantly, one can argue that there is certainly equal evidence in Emerson's texts to suggest that the human will to power is always conclusively reined in by Emerson's unchanging faith in the "moral law." There is much to suggest that it is really not a voluntaristic conception of action, will, or power that Emerson ultimately advocates but something closer to a Buddhistic negation of the will, what critics have usually referred to as Emerson's "mystical tendencies." Emersonian action and identity seem, rather, to be the function not of a Schopenhauerian or a Nietzschean will but of a wise passiveness, what Emerson extols as reception, abandonment, or acquiescence. Lawrence Rosenwald, for instance, argues that Emerson's identity as an artist "is the product of surrender, of self-abandon; it is opposed to self, to will, to thought." What is "most radical about Emerson's thought," Richard Grusin writes, is precisely Emerson's "conviction that all action involves the surrender of agency, [that] all expressions of conscious will involve the relinquishment of will." Cavell, focusing on Emerson's claim that "Our thinking is a pious reception" (CW, 2:195), suggests that Emersonian thinking is "thinking as the receiving or letting be of something, as opposed to the positing or putting together of something, as this is pictured most systematically in Kant's ideas of representation and synthesis, and most radically in Nietzsche's will to power."[17]

There is much in Emerson to support such readings. "My whole philosophy," as Emerson once put it himself (in a sentence that has helped to diminish his reputation ever since), "teaches acquiescence and optimism"

(CEC, 304). All "real power," he can imply, is "spiritual power" (W, 10:47). Emersonian power can seem to be something that either transcends the individual will ("Character teaches above our wills" [CW, 2:34] and "over our heads" [CW, 2:169]) or something that proceeds indifferent to the will's exertions, or streams beneath it, through the intuition or unconscious ("Power keeps quite another road than the turnpikes of choice and will, namely, the subterranean and invisible tunnels and channels of life" [CW, 3:39]). The high will of the moral law (a higher will than the individual) is, Emerson writes, "alive and beautiful . . . [and] works over our heads and under our feet" (CW, 3:166). "A higher law than that of our will regulates events; . . . our painful labors are unnecessary, and fruitless" (CW, 2:81).

Even the nonconformist aggressiveness of an essay like "Self-Reliance" can appear to give way to what David Robinson calls "a stance of humility": "Why then do we prate of self-reliance?" Emerson concedes, halfway through the essay, "To talk of reliance, is a poor external way of speaking. Speak rather of that which relies" (CW, 2:40).[18] "What am I?" he asks, "What has my will done to make me that I am? Nothing. I have been floated into this thought, this hour, this connection of events by secret currents of might and mind, and my ingenuity and wilfullness have not thwarted, have not aided to an appreciable degree" (CW, 2:194–95).

"Our moral nature," Emerson writes, "is vitiated by any interference of our will" (CW, 2:78). "Our action is overmastered and characterized above our will by the law of nature" (CW, 2:64). As Emerson adds immediately after the remarkably Nietzschean celebration of the aristocratic will cited previously, "Will is always miraculous, being the presence of God to men" (W, 12:46). This theocentric will is, it would appear, something quite other than Nietzsche's heroic, and godless, individual capacity for mastery and self-discipline. "Real master[s]," Emerson suggests, are defined by their receptivity to the infinite strength of God, the Over-Soul, the "eternal Cause" or "central intelligence." Mastery of this kind requires a "renunciation of Will" (EL, 3:312), a surrender of self so that a higher power may use us (W, 7:295). Caesar and Napoleon conquered not through willpower but through the "annihilation" of self (CW, 2:78–79).

Artistic creation would appear to involve a similar abnegation of will or labor. "The poet," Emerson claims, "must be a rhapsodist: his inspiration a sort of bright casualty: his will in it only the surrender of will to the Universal Power" (CW, 1:132). The poet "works to an end above his will" by means "which are out of his will." The production of a poem is "miraculous at all points." There can be "no practical rules," no "working plan." "It is as impossible for labor to produce a sonnet of Milton, or a song of Burns, as Shakespeare's Hamlet, or the Iliad" (W, 12:71–72). Emerson praised Michelangelo and Newton because their work seemed "rather a part of Nature than arbitrary productions of the human Will" (EL, 1:99).

He censured Goethe because he was "incapable of a selfsurrender to the moral sentiment" (CW, 4:163). Each man must learn, he said, "that he is here not to work, but to be worked upon" (CW, 4:105).

. . .

Does Emerson, then, contradict himself? He seems, on the one hand, passionately committed to the nineteenth-century doctrine of work and self-determination. He appears to uphold a characteristically nineteenth-century belief in a radical voluntarism—a philosophy of Will—and a radically humanistic pursuit of self-empowerment. Yet he seems to advocate, on the other hand, the rejection or transcendence of work, the rejection of voluntary exertion in favor of *"supervoluntary"* effects (W, 12:72). His essays may be read as a sustained argument against "spectator theories of knowledge," a rejection even of those aesthetic theories that depict art as a function of the mystical loss of self-control. Yet he also celebrates the passive attitude of spectatorship and reception. He urges us fervently—pragmatically—to use, test, meet, resist, antagonize, oppose, counterbalance, cope with, and overcome the hard facts that confront us, to counter the violence from without with an equal violence from within. Then he asks us to renounce our will.

He preaches self-reliance in one paragraph, God-reliance in the next. He endorses the labor, the complex discipline of self-creation, then calls for the yielding up of that self to some "vaster mind and will" (CW, 4:20)—be it God, Nature, or the "highest unity" (CW, 4:163). He encourages us to build our own world, then asks us to surrender ourselves to another world. At times it seems that some form of action is the only response to the world or to other people that Emerson can recognize as real or legitimate—that the exhortation to further action is his single, incessant message. ("New actions," he claims—and it is an extraordinary claim—"are the only apologies and explanations of old ones, which the noble can bear to offer or to receive" [CW, 3:60]. "I do not see how any man can afford, for the sake of his nerves and his nap, to spare any action in which he can partake" [CW, 1:59]. "What a man does, that he has" [CW, 2:83]. It is not even particular actions Emerson prays for, but "the spirit that sheds and showers actions, countless, endless actions" [CW, 1:177].)

At other times he seems the very spokesman for what Carlyle abhorred as "Hindoo-like passivity" (what Emerson himself could dismiss as moribund "Orientalism" or "Chinese stagnation").[19] No writer enshrines "practical power" more than Emerson does, yet there is no writer who can sound, at the same time, so profoundly suspicious of it. He speaks, one moment, the martial language of hard power and, the next moment, the Buddhistic or mystical language of self-negation. He can seem in one paragraph almost indistinguishable from Nietzsche, in the next, almost indistinguishable from Plotinus. He can appear to espouse, on one page, a revolutionary—indeed, a willfully dangerous, or perverse, Nietzschean brand of modernism—and on the next page seem to favor an outdated Transcendentalism, a genteel "last gasp of classical idealism," as Peter Carafiol has described it.[20]

This is, I think, the central paradox, the Gordian knot that every critic of Emerson must sooner or later confront. It is, to switch metaphors, the sphinx to which anyone attempting to understand Emerson must hazard some response—for the reader encounters it, in some form, on virtually every page of his prose.

It is, as I have already suggested, a paradox that has been noted repeatedly by Emerson's readers. "Moonshiny as it in theory may be," Melville concluded of Emerson's Transcendentalism, "yet a very practical philosophy it turns out in effect." Lowell painted him as a curious hybrid: a Yankee "Plotinus-Montaigne" whose shrewd wit existed in a Transcendentalist mist ("E. sits in a mystery calm and intense, / and looks coolly around him with sharp common sense"). O. W. Firkins made the same point in his more orotund style: "Where but in Emerson can we find a reverence for the solitary vision which exceeds that of the ascetic and devotee united with an esteem for the varied, palpable, objective fact, which the investigator or commercialist might recognize as adequate?" "Here is Emerson, then," Ray Benoit writes, "what he offers with his right hand, an emphasis on the vertical otherworldly, his left hand withdraws with an emphasis on the horizontal worldly. For every step forward there seems to be one backward": "The idealists dismiss Emerson as a pragmatist and the pragmatists dismiss him as an idealist. . . . [W]hat does the reader do when he discovers that two exactly opposite philosophies claim him[?]"[21]

This is, as I have said, a crucial question to which a variety of defensible responses may be made. Before turning to those possible responses, however, I should note that there has traditionally—as Benoit's description and my own discussion of the different Emersons depicted by Santayana, Henry James, Dewey, and Stephen Whicher suggest—been debate over just what, precisely, in Emerson constitutes a step forward and a step backward, just what in his thought is living and what is dead. Given the ideological age in which we live, the two schools of interpretation—Emerson as pragmatist, Emerson as idealist—are likely to become even more pronounced. There may well emerge, in even sharper distinction than heretofore, "Right" and "Left" Emersonians: those who emphasize Emerson as idealist, guardian of the absolute, moral law; and those who emphasize Emerson's apparent rejection of metaphysics and metaphysical truth and his attendant vision of a world that can and must be molded according to—a world that is meaningless without—the dictates and the shaping power of the human will.

Yet if this happens it will not only be the result of current academic culture. It will also be the inevitable outcome of emphasizing Emerson's place in the mainstream of nineteenth-century intellectual history. For it is only in that context that Emerson can clearly be seen not as a cheerful monist or well-balanced soul but as another key nineteenth-century mind whose work seems to contain sufficient ambiguities or contradictions to inspire opposing, Right and Left, schools of interpretation. (Revisor-philosophers like Rousseau or Thoreau are often, Cavell notes, "contradictory sensibilities" who "may appear as radically innovative . . . or radically conservative.")[22]

Hegelian philosophy, the century's ultimate idealism, has produced precisely the same debate. It has given birth to the same contradictions we come to at the crux of Emerson's Transcendentalism. Like Hegel, Emerson may be radically transcendentalized or radically detranscendentalized—without straying from or misreading the texts themselves. It would seem to depend, as Benoit remarks, "on how you choose your quotations." Hegel and Emerson both appear to offer sufficient textual evidence to be taken as radical idealists or radical pragmatists, as (fundamentally) Christians or (fundamentally) humanists, as transcendentalists or antitranscendentalists, as the nineteenth century's absolutists par excellence or as extreme relativists, as foundationalists or antifoundationalists, as theocentric mystics or as two of the century's greatest prophets of human self-determination. As Solomon observes of Hegel, in a statement that is every bit as relevant to Emerson: "It is not always clear to what extent the image [in Hegel's philosophy] is the humble Vedic vision of losing ourselves in a force much greater than ourselves—in 'the All'—and to what extent it is the egomaniacal image of the self as everything."[23]

Dewey's response to this interpretive dilemma as it was exemplified in Emerson's putative idealism was, as we have seen, to conclude that Emerson was at heart pragmatic. According to Dewey, there was a basic, hard-headed, aggressive (and progressive) pragmatism in Emerson's thought that was all too easily overlooked. Emerson's writing was itself to blame, for it constituted an ambiguous compound of idioms and tones that was seriously misleading: it lent itself to embezzlement by those who wished to claim Emerson as a genteel idealist.

Many of Emerson's most recent critics—Porter, Ellison, Hughes, Poirier, Donoghue, West—emphasize a similarly aggressive, voluntaristic, pragmatic Emerson. As Harold Bloom suggests, "Emersonian Transcendentalism is not a transcendence at all." Emersonianism must be considered, Bloom argues, fundamentally a radical, Romantic humanism—a "humanism which seeks our renewal as makers." It is not transcendence or immanence that Emerson heralds, not "the Divine . . . either *in* the world or above and *over* the world," but a divine that can be attained only "*through* the world": a humanized divinity (if it can then be called divinity at all) that is, as Whitman or Hart Crane discovered, a matter of the "ebbing out" and "flowing in" of the energies of the human imagination or of the distinctly human capacity to renew and remake.[24]

William James had a tougher, often an exasperating, time dealing with these apparently contradictory sides to Emerson's thought. James, as it is now clear, read and reread, marked, and indexed nearly all of Emerson's essays and lectures. But Frederic Carpenter's valuable study of James's extensive marginalia suggests that he early on gave up trying to reconcile the two Emersons. "Throughout his life," Carpenter writes, "James praised the pragmatic Emerson, but disapproved the transcendentalist." James's failure to unify these two tendencies in Emerson's thought under any single rubric is reflected in the method of indexing he finally settled on. He indexed those transcendental passages and essays that he categorized as "against my philosophy" under such titles as monism, abstract unity, absolute thought, or the ONE. Under the title pragmatism he indexed those paragraphs containing the word "action" or "deeds." He similarly approved of those passages emphasizing the present tense, psychic energy, expansiveness, or power in general.[25]

The reader can choose another option when faced with "two exactly opposite philosophies" on the same page or in the same essay: "He brushes [Emerson] off," as Benoit says, "as a befuddled thinker, sincere but befuddled." The readiness of criticism to brush Emerson off in just this way has been one of the major legacies of the anti-Emerson tradition. Kenneth Marc Harris accurately notes the existence of an apparent "general rule in Emerson studies that evidence can always be found to contradict the most carefully considered conclusions." Donoghue, for instance, remarks that Emerson "can be quoted to nearly any purpose." As Maurice Gonnaud more caustically states it: Emerson's failure to arrive at "an ultimate effort of synthesis"—his "perennial defect"—"is also the good fortune of his critics, who in consequence can find in his work material to justify several contradicting interpretations with equal plausibility."[26]

One might wish to argue that such inconsistency is further evidence of the expansive nature of Emerson's imagination, what I have discussed as the assimilative psychology of the Emersonian overman: evidence of Emerson's attempt to leave nothing in life unrepresented, to include in his enterprise the record of as many moods and perspectives as possible. But the assumption that he is incoherent, now one of the commonplaces of Emerson criticism, has usually not been offered in Emerson's defense. Conclusions like Whicher's—that "The more we know him, the less we know him"—have usually not come as part of an effort to understand Emerson as a less systematic but no less serious thinker than, say, Kant, Locke, or even Edwards. (This is the kind of defense, for instance, that Erich Heller makes for the fiercely personal, but no less philosophical, work of a Pascal or a Nietzsche, as opposed to a Descartes or a Kant.) Nor have such comments generally been offered as part of an effort to place Emerson more clearly against the background of his time. Emerson's failure to achieve an "ultimate synthesis" of his beliefs has generally been taken as further proof of unique intellectual and temperamental flaws rather than as evidence of a quite general and characteristic mid-nineteenth-century failure to achieve any such philosophical synthesis. (This is the argument I shall suggest in this chapter and, more extensively, in chapter 6.)[27]

The presumption that anyone can find anything in Emerson, that any interpretation can be made to stick, has really operated as just another way of claiming that Emerson is simply too foggy to bear much more than historical scrutiny. It is another way of concluding, as Cavell puts it, that "to bear interpretation [is] simply beyond him."[28] Like those other axioms of Emerson studies (his childlike optimism, his escapism, his blindness to evil) that perpetuate the anti-Emerson tradition, one would like to see it left behind—or at least sufficiently questioned that it can no longer be repeated as self-evident.

Yet another response can be made to the problem of Emerson's apparent contradictions. It, too, has become one of the standard conclusions in Emerson scholarship—which is hardly surprising, for there are innumerable passages in which Emerson appears to offer exactly the same interpretation himself. According to this interpretation, there is, finally, no contradiction between the transcendental and pragmatic, the idealist and empiricist, strains in Emerson's thought: the two are actually united, as Benoit argues (and as Emerson critics have often agreed) in a "mutual harmony . . . in a higher third realm where the opposition ceases though neither item is reduced to the other." This "union of impossibilities" (CW, 4:31) or "bipolar Unity" (JMN, 7:200), as Emerson refers to it, constitutes what Benoit calls a "monistic dualism," "dualistic monism," or "oneness of two." It has roots in Plato, in Coleridge, and in Wordsworth, and it exemplifies what Benoit identifies as "the romantic calculus": Romanticism's belief that spirit and matter, permanence and change, the monism of idealism and the dualisms of empiricism, can be united in a "distinctly mystical" higher synthesis that sacrifices the opposing priorities of neither component.[29]

Such a resolution decrees that there is, ultimately, no inconsistency in Emerson's advocacy of action and abandonment, work and acquiescence, a strong will and will-lessness, or power and passiveness. The greatest passivity is the greatest power. Human will is, when dependent on the moral sentiment, only another form of inexhaustible divine power. The two are joined in a productive, vital harmony—"a Coleridgean reconciliation of opposites in a dynamic unity," as one student of Romantic thought has identified it. What appears to be the gnawing contradiction in Emerson is, then, more correctly perceived as a kind of closed circle encompassing both will and will-lessness, individual action and divine decree, in a harmony that can be nothing but moral—and, ultimately, energizing. Such a synthesis acts as an always-flowing system of power that unites human and divine force along the single circuit of the moral law. Within this monistic/dualistic circle, acts of abandonment are acts of will. "Diametrically opposed positions," as Grusin says, "are seen to adhere in a single yet also double act."[30]

William James defined this dynamic relationship between individual soul and universe as the essence of the "Emersonian religion," the Emersonian moral law: "The universe has a divine soul of order, which soul is moral, being also the soul within the soul of man."[31] By "abandonment" or "selfsurrender to [this] moral sentiment," the individual can then tap into divine force. Thus, as Emerson more simply states it, "self-reliance, the height and perfection of man, is reliance on God" (W, 11:236). "Self-trust . . . is a trust in God himself" (W, 10:65–66). Man's intellect and the moral sentiment are unanimous: "the wiser a man is, the more stupendous he finds [this] natural and moral economy, and lifts himself to a more absolute reliance" (CW, 4:99).

. . .

This is, without any doubt, one theory of power that can be found throughout Emerson's writing. It can provide a compelling holistic vision—what Firkins calls Emerson's "successful practice of unbroken commerce with omnipresent deity." It offers what Sherman Paul calls an Emersonian unity of vision: "a living connection between the horizontal-worldly and the vertical-otherworldly." In a professedly Catholic reading of Emerson (which, tellingly, accommodates itself quite easily to this strain in his thought), Robert Pollock speaks of this synthesis as Emerson's great synoptic vision, the achievement, in an age in which the spiritual life seemed threatened, of "an all-inclusive and organic consciousness," "a reconciliation of inward spirituality with the cosmic sense."[32]

This holistic or synoptic vision is surely a major part of what Firkins calls Emerson's secret, the secret of what has often seemed a uniquely powerful yet enigmatic appeal. But although this is, undeniably, one Emersonian theory of power, there are several reasons why we should hesitate to settle on it as *the* theory or the resolution of the central contradictions I have been pointing out.

The resolutions that such an interpretation brings to Emerson are, finally, too neat and too simple. This closed, transcendental system of essentially theistic Unity describes a part of Emerson's philosophy and explains part of his appeal. But if it is taken, as it often has been, as the definitive synthesis applicable to the whole of Emerson's thought—adequate to the many complications and problems his thought and rhetoric present—then it reduces him and robs him of much of his interest, much of what is radically new in his ideas, much of what is most alive to us today. It is a transcendental interpretation of Emerson that has, for a century and a half, made Emerson's thought and writing seem much purer in conception and execution than they actually are. It has tended to locate his thinking, specifically his meditations on power, outside the currents of mid-nineteenth-century philosophy and has defined it as timeless, mystical, and more purely theocentric than it is. It has flattened out the many extremes—the consciously experimental, the extravagant and dangerous nature of his rhetoric—and made the task of interpreting him much less treacherous than it actually is. It has made his writing seem, in Packer's phrase, less "strange and difficult"—and less historically complex—than it is.[33] The scholarly acceptance of this interpretation has, in short, been one of the cornerstones of the anti-Emerson tradition and a positive hindrance to appreciation. It has been one way of reading Emerson that has allowed generations of critics to condescend to his work as possessing mainly historical interest, less depth or relevance than Melville or Hawthorne, and not much that requires continued critical scrutiny or debate.

The holistic interpretation of Emerson reaffirms Santayana's and Henry James's version of Emerson. It does not, it seems to me, sufficiently take into account the progressive—though confusingly articulated—philosophy of the future, or pragmatics of the future, that Dewey and others have found in Emerson. Nor does it adequately account for that startlingly original expression of "man's entire independence" or the extreme voluntarism that Whicher, Donoghue, and several other critics, old and new, have glimpsed hovering conspicuously behind the clouds of Emerson's holistic or moralistic language. It has, for much too long, deemphasized the important links between Emerson and Nietzsche. It has provided a rationale for ignoring or explaining away the more extreme, but salient, ramifications of Emerson's philosophy of power. Most significantly, it has made possible the widespread underestimation of the much more extensive middle ground of Emerson's thought—call it pragmatism or call it a midcentury philosophy of will or action—that is neither Transcendentalism nor extreme Nietzscheanism.

Packer correctly notes that resolving the self-reliance/God-reliance contradiction by interpreting it as a monistic/dualistic paradox resembles the resolution Christianity finds in the paradox of the Incarnation. For the paradox on which this transcendental resolution is based is fundamentally an orthodox, Christian one: the surrender of the self to a higher power is an act of faith that makes possible the regeneration of that same self. This describes, as John Reed observes, a "traditional theism." It is an old story. "The world is the product of one will and one mind and the future will be good for the man who sees himself as the conduit through which the will of God flows. This is the old lesson that man's freedom comes through his submission to God's will, manifest for Emerson in the Law of Nature and its Beautiful Necessity. Obedience is freedom." The "familiar paradox of self-suppression as a means to self-fulfillment" was the commonplace response by Victorian religious moralists to the century's continuing debate over free will. It is—as Reed's survey of the vast body of sermons, tracts, and books on the subjects suggests—a traditional Christian resolution, founded on Christ's own filial self-surrender as a paradigm for human conduct.[34]

Readers like Pollock take the reassertion of this ancient tradition as an unqualified, philosophical triumph—a sorely needed, modern-day reconciliation comparable to that attained in medieval Christian thought. But Charles Feidelson's negative evaluation has been much more typical, and it is still very much alive in Emerson scholarship. Feidelson, accepting this drive "to reduce multiplicity to unity" as the last word on Emerson's thought, concludes that Emerson's enterprise was destined to fail, morally and aesthetically, because it was, in its very inception, stubbornly anachronistic. "For, as [Emerson] was perfectly aware, he was running counter to the mental habits of over two centuries. . . . [H]e was trying to describe an ancient way of seeing by means of a modern vocabulary which had been designed to repress it." Most readers who have settled on a holistic Emerson have, like Feidelson, seen such holism as an intellectual liability or retrenchment, a "facile harmony," aloof from and ill equipped to address effectively the complications of its time. As Feidelson puts it: "Instead of going on . . . to make the most of paradox, Emerson usually beat a hasty retreat into transcendent unity."[35]

The holistic interpretation of Emerson (the interpretation that sees him as solving or transcending the contradiction between the shaping and the submissive will, between working and being worked upon, between self- and God-reliance) manages to free his ideas from the most fundamental contradictions of his age. Such dichotomies are, however, the very stuff of Emerson's art and thought. They are the complex source of his rhetorical power and of the intrinsic (and historical) interest he still holds for us. They are contradictions that his essays quite consistently reflect and exploit, despite his professions to (or, more often, his longing for) the contrary. It is hardly surprising that, given the holistic interpretation, Emerson's ideas begin to seem like genteel regressions, out of touch with the tensions of their time, with little to tell us about the fragmented course of Western intellectual tradition in his own day or since and with little to offer us in the way of philosophical or moral direction today. Emerson comes indeed to seem the intellectually minor figure, the Boston "naïf" Henry Adams rejected. Like the mild Unitarianism Adams scorned, he seems to have "solved the universe" and escaped, or simply turned his back on, the central philosophical ruptures that define the nineteenth century.[36]

For the nineteenth century was not an age in which holistic philosophies, syncretic systems, or post-Kantian forms of metaphysical idealism managed to sustain their integrity or significance for very long or even to succeed on their own terms. The overreaching, omnisynthetic philosophies of Schelling and Hegel were, rather, replaced, in an extended period of philosophical crisis and transformation, by new philosophies of will—by Schopenhauer, Marx, and Nietzsche. The 1830s, the decade in which Emerson began his career as essayist and lecturer, was also the decade that witnessed the death of Goethe and Hegel and the "collapse of Idealism" that "plunged philosophy into a profound identity-crisis which has persisted up until the present day."[37]

"Metaphysical idealism," Richard Rorty notes, "was [only] a momentary, though important, stage in the emergence of romanticism." The romanticism that resulted was, by the end of the century, *aufgehoben,* as Rorty says, in the pragmatism of Nietzsche and William James.[38] Emerson has far too often been pushed backward—away from Nietzsche and James—into the absolutism of the earlier German Idealists, into pantheism, or into monistic/dualistic syntheses that seem to belong more to the Middle Ages than to the mid-nineteenth century. It is a decontextualizing, a narrowing and refining of his ideas that inevitably discredits him. What still needs to be emphasized and recovered is the crucial role Emerson played as a mediating figure between Schelling and Hegel, on the one hand, and Nietzsche and James, on the other: between an idealism that was shattering under the century's new emphasis on human power and self-transformation and the philosophies of will and use that came to replace them. What needs to be recovered is what Emerson achieved and failed to achieve in the attempt (forced on him by his position as a mid-century thinker) to mediate between the idealist's urge to Unity, to Truth, system, and Over-Soul and the century's increasing stress on the primacy of the will, its conception of man as his own maker, its doctrines of labor and work, its philosophies of action and practical power.

It is not, as is so often alleged, that there is a general incoherence behind Emerson's ideas—a fogginess that allows any and all interpretations to be imposed on him. It is rather that his texts occupy so complicated, so mediatory a position, expressing as they do and building on the same contradiction—really a family of inseparable dualities—that besets the nineteenth century generally. Under the whole of Emerson's thought, through one essay after another, there runs that persistent contradiction, replicating itself in a sequence of related oppositions that are all, finally, of a piece. We may identify it as the contradiction between the Over-Soul (God-reliance) and self-reliance, between a tender-minded and a tough-minded philosophy, between Transcendentalism and Pragmatism, between Romantic Vedantism and radical humanism, the conflict between a philosophy that seeks atonement and one that seeks something against which to react.

I have suggested previously the way Emerson can seem not to be fully aware of the originality or ramifications of his theory of pragmatic use and resistance. His concern for the intellectual and cultural value of human power often seems to emerge tentatively, half-clothed in the vestments of an earlier idealism. He was, Carafiol remarks, "suspended between old meanings of his language and new circumstances." His resemblance to Nietzsche in this regard is striking. Arthur Danto's description of Nietzsche's philosophy—full of "odd dissonances . . . like architectural disharmonies in a transitional church"—provides us with a useful image, a way of picturing Emerson's own mediating position as a mid-nineteenth-century mind.[39]

In her examination of Emerson's public reception, Mary Kupiec Cayton suggests that Emerson has been "systematically misconstrued" by different "discourse communities." First his audiences, Cayton argues, then reformers and scholars have "appropriate[d] his discourse to their own ends" and imposed on him their various agendas. It would be more accurate to say that Emerson's texts *invite* specific contradictory readings. There are in his texts, as there are in the writing of so many other post-Enlightenment thinkers, certain profound dichotomies (one may consider them evasions or confusions)—breaking points where attempts at system making, unity, or the achievement of universal truth no longer hold together. Although the nineteenth century was, until its closing decades, a great age of system making, and of great hopes for final syntheses, it was also an age haunted by the failure of such hopes and by the overturning or reduction of universal theories. Solomon speaks of the epoch between 1750 and 1850 as witnessing the "first signs of [the] disintegration of the grand abstractions which constitute [the] bourgeois family of ideas." These were the very abstractions that the culture of the period again and again pushed to their ultimate conclusion—only to discover their inevitable breakdown.[40]

The century's thought is defined by a recurrent pattern, one that begins in the late eighteenth century: the inner contradictions of an attempted synthesis or holistic vision become evident and invite contradictory interpretations (right versus left, theistic versus secular, transcendentalist versus empiricist). Or they invite further attempts to correct, complete, or rewrite entirely the original synthesis. Thus Fichte, Schelling, and Hegel try, one after the other, to heal or reconcile, once and for all, the unresolved contradictions in Kant or in each others' philosophies. Hegel's Absolute, the grandest universal of all, is finally attained, only to decompose into antagonistic Hegelian*isms*.[41] Schopenhauer, Feuerbach, and then Nietzsche push to its limits a voluntarism that was already latent in Kant and his successors. A similar phenomenon occurs in the history of Marxism and Darwinism. In the case of such extravagant writers as Carlyle or Nietzsche, the inherent ambiguities of their thought and the deliberate extremism of their rhetoric have allowed sharply different readers, in their time and ours, to claim them as their own.

Beneath Romanticism's "urge to system," beneath its wish for nothing less then the absolute unity of the modern world, there exists, as Thomas McFarland suggests, the deeper reality of "incompleteness, fragmentation, and ruin." No wonder it was an age that, while positing one syncretic or organic paradigm after another, remained "fascinated by polarities and dualities": fascinated by supermen and submen, power and impotence, strong wills and will-lessness, healthy souls and sick souls, a fierce humanism and a lurking antihumanism, "the anthropocentric conceit" and the apocalyptic anticipation of the end of man.[42] It was not a century of resolutions, though innumerable philosophical resolutions were offered, but rather an era of omnipresent debates in which irreconcilable premises went unresolved. Nineteenth-century narratives, historical, fictional, and scientific, return time and again to the age's abiding paradox: the conviction that "the exercise of individual human will" is "central to all human endeavor" and the concurrent faith that "the highest function of that will" lies in its subordination "to some higher power, institutional, moral, or theological."[43] Against this larger backdrop we can see that the midcentury's contradictions were, precisely, Emerson's. His texts do not represent the transcending, harmonizing, or escape from these obstinate polarities. If they did, he would be a much less interesting, an easier, writer than he is—and those readers who profess to finding such resolutions usually claim only secondary importance for him.

His difficult texts suggest, instead, the extent to which his work reflects, takes as its starting point, and accepts as its medium the century's "rich historical confusion."[44] This is one roundabout way of claiming that his prose, as art, meets the criterion R. P. Blackmur once recommended: "that there must be an underlying equivalence between the art and the complexity of what the artist . . . had seen."[45] The point should no longer need to be made; but the notion that there is no such equivalence in Emerson's work, that his thickly bandaged eyes saw too little, and that he left the task of articulating the deeper tensions of his time and place to a Melville or Dickinson dies hard.

In essay after essay Emerson made the most of paradox. If we fail to recognize that, we shall fail to appreciate the degree to which his work acknowledges and even stakes out the limits of the century's double consciousness. Increasingly, criticism finds confirmed and explored in his prose the major philosophical cruxes of modern thought. Most relevant in the context of this study is, as I have suggested, the midway or mediating position Emerson occupies between an earlier idealism and what we generally think of as a late-nineteenth-century "pragmatic-economical view of the human mind."[46] But other recent approaches have similarly located his work in terms of the major intellectual conflicts of its time, conflicts that are still with us.[47]

Allan Megill's study of that "epoch in modern Western intellectual history" that runs from Nietzsche to Derrida further clarifies the way in which the will/will-lessness, transcendentalist/pragmatist, actor/spectator dichotomy is one of the most deeply rooted contradictions of the post-

Enlightenment, post-Romantic world. Megill's subject is what he calls the "aestheticist" tradition of philosophy: that tradition that takes art (and the work of art) as the primary paradigm for human experience. The aestheticist tradition attempts "to expand the aesthetic to embrace the whole of reality."[48] It is exemplified, at its most extreme, in Nietzsche's claim that reality, truth, and value are not matters of fact or nature but the result of some form of human work—they are works of art, works of interpretation, products of the will to power.

This emphasis on the radically mediated, radically man-made nature of the world leads, Megill suggests, to radically opposed positions. And those radically opposed positions define the schism I have been tracing in Emerson's own "aestheticist ontology"—in his assertion of a malleable, always usable, always humanly mediated world. On the one hand, Megill writes, the aestheticist tradition leads "in the direction of passive contemplation": "since the world is a work of art we ought to relate to it as we do to works of art. . . . That is, we ought to stand before the world in awed rapture, allowing it to manifest its deeply veiled truth." On the other hand, the aestheticist ontology leads in an "activist direction" that stresses radical creativity over contemplation: "all human activity comes to be interpreted on the model of the creativity attributed to the (Romantic) artist, who himself stands as the successor to the radical creativity of God."[49]

. . .

There are other reasons why we should hesitate to take what I have been calling the holistic and theocentric interpretation of Emerson as an adequate account of the whole or even the primary tendency of his thought. Those readers who settle on him as a preeminently "God-intoxicated" man (the epithet Novalis used to describe Spinoza) push him, as the origins of the phrase would suggest, backward in history to centuries in which a writer's reliance on a theistic rhetoric does not present the same problems it does in the nineteenth.[50]

Emerson's reputation as a religious thinker is, to be sure, one of the key foundation stones of the Emerson image. He is, John Morley writes, "one of the privileged few whom the reader approaches in the mood of settled respect, and whose names have surrounded themselves with an atmosphere of religion."[51] But there exists, as every student of Transcendentalism is aware, a long tradition of readers who have criticized Emerson for retaining little *but* the *atmosphere* of religion.

There have always been critics who have complained of a pernicious ambiguity in the way Emerson appropriates an apparently Christian vocabulary for his own unchristian ends. "For though he builds glorious temples," Lowell joked, "'tis odd / He leaves never a doorway to get in a god." His Unitarian opponents accused him of egotheism. Orestes Brownson charged that he "unchristianizes Christianity, makes it an element of human nature." "Modern transcendental idealism, Emersonianism, for instance," William James observed, "seems to let God evaporate into abstract Ideality." In the twentieth century, Yvor Winters concluded that "the religious experience for Emerson was a kind of good-natured self-indulgence": Emerson and Whitman were "moral parasites upon a Christian doctrine which they were endeavoring to destroy." Oliver Wendell Holmes, anticipating Winters's criticism, once remarked that Emerson was "an iconoclast without a hammer, who took down our idols from their pedestals so tenderly that it seemed like an act of worship." He "reduced the religious experience," Porte writes, "to a reaffirmation of Christian ethics." Emerson's true religion was, according to Bloom, an Orphic or Gnostic belief in "the American More-than-Christ who is *to come.*" He can be classified neither as a Christian "nor even a non-Christian theist in a philosophic sense." "Augustine . . . made a church," Quentin Anderson observes; "Emerson undertook to bring one down." He was shrewd enough, in his "transvaluing [of] religious values," to "let the formerly religious down easily by using just enough of the vocabulary of religion to reassure his hearers, and not enough to trouble their sleep."[52]

What needs to be stressed is that Emerson and those he influenced were not the only writers of their time to inspire such caveats. The habit of using a traditional religious terminology in the advancement of ideas that are neither traditional nor Christian, nor even religious, is one of the distinguishing features of post-Enlightenment philosophy and literature. We need to be extremely cautious in reading the German tradition, particularly, because so many of its thinkers who were thorough humanists continued to call themselves religious and speak as if they were. "If the language of Christianity still pervaded German philosophy [in Hegel's time]," Solomon notes, "the substance had long ago been altered beyond recognition." "Even such vehement atheists as Schopenhauer and Nietzsche would continue to use the language of 'redemption' and 'spirit.'"[53]

The scope of religion in the nineteenth century was not narrowed, Mandelbaum suggests, but broadened to the point of meaninglessness: "religion came to be identified with whatever ranges of feeling and of moral aspiration were of most significance to man." Thus Kierkegaard, assessing the post-Hegelian tradition in 1846, complained that it had functioned as a Trojan horse, undermining Christianity and religious thought in its purported attempt to defend it. "[T]he entire Christian terminology," he declared, "has been appropriated by speculative thought to its own purposes. . . . The concepts have been emasculated and the words have been made to mean anything and everything." If Hegel's attempt to "do justice to faith and make peace with religion" were to succeed, Kierkegaard warned, "then it would have the ironical fate that precisely on the day of its triumph it would have lost everything and entirely quashed Christianity." The German tradition finally did succeed in delivering the coup de grâce to traditional theism in Marx's vision of man himself as the highest and only divinity. "The divine essence," as Ludwig Feuerbach expressed it, "is nothing else than the human essence." As British Hegelian T. H. Green phrased it, "God is our possible or ideal self." It is characteristic of a century used to defining religion primarily in terms of its capacity to inspire the human spirit that Feuerbach had no difficulty in continuing to value religious feeling as the emotion that gives man his highest worth.[54]

Protestant asceticism can be, as Max Weber demonstrated, ultimately worldly. "It is of the essence of Protestantism and of German philosophy," Santayana writes, "that religion should gradually drop its supernatural personages and comforting private hopes and be absorbed in the duty of living manfully and conscientiously the conventional life of the world." The metamorphosis of German and American transcendentalisms into radical humanisms was simply, Santayana concluded, the inevitable outcome of Protestantism's deeply rooted belief in a man-centered God and an anthropocentric universe.[55]

It is not necessary to enter into the continuing scholarly dispute over Emerson's relative conservatism or radicalism from the perspective of Unitarian tradition. My point is that Emerson, though he has been studied in the contexts of mysticism, pantheism, Neoplatonism, idealism, orthodox and liberal Christianity, and even Judaism, belongs above all in that tradition of late-eighteenth- and early-nineteenth-century writers and thinkers whose dependence on a religious vocabulary (whose very attempt to provide a rational proof of religion, a new exploration of God, or a new apology for Christianity) can be profoundly misleading.[56] It would be possible to read or teach Blake, Wordsworth, Shelley, Carlyle, Fichte, Schelling, Hegel, Thoreau, or Whitman anachronistically. One could take their usage of religiously pretentious terms like spirit, Over-Soul, the absolute, Unity, "ever-blessed Oneness," faith, redemption, holiness, even God (or "the God within") as meaning more or less the same thing as they might in a poem by John Donne. This would be to forget, however, that they wrote in an age that was moving from "the demise of religion" to "a thoroughly human world," a "watershed moment in Western thought," as Kenneth Burke puts it, when theistic "vocabularies of motive" were being replaced by naturalistic ones.[57]

Carlyle's theistic, often absolutist, rhetoric—Philip Rosenberg writes of his deep attraction to "some sort of absolute God principle"—offers an instructive case in point. Carlyle's oracular rhetoric, his jeremiads, his spiritual biographies, his apostrophes to the Infinite and to Divine Mystery, rely consistently on a religious vocabulary and on Biblical tradition. But his actual definitions of divinity are so ambiguous or contradictory—God and the world, divine and natural power, are so equated—that a situation is created in which, as Rosenberg puts it, "one of the terms is redundant." Kenneth Burke, attempting to resolve a similar ambiguity or merging of opposite terms as it occurs in Spinoza's philosophy, suggests that we must ask, "Which of the two equal terms [is] foremost?" Rosenberg directs that question to Carlyle and concludes that "from the moment he asserted the transcendental identity of god and the forces at work in the natural, historical world, his theology became a redundancy which we can well afford to ignore."[58]

Peter Dale refuses to draw a conclusion quite that extreme, but he reaches the same impasse. The tendency of nineteenth-century thought, he argues, was always toward the collapsing of the division between history as the actualizing of divine force, the Divine Idea, and history as the product of man's own heroic endeavors. Carlyle's writing reflects this tenuous balance between a "complete [fully humanistic] historicism" and "the saving notion of a permanent [Divine] Idea behind the flux" of historical change. It reflects, as well, the conflict between Carlyle's strong attraction to an irrational, "distinctly mystical approach to the Absolute" and his commitment to that post-Kantian, German idealist movement that "worked ultimately against the religious interpretation of the Idea or the spiritual" and points, instead, in the direction of the "human will and spiritual self-determination." "The unique interest of Carlyle's position in the context of nineteenth-century intellectual history," Dale writes, lies in the complicated interplay in his thought between "the more conservative, Neo-Platonic, and/or religious impulse looking back toward Coleridge and the English romantics and the 'Kantist' impulse looking forward to Nietzsche's elimination of God in favor of placing the 'whole drama of fall and redemption' within the spiritual power of man's finite will."[59]   *VIP!*

Assessing the ambiguities in that interplay forces the reader, Dale suggests, to look for the "general rhetorical bias" in Carlyle's texts. Carlyle may endeavor to retain in some form his family's Calvinist reverence for an all-powerful Deity: but his rhetorical bias seems to fall in the opposite direction, toward a Nietzschean philosophy of will, an existentialist commitment to man's "capacity to *act* and to *make* in the face of a hostile universe."[60]

It would be wrong to underestimate the differences between Carlyle's position and Emerson's. But I would argue that the broad philosophical and theological contradictions Rosenberg and Dale identify in Carlyle's thought are quite evident in Emerson's as well. And the final Carlylean rhetorical bias in favor of man's capacity for action and self-determination, in favor of a necessary and fruitful antagonism between mind and nature, human will and what it resists, seems, as I have been attempting to argue, no less conspicuous in Emerson's essays.[61]

Let us return then, keeping in mind this principle for reading Carlyle, to questions I raised earlier in this chapter. For the way we interpret Emerson's putatively holistic, theistic vocabulary must take into account, as any interpretation of a Hegel, Carlyle, or Nietzsche must, the general rhetorical bias of his thought as a whole. Does Emerson's rhetorical bias suggest that Will—the search after power—is his ultimate moral principle? Is Emerson's moral law ultimately the will to power? If it is, then much in our traditional conception of Emerson will certainly need to be redefined. We shall need to ask what, then, is moral about his moral law. We shall need to decide if will and power can constitute a moral principle at all and if Emerson's moral law is not, in large part, a confusion of terms or a misnomer, in the way his titles and terminology often are. We shall need to reconsider the implications of such a philosophy. And we shall need to decide if it deserves to be categorized as an idealistic transcendentalism, in the way Emerson scholarship has usually categorized it.

How close does Emerson come to a Nietzschean voluntarism that defines truth not in terms of preexisting ideas or universal laws but in terms of the feeling of power it instills, the degree of life-preserving mastery it provides? To what extent has Dugald Stewart's moral sense become, in Emerson's hands, no longer a defense against Lockean psychology but something with closer affinities to the later nineteenth-century turn away from epistemology and metaphysical idealism to "life-philosophy," to a philosophy that replaces God and supernatural force with an intensified concern for purely human potential?[62]

It becomes a nice question, as one scrutinizes those many passages in which Emerson speaks of the moral law, just where the rhetorical bias lies. For what appears to draw Emerson so strongly and consistently back to the moral law is not its value as a source of divine truth or morality but its utter reliability as a source of human power: the feeling of mastery, of renewed creativity; the will to resist, overcome, and appropriate that it bestows. Emerson's "cognitive apparatus" seems, in Nietzschean terminology, "directed not toward knowledge but rather toward mastery and possession."[63] "Strength enters," Emerson writes, "as the moral element enters" (W, 12:61).

Emerson's invocations of humility and pure acquiescence have the habit of turning into "almost Nietzschean proclamation[s]," as Gonnaud puts it, of the strength of character.[64] "The Sovereignty of Ethics," cobbled-together text that it is, is still an instructive example, for it follows that typically Emersonian pattern and involves the same ambiguities. As the title suggests, it is, purportedly, yet another testament to the moral law. "I see," Emerson writes, "the unity of thought and of morals running through all animated nature. . . . The high intellect is absolutely at one with moral nature" (W, 10:184–85). But self-surrender to that higher unity is being celebrated, as quickly becomes clear, not for the inherent worth or beauty of such moral unity but for the power it gives back. "The animal who is wholly kept down in Nature has no anxieties," Emerson continues: "By yielding, as he must do, to it, he is enlarged and reaches his highest point" (W, 10:184). The essay's true subject is, of course, precisely such enlargement. It is about the sovereignty of man, not the sovereignty of ethics—about the perfect health, the expansion and apotheosis of the human spirit. The essay ends by envisioning a new, "superhuman" form of life (W, 10:214). Even Emerson's most pious and humble-sounding essays—like "Compensation" or its companion piece, "Spiritual Laws"—typically end by reaffirming the will, the growth of character, the strength of thought, the necessity of work, the necessity of converting one's losses to new power, the imminent arrival of some form of mastery or Caesarlike dominion.

Emerson often, Robinson argues, balances a stance of humility with what might be called a stance of dominion or uprightness. Take, for instance, the famous, parallel closing sentences of "Self-Reliance": "Nothing can bring you peace but yourself. Nothing can bring you peace but the triumph of principles." The first sentence implies a quietistic atonement of "individual self with a universal or abstract Self underlying it." But the final sentence suggests a necessary dualism, a reaction of self against some form of opposition. Like many of Emerson's essays, "Self-Reliance" ends with the image of conflict and victory, the conversion of opposition into opportunity. "To say," Robinson writes, "that 'nothing can bring you peace but yourself' is to evoke quiet self-possession. To call peace a 'triumph of principles' is to suggest a struggle." This dichotomy marks the entire essay: a vocabulary of acquiescence coexists alongside a vocabulary of "barriers, obstacles, entanglements" that implies "opposition, will, and action."[65] Where, then, does the rhetorical bias fall? Where does it fall, to take another example, in Emerson's famous recommendation that our knowledge of our "relation to the world" is best arrived at "by untaught sallies of the spirit, by a continual self-recovery, and by entire humility" (CW, 1:39)? Is the emphasis on "entire humility" or on the struggle implied in "continual self-recovery" and "sallies of the spirit"?

Emerson's means, Robinson concludes, "may be those of surrender, but the ends are those of assertion, strength, pragmatic result."[66] If this is true, then the contradiction between means and ends raises a host of questions with profound implications for the way we see Emerson. What does it mean to yield oneself to the perfect whole if the outcome of such abandonment is some form of empowerment: not self-abnegation but the reassertion of identity? What does it mean to advocate passivity—in a way that can sound ascetic, sound like transcendence, sound like acceptance of a power higher than the human, sound like the Buddhist principle of negation (the denial of the will), what Schopenhauer extolled as Nirvana (self-extinction)—if what is gained in such apparent powerlessness is a renewed form of power and will, a new superhumanity? What does it mean to preach acquiescence, the renunciation of "our bloated nothingness" and our humble obedience to a higher wisdom ("Let us lie low in the Lord's power") if what is being celebrated is not the humbling means but the ultimate, powerful result, the certain access to "the stream of power" such apparent selflessness guarantees (CW, 2:93, 81)?

Evelyn Barish, arguing against a Nietzschean interpretation of Emerson, suggests that "The sense of strength [Emerson] aimed to describe existed . . . only in a God-centered universe; never did he imagine a sense of self whose only referent was itself." But Emerson's ideas are rarely so pristine or so unequivocally expressed as this. Settling with such certainty the contradictions involved in the self-reliance/God-reliance paradox only simplifies Emerson's complicated position as a midcentury thinker. Reading him in this way ignores the problematic nature of much of the putatively God-centered rhetoric of nineteenth-century writing. It downplays the way in which his prose remains so tricky, so transitional a medium, changing meaning or connotation with each use, through "gradual modulations of meaning, alterations of emphasis, reapplications of old terms in new and transforming contexts."[67]

Innumerable passages could be adduced where the rhetorical bias seems to fall not on self-surrender or a mystical transcendence that takes us away from "the things of this world," as Philip Gura puts it, but on the need for ever-continuing work and struggle.[68] In his "Introductory Lecture" to "Lectures on the Times," for instance, Emerson invokes the "mysterious fountain of the moral sentiment" but seems most rhetorically passionate in his affirmation of the creativity, the life, the "unbounded energy, unbounded power" that sentiment provides (CW, 1:174). In "The Over-Soul" Emerson calls for abandonment to "moral beatitude" but celebrates "the royal road to particular knowledges and powers" such abandonment insures (CW, 2:164). In "Circles" he speaks of union with divine power but rejoices because such moments confer "an energy of mind . . . commensurate with the work to be done" (CW, 2:187–88). In "Worship" the "moral sense" is described as that principle that decrees "we are not to do, but to let do; not to work, but to be worked upon"—but we are then assured of the strength, the "vast and sudden enlargements of power" such submission guarantees (W, 6:212–13).

One of Emerson's best-known testimonies to the way of abandonment comes at the close of "Circles." But where does the rhetorical bias fall, on the humility that comes in forgetting ourselves or on what Emerson calls "the facilities of performance"—his desire to "draw a new circle," to "do something without knowing how or why"? Is the emphasis on acquiescence to a supernatural power or on the call for heroic self-assertion ("Nothing great was ever achieved without enthusiasm"), great victories (like Cromwell's), great deeds (the "great moments of history"), and great works ("the strength of ideas, . . . the works of genius") (CW, 2:190)?

William James believed that passivity was one of the four characteristics of mysticism: "the mystic feels as if his own will were in abeyance, and indeed sometimes as if he were grasped and held by a superior power."[69] The following 1837 journal passage, with its invocation of self-renunciation and atonement with the Universe, would appear to advocate a similar ebbing of personal will before a superior All. But it is also a wholly Emersonian lesson, not in passivity but in the doctrine of use. It teaches us how to bear it well, how to use, confront, and make the most of disgrace, defeat, and "calamitous days." So we need again to ask where the rhetorical bias falls. Does it favor the dissolving of personality and "keeping the habit of the observer"? Or does it incline to Emerson's advice never to relax our watchfulness, to record confidently the mere phenomena of loss so that we might eventually oversee ourselves "like a god," so that we might turn adversity to profit, "harvest our losses" (a wonderful, thoroughly Emersonian image), and achieve some sovereignty over "the whole game"? The metaphors are curiously, but characteristically, mixed. Unity appears to be the goal, but the passage's imagery relies on consistent dualisms—struggle, victory, mastery of the game. Once again, life is conceived as a contest of wills.

> I claim to be a part of the All. All exterior life declares interior life. I could not be but that absolute life circulated in me & I could not think this without being that absolute life. The constant <strife in> warfare in each heart is betwixt Reason & Commodity. The victory is won as soon as any soul has learned always to take sides with Reason against himself; to transfer his Me from his person, his name, his interests, back upon Truth & Justice, so that when he is disgraced & defeated & fretted & disheartened & wasted by nothings, he bears it well, never one instant relaxing his watchfulness, & as soon as he can get a respite from the insults or the sadness, records all these phenomena, pierces their beauty as phenomena, and like a god oversees himself <as a valley>. Thus he harvests his losses & turns the dust of his shoes to gems.
>
> Keep the habit of the observer & as fast as you can, break off your association with your personality & identify yourself with the Universe. Be a football to time & chance[,] the more kicks the better so that you inspect the whole game & know its uttermost laws. As true is this ethics for trivial as for calamitous days. (JMN, 5:391)

Just where Emerson's rhetorical bias falls is, as I have taken some pains to suggest, arguable. What is not disputable, it seems to me, is how ambiguous and problematic Emerson's descriptions of working and being worked on can be—which is to say that a holistic interpretation or any interpretation that defines Emerson's thought as *wholly* any one thing or the other will be wrong. His writing constitutes, rather, a tense, rhetorically powerful amalgam of disparate elements.

The previous chapter emphasized how difficult it can be to pin Emerson down rhetorically. I end this chapter by emphasizing how difficult it can be to pin him down philosophically. Close study of Emerson's thought seems inevitably to reach a point at which the traditional philosophical categorizations appear to blur into one another. One may choose, as I have previously noted, to regard Emerson's philosophy of work as "Apollo's child's play"—or as symptomatic of a traditional, idealist preoccupation with "the power of Thought and of Will" (CW, 1:201). There is a sense, as Danto suggests, in which even Nietzsche's philosophy of will may be defined as a "*dynamic* idealism" with salient affinities to Berkeleian idealism. But Danto also identifies that same philosophy, with its aestheticist ontology, its determination to master and find a "new way to [say] 'Yes'" to a world in which all meaning is humanized, in which all meaning depends on some version of human force, as a form of nihilism.[70]

I would argue that similar ambiguities, as they exist in Emerson's texts, are in themselves sufficient evidence of a rhetorical bias in favor of pragmatism. A pragmatic world view, as Rorty observes in a useful attempt to define the term, will always work to undermine "the traditional distinctions between reason and desire, reason and appetite, reason and will."[71] Thus Emerson can speak synonymously of the Will and the Moral Sentiment (CW, 1:187), define "the atmosphere of moral sentiment" as "the kingdom of the will" (CW, 4:54), speak of the moral law as "the spring of all power" (CW, 1:181), and stress consistently the "energy of the Highest Law" (CW, 2:160).

CHAPTER

6

Detranscendentalizing Emerson

> Our own inevitable concern with synthesis finds [Emerson's] delight in the flux . . . exaggerated, reckless, . . . even meaningless.
>
> —*F. O. Matthiessen, "American Renaissance" (1941)*
>
> Emerson is important not for any solutions proposed by his aphorisms, but for the trouble and contradictions into which his aspirations put him.
>
> —*Richard Poirier, "The Renewal of Literature" (1987)*

"The de-Transcendentalization of the Emerson Image": thus Lawrence Buell christened the major tendency of Emerson criticism in the 1980s—a trend that has certainly continued into the '90s.[1] There was, Buell concluded in 1984, much to celebrate. A diverse array of fresh approaches was rehumanizing, recontextualizing, rehistoricizing an amber-embalmed literary icon. The unexpurgated texts, the complexities of the life and work of the writer who had remained, through most of the twentieth century, a "sacred relic"—a priggish "nice, dry, clean mind"—were being recovered.[2] But Buell's sympathetic appraisal of the Emerson revival also came with an important reservation. A detranscendentalized Emerson was also a fashionable Emerson, a presentist Emerson, an Emerson most suitable for a "1980s mentality." Emerson's writing is, as Buell put it in his closing remarks,

> very likely to provoke present-minded responses that seem powerful at the time but give way to others as the intellectual climate changes. Emerson vis-à-vis Kierkegaard yields to Emerson vis-à-vis social radicalism which yields to Emerson vis-à-vis Nietzsche and Derrida and so on through the succession of dominant isms.[3]

That certainly sounds like a reasonable reservation to bear in mind. Literary scholarship over the past quarter-century has witnessed a relentless "succession of dominant isms." Who has not, in its wake, grown wary of intellectual trends? Interpretation of any kind must always strive to remain self-conscious about its own, inevitable present-mindedness. But there is also reason to suspect that the equation Buell makes—a detranscendentalized reading of Emerson is (merely) a present-minded reading—is too simple, especially in light of those many ironies that surround Emerson's canonization.

Deshrining the Concord Sage is, for one thing, an old and venerable tradition in American literary history. Emerson's Transcendentalist image has, from his own time to ours, so eclipsed his works themselves that his best readers have been ready to resist the image in order to give his extravagant texts the full, skeptical hearing they invite. (If a detranscendentalized Emerson sounds suspiciously like the imposition of the latest-model theory, we need to keep in mind just how extreme and stubbornly ahistorical the Transcendentalist image was to begin with.) The current Emerson revival owes much to a long tradition of writers and critics—Melville, Lowell, Hawthorne, Thoreau, Whitman, Dickinson, and William James can all, at one time or another in their careers, be counted among them—whose skeptical (detranscendentalizing) resistance to Emerson has given us an understanding of the contours and ramifications of his thought obscured by his nineteenth-century canonization as an "angel" and "beautiful transparent soul."[4]

Emerson's best critics continue to take as their starting point the profound disparity that has always existed between his image and his essays themselves. The enshrinement of Emerson the man, Joel Porte argues, has resulted in the "neglect of the literary particulars": "the meaning and value of Emerson's work have typically been overshadowed, and frequently undermined, by an emphasis on his example and personal force." Stanley Cavell proposes that Emerson's very canonization and American culture's failure to believe in "its capacity to produce anything of permanent value" have kept him invisible. Emerson and Thoreau are, he writes, "unknown to the culture whose thinking they worked to found." They "taught us the tongue, established American thinking—and they are repressed." "Emerson has been," Richard Poirier writes, "a pervasive presence, but he has not been allowed to *be* Emerson"; "Emerson's writing makes claims upon us to which we have not yet sufficiently responded."[5]

"De-Transcendentalizing the Emerson Image" cannot, in other words, simply be described as the activation of the latest "ism" or the latest "de." It has, on the contrary, always been a prerequisite for reading him. Nor is the present moment in Emerson studies simply the latest revolution of the wheel of critical fashion. It represents, rather, a unique moment in literary history, one that has not occurred before and will not occur again. For the first time, scholars have, as a whole, been distanced from the vagaries of the Emerson image and the prejudices of Modernism and the New Criticism (which underestimated Romantic literature generally). For the first time, Emerson's unexpurgated journals, notebooks, and lectures have been widely available.

We cannot, therefore, accurately speak of a transcendentalized Emerson that has been agreed on as the standard interpretation, one that now faces the challenge of a detranscendentalizing criticism and will, tomorrow, face other "isms." A standard interpretation of Emerson's work is only now coming into being, at least in the way that has occurred for many of the other authors we usually include in the American canon. Detranscendentalizing Emerson represents a collective evaluation of Emerson's words and ideas (not the image) that has not taken place before, an evaluation that is finally giving his texts the kind of scrutiny that Cooper's, or Hawthorne's, or Melville's have received.

There are other reasons for not taking Emerson's detranscendentalizing as simply present-minded theorizing. Our primary term itself, "Transcendentalism," has long been a source of confusion. To speak of *de*transcendentalizing implies that there exists an original meaning for Transcendentalism sufficiently clear and stable enough to be deconstructed. This, notoriously, is not the case. An anthology could be compiled of all those contemporary accounts of New England Transcendentalism that portrayed "Giant Transcendentalist" as an emperor with no clothes, or at least, as Hawthorne remarked, without comprehensible form, features, or substance: "it is the chief peculiarity of this huge miscreant, that neither he for himself, nor anybody for him, has ever been able to describe them." Transcendentalism has always been what Arthur Lovejoy called a "great catchword"—seminal precisely because it is so "equivocal" or "multivocal." It remains, Thomas McFarland notes, "one of those vast general words . . . that we allow to be thrown about mightily by almost anyone able to string sentences together."[6]

The century and a half in which Emerson has been institutionalized and endlessly classified has, however, made a working definition possible. The *Transcendentalist* Emerson has been many things, but most fundamentally that term has been used in descriptions of him as a *syncretic*—what McFarland calls a "reticulative"—thinker. That is the pivotal feature around which turn those conceptions of him as Romantic idealist, monist, pantheist, Edwardsean mystic, Platonist, Neoplatonist, Hindu, Buddhist, Confucian, saint, beautiful and serene soul, Arnoldian moralist: Emerson as affirmer of Swedenborgian correspondence and Unity of Being, Emerson as organicist reconciler of consciousness and nature, Emerson as believer in the "total integration of the universe," preacher of the doctrine that "the business of all mankind [is] to act in harmony with the movement toward . . . final unity."[7]

Criticism's current questioning of such syncretic claims is clearly one of the trends Buell has in mind when he suggests that a detranscendentalized Emerson is most in keeping with a contemporary mentality. This skeptical, contemporary mentality, and its continuing influence on Emerson studies, is, at least in part, the subject of this chapter. The argument I shall make—that Emerson can be more accurately described as a post-idealist than a Transcendentalist—makes extensive use of a number of recent critics whose work has been shaped, if only indirectly, by deconstruction and by literary theory's current skeptical or negative turn.

But it must be stressed that even this mode of detranscendentalizing is no purely present-minded phenomenon. Detranscendentalizing Transcendentalism was an essential characteristic of the movement itself. American Transcendentalism, with its keen, provincial self-consciousness, its relish for self-dramatization (as the examples of Emerson, Thoreau, Fuller, and Alcott—not to mention Whitman—will attest), must be defined in terms of its own ironic sense of itself—its acute awareness of its own extravagances and the self-skepticism and satire it intentionally inspired. "Imaginative excess coupled with the ability comically to deflate one's own excesses"—the juxtaposition of hyperbole and irony, extravagance and truth-seeking—is, Porte suggests, nothing less than Transcendentalism's defining feature.[8] It is also an essential pattern in Emerson's prose.

Emerson's own most famous attempt to define "The Transcendentalist" is, for instance, among other things, an exercise in detranscendentalizing. The transcendental vision of cosmic unity is certainly there (Emerson defines Transcendentalism as post-Kantian "Idealism as it appears in 1842" [CW, 1:201]). But it is balanced by Emerson's recognition that there exist only "harbingers and forerunners" of a "purely spiritual life" (CW, 1:206), his complaint that idealistic youth never fulfills its promise (CW, 1:209), his concession that the Transcendentalist's faith in a universal moral law rarely lasts for more than an hour (CW, 1:213). Emerson is careful never to identify *himself* as a Transcendentalist, and his seriocomic portrait of the Bartleby-like young man determined to "sit in a corner and *perish*" (CW, 1:212) is a shrewd critique of the potentially self-destructive nature of idealistic protest. (Emerson was often, as David Bromwich notes, "the cruelest satirist of his own followers."[9]) "The Transcendentalist" ends in a climactic vision of cosmic unity to come. But if Emerson has played the prophet, so too has he played the satirist, providing, throughout the essay, a dramatic sense of the overstatement, the unsustainable claims, the "cant and pretension . . . and moonshine" (CW, 1:215) of the idealism he describes.

According to Sherman Paul, "The affirmative was [Emerson's] constant . . . mode of expression."[10] And, to be sure, an affirmative rhetoric plays a crucial role in "The Transcendentalist" and in all of Emerson's essays. But there exists always an alternate rhetoric that laments, even mocks, the "hidden fragmentations" beneath Emerson's syncretic affirmations: an at times elegiac, at times satiric, mode that makes clear the difficulties, even the impossibility, of idealism.[11] Transcendentalizing followed by detranscendentalizing, claiming then disclaiming, defiant self-inflation that invites an antiphonal deflation: this, not a monotone of affirmation, is the essential rhythm in Emerson's essays. "These two states of thought," Emerson remarks, "diverge every moment, and stand in wild contrast" (CW, 1:213); the Transcendentalist's idealist vision remains "the tendency, not yet the realization" (CW, 1:214). Such ironic self-awareness is testament not to an unalloyed idealism but to the conflicted, deconstructive consciousness Paul de Man identifies in Romantic poetry. The "monistic dream of a world in which desire and its object, the forms of the mind and the stuff of reality are continuous" remains a desire, a prophecy, a *dream*—the "intent of consciousness," not reality.[12]

Recent critical theory in the humanities and what Michel Foucault called "the human sciences" is skeptical of idealism and transcendentalism, skeptical of affirmations of the unity of the mind or the self. It deconstructs, detranscendentalizes, deidealizes, deabsolutizes, demystifies. It is skeptical of claims to wholeness, completion, and atonement, skeptical, as Buell notes, of a "visionary-prophetic impulse" that can claim "unmediated vision" or "unmediated expression of vision." It is "based on the notion of discourse as fractured." It leans toward what J. Hillis Miller defines as the antimetaphysical as opposed to the metaphysical approach: it looks not for organic unity but for the way in which purported syntheses "break down into contradictory elements." As Donald Pease comments, "Contemporary criticism, no less than quantum physics, elevates uncertainty into a principle." Recent "theories of undecidability," as one critic has put it, "have changed the interpretive practices of many within the discipline: instead of looking for unities, they look for disunities, contradictions, incoherencies." "We require," Hayden White writes, "a history that will educate us to discontinuity more than ever before: for discontinuity, disruption, and chaos is our lot."[13]

Jerome McGann, for example, argues that "Romanticism is characterized not by its reconciliations, its artistic completeness, but by its *Sehnsucht,* its fragmentations: by its aspirations toward that condition of reconciliation which Hegel [in his "Introduction to the Philosophy of Art"] ascribes to it." The professed Romantic longing for "Harmony," for "a completeness of idea, a completeness of culture, perfection of art . . . , 'Unity of Being,'" is just that—the longing only, or "aspiration toward completeness." The expression of such hypothetical unity is, for McGann, part of "the Romantic ideology"—and criticism should not repeat that ideology in "its own ideological terms" but seek to reveal its explicit or implicit contradictions and ambivalences. Romantic theories, W. J. T. Mitchell suggests, cannot be "taken at face value; none of their self-representations of mastery, comprehension, utopian perfection, or imaginative freedom can be accepted as reliable guides to the understanding of their work."[14]

For Tilottama Rajan, the "belief in the unity of consciousness and nature" we associate with Romantics like Coleridge and Schelling is fundamentally "a defensive reaction." Romantic rhetoric of synthesis—the language of affirmation—is, as Paul de Man argues, *intentional* in structure: the attempt of poetic language to claim an organic view of itself "as a natural and therefore real construct" is "doomed in advance" because poetic language is "unable to give a foundation to what it posits except as an intent of consciousness." "The characteristic of the Romantic text," Rajan writes, "seems to be that it exists on two levels of awareness, often to the point of self-contradiction." To deconstruct such a text, as de Man says, "always has for its target to reveal the existence of hidden articulations and fragmentations within assumedly monadic totalities." Or, as Rajan puts it, "To deconstruct a text is thus to assume that it is a disunified and contradictory structure tacitly involved in contesting its own meaning." "The surface commitment to transparency that runs through Romantic thought," Allan Megill writes, "tends to be undercut by an uneasy sense of the obstacles standing in the way of this transparency."[15]

To detranscendentalize Romantic texts in this sense, then, is to remain skeptical of claims to unity or resolution—to see such claims as (to use Emerson's own term) essentially "prospective," something longed for, taking place only provisionally, or taking place in the future, not the present. To interpret Romantic literature in this way is to be alert to the sense Romantic writers express of the obstacles standing in the way of their professed aspirations. Recent Emersonians, as Buell notes, see Emerson "as more a struggler than an affirmer" and show "a relish for the elements of . . . nonresolution in [his] prose."[16]

This is one reason Stephen Whicher's influential thesis—for forty years now one cornerstone of the Transcendentalist interpretation of Emerson—has come to seem simplistic. Whicher's paradigm (a young, Transcendentalist/idealist Emerson and a mature, skeptical Emerson) overlooks the convergent voices of affirmation and doubt, the concurrent impulses toward unity and fragmentation that run through all of Emerson's essays (and, as the critics I have cited would suggest, through many if not all Romantic texts). The Whicherian approach evades, as Julie Ellison states it, "the central interpretative problem, namely, the constant tension between freedom and fate, convention and rebellion *within* each essay." Romantic texts, Ellison writes, "are now regarded as philosophically unstable, psychologically ambivalent, and ideologically mixed. In this context, teleological readings of individual careers as moving from light to darkness or darkness to light become unworkable."[17]

If it is simplistic to speak of Emerson's Transcendentalism solely in terms of a syncretic or reticulative voice—because transcendentalizing

and detranscendentalizing impulses are always concurrent in Emerson—
neither should it be assumed that Romantic literature in general can be defined as a transcendental movement that has now been detranscendentalized by poststructuralist theory. "The current debate between organicist
and deconstructionist critics over the nature of Romanticism was," as Rajan argues, "originally waged by the Romantics themselves and was not resolved in favor of either side."[18]

The current debate of which Rajan writes is best epitomized in the opposing views of M. H. Abrams and J. Hillis Miller. Romanticism, according to Abrams, is fundamentally a secularized rewriting of the "great circle" of Neoplatonic Christianity, "with its vision of a return from sin to
primal unity." Romantic writers begin in communion with nature, became
separated from it, but make their way back: "We move from alienation,
through spiritual crisis, to a redemptive reintegration with the cosmos and
with our own possibilities." Miller has attacked this view for ignoring Romanticism's "disturbing underside"—most particularly the way Romantic
writers anticipate the twentieth-century's preoccupation with disunity. As
Miller puts it, Abrams "perhaps takes his writers a little too much at face
value, summarizes them a little too flatly, fails to search them for ambiguities or contradictions in their thought." In "the various hesitations and un-
certainties of the Romantics," Miller finds, instead, "a denial of the notion
of primal unity to which, on a manifest level, they seem to be solidly committed."[19]

The Abrams-Miller debate is not new. It is the latest version of an opposition that has occurred whenever a definition of Romanticism has been
attempted: it reflects, as Rajan suggests, a dichotomy within Romantic literature itself. Arthur Lovejoy and René Wellek, taking positions analogous
to Miller's and Abrams's, waged the same argument in the first half of the
twentieth century. As McGann observes, "The difference of opinion sepa-
rating Wellek and Lovejoy merely epitomizes the general terms in which
critics had been discussing the problem of Romanticism for decades."

> What we have come to call Romanticism in literature [McGann writes]
> was a movement born in an era marked by radical sets of conflicts and con-
> tradictions. Later scholars and critics who have labored to define and under-
> stand these phenomena have, not unexpectedly, turned up a mare's nest of
> problems. The extremity of these discussions seemed to be reached in the po-
> sitions taken by Lovejoy, on the one hand, and Wellek on the other. Both ar-
> gued that Romanticism . . . comprised a vast and heterogeneous body of ma-
> terial; . . . but where Wellek saw a basic unity in that diversity, Lovejoy
> argued that critical rigor permitted nothing less precise than a careful "dis-
> crimination of Romanticisms." . . .
>
> In *The Great Chain of Being* Lovejoy had no difficulty showing, from
> original Romantic documents, that Romanticism was a movement which at-
> tacked received ideas of uniformity, standardization, and universality with

"the idealization of diversity," with a program which set the highest value upon the unique, the peculiar, the local: what Schlegel called "the abnormal species of literature . . . even the eccentric and monstrous." Wellek, on the other hand, pursued his investigations under the influence of the integrative impulse present in the earliest programmatic Romantics.[20]

Romantic poetry and philosophy, Rajan suggests, tries "to construct a metaphysics of integration" (as Abrams argues); but it also "anticipates the recognitions of existentialism . . . , of . . . radical modernism," and of deconstruction. Poststructuralist and deconstructive critics have not been the only ones, however, to note that "chaos and discontinuity" can seem "at least as primary as organic unity" in the Romantic period.[21] Seventy years ago, Alfred North Whitehead commented on the way in which the most profound thinkers in the nineteenth century seem to be defined not by the achievement of synthesis but by the irresolvable contradictions they faced and the obscurity that resulted:

> In the earlier times the deep thinkers were the clear thinkers—Descartes, Spinoza, Locke, Leibniz. They knew exactly what they meant and said it. In the nineteenth century, some of the deeper thinkers among theologians and philosophers were muddled thinkers. Their assent was claimed by incompatible doctrines; and their efforts at reconciliation produced inevitable confusion.[22]

Émile Bréhier characterized the period between 1800 and 1850 as a time of great claims to philosophical synthesis and of simultaneous despair over the failure of those claims. The first half of the nineteenth century, Bréhier writes, was a time of "heavy systems." "There was an extraordinary flowering of vast, constructive doctrines, which claimed to reveal the secret of nature and of history and to acquaint man with the law of his destiny, individual and social." But "the unreasonable goals of the philosophical speculation of the period had as their counterpart despair and renunciation." Sénancour complained of boredom, his weak will, and the painful consciousness of "the contrast between what is felt, between the barrenness of what usually is present and the fullness of what is envisioned."[23]

Emerson, too, repeatedly diagnosed the midcentury's disease as lack of will, the penchant for Hamletizing, and the "double consciousness" (CW, 1:213). "This *Ennui,* for which we Saxons had no name, this word of France has got a terrific significance. . . . [B]efore the young American is put into jacket and trowsers, he says, 'I want something which I never saw before;' and 'I wish I was not I'. . . . [The young American's] inaction [arises] out of a scorn of inadequate action . . . , the contrast of the dwarfish Actual with the exorbitant Idea" (CW, 1:180–81). Any definition of Romanticism, or of the Transcendentalism we ascribe to Emerson, will need to take into proper account these omnipresent, contrasting states of mind—transcendental and de- (or anti-) transcendental. "Romantic literature," as Rajan writes, "is better seen as a literature involved in the restless process of self-examination, and in search of a model of discourse which accommodates rather than simplifies its ambivalence toward the inherited equation of art with idealization." Rajan, turning to German theory for the vocabulary that can best "name the specters that haunt an ideal art," suggests the aesthetic ideas of Schiller, Schopenhauer, and Nietzsche as models for gauging and classifying the claims of an organic or transcendental art.[24]

Less schematic and much broader in scope is the distinction McFarland makes between the nineteenth century's "need for reticulation" (the achievement of synthesis or unity of some kind) and the concurrent predominance of "diasparactive" forms and "fragmented modalities." McFarland's thesis, expanded now in a series of books, seems to me as important a contribution to our understanding of the Romantic movement as anything published during the last thirty-five years. Because it provides what I think is an essential background to Emerson, and is central to my own argument, it deserves to be explained in some detail.

In his earlier study, *Coleridge and the Pantheist Tradition,* McFarland emphasized the systematic unity that Coleridge, "and almost all other thinkers of his era, accepted as the necessary condition of any intellectual activity at all." The "urge to system," whether, "as in Hegel, fully enunciated, or, as in Coleridge, merely implied," was a reflection of the epoch's "need to harmonize, to tie things together—what we may call the need for reticulation." The "whole thrust to unity so characteristic of Romanticism"—the revival of the *coincidentia oppositorum* in literature, "the rise of pantheism in religion, of synaesthesia in art, of democracy in politics, of system in philosophy"—may all, McFarland suggests, be considered "an intensification of the reticulative need."[25]

In *Romanticism and the Forms of Ruin: Wordsworth, Coleridge, and Modalities of Fragmentation,* McFarland proposes a "diasparactive" consciousness (from the Greek verb "to rend in pieces" or "to sunder")—not as a refutation of his earlier emphasis on "the omnipresence of system" but as its "necessary complement." The reticulative and diasparactive are finally the two tendencies, the two consciousnesses, that define the Romantic mind—divided, but confluent and necessary to each other's existence. Like Rajan, McFarland sees the reticulative need as a reaction formation, an exercise in "the mechanism of denial," a defensive reaction to a powerful sense of disintegration. "The existence of so powerful a [reticulative] need suggests that the situation actually obtaining must be the contrary of unity: that is, one of fragmentation, of things not tied together, not harmonious, and not architectonically ordered." "Upon closer examination," McFarland writes, "the doctrine of organic form is seen to be unsuccessful in its attempt to bridge the power of the diasparact—indeed, is seen to exist precisely as a kind of despairing response to that power."26

On every front—philosophical, religious, political, economic—the nineteenth century offered not the possibility of a unified or powerful self but "a mounting pressure on the ego" that needed to be confronted, coped with, in some way resisted or overcome. The Romantic commitment to Unity, to reconciled oppositions, exists as a reaction formation in the face of "a single truth that constitutes the Romantic core." That single truth, which became more apparent as the century wore on, is "the diminishment of man's sense of self and its value."27 Like Rajan, McFarland turns to German theory—Hegel's definition of "the unhappy consciousness"—for the most perceptive commentary on the gap between transcendental claims and the ironic awareness of ineluctable conflict:

> For incompleteness, fragmentation and ruin—the diasparactive triad—constitute the deepest underlying truth of Romanticism's experience of reality. The normative awareness of the century as a whole was what Hegel termed "das unglückliche Bewußtsein," the unhappy consciousness. And the unhappy consciousness was a consciousness of irreconcilable conflict—was [in Hegel's words] "the consciousness of self as a divided nature, a doubled and merely contradictory being." As . . . [Edward Bostetter] has urged, "even a cursory examination of the writings of the major Romantic poets reveals that the traditional view is seriously oversimplified and misleading. . . . What seems at first glance triumphant affirmation, is revealed on closer observation as a desperate struggle for affirmation against increasingly powerful obstacles."28

I have, throughout this study, argued along lines congruent with McFarland's approach to Romanticism. I have examined the psychology of self-overcoming, self-strengthening, and resistance to adversity, failure, metaphysical flux—all that threatens the ego—that lies, as a defensive reaction, at the core of Emerson's writing. I have argued that Emerson's affirmations of power are never simply retreats into the ideal or projections of a serenely unbridled ego. I have suggested that Emerson's psychology is the embodiment of Kenneth Burke's principle that every imaginative act originates "in terms of a situation and as a strategy for confronting and encompassing that situation." I have suggested that every Emersonian claim to power arises out of a particular situation—some perceived threat to human force, some fear for "the decay of humanism," fear for "the diminishment of man's sense of self and its value"—and is meant to represent some strategy for coping with that situation.29 What needs to be stressed, in concluding this section, is the way Romantic Transcendentalism or Organicism, for all its claims to unity, actually depends on an underlying, profound sense of disunity. In other words, transcendentalizing and detranscendentalizing were, in the Romantic period, complementary, mutually sustaining modes of perception.

To argue that Emerson is inconsistent, that there are profound contradictions in his thought, is nothing new. It is a (detranscendentalizing) criticism made by Emerson in his own works, a criticism he invited throughout his career, thereby inaugurating a central tradition in Emerson criticism. The attempt to explain or account for his contradictions has become a common starting point for his critics. What have changed over the past two decades are the assumptions about Romanticism, about the nineteenth century, about literature and literary interpretation in general, that critics have brought to the pivotal problem of Emerson's "double consciousness."

The two epigraphs that begin this chapter epitomize those differences. The first quotation represents an approach that takes "reticulation" (the achievement of synthesis or unity) as the fundamental concern of literary interpretation generally, as the underlying goal of Romantic literature as a whole, and as the primary goal of Emerson's own writing and aesthetic in particular. Although it is an approach acutely sensitive to divisions in Emerson's thought, it evaluates his writing in monistic terms: Emerson's aesthetic goal is to make "the word one with the thing"; to "unite the solid with the ethereal"; to span "the gap between the two poles of thought . . . , fact and abstraction, the many and the One, society and solitude"; to reassert the "mystical" synthesis of understanding and soul, mind and feeling, that has been sundered in America since the death of Jonathan Edwards and "the breakdown . . . of the Puritan synthesis."[30] The drama in Emerson's writing, the drama the critic needs to recapture, lies in Emerson's movement toward wholeness, toward organic unity.

"Organic wholeness," Matthiessen writes, "was what [Emerson] admired most." Matthiessen applies Emerson's own professed syncretic aspirations ("in good writing, words become one with things") as the critical standard for assessing his writing. What he finds, however, is not synthesis or wholeness but further contradiction. And because Emerson's professed desire for unity is used as the criterion, his actual writing can only be faulted. Emerson ends up hoist by (what Matthiessen has taken as) his own petard. What Matthiessen finds is a "drastic paradox": Emerson's organic aesthetic does not seem to shape his own practice. "We can hardly assess Emerson's work in the light of his theory of language and art," Matthiessen concludes (though this is precisely what he has done), "since there is such disproportion between his theory and any practice of it." It is in the sensuous particulars of Thoreau's writing that Emerson's theory finds its true embodiment, according to Matthiessen, although his description of Thoreau's achievement suggests how much his discussion of

Romantic ideas actually owes to an Eliotic, New Critical sensibility. Thoreau, with his dogged respect for facts, successfully made the word and the thing one—thereby uniting "thought with sense impression, the immediate feeling with the reflection upon it." He achieved, like Donne in the seventeenth century, T. S. Eliot's ideal of a "unified sensibility."[31]

Matthiessen is painfully aware of Emerson's "inveterate habit of stating things in opposites," but he never wavers in his conclusion that reticulation is the aesthetic goal, the primary shaping mode of perception informing Emerson's thought and his practice as a writer, even though monistic terms do not, finally, serve Emerson well and do little to account for his contradictions. Matthiessen ends up reasoning in the way that has so often, as Porte argues, undermined the meaning and value of Emerson's work: by emphasizing the Emerson *image,* by affirming the wholeness, not of the writing, which is judged a failure in its attempt to find a syncretic form, but of the personality. Although Emerson "never created a form great enough to insure that his books will continue to be read," the genius of his personal example is "uncontestable." "The danger now," Matthiessen writes, "is that in the multiplicity of his conflicting statements, we shall miss the wholeness of character lying beneath them." Matthiessen's criticism of Emerson as a failed organicist also involves a moral criticism. Emerson's inability to unite idea and experience encouraged him, Matthiessen says, "to ignore experience whenever it was in harsh or ugly conflict with his optimism."[32]

My aim is not to diminish Matthiessen's achievement: *American Renaissance* continues to deserve—richly deserve—its canonical status. But Matthiessen's discussion represents an approach to Emerson that is still common, even though it is the Emerson chapters in *American Renaissance* that now seem most dated. Those critics who have followed Matthiessen, expanding the argument that Emerson can be best understood as an organicist, have faced the same problems.

Richard P. Adams's important essay, "Emerson and the Organic Metaphor," is a good example. Adams intends to correct those interpretations of Emerson that account for his contradictions by deferring to "some unexplainable, perhaps mystical, consistency in his character." It is Emerson's organic theories, his reliance on Romanticism's "organic principle," Adams argues, that can best be used "to explain his meaning and to evaluate his aesthetic achievements." But Adams, like Matthiessen, finds that Emerson, more often than not, fails to practice the organicism Adams takes as his master term. *Nature*'s language "fails to assimilate the organic idea which it struggles to express." In the first *Essays* and in "most of Emerson's work . . . there are gaps, perhaps in his thinking, certainly in his writing, left unfilled." Few of the essays "have anything like the organic unity which the New Critics and their predecessors in the romantic tradition have taught us to expect." They "lack the very qualities of structural relatedness . . . and unity which Emerson considered the most important attributes of the universal reality." "Nevertheless," Adams concludes, "I believe Emerson was a great writer."[33]

Unfortunately, Adams winds up practicing the very strategy he has criticized, the same tactic Matthiessen employed: Emerson's greatness has to be located *outside* his actual writing. Like Matthiessen, Adams suggests that it is in other writers that Emerson's greatness is most evident—in writers like Melville, Henry James, or Faulkner, who "have practiced Emerson's method more consistently, and to better effect, than he was able to do himself." And although Adams criticizes other critics for rescuing Emerson from his contradictions by appeals to the ineffable, his organic interpretation leads him to a similar, semimystical position. Emerson's essays are organic but never "perfect organisms in themselves." They must be appreciated as part of a "macrocosmic," "universal" unity larger than any single, human composition.[34]

The other possible explanation Adams offers for Emerson's contradictions is the now common argument that the essays move "back and forth, or up and down, from statements of diversity to declarations of unity and back again to diversity" in a "dialectic unity." Yet one wonders if the various syncretic explanations Adams provides are really true to his own experience of Emerson's writing: he values most the essay in which Emerson moves furthest away from organic principles. "He was at his best," Adams says, in "'Experience,' where he admitted most liberally the confused and contradictory character of human life and refrained from building on it any further in the direction of unity than the nature of his materials permitted."[35]

Adams's organicist approach leads him, as it did Matthiessen, to aesthetic *and* moral criticisms of Emerson. Emerson's writing fails to achieve a union of ideas and experience, just as his moral vision neglects pain and tragedy. The essays, in their search for unity, ignore "the confused, weltering world we live in." The "cosmic optimism," the premise that all things are "ultimately organized in perfect unity," seems unearned: "it is a unity that we cannot see, and that Emerson cannot show us." Emerson's premise of "final unity," Adams writes, is forced on the facts of experience "in such a way as to do them violence." Adams is, like Matthiessen, clearly aware of Emerson's many contradictions; nevertheless, he ascribes to him an ultra-organicist vision of total harmony, then condemns him for "reckless . . . celebration of the perfection of the universe."[36]

This chapter's second epigraph, from Poirier's *The Renewal of Literature,* typifies the current, detranscendentalizing tendency in Emerson criticism. Poirier's interest in Emerson's contradictions, not his proposed resolutions, characterizes the recent criticism that takes organicism as neither the defining principle of Romanticism nor the fundamental concern of criticism. Richard Adams criticized Emerson for pronouncements that came recklessly or too easily; recent criticism emphasizes the struggle and complications, the antagonism and resistance, involved in Emerson's affirmations. A monistic or organic critical framework, one that defines the central drama in Emerson's writing as the reticulative movement toward wholeness, has, more and more, been replaced by a criticism aware of the diasparactive context of Emerson's thought.

"With so fervent a vision of transcendence," as Harold Bloom put it in 1982, "there must be an implication of a radical dualism, despite Emerson's professed monistic desires, his declarations that he is a seer of unity." That may well serve as a summary statement for much Emerson criticism in the last twenty years. Increasingly, critics have stressed Emerson's "antagonizing mind" (CW, 3:39)—not his "professed monistic desires" but the dualisms that are a vital and necessary part of his thought. Increasingly, it has been Emerson's "metamorphic religion of power," as Bloom calls it, not his vision of final unity that critics have taken as his true legacy.[37]

The Renewal of Literature is a case in point. Poirier's recovery of a neglected, pragmatic, and agonistic Emersonian tradition embodies, in a multitude of ways, the recent critical trends I have highlighted; it may well represent something of a watershed, an influential culminating moment in the detranscendentalization of Emerson and a turning point for Emerson criticism as a whole. Like Bloom, Poirier takes the radical dualism evident in Emerson's always-antagonizing mind as central. Poirier is most concerned with "the Emersonian vocabulary of 'fact,' 'action,' and 'power'" and sees Emersonian identity, both personal and literary, as originating in the act of resistance. Emerson's central tropes are not syncretic but the tropes of "breakage, displacement, and disappearance." That accounts, Poirier argues, for the intentionally antiorganic, "characteristically Emersonian blur" in Emerson's prose: "Within a given paragraph, he tends not to develop an argument in the direction already laid down by a previous remark but to veer away from it, as from some constraining influence."[38]

According to Poirier, two contesting voices—one self-affirming, reticulative, transcendental; another self-effacing, diasparactive, and antitranscendental—resound through Emerson's prose. Ultimately, Emerson's commitment to "breakage, displacement, and disappearance" is so deep, his distrust of all "the codifications of life" so intense, that he implies a writing off of the self—an antihumanistic vision that throws into question "any settled, coherent idea of the human," including "the very idea of Man" and the authority of literature itself.[39]

Poirier is here preceded by several readers who have noted Emerson's preoccupation with power—his apparent *Bemächtigungstrieb* (instinct for mastery) or his Nietzschean ideal of *Selbstüberwindung* (self-overcoming). But in his conception of an Emersonian commitment to writing as essentially reactive—existing in those acts of "resistance," "antagonism," "transition," and "abandonment" through which literature simultaneously effaces and renews itself—Poirier is most immediately preceded by Julie Ellison. "Like all true Romantics," Ellison argues, Emerson "alternately celebrates discontinuity and wishes it could be teleologically resolved." But "his preference is clearly for antagonistic differences rather than organic integrations": the "oppositional tendency is one of the spiritual laws of [his] prose." Ellison has carefully charted the continuously reenacted pattern in which Emerson longs for or seems to come close to some kind of unity of conception or tone, or a final, monistic vision of resolution, only to return to a vision of conflict or "binary opposition" in which discontinuity and aggression can be reembraced and continued.[40] Ellison provides what may serve as another summary statement of recent dualistic interpretations of Emerson:

> [Emerson's] expressions of an optimistic faith in dialectical synthesis should not be honored over his periodic recognitions of irreconcilable polarities. He alternates between the hope for transcendent resolutions and skepticism toward them. When antitheses do issue in synthesis, it rarely endures for more than a paragraph; contradiction is no sooner resolved than it is repeated. Dialectic, by definition, cannot mean mere alternation, and so necessarily misdescribes prose that accumulates but does not progress. Emerson's writing can just as well be called anti-dialectical, for its possible unities continually break apart into antagonistic opposites.[41]

Barbara Packer sees Emerson as ultimately transcending dualism, but her own influential close reading of the major essays is similarly focused on the "unresolved contradictions, [the] cracks not to be soldered or welded." Packer's analysis of Emerson's rhetoric remains the single most important counterstatement to Matthiessen's thesis that Emerson was, in theory at least, an organicist. Emerson's rhetoric, Packer claims, is not, nor does it aspire to be, syncretic. Instead, it promotes and exploits its lack of connections, its indeterminacy of tone, its breakings of decorum. What Henry James and Matthiessen criticized as Emerson's formlessness, Packer sees as an often-calculated refusal on Emerson's part to provide transitions or explanations. Emerson, Packer argues, could be deeply skeptical "about the capacity of language to embody truth." He recognized that language is indeterminate, that words "cannot cover the dimensions of what is in truth. They break, chop, and impoverish it" (CW, 1:28). His famous laconism offered its own higher reasoning. As a rhetorician, Emerson "celebrates the virtues of absence, the exhilarations of discontinuity."[42]

There are other critics I could include at this point, critics whose work over the past two decades exemplifies the current shift of emphasis away from Emerson's attempts at resolution and toward the at times self-effacing, at times creative, antagonisms in his prose.[43] My main point, however, should be clear. The transcendental and organic terms in which Emerson has traditionally been read and taught are simply too limited to do justice to the complexity of his thought. They are too limited to do justice to Romantic writing generally, and they always have been.

The interpretation of Emerson as a fundamentally syncretic or organic thinker has, as I have argued, led repeatedly to a critical dead end. Emerson's actual writing fails to exemplify its professed organic theory, and it is therefore devalued. At the same time, Emerson is condemned because his purported organicist faith in the ultimate relationship "between the apparently incompatible facts of experience" is morally naive.[44] It seems impossible, given the organicist framework, for Emerson to escape punishment.

The perception of Emerson as an organicist—a major component of the Emerson image—also plays a prominent role in a long tradition in which Emerson's thought has been radically dehistoricized. That Emerson speaks an eternal, transcendent wisdom, one that was peculiarly immune to the intellectual currents of its time, became one of the unshakable commonplaces of Emerson's nineteenth-century hagiography. It survived as part of the Emerson image in the twentieth century, and it can be detected even in the work of the most scholarly of Emerson's critics. That image of a hieratic, bodiless Emerson, an Emerson who will somehow always elude critical or historical comprehension, surely echoes in the background of Whicher's warning to critics ("The more we know him, the less we know him") or his acknowledgment that "the story of [Emerson's] thought" seems to exist "like an episode from a vanished past," outside the mainstream of modern, or post-Enlightenment, intellectual history.[45]

Even in Whicher's contention that Emerson's thought had a "personal," not a "logical," structure, that it existed in the extreme psychological states of "transcendence or despair," "entire assurance or . . . none at all," one senses some unwillingness or unreadiness to see Emerson against the background of the larger patterns of Western thought, of idealist philosophy particularly, from 1820 to 1860. Even Jonathan Bishop's speculation that Emerson's nineteenth century was a more unified age than our own, one more appropriate for Transcendentalism's "perennial philosophy," or his evaluation of Emerson's career primarily in terms of its Romantic and Victorian periods, suggests an unwillingness to evaluate Emerson's "idealism" in the larger context of post-Hegelian philosophy.[46]

One may agree with Henry James that Emerson is finally an "irreducible spirit" or with Whicher that "there is something enigmatic about most American authors" and still wish for a firmer sense of historical and intellectual context than that underlying the Transcendentalist-organicist image of Emerson. E. R. Curtius, for example, defined Emerson's vitalism as bringing all things together in one great, timeless harmony. Although

Curtius perceived a connection between Emerson's monistic, spiritual vision and a Balzacian "Theory of the Unity of the All," he concluded that Emerson's essays exist "alien . . . and remote, like the 'beautiful children of God.' . . . If we try to find a respect in which they are connected with another intellectual production of the period, almost nothing valid presents itself." Paul Elmer More, confirming Emerson's saintly links to Plato, Buddha, and Jesus, similarly maintained that "the truth that Emerson proclaimed is the old, old commonplace that has arisen before the minds of sages and prophets from the beginning of time." John Jay Chapman, who left us an incisive record of what Emerson meant to another nineteenth-century American, belied the specificity of his own historical account when he concluded that the perfectly serene sage who spoke only eternal ideas was free "from the tangles and qualifications of circumstance": "It is as if a man had been withdrawn from the earth and dedicated to condensing and embodying this eternal idea—the value of the individual soul—so vividly, so vitally, that his words could not die. . . . [H]is philosophy . . . consisted of a very simple drawing together of a few ideas, all of which had long been familiar to the world." ("The fancy that the good, the true, the beautiful . . . are somehow connected together and are really one thing," Chapman continues, was "the cornerstone" of Emerson's thought.)[47]

For Santayana, too, Emerson's syncretic thought ("the unity of all minds in the single soul of the universe, which is the same in all creatures") existed in a sacred void:

> If we ask ourselves what was Emerson's relation to the scientific and religious movements of his time, and what place he may claim in the history of opinion, we must answer that he belonged very little to the past, very little to the present, and almost wholly to that abstract sphere into which mystical or philosophical aspiration has carried a few men in all ages. . . . He belonged by nature to that mystical company of devout souls that recognize no particular home and are dispersed throughout history.[48]

Interpreting Emerson's "idealism" as the declaration of eternal Unity of Being, pantheistic Harmony, cosmic optimism, mysticism, Platonism, or Neoplatonism obscures the persistent divisions, the complex conflict of voices and impulses, that characterize his writing. It ignores the immediate philosophical context of the early and middle nineteenth century, decades in which the fractured course of European thought, of German idealism particularly, mirrors precisely the fundamental contradictions in Emerson's writing. Emerson's idealism, what we take as his Transcendentalism—his syncretic or organic aspirations, his famous affirmations—was "idealism as it appears in 1842." It needs to be viewed against the larger backdrop of European thought from 1820 to 1860, the decades in which the collective system making and vast hopes for final, philosophical synthesis that

characterized the late eighteenth and early nineteenth centuries were yielding to a new concern for what Emerson called "practical power," giving
way to philosophies of will, new philosophies of power, a new "anthropology."

Discussions of Emerson as an organicist generally proceed as if he wrote
not in the mid-nineteenth century but several decades earlier, when the
work of defining a sympathetic or organic imagination and an inclusive,
synthetic philosophy reached its apex. But the great age of idealistic synthesis, the age that produced the German and English conception of a
"creative imagination," was beginning to wane and move toward a point
of crisis before 1820. By 1836, when Emerson published his first book, the
ambitious, syncretic philosophical projects of Schelling or Hegel were being replaced by the search for a new elemental force, the search for "the
motive power in a world which everybody agreed was a dynamic one."
The mid-1830s and early 1840s, the decade Whicher defined as Emerson's
transcendental period, were precisely the years in which European idealisms were undergoing crises and transformations. It was, John Toews
writes, "a radical turning point in western man's experience and self-consciousness." Those were the decades in which Hegelian idealism, the most
significant synthesis of the transcendent and the immanent achieved in the
Romantic period, broke down in "the transition from 'the actualization of
the absolute' to the 'self-actualization of man,' from the incarnation of the
transcendent in the immanent to the self-production of man's immanent
essence in concrete historical existence." With the post-Hegelian recognition of man's "transcendental 'homelessness'" there came a new "commitment to the necessity or at least possibility of a completely immanent, natural, and/or historical actualization of human redemption."[49]

It was during this period, the years in which Emerson began his career
as a writer, that Hegelian idealism—the central example of the "hunger for
unity" that marked the German Romantics—was "inverted" or "reduced"
in Left Hegelian humanism and eventually was turned on its head by
Marx. "Hegel's rhetoric about 'system' and '*Wissenschaft*,'" Richard
Rorty writes, was not the part of Hegel's work that "mattered to Marx, or
more generally, to the historical and political thought of the nineteenth
century. What mattered were precisely those parts that turned away from
the knowledge of nature, from the phenomenon of the New Science, to the
historicist self-understanding and self-determination of human beings."[50]
The root contradictions, patterns, and transformations in Emerson's
thought, however they may form a purely "personal structure," must also
be seen as incorporating and echoing the major philosophical transformations of the nineteenth century. What was left behind as the century pro-
gressed was, as Rorty suggests, the Hegelian wish for synthesis, for system
and *Wissenschaft*. What gained strength was that part of Hegelianism that
stressed human self-determination. Emerson's essays, composed during a

crisis point for idealistic philosophy in Europe, record the longing to follow both those paths—and they are philosophically confused (but quintessentially of the middle nineteenth century) because of it.

I do not dispute René Wellek's well-known conclusion that American Transcendentalism cannot "be described as a *result* of German idealism" (my italics). Yet Wellek's conviction that the Transcendentalists "should not be coupled with German philosophy," that "the ancestry of Transcendentalism includes almost the whole intellectual history of mankind," ultimately reaffirms the image of the sage who exists out of time, out of history. The "better understanding and higher evaluation of the Romantic and nineteenth-century writers" that characterizes the present moment in criticism has been gained, as Geoffrey Hartman notes, by the correction, over the past decades, of the Anglo-American "forgetting of Romantic . . . especially German Romantic, thinking." The more Romantic writing is considered outside the central intellectual trends in the late eighteenth and early nineteenth centuries and apart from the German tradition that lies at its core, the more it tends to be underestimated as only mysticism or nature poetry. This has been especially true in the case of Emerson, who still exists in the public mind as a "Yankee Kahlil Gibran." I am arguing for context, not direct influence. Emerson throughout his career remained cheerfully recalcitrant to any direct study of German philosophy: Hegel's headache-inducing "dry bones of thought" were no exception. But the first half of the nineteenth century, though Emerson christened it "the age of Swedenborg," was more correctly, as Matthiessen observed, the age of Hegel and the transformations of Hegelian idealism.[51]

The course of German idealism from Kant into the nineteenth century represents, David Simpson writes, "the movement away from concentration on the unchanging operations of mind towards the positing of some dynamic and practical version of what Schopenhauer calls the 'will.'" That pattern is already evident in the eighteenth century in Fichte's treatment of the "drives" *[Trieben]* and "the one indivisible primary force *[Grundkraft]* in man" and in Schelling's conception of "force" *[Kraft]*. "The general tendency observable in the history of philosophy between Kant and Hegel or Schopenhauer [is] roughly speaking a movement from an emphasis on knowledge to an emphasis on will." It "seems undeniable," Simpson notes, "that [the philosophies of Fichte, Schelling, Hegel, and Schopenhauer] more and more admit, even as they qualify, what we may call a philosophy of will—by which I mean one more and more explicitly founded upon the modifications enacted upon subjectivity by interest and appetite, by history or ideology, by the unconscious."[52]

The seeds of the nineteenth century's turn toward radical "anthropologization" were already laid in the eighteenth century's expressivist notion of true freedom as residing only in the authentic expression of the deepest, the organic, the true and "natural" self. The expressivist notion of freedom (incorporated by Kant, transposed by Hegel and again by Marx) "turns into the idea that human nature is not simply a given, but is to be made over." "The great expressivist protests against the course of modern civilization," Charles Taylor writes, "have incorporated this notion of willed transformation of nature, both human and external, as an essential part of man's fulfilment." From the revolutionary transpositions carried out by the Young Hegelians of the 1830s and 1840s and the Promethean ideology of Marxism, to anarchism, to fascism, the "expressivist anthropology" of the late eighteenth century has resulted in movements both political and artistic that have stressed "the release of pent-up 'elemental' forces in man."[53]

Emerson's thought reflects that same course of deflection from the earlier idealistic conception (found in Herder and the German Romantics) of some Divine Unity, Divine Absolute or One, some immanent "World-Spirit" of which "the inner forces of man, the hidden drives and secret power in all things" are the expression, to a new, narrowed focus on what Marx emphasized in his conception of *"praxis"*—a new concern for *man's* capacity for changing himself and changing history.[54] In its general outline of Marx shattering and turning Hegelian idealism upside down or in the traumatic course Emerson is forced to take in "Experience" (and throughout his essays), from some longed-for unity to a consciousness of a very human fragmentation, to the new prophecy that "the *true romance* which the world exists to realize, will be the transformation of genius into practical power" (CW, 3:49; my italics), the movement is in essence a kind of "Fall of Man" (CW, 3:43), as Emerson says, from the old "romance" of a religious or quasi-religious or Hegelian synthesis or wholeness of vision to a new consciousness that carries its own compensation of radical self-determination.

"Detranscendentalizing Emerson" may sound like a thoroughly chronocentric (or present-minded) exercise, another manifestation of the hermeneutics of suspicion now predominant within the academy. That is unfortunate. For Emerson's detranscendentalization is a necessary process that can help us restore the "historical ecology" of his thought.[55] For historically it is more accurate to think of Emerson as a post-idealist (or post-transcendentalist); that designation will take us further in our efforts to understand the complexities of his thought and the entanglements he faced as a nineteenth-century thinker than will the relatively ahistorical and one-dimensional tags of idealist, organicist, and Transcendentalist, though those are now well-established pieces in the Emerson image. That there are fundamental contradictions in Emerson's thought is, it seems to me, undeniable: they are, I am arguing, best understood as contradictions faced by any would-be syncretic philosophy in the post-Hegelian, mid-nineteenth century—an epoch in which transcendental systems were detranscendentalized or reshaped and redefined (according to their own implicit tendencies) as philosophies of will.

The massive nineteenth-century attraction to what Bréhier calls "heavy systems"—the effort on the continent and in England to find a new synthesis of knowledge, a new science, a new and effective cosmic vision for the age—was very much a part of the American Transcendentalists' hope to lay the groundwork for the perfect community and state. It defines the transatlantic background for Thoreau's attempt to find "the only true America," forge the foundation of "a true expression," discover a "Realometer," present a "true account" of the facts of life, and write the perfect, apocalyptic book.⁵⁶ It underlies, as well, Emerson's longing to utter the "truest word ever spoken," attain "the science of the real" (CW, 3:8), and find, at last, the one "true theory" that "will explain all phenomena" (CW, 1:8).

The "paramount intellectual influence" of the modern age, as Emerson put it in 1840, was the synthesizing, systematizing "genius of the German nation": German intellectual activity encompassed "poetic . . . scientific, religious, and philosophical domains." Modern literature in general was characterized by its Germanic "insatiable demand for unity—the need to recognize one nature in all the variety of objects,—which always characterizes a genius of the first order." Emerson singled out Goethe—poet, naturalist, and philosopher—for his talent for uniting in himself all the tendencies of the age. Goethe succeeded in reconciling the age's encyclopedia of facts ("What he could so reconcile was good; what he could not, was false").⁵⁷ Emerson clearly had a new kind of Goethe in mind when he spoke, in 1841, of "some profound and all-reconciling thinker" to come (CW, 1:176).

But fundamental tensions and ambiguities were, as David Simpson suggests, "necessarily apparent in any nineteenth-century system with . . . total [syncretic] aspirations." In Hegel's vast synthesis those contradictions had to be included as necessary moments in the larger dialectic: "the Absolute" *was,* in fact, "the labor of the concept," the "drama of . . . [the] testing out" of contradictory visions. "It is . . . part of [Hegel's] theory that, whilst the evolution of *Geist* may indeed be received as a synthesis of reason and faith, it is yet obliged to reveal within itself all the traces of the forms of thought it purports to transcend. Such inclusiveness is the very essence of sublimation and remembrance, *Aufhebung* and *Erinnerung.*"⁵⁸

It was Hegel's ambition to reconcile the contradictions of thought and philosophy, self and nature, man and God, his attempt to synthesize philosophy, art, politics, history, economy, science, and religion into a single cosmic vision, "cheerful & large" (as Emerson phrased it [JMN, 11:187]), that roused Emerson's as well as Whitman's interest in him. Hegel's titanic effort to achieve a final synthesis and the "decomposition"[59] of that synthesis after 1820 makes Hegelian idealism an essential background against which Emerson's "idealism" and the claims and high hopes of Transcendentalist writing must be measured. For what defines Emerson's thought is *not* its success as an organic, omnisynthetic philosophy or cosmic vision (though the often-expressed *longing* for such resolution *is* characteristically Emersonian) but its significance as a post-Hegelian or post-idealist philosophy of will, or, to use the phrase usually applied to Nietzsche, "philosophy of power."

Emerson was, as I have suggested, drawn to both the Hegelian desire for synthesis and the mid-nineteenth-century's new emphasis on human self-determination. He welcomed consequently—as has often been noted—both system making and system breaking. "To break all prisons" (EJ, 248) and "unsettle all things" (CW, 2:188) were two of his rhetorical goals. "The system grinder," he declared, "hates the truth" (EL, 1:327). Fixed creeds, Emerson says, are a "disease of the intellect." We err if we stop to weep with those who are "infirm of will," for truth and health come in "rough electric shocks": "Power ceases in the instant of repose; it resides in the moment of transition from a past to a new state, in the shooting of the gulf, in the darting to an aim" (CW, 2:45, 44, 40). Valor, Emerson says in "Circles," "consists in the power of self-recovery." That ceaseless process of self-recovery that is Emerson's definition of identity is founded on the recognition that there is nowhere anything final. In order to gain the power of identity that universal flux can confer, man must relinquish his hope for absolute meaning and place himself in the position of anticipating always a new truth that will displace "his past apprehension of truth." He must resolutely accept "that his laws, his relations to society, his christianity, his world, may at any time be superseded and decease" (CW, 2:183).

But if Emerson loved formless energy for its own sake, he also revered the "methodizing mind" (W, 12:20) and loved "whatever affirms, connects, preserves" (CW, 4:96).

> Not only man puts things in a row, but things belong in a row. . . . It is certain that however we may conceive of the wonderful little bricks of which the world is builded, we must suppose a similarity and fitting and identity in their frame. It is necessary to suppose that every hose in Nature fits every hydrant; so only is combination, chemistry, vegetation, animation, intellection possible. Without identity at base, chaos must be forever. (W, 12:20)

Emerson's reading in Goethe had encouraged his prominent interest in science and scientific laws. According to his editors, he took "the great fact of 'modern history' [as] the emerging discovery in every department of life of 'certain external laws'" (EL, 2:5). "The most striking trait of modern science," he contended, "is its approximation towards central truths" (EL, 2:27). "This reduction to a few laws, to one law, is not a choice of the individual. It is the tyrannical instinct of the mind. . . . The immense variety of objects is really composed of a few elements. The world is the fulfilment of a few laws" (EL, 2:23, 25). The new laws of electricity and magnetism, the systems of Newton, Hooke, Boscovich, and Davy—"all these, whether they are premature generalizations or not, indicate the central unity, the common law that pervades nature from the deep centre to the unknown circumference" (EL, 2:29).

But Emerson was not really interested in resting in final scientific or positivistic laws. What ultimately moved him about the idea of science or system making was—it is that characteristic turn of his thought we have seen so often before—the *effect* it had on the will of the individual, the sense of power it conferred:

> Every system of faith, every theory of science, every argument of a barrister, is a classification, and gives the mind the sense of power in proportion to the truth or centrality of the traits by which it arranges. Calvinism, Romanism, and the Church of Swedenborg, are three striking examples of coherent systems which each organize the best-known facts of the world's history, and the qualities of character into an order that reacts directly on the will of the individual. (EL, 2:25)

What most concerns Emerson is not synthesis, metaphysical systems, or natural history but the practical effect, the power a "domesticated" or anthropomorphized knowledge brings with it. "I want not the logic, but the power, if any, which [metaphysics] brings into science and literature; the man who can humanize this logic, these syllogisms, and give me the results. . . . My metaphysics are to the end of use. I wish to know the laws of this wonderful power, that I may domesticate it" (W, 12:11–14).

Hegel's idealistic synthesis succeeded on its own terms.[60] Emerson's thought—drawn to both the systematic coherence Hegel's theory represents and the contrary desire to resist any final system—often fails to satisfy its own inclinations and fails to reconcile its contradictions or its own habitual "dialectic." (Recall Ellison's hypothesis that dialectic misdescribes Emerson's dualisms. The possible unities his writing offers "continually break apart into antagonistic opposites.") A thorough comparison of Emerson's brand of putative idealism with Hegel's would reveal, I think, the ways in which Emerson fails to reconcile the crucial contradictions in eighteenth-century idealism that Hegel recognized and attempted to resolve. Hegel believed that he had definitively bridged the central breach in Kant's philosophy: the division between inclination and reason, the expressivist ideal of freedom and the Kantian conception of the freedom of moral autonomy. Any philosophy that failed to heal that division would be condemned, Hegel prophesied, to a "bad infinity"—a Romantic, limitless creativity or subjectivity that hamstrings itself of the ability to find and settle on a true expression of itself.[61]

Emerson's thought often seems to arrive at that God-forsaken landscape, as Hegel called it, where the Romantic spirit remains self-divided, the victim of shifting "moods," craving an authentic self-expression yet in love with the endless cycle of destructive and creative force. "By going one step farther back in thought," Emerson writes in a pronouncedly Hegelian moment, "discordant opinions are reconciled, by being seen to be two extremes of one principle." But he then proceeds to annex the characteristically Emersonian conclusion that there can be no conclusion, no final, Hegelian synthesis—"and we can never go so far back as to preclude a *still higher vision*" (CW, 2:183; my italics).

This is an often-overlooked pattern of his thought we have seen before. Emerson's writing, like Thoreau's, remains haunted by its own ironic sense of "prospectiveness," its lament for life's lack of wholeness and its concurrent anticipation of some ultimate theory or vision that will reconcile oppositions, unify humanity's fragmented powers, and usher in the new birth of the individual and a reawakened literature and society. "The structure, tone, and themes of Transcendentalist writing," as Buell states it, "all convey a strong but precarious sense of imminent fulfilment. The possibilities are boundless, but nothing may come of them; the world is full of meaning, but that meaning is yet to be disclosed." "Every intellection is mainly prospective," Emerson insists: "Its present value is its least" (CW, 2:197). "All promise outruns the performance. . . . Every end is prospective of some other end, which is also temporary; a round and final success nowhere" (CW, 3:110).[62]

Unable to achieve, and ultimately uninterested in attaining, even within its own limits, any final "central Unity" (CW, 1:28), Emerson's thought takes as its true subject the recording of the "law of undulation" (CW, 2:197) that governs its own wavering, irreconcilable energies or, as he often called them, his "moods." It is an appropriate, if, on Emerson's part, struggle-filled and at times painful, solution for an American mind in the middle of the nineteenth century. It incorporates in its own way the century's search for general, natural, or scientific laws—for theories of chemical, biological, historical, economic, and psychological force—and anticipates and influences William James's devaluing of absolutism and "building-block" theories of the universe.

Like James's philosophy and psychology, Emerson's essays are steadfastly anthropocentric. They aim for a pragmatic effect; they hope to see the force of their own genius transformed into practical power. Nature, when properly used, Emerson writes, is "medicinal," "a cordial of incredible virtue" (CW, 1:13, 10). The same can be said of Emerson's prose. It addresses itself, ultimately, not to an absolute World-Spirit or Over-Soul but to the health and force of the individual will.

For Hegel, "the need for philosophy *is* the need for the restoration of harmony."⁶³ *Phenomenology of Spirit* records the "Ideal's" gradual comprehension of negativity and its own dualities, its ultimate evolution to its closure with and in a final purpose or "Absolute Spirit." The Hegelian synthesis looks for the realization, the completeness, of Geist, not man. Emerson, as a child of the first half of the nineteenth century, longed for that kind of philosophical harmony. He enjoyed his own absolutist rhetoric of the Over-Soul, claimed for himself the role of "affirmer of the One Law" (JMN, 8:8), professed repeatedly his syncretic and organic aspirations; but the ultimate concern of his essays is the generation and affirmation of power, identity, man.

Emerson's dualisms were necessary: if the life of "division" (CW, 2:160), the "double consciousness," were to end, if the timeless unity that is always postponed were ever attained, the time-bound *drama* of the individual's search for power and a well-grounded self would cease. The self would no longer have divisions or resistance to react against; the very basis of identity would be threatened. A definitive expression of the moral law at the heart of the universe would be achieved, but the process of the generation of always-new reservoirs of force—the process in which Emerson's "radically anarchic" theme of "man's entire independence," his "freedom and mastery"⁶⁴ is, again and again, acted out—would be annulled and replaced by a static and stagnant world of atonement.

The paradoxical Emersonian longing for the integration of some kind of religious Unity or vision of an Absolute with a fierce affirmation of autonomous individuality may be characteristically American. That driving contradiction may make him one of our most representative voices. In his comprehensive study of the subject, Ronald Martin notes the curious way in which such quasi-scientific and metaphysical "universe-of-force" theories as Spencer's synthetic philosophy or John Fiske's Spencer-and-Comte-derived "Cosmic Philosophy" came to be overwhelmingly influential in America in the last quarter of the nineteenth century—popular primarily for the way they fulfilled an American hunger for some manner of reconciliation (however superficial) between the new science and the old religion. Emerson's attempt to unite God-reliance and self-reliance, absolutism and pragmatism, a philosophy of atonement and one of resistance, foreshadows that later chapter in American cultural history. It might be argued that the often enigmatic attraction Emerson's writing has exerted is due to something like the sheer rhetorical and metaphorical effectiveness of a John Fiske—the ability to combine the great "peace-conferring power" of an absolutist rhetoric with a rhetoric of mankind's own reactive, self-determining force into a single, ambiguous rhetoric of force. It is a rhetoric that "reads well," as Kenneth Burke says, one that makes for good "medicine."⁶⁵

CHAPTER

7

The Rhetoric of War

There is nothing real or useful that is not a seat of war.

—*Ralph Waldo Emerson, "Character" (1844)*

I conclude by returning to an idea that runs, as we have seen, through much of Emerson's work, appearing often in quite unexpected contexts. It was not simply war in its literal sense that appealed to him but war's agonistic psychology: war in its sublimated or internalized forms. And this marks Emerson, once again, not as an eccentric Transcendentalist but as a mind quintessentially of its time. For war was, like power itself, one of the nineteenth century's master tropes. It functioned as a particularly rich, if elusive, metaphor, an analogy that could be relied on for all manner of uses, regardless of whether or not those uses dissolved the boundary between the figural and literal meanings of the word. His attraction to war in all its forms may be considered a final test case for my central theses: that his thinking is, despite his professions of unity, essentially dualistic, founded on the belief that conflict is necessary and, ultimately, creative; and that he conceived of the universe as a system of antagonisms, a discipline for the strengthening and defining of the self.

His attraction to war also serves as a last, as a particularly appropriate, testament to that most extreme, that curiously contradictory, tendency we have glimpsed throughout this study: the impulse to efface the self that seems to exist beneath the surface of any philosophy of power, be it Emersonian or Nietzschean.

The Romantic imagination, Santayana concluded, will always seek that life of strife and contradiction in which the mind may find fresh resistances by which to wound and test itself. It will settle, inevitably, on "universal battle" as its native element, its most "soul-satisfying expression."[1] Like Nietzsche (who was in the habit of jotting his own militaristic aphorisms in the margins of his Emerson), Emerson provides ample, if often overlooked, testament to Santayana's thesis. "We want to be expressed," he wrote in his journal in 1841, brooding on the Abolition problem, "yet you take from us War, that great opportunity which allowed the accumulation of electricity to stream off from both poles, the positive and the negative" (JMN, 8:116).

"The world," Emerson insists, "is a battle-ground; every principle . . . a war-note" (W, 10:87). "War is the natural state of man & the nurse of all virtues" (JMN, 5:421). The individual is "born into the state of war," and culture must attend to "the arming of the man" (CW, 2:148). The warlike part of human nature is "always the attractive, always the salient part" (EL, 2:241). "Self-trust" is "the state of the soul at war" (CW, 2:149). Man's inner life is a perpetual psychomachia; his relationship with his world, the conflict of counterbalancing powers. "This floor holds us up by a fight with agencies that go to pull us down. The whole world is a series of balanced . . . antagonisms" (JMN, 11:371). "Nature is upheld by antagonism" (W, 6:254), and war is only natural.

No one has yet compiled an anthology of Emerson's meditations on war, but there is no dearth of material. Throughout his life, Emerson reflected often on the reasons for our "invincible respect for war" (W, 10:37). Why are a civilization's greatest intellectual achievements, its "triumphs of peace" (W, 6:71), so closely linked to military greatness? Why is war such a "potent alterative" or "tonic"—physically, intellectually, morally (JMN, 15:379)? Why in the midst of even "the most accumulated culture" do we remain so attracted "to the sound of any drum and fife" (W, 10:38)? Why do "the finest and softest arts" require the "tension" of war's "stern conditions"—or "some analogous vigor" (W, 6:71)? Why "in any trade, or in law-courts, in orchard and farm" do "they only prosper . . . who have a military mind, who engineer in sword and cannon style" (W, 10:38)?

War simply is, as Emerson remarked in 1854, "a part of our education, as much as milk or love, & is not to be escaped" (JMN, 13:344). Emerson always sought a philosophy "of fluxions and mobility" (CW, 4:91); war, as the most violent form of change, was the extreme embodiment of that philosophy. War, by breaking "immovable routine," shatters rotten systems and fosters cultural renewal, allowing things "to take a new and natural order" (W, 6:254). War, as he put it in 1841, breaks up "the Chinese stagnation of society, and demonstrates the personal merits of all men" (CW, 1:198).

This idealization of struggle and soldiery was hardly confined to Emerson. The vision of the universe as a gigantic *bellum omnium contra omnes,* a place of constant struggle in which the human race is "always and everywhere at variance with itself . . . , everything a hunter and everything hunted," was deeply characteristic of Schopenhauer's philosophy, characteristic of Darwin's, Marx's, and Nietzsche's—to name just a few of Emerson's nineteenth-century contemporaries or near contemporaries.[2] War was, according to Nietzsche, "indispensable." War's torrents of power "turn the wheels in the workshops of the spirit with newfound energy."

The "feeble humanity" of nineteenth-century Europe would, he predicted, require "the greatest and most terrible wars" for its culture to regenerate itself (HH, 1:477). "You should love peace as a means to new wars," proclaims Zarathustra, "and the short peace more than the long. . . . War and courage have accomplished more great things than love of the neighbor" (Z, 1:10).

Such statements remind us how profoundly Emerson's rhetoric of war, like his more general preoccupation with power, mirrored the main currents of nineteenth-century thought. Jacques Barzun explains the situation this way: after 1848 all Europe had entered a period of conspicuous malaise—revolution in Austria and Italy, violence in Ireland, the Crimean War, the failure of the German Assembly—disorders in part created, and continually worsened, by the Darwinian and Marxist visions of evolution through strife and struggle. "The suffering, impatience, sense of weakness" of the period "were creating a temper favorable to all programs of force. . . . An infinity of cures were proposed . . . but they now had a common factor: the use of force." The worship of force and the ideal of "the struggle-for-life" culminated between 1870 and 1914 in "the poeticizing of war" and, inevitably, in the first "world war." By the second half of the century, Barzun concludes: "War [had become] the symbol, the image, the inducement, the reason, and the language of all human beings on the planet. No one who has not waded through some sizable part of the literature of the period 1870–1914 has any conception of the extent to which it is one long call for blood, nor of the variety of parties, classes, nations, and races whose blood was separately and contradictorily clamored for by the enlightened nations of the ancient civilizations of Europe."[3]

Real war was for Emerson, in principle at least, a violation of the common soul of all men. "It will no doubt be found out one day," he prophesied confidently in 1838, "that men cannot go to war with men any more than fathers can shoot or poison their children and keep the reputation of sanity. . . . The injured party and the injurer have one heart" (EL, 2:286). "But is not peace greater than war and has it not greater wars and victories? . . . To wish for war is atheism" (JMN, 8:242). We have arrived, however, at one of the ironies of the saintly persona Emerson impressed on his contemporaries. The benign seer whose beacon of "the ideal life" provided spiritual sustenance for the young martyrs of the Civil War also formulated, as part of his philosophy of individual power, a philosophy of war.[4] "Long before Federal and Confederate soldiers began to slaughter each other . . . Emerson worked out his dialectic of war and peace, and he had no difficulty accommodating it to American facts."[5]

Emerson's reverence for the stupendous energies war set flowing must not be overlooked as a significant contribution to a nineteenth-century worship of force that could all too easily translate into a literal militarism. His exultation of war's positive powers is undoubtedly linked to the millennial glorification of war that took place in his own country (in a gradual, often unconscious acceptance of an impending "general divine war") in the years leading up to the Civil War—but it is linked, as well, to the general "poeticizing of war" that took place in fin de siècle Europe.[6] Much has been written to document Emerson's place in an American millennial tradition, but we should not forget that there is nothing unique about America's tendency to interpret history according to an apocalyptic framework during times of crisis. In the twentieth century Yeats praised war, as Emerson and Nietzsche had, as the great opportunity for cultural purgation and renascence: "The danger is that there will be no war. . . . Love war because of its horror, that belief may be changed, civilization renewed."[7]

Emerson was certainly a key source for the rhetoric of force, the conception of life-as-battleground that Nietzsche was to make his own. But his vision of war as the prime symbol for the life of heroic activism probably found its most complete and systematic statement in William James's popular, still influential essay, "The Moral Equivalent of War."[8]

James was a pacifist, but war's *strong* life" fascinated him. He deplored the actual bloodbath of history but lamented the closing of "the supreme theatre of human strenuousness" that war's end would bring. A utopian literature of pacifism would, he feared, promote an insidious "pleasure economy." It would open the door to "ubiquitous inferiority," degeneration, and the loss of "manliness." Actual war making was barbaric. But the "fear economy" of the warlike state was worth celebrating for its "merciless scorn" of such inferiority. War stimulated men's "spiritual energies." It served as the best theater for self-strengthening, the most effective method for the creative disciplining of whole societies.

War had, so far, provided men and nations with one of their best mechanisms for converting weakness to force. "Taking human nature as a whole," James said, "its wars are its best protection against its weaker and more cowardly self." He quoted approvingly S. R. Steinmetz's "Philosophie des Krieges": war was "an ordeal instituted by God" to determine the strongest. It was by nature—so James quotes Steinmetz—an apocalyptic judgment that revealed each participant's moral and physical strength: "World history is the last judgment" *("Die Weltgeschichte ist das Weltgericht")*. War was, in effect, not primarily a negative force, an obstacle to civilization, but a creator and ensurer of healthy cultures. It did not temporarily break the peace but made possible a stable, continuous generation of national and personal force: "War, according to this author . . . is the essential form of the State, and the only function in which peoples can employ all their powers at once and convergently."

Concluding that "the martial virtues" originally gained in war were "absolute and permanent human goods," James proposed a peace corps in which the nation's youth would be conscripted for the war against nature—"to road-building and tunnel-making." The "military ideals of hardihood and discipline" would thus "be wrought into the growing fibre of the people."

James had, we need recall, read through, marked, and indexed Emerson's essays seven years earlier, in preparation for his address for the Emerson centenary. He was clearly echoing Emerson's belief that war's destruction could provide compensatory creation, his certainty that beneath the surface bloodshed of battle there lurked "a great beneficent principle," advancing the cause of civilization. For Emerson war was above all useful as a symbol of self-help, a symbol of the "self-defended being" born of a state of resistance:

> What does all this war, beginning from the lowest races and reaching up to man, signify? Is it not manifest that it covers a great and beneficent principle, which Nature had deeply at heart? What is that principle?—It is self-help. Nature implants with life the instinct of self, perpetual struggle to be, to resist opposition, to attain to freedom, to attain to a mastery . . . of a permanent, self-defended being. (W, 11:154–55)

> The student of history acquiesces the more readily in this copious bloodshed . . . when he learns that it is a temporary and preparatory state, and does actively forward the culture of man. War educates the senses, calls into action the will, perfects the physical constitution. . . . [It] shakes the whole society until every atom falls into the place its specific gravity assigns it. (W, 11:152)

The assumption of war as a natural state for man, as it is for beasts, the identification of "the perpetual struggle to be" with military triumph, the sanctioning of war as "within the highest right" (W, 11:342), Divine Providence's ritual separation of the strong from the weak, and nature's way of shaking society's atoms into their proper place in a natural hierarchy—the rhetoric here is unmistakably akin to that adduced by Barzun in his discussion of a European poeticizing of war that took as its philosophical and "scientific" imprimatur the evolutionary ethos of perpetual struggle as it was summarized in Darwin and in Herbert Spencer.[9]

The most dramatic of Emerson's eulogies to war is his "Harvard Commemoration Speech" of July 1865. The Civil War, as Emerson painted it, had gloriously awakened all "the energies that have slept in the children of this country" (W, 11:341). It was the welcome apocalyptic unsettling that destroyed the old and created new power and character. That he chose, barely three months after Lincoln's assassination and before an audience whose college had lost ninety-three of her sons on the battlefield, to praise war as culturally and individually energizing, the ritual that lifted the true men of force "into their true places," may seem odder to us now than it did then. But we need bear in mind the "Federal Epic" that, according to

Daniel Aaron, constituted the North's (and particularly New England's) mythic perception of the conflict. The outcome of what Oliver Wendell Holmes called "our Holy War" vindicated the Union side; the martyrdom of the North's Illinois Savior was the proper conclusion to the conflict's Miltonic plot.[10] Massachusetts, of course, had long since grown accustomed to hearing, in the sermons of the Puritan Jeremiahs, disaster interpreted as God's penance on an "erring and immoral nation":

> The old Greek Heraclitus said, "War is the Father of all things". . . . War passes the power of all chemical solvents, breaking up the old adhesions, and allowing the atoms of society to take a new order. It is not the Government, but the War, that has appointed the good generals, sifted out the pedants, put in the new and vigorous blood. The War has lifted many other people besides Grant and Sherman into their true places. Even Divine Providence, we may say, always seems to work after a certain military necessity. . . . The proof that war also is within the highest right, is a marked benefactor in the hands of Divine Providence, is its morale. The war gave back integrity to this erring and immoral nation. It charged with power, peaceful, amiable men, to whose life war and discord were abhorrent. . . . What an infusion of character [went] down to the ranks! (W, 11:341–42)

It would be a misreading of Emerson, however, even in the face of such spirited acceptance of not only the idea of metaphysical war but also war itself, to reduce his vision of universal antagonism to warmongering. Emerson denounced militarism as "rude and puerile," an ultimately self-destructive process (W, 7:290). He was confident that history showed war's inevitable decline. Universal peace would eventually be reality, and to hope for it was no visionary scheme. "Nothing is plainer than that the sympathy with war is a juvenile and temporary state," he said in 1838. Civilization would prevail over barbarism, "liberal governments over feudal forms" (W, 11:156, 161). His belief that negative force could be harnessed and converted to positive force allowed him to see war as the birth pangs for the unfolding of greater, civilized human powers. In "the eternal germination of the better," man would leave behind his "tiger and . . . shark" nature and unfold the "new powers, new instincts" that were really "concealed under this rough and base rind" (W, 11:160). "We can harness . . . evil agents, the powers of darkness, and force them to serve . . . the ends of wisdom and virtue." The "index of high civilization" is "that tendency to combine antagonisms and utilize evil" (W, 7:30, 25). Thus "war subsides into engineering." Commerce transforms war's aboriginal force into constructive energy: "The progress of trade has been the death of war, universally" (EL, 2:214, 81).

Emerson was hardly above jingoism, and he enjoyed the smell of gunpowder when he visited the Charlestown Navy Yard at the beginning of the Civil War; but what most attracted him to the idea of battle was its symbolic value. American writers, Aaron argues, managed, like most of their fellow Americans, to drape the Civil War in myth and to transmute its actuality into symbol.[11] Emerson was no exception. His doctrine that all existence was fundamentally emblematic—that "we are symbols and inhabit symbols"—his worship of "the primal springs," the incessant cycle of destruction and creation that was the core and "secret of the world" (JMN, 14:179), and his belief in a cosmic moral law all combined to decree that he perceive the Civil War, *any* war, or any act of human destructiveness as primarily a symbol of pure power that could be transmuted into greater human force.

War was also something more than a source of power. It was a symbol of the Apocalypse. God, according to the New Testament, would put an end to human time with a cosmic battle to be followed eventually by a new heaven, a new earth, and God's final reign. When the writers of the Romantic period internalized this apocalypse they kept and, under the spell of the French Revolution, expanded the military rhetoric. The French Revolution was, as M. H. Abrams has noted, the preeminent and immediate inspiration for the imagery of apocalyptic battle that runs throughout Romantic literature. Blake displaced the revolution from the battlefield to "intellectual War." In Fichte's philosophical system, the apocalyptic struggle between the ego and the nonego, the "endless striving" of the ego against nature toward an ever-approachable but never-quite-achievable victory, is "couched in metaphors of *Machtpolitik*—a power language of challenge, conflict, and the struggle for mastery between two hostile forces."[12] A similar power language can be found in Hegel.

Emerson was heir as well to the Puritan tradition of saintly warfare. "I am come not to send peace, but a sword" [Matt. 10:34], Christ had spoken. "Permanent warfare," Michael Walzer writes in *The Revolution of the Saints*, "was the central myth of Puritan radicalism." The internalizing of "the discipline of warfare" in the soul of the believer was the underlying goal of the tradition of religious radicalism that Emerson inherited.[13] Martin Luther was, for Emerson, the perfect example of a Protestant warrior who had sublimated his warlike genius into more civilized forms: "[Luther] achieved a spiritual revolution by spiritual arms alone" (EL, 1:140, 127). Emerson's own repeated linking of speakers, poets, scholars, and soldiers has not gone unnoticed.[14] If the pugnacious Thoreau claimed that the art of composition was "as simple as the discharge of a bullet from a rifle," the Puritan warrior in Emerson longed for a pulpit from which he could deliver the "sharp artillery" of his eloquence (JMN, 7:265).[15]

The war Edward Johnson's "soldiers of Christ" had waged against unbelievers and the colonial American wilderness was still alive, in its internalized form, in William Ellery Channing's 1824 espousal of "The Christian Warfare."[16] "Christianity arms us with no weapons for the destruction of our brethren," Channing declared. "The conflict is within. It is war with our own hearts." But it was not only the tradition of battle displaced into spiritual combat or rhetorical power on which Emerson drew. American Christians had, since the Cromwellian Revolution, translated their apocalyptic rhetoric into real weapons and employed the Bible to vindicate their real wars. The spokesman for the American Revolution had hastened to locate the new nation "in a grand apocalyptic interpretation of universal history, the only conceptual framework acceptable to a people still rooted in the providential assumptions of the English Reformation."[17] During the Civil War years, when God again unsheathed "His terrible swift sword," the rhetoric of millennial and saintly battle was massively resurrected. In the decades that led to the war, millennialists in America may have talked of man's peaceful natural progress toward a postmillennial utopia, but almost always they came back to the necessity for apocalyptic warfare.[18]

The eighteenth-century mind, Michel Foucault writes, embraced not only the idea of the "primal social contract" between men but also "the military dream of society" that took as its model not the state of nature but the meticulously and mechanically organized army camp, where power was invested in the discipline of the individual soldier. The army in the eighteenth century was a real force and also "a technique and a body of knowledge that could project [its] schema over the social body." The eighteenth-century idealization of the Roman republic referred not only to the classical notion of jurists and counselors of state but also to the Roman legionnaire and armed camp.[19]

"Power" and identity, by Foucault's definition, are not "built up out of wills (individual or collective)." "Power is not an institution, a structure, or a certain force with which certain people are endowed; it is a name given to a complex strategic relation in a given society." "The individual is not a pre-given entity which is seized on by the exercise of power. The individual, with his identity and characteristics, is the product of a relation of power exercised over bodies, . . . movements, desires, forces."[20] Power in a modern society is not, Foucault claims, "repressive," is not imposed on the bodies of subjects by sovereigns, as it was in what Foucault calls the "classical," premodern age. Rather, in ways that are "subtle, effective, and economic" it sets in motion individuals, rituals, systems, bureaucracies, and forms of knowledge that will perpetuate themselves. Power produces identity, "produces reality."[21]

In our legal systems, for example, as the interest of the court focused increasingly on the defendant's *motive* and less on fitting each crime to a specific catalog of penalties that determined the particular punishment automatically, there came into being a modern notion of "humane" treatment and "humanity," increased interest in the unconscious self, and the modern, secular conception of that noncorporeal substance called a "soul." Soul in this sense has little to do with the soul as Christian theology conceives it. It is, rather, a working notion of individuality through which the legal and penal system can proceed, a standard by which it can distribute its verdicts and punishments. Through this system of power a particular notion of a private "self" is produced, along with a form of knowledge (the legal system) that will continue to reaffirm and perpetuate that self.[22]

Similarly, our institutions and sciences of mental health ultimately help to produce our ideas of what individualizes a "self" ("when one wishes to individualize the healthy, normal and law-abiding adult, it is always by asking him . . . what secret madness lies within him, what fundamental crime he has dreamt of committing"). Our modern fabrication of "sexuality" constitutes, in its "intensification of the body," another crucial "affirmation of self."[23]

Each of the central "technologies of power" that arose in the late eighteenth or early nineteenth century to produce for man a particular definition of a self is fundamentally linked to "the military dream of society," with its emphasis on the disciplining of the individual body of the soldier. (The turn of the eighteenth century marks, for Foucault, the beginning of the modern era of "identity" from which we are only now breaking free.) "Discipline," Foucault writes, "'makes' individuals; it is the specific technique of a power that regards individuals . . . as instruments of exercise." Discipline emphasizes the body as "the bearer of forces." Our wholly modern "science" of sexuality, our schools, prisons, courts, hospitals—each exemplifies to some degree, or has its origins in, the "militarization" of society, the militarization of the body and our conception of a private self. The school as it developed through the nineteenth century was, like the army, a machine: a machine for learning. It "exercised" its individual pupils, extracted from them their maximum "force."[24]

Foucault—our contemporary philosopher of power—represents, of course, an understanding of identity directly opposed to the Emersonian psychology I have been trying to recover. Identity for Emerson was hardly the function of "a complex strategic relation in a given society"—not, at least, in the poststructuralist way in which Foucault conceives it. Human power was, for Emerson, sublimely interior. It was Carlyle's obstinate groping in "the obscure recesses of power *in* human will" and his returning to reaffirm "the might that is *in* man" (JMN, 5:290; my emphases) that won Emerson's admiration. The "main interest of history" for Emerson was the discovery of the "primal springs" of "human power" (JMN, 5:410–11; JMN, 14:179). Within every individual lay a measureless residuum of force, always "unknown, unanalyzable" (CW, 2:182). And it was the obligation of society to nurture and distill that pure force of humanity: "the end of culture is . . . to train away all impediment and mixture [in the individual] and leave nothing but pure power" (W, 6:134). Foucault's theories offer a radical antidote to this nineteenth-century idealization of an innately human identity.

Yet Foucault's ideas on this point—however confirmable they may ultimately prove—appear to have remarkable pertinence in the case of Emerson's militarized rhetoric. For Emerson's essays seem persistently to embody that principle Foucault identifies as the defining characteristic of modern man: his labor to define himself through the "exercising" or "disciplining" of the individual. The goal of education for Emerson was to draw forth from the student the "fullness of [his] power." Even the domestic household was "a school of power" (W, 10:148, 128). A "new view" or new kind of *"Culture,"* Emerson announced to his Boston audience in 1837, was in the process of remolding "metaphysics, theology, science, law, trades, and professions." The end of that culture was the "unfolding" of man's nature *"by exercising,"* as Emerson emphasized it, "his latent power." "The true culture is a discipline so universal as to demonstrate that no part of a man was made in vain" (EL, 2:215).

Emerson, consciously or unconsciously, incorporated in his prose the subtle and influential rhetoric of "the military dream of society" by which man in the modern era was, as Foucault's analyses suggest, establishing his individuality. "The charm of war" for Emerson was "self-subsistency"— "for this self-subsistency is essential to our idea of man" (W, 11:173). It is worth noting that Andrew Jackson, whose name has become synonymous with the decades in which Emerson wrote his most important essays, favored compulsory military service and attempted, as Michael Paul Rogin observes, "to diffuse military discipline and ardor throughout the population." Jackson, Rogin suggests, was heir to the modern and Puritan definition of the family according to military terms. He attempted to replace, particularly in his own life, the family with the army as society's central "school of power" and foundation of identity:

> The shift in Europe from a medieval, communal, clan existence to the child-centered, conjugal family had increased the role of the army both in child-rearing and in nation-building. Adolescents in the late eighteenth and nineteenth centuries were meant to acquire discipline in the army. The army substituted shared ego ideal (the leader) and shared desire (for conquest) for actual family blood ties. In the symbolism of seventeenth-century Puritan militants, men left the profane family world to do battle against the devil. . . . Puritan theology shifted God the father and the family father from loving, organic presences to military enforcers of command and obedience. Jackson was heir to these traditions, and they played a powerful role in his personal history.[25]

A similar case can be made for Emerson's rhetorical utilization of those other "technologies of power"—natural, technological, sexual, and economic force—that absorbed the energies of antebellum America. Emerson remained assured, as Henry Adams at the end of the century did not, that those intimidating powers surrounding man would remain "nicely adjusted" to the strength of the human mind (EL, 1:37). One of the key ways Emerson diffused them of their force, and so kept in equilibrium what Perry Miller defined as the nineteenth century's crucial struggle between mind and nature, was by incorporating them into his prose as the very rhetoric by which he affirmed mankind's superiority.

Emerson's philosophy of power was the example par excellence of what Foucault has classified as a fundamentally nineteenth-century "philosophy of identity": one of the "arrangements of knowledge" or "human sciences" by which mankind has, for approximately the last two hundred years, given itself a particular "humanity."[26] Emerson's "search after power" was one of the century's many attempts to justify "man" to himself: an attempt to construct a particular theory and rhetoric by which man could confirm himself and all his powers.

Emerson's rhetoric of war was one subcategory of his rhetoric of power—the symbolic language with which he painted for nineteenth-century man a portrait of an anthropocentric universe, bestowed on him his identity as the central force in nature, and posited the cultivation and exercise of human power as the highest good and end of existence. The "fact which commands our attention," he proclaimed in 1834, "is the manner in which man is led on by his wants to the development of his powers and so to the possession of the globe": "that Man who stands in the globe so proud and powerful is no upstart in the creation, but has been prophesied in nature for a thousand thousand ages before he has appeared; . . . from times incalculably remote there has been a progressive preparation for him; an effort, (as physiologists say), to produce him; the meaner creatures, the primeval sauri, containing the elements of his structure and pointing at it on every side, whilst the world was, at the same time, preparing to be habitable by him" (EL, 1:41, 29).

It may be that it is impossible to speak of human action, time, or change without using an agonistic rhetoric. The point and counterpoint of discourse itself seem to duplicate the give-and-take of combat. The dialectic of discourse and history—even pacifist rhetoric in times of peace—hides, Kenneth Burke notes, a "militarist core."[27] The Heraclitean conception of war or strife as the father of all things—a metaphor that inspired both Emerson and Nietzsche—suggests that all human history can be interpreted *sub specie belli*. "Life *is,* in fact, a battle," Henry James said. Even James's cerebral drawing rooms are the stage for an artful rhetoric of warfare and aggression.[28]

Foucault's studies of the way political power arises and deploys itself in modern societies led him to take as the "symbolic field" by which man constructs his institutions not the structuralist model of language and signs but "that of war and battle." Politics is, according to Foucault, the inversion of Clausewitz's formula: "the continuation of war by other means." Political power is "a sort of generalized war which assumes at particular moments the forms of peace and the State." A peaceful society has not transcended the state of war, only transformed and internalized it. Peace is "a form of war, and the State a means of waging it."[29]

Foucault's hypotheses are intended to demystify war; they attempt to exorcise war from our subconscious and clarify the symbolic value we attach to it. Burke's *A Grammar of Motives* has a similar aim: "to purify warfare" (*"ad bellum purificandum"* is the book's motto), to make definite the distinction between war as act and war as symbol.[30] The prevalent tendency of the modern imagination has, however, been the contrary. Increasingly, our apocalyptic poets and writers have confused war's literal and figural meaning. They have conceived the world in terms of catastrophe, Armageddons, and the end of time without taking or intending that their rhetoric be taken literally. "When I was writing *A Vision,*" Yeats said, "I had constantly the word 'terror' impressed upon me, and once the old Stoic prophecy of earthquake, fire, and flood at the end of an age, but this I did not take literally." This tendency to internalize and not take literally an apocalyptic rhetoric is, Frank Kermode writes, "characteristic of the attitude not only of modern poets but of the modern literary public."[31]

Emerson and Nietzsche may indeed write in a way that confuses war's reality and its symbolic value. But it is a confusion they share with much of Western tradition over the past two centuries. This makes them particularly instructive case studies for a far more extensive problem. Consider, for instance, Nietzsche's employment of a rhetoric of war and the difficulties it creates, the misinterpretation it invites. Few have employed the language of force with Nietzsche's skill. And a language of force is undoubtedly the most rhetorically effective, the most dramatic vehicle—the aesthetically appropriate way—to communicate a Nietzschean belief in the "will to power" as the basic biological impulse of all living organisms. Even the most graceful, the most peaceful, culture, Nietzsche claims, will require the noble "cruelty" involved in man's quest to overcome and perfect himself. Nietzsche's often-misunderstood use of military imagery clearly refers to this interior struggle for *self*-perfection. ("If you cannot be saints of knowledge," he declares, "at least be its warriors. . . . I see many soldiers: would that I saw many warriors!" [Z, 1:10].) Those who externalize that impulse into real wars, real soldiery, and thereby escape the task of self-examination only admit their weakness.[32] Yet Nietzsche's rhetoric leaves him acutely vulnerable to misinterpretation. Whatever inner warfare he may have in mind, he still defines and celebrates man as an essentially military animal. The "warlike nature" he upholds may be meant in its symbolic sense—may be intended merely as a metaphor for what Emerson extols as "self-subsistency"—yet it seems to invite a far more literal, a far less sophisticated, interpretation.

Barzun suggests that Nietzsche's words were "violent and his metaphors military" because he was forced to "make his contemporaries understand by using the language of competition and struggle which they already knew."[33] But I think we have to go somewhat further than this to understand properly the kind of imagination of disaster that a writer like Nietzsche exemplifies. Nietzsche's apocalyptic imagination was, like Emerson's, much more than a reaction to the cant of a Darwinian age. It answered, I would argue, to those darker needs of the imagination Kermode identifies in *The Sense of an Ending*. I am referring to the ultimately self-effacing tendencies Kermode discerns: the potentially madness-inducing desire to impose *kairos* on *chronos;* the drive to transform time, through literature, into a state of "perpetual crisis" and thereby deny human, day-to-day reality; the paradoxical need of the Romantic imagination, so tirelessly preoccupied with affirming a "Self," to turn back on that self, to contemplate and warm to the idea of self-annihilation.[34]

We have seen this underlying impulse to "write off the self" (as Richard Poirier calls it), this attraction to failure, this need to confront life-threatening force, before. It seems to exist as a running, yet necessary, counterpoint to Emerson's more dominant theme of self-assertion. Any psychology of self-empowerment that requires self-overcoming, any philosophy that demands some daily calamity for every self-recovery, seems destined—in either its Nietzschean or Emersonian varieties—to harbor this anti-humanistic streak beneath its vehemently humanistic exterior. We may consider it a fundamental, if recessive, principle of Emerson's thought.

William Graham Sumner, who, in the last years of the nineteenth century, fought with Yale's president Noah Porter for the right to use Spencer's *Principles of Sociology* in his classroom, was as drenched in Darwinism as anyone else in the century and was staunchly committed to the idea of self-seeking as man's primary instinct. But Sumner was a professor of political and social science, not, like Emerson or Nietzsche, an apocalyptic prose-poet. He was quick, in 1903, to draw a firm line between war as symbol and war as that reality that, if ritualistically pursued, can only plunge civilization "into an abyss of wasted energy and wealth."

In his essay on "War," Sumner restated ideas Emerson had put forth in his earlier lecture of the same title. He often appears to be, like William James in 1910, echoing Emerson directly. War (Sumner takes the American Civil War as a prime example) can be productive and, in many ways, benevolent. It allows, he suggests, "new social powers [to] break their way and create a new order." "Military discipline educates; military interest awakens all the powers of men. . . . [T]he student is tempted to think that even a great social convulsion is worth all it costs." "But," Sumner adds, refusing to let the matter rest there, "war and revolution never produce what is wanted . . . , only some mixture of the old evils with new ones." In modern times, Sumner notes, man has more than ever organized his activities and collective identity around the preparation for war. "Never, from the day of barbarism down to our own time, has every man in a society become a soldier until now." But this notion of politics as the constant ensuring of "the state of readiness for war" only absorbs "all the resources and activity of the state" in a fallacious, doomed ritual. The answer can only lie, he concludes, in a new emphasis—an emphasis not on the dramatic symbolic value of conflict and its vivid rhetoric but on great statesmanship. "A wiser rule would be to make up your mind soberly what you want, peace or war, and then get ready for what you want; for what we prepare for is what we shall get."[35]

We have, of course, come back to the interpretive problems I raised in chapter 4. How literally are we to take Emerson's metaphors? Should we subscribe to his vision of war as a juvenile stop on man's evolution to civilization and at the same time think, as he does, in a power language of ceaseless struggle for superiority? Does Emerson's symbolic language *sanction* militarism, holy wars, *Machtpolitik?* To which Emerson should we listen: the Emerson who preaches the abandonment of the will to "the ever blessed ONE," or the Emerson who dearly loves the warlike energy of men and the natural law decreeing that in a world of balanced antagonisms "there is always room for a man of force"?

F. O. Matthiessen several decades ago suggested the link between Emerson's "indiscriminate glorification of power" and the "predatory career" of that great admirer of Emerson, Henry Ford. Critics have generally noted, if only in passing, the potential dangers of Emerson's "imperial self." During the political upheavals of the late 1960s Maurice Gonnaud predicted that, if "responsible citizens" could see through Emerson's superb manipulation of words to "the self-righteous supporter of violence" beneath, it would be the saintlike sage of Concord, not the nefarious authors of *Huckleberry Finn* or *Sister Carrie,* who would be banned. In 1981 Bartlett Giamatti blamed Emerson for America's "worship of power as force." In a nuclear age, when one person can wield the power to destroy millions, Emersonian individualism may be more dangerous than anyone in the nineteenth century could have foreseen.[36]

Such criticisms will probably only increase. But they will need, if responsibly made, to take into account the complex rhetorical problems I have noted. They should be made in the awareness that Emerson's prose is a central example of that "language of paradox" and ambiguity shared by many of the writers of the American Renaissance and by Romantic writing in general. As Perry Miller reminds us: "to take Emerson literally is often hazardous."[37] I have said much already about this issue, but some points require amplification.

Emerson was, for one thing, well aware that metaphorical extravagance could be dangerous. In a journal passage of 1841 he issued what amounts to a warning to his readers (and himself) to take care lest the apocalyptic poet, in his love of verbally upheaving and tossing all things, attempt to translate his metaphors into reality (JMN, 8:43). Emerson shared Poe's desire to carve out for his art its own self-contained "Domain of Arnheim"— not a realm where a poem was a clockwork, mechanical creation but a clearly boundaried space in which discourse answered only to its own rules. The idea that his metaphorical "paintings" might be taken by ardent readers as reality or a reality-to-be made him retreat nervously behind the disclaimer that he was not a prophet, a preacher, or an ethical teacher but an *artist*, first and last only a prose "painter": "People came, it seems, to my lectures with expectation that I was to realize the Republic I describe, & ceased to come when they found this reality no nearer. They mistook me. I am & always was a painter" (JMN, 9:49).

When Whitman called his magnum opus a "language experiment" he put *Leaves of Grass* in the same category in which Emerson had placed his own work. Emerson was quick to distinguish his own vocation from the work of social reformers like Horace Greeley and Albert Brisbane. ("They are bent on popular action: I am in all my theory, ethics, & politics a poet and of no more use in their New York than a rainbow or a firefly.") And he complained when he felt he had become "known & fixed" as a "Transcendentalist": "So that I have to begin by endless disclaimers & explanations—'I am not the man you take me for'" (L, 3:18). "I am always insincere," he demurred, "as always knowing there are other moods" (CW, 3:145). At critical junctures in his writing, when he worried that his prose might be taken as doctrine by literal-minded readers, he made it clear that he intended his essays to be the platform where he was bound to no criterion outside his *"Whim"* (CW, 2:30) or the caprice of his moods:

> I am not careful to justify myself. . . . But lest I should mislead any when I have my own head, and obey my whims, let me remind the reader that I am only an experimenter. Do not set the least value on what I do, or the least discredit on what I do not, as if I pretended to settle anything as true or false. I unsettle all things. No facts are to me sacred; none are profane; I simply experiment, an endless seeker, with no Past at my back. (CW, 2:188)

Emerson dreamed of the kind of rhetorical power that could profoundly move and agitate an audience. But he winced at the moral responsibility of the preacher. One of the documents that best reveals this side of his nature is the letter he wrote Henry Ware Jr. three months after the Divinity School controversy. "I have always been," Emerson pleads (in a memorable phrase), "a chartered libertine." Although he has longed from his youth "to put on eloquence as a robe" (JMN, 2:242), he now offers the very difficulty, the unsystematic nature of his writing ("my very incapacity for methodical writing") as a rationale for not being taken seriously as a moral instructor. He has had the freedom "to worship and . . . to rail" because his rhetorical "nonsense" is too inaccessible to be considered dangerous by "the institutions and mind of society": "I have appreciated fully the advantage of my position, for I well know that there was no scholar less willing or able to be a polemic" (L, 2:166–67).

This effort of Emerson to deny responsibility for the literal implications of his rhetoric—by stubbornly insisting on its properly belonging in the realm of art, not "polemic"—will undoubtedly, and understandably, appear to some as mere hypocrisy. However it is judged, it should, I think, be understood as one symptom of a larger need: Emerson's need to back off from any potential obligation that could reduce his ability to express himself "abundantly, not dwarfishly and fragmentarily" (CW, 3:22). Such obligation could come as the request to commit himself politically, morally, emotionally, or, as readers of his journals know, in the simple form of unannounced visitors, house guests, or anything that took up his time in "miscellany." The pattern of provocation followed by the refusal to accept responsibility certainly marks Emerson's relationships with his three most famous disciples—Thoreau, Whitman, and Fuller. It was, no doubt, the trait Henry James had in mind when he remarked, with equal insight and wit, that Emerson "liked to taste but not to drink—least of all to become intoxicated."[38]

In this deeply characteristic pattern of alternate enthusiasm and reticence—a trait of which he was quite aware—the idiosyncrasies of Emerson's personal temperament and his aesthetic as an artist become one. It is difficult to know whether one dictated the other or whether the two shaped and influenced each other during Emerson's development as a writer and as a man.

Emerson's devotion to pursuing his own whim was intended ultimately, however, to serve a higher purpose than his personal gratification or his autonomy as an artist. Like Whitman and Thoreau, he nationalized his quests. The "American mind" Emerson perceived as still "a wilderness of capabilities" (JMN, 10:77)—and he dedicated himself, as a writer, to exploring the spectrum of possible identities for what Crèvecoeur called "the American, this new man." William Ellery Channing, Emerson, Thoreau, Fuller, Melville, and Whitman were only the most famous writers of the antebellum decades to demand a national literature that could provide new mythologies of the self. Behind Emerson's repeated calls for a life and art of "endless experiment" lies the era's search for originality, for cultural independence from Europe. Emerson required, like Whitman's expansive persona, the imaginative space to explore even the dangerous potentialities of his own nature. He required the freedom to express his "fantasies of size, power, violence, debauchery, and fertility," the license to take up and toss aside potential identities that lay beyond the bounds of traditional morality, without worrying that he would be imitated by disciples or naive readers who took him solely at his literal word or expanded the expression of a transitory mood into dogma.[39]

To create an identity is, for a writer, to create a particular kind of rhetoric. Emerson needed a medium in which he could test out a variety of identities and the often extreme or inconsistent rhetorics those identities required. The aesthetic Emerson worked out in his essays and journals is both prophetic (a declaration of cultural independence and a prophecy of what the new national art would be) and defensive: a defense of his own rhetorical experimentation. "In some sort," he wrote, "the end of life, is, that the man should take up the universe into himself, or, out of that quarry leave nothing unrepresented, and he is to create himself" (JMN, 11:440–41). The aesthetic he arrived at was a further refinement of his doctrine of use. It allowed him to assimilate Martin Luther and Napoleon, George Fox and Hercules, Swedenborg and Montaigne—any of the antithetical symbolic personalities with which he filled his pages—to piece together a "representative self." He was free to move from one hero to the next, from one rhetoric to another—from a rhetoric of war to a rhetoric of quietism, from a God-oriented to a radically self-oriented rhetoric, from the tones of Old Testamental prophecy to the ironic play of his whim.

There is, consequently, not one Emerson but many: his legacy to the writers who followed him was, as Poirier states it, "a compendium of iconographies."[40] His rhetoric is really many different rhetorics melted into one. (By *rhetoric* I simply mean his figurative language: the voice or voices he projects—through that figurative language—to persuade and engage the emotional response of his audience.) Alongside a rhetoric of power are a Neoplatonic, biblical, and bucolic rhetoric; a neoclassical rhetoric; and a rhetoric of the sublime and beautiful—a rhetoric of manifest destiny and the millennium, the accents of the *Bhagavad-Gita,* German idealism, and a Yankee brand of American humor. Others could be added to the list.

Any attempt to dissect Emerson's rhetoric will soon come to these different Emersons—and eventually to those root contradictions I have tried to sort out in previous chapters: the fundamental contradiction between God-reliance and self-reliance, Transcendentalism and pragmatism, a philosophy that seeks atonement (and desires to be worked upon) and one that seeks something to react against (and something, always, to "work up"). It is this contradiction that allows Emerson to champion the course of man's exuberant rise to "civility and power" on one page and on the next praise "Sleep" for its destruction of the "individual will" [EL, 2:295–309]). It is this attraction to contrary impulses that allows him to claim, in the same breath, "I am God in nature; I am a weed by the wall" (CW, 2:182).

Whatever one thinks of his welding together of an arsenal of potentially self-repellent rhetorics, it has retained its expressive power. But for some, the moral cracks in that rhetorical amalgam have been difficult to over-look. Some of his most intelligent readers have discerned, beneath the pi-ous clouds that have descended around his name, a strangely evasive and duplicitous figure. Melville placed him in his pantheon of American confi-dence men. James Russell Lowell saw in him a "Plotinus-Montaigne," the Janus-faced coupling of Neoplatonist and skeptic. "The man has *two* faces," Jane Welsh Carlyle complained, "which are continually changing into one another like *dissolving views*." At bottom, Santayana observed, Emerson's prose is rhetorically powerful but contains "no doctrine at all." Yvor Winters called him a fraud. He endlessly transcends "his own conclu-sions," Charles Feidelson writes: he remains "as much for good as for ill, a 'man without a handle.'"[41]

$\mathbf{A}$n apocalyptic style (one that remains oblique, remains diffi-cult to pin down when we most want to pin it down) can provide, as Ernest Tuveson observes, the greatest reassurance to a nation in crisis and uncertain of its future. Only half the logic can be grasped, but the divine plan is always there beneath the deliberate "mixture of clearness and ob-scurity": "God has neither left us without compass and map, nor made us robots of his will. We make history ourselves although we are under the inspiration of grace . . . by a path marked out in advance."[42]

This strong apocalyptic impulse may help explain the difficult styles of several nineteenth-century "sages": Thoreau's hope "to attain to obscu-rity," Whitman's "indirection," Emerson's contradictions, Nietzsche's de-cision to write in excess or, as he put it, "in blood." But Emerson's style was, like Nietzsche's, also shaped by his acute awareness of the "disinte-gration of the symbol"—the tendency of language, especially doctrinal and religious language, to ossify into mere "rhetoric."[43] Like Nietzsche, who similarly intended his writing be a cultural force or "destiny," Emerson was determined that his essays should constitute a sacred text that would survive him as a self-perpetuating source of spiritual influence and power. "I flow down forever," he wrote in his journal, "a sea of benefit into races of individuals" (JMN, 7:435). It was an age, however, when the old reli-gions had become so much "trite rhetoric," at last "nothing but an excess of the organ of language." Like Nietzsche, Emerson realized that rhetorics become institutions, heroes become bores, and gods die and become op-pressive religious hierarchies when they are turned into dogma:

> Here is the difference betwixt the poet and the mystic, that the last nails a symbol to one sense, which was a true sense for a moment, but soon be-comes old and false. For all symbols are fluxional; all language is vehicular

and transitive, and is good, as ferries and horses are, for conveyance, not as
farms and houses are, for homestead. . . . The history of hierarchies seems to
show, that all religious error consisted in making the symbol too stark and
solid, and was at last nothing but an excess of the organ of language. (CW,
3:20)

Nietzsche too hoped to find a type of rhetoric that could be always
transitive, capable of resisting codification into the very systems of inherited cultural values he was attempting to lay bare. He took as his primary
task, Gilles Deleuze suggests, the construction of a discourse "that does
not and will not allow itself to be codified." In an aphoristic style hard
enough to resist "the teeth of time" (HH, 2:168) he was able to find his
own fluxional medium. "All events in the organic world" were, for Nietzsche, "a subduing . . . and all subduing and becoming master involves a
fresh interpretation, an adaptation through which any previous 'meaning'
or 'purpose' are necessarily obscured or even obliterated" (GM, 2:12). As
the reader's own force of mind is brought to bear on the gaps and disharmonies in Nietzsche's texts there comes into being the always fresh "ar-
rangement of forces" (WP, 633) duplicating that dynamic flow of appear-
ances Nietzsche called "the will to power."[44]

George Woodberry recognized that Emerson's prose aimed at something similar: "he was interested rather in the energy of ideas than in ideas
themselves."[45] We may import the Derridean terminology of deconstruction to describe this underlying pattern in his prose, but Emerson's own
descriptions suggest the same thing. He spoke often of the disconnection,
the self-contradiction he attempted to introduce into his paragraphs and
sentences. "A little guessing does [the reader] no harm," he once remarked, "so I would assist him with no connections." To Carlyle he acknowledged that he wrote "paragraphs incompressible, each sentence an
infinitely repellent particle" (CEC, 185). "If you desire to arrest attention,
to surprise, do not give me facts in the order of cause & effect, but drop
one or two links in the chain, & give me with a cause, an effect two or
three times removed" (JMN, 7:90). His own wry comment on his style—"I
found when I had finished my new lecture that it was a very good house,
only the architect had unfortunately omitted the stairs"—mocked his fondness for a prose so "faultily" constructed that we might say it was meant
to be self-destructive, to fall apart like a chain with missing links, or, like a
house without stairs, to defeat any attempt to pass through it.[46]

At its most intensely fragmentary and aphoristic, Emerson's prose seems
to attain that "primal realm of being—pure energy . . . unincarnate life,"
and we are in the presence of a volatile medium beyond and resisting language.[47] His syntax can create, David Porter notes, that "condition of
agentless process and power that attracted Nietzsche so strongly."[48]
Thoreau was equally possessed by the desire to transcend the flesh of expe-

rience and the flesh of words. However hard he grasped at the facts of the natural landscape, he desired, as Perry Miller once remarked, to consign, ultimately, his beloved nature to oblivion. "He strove to transcend not only experience but all potential experience; had he achieved what he intended, he would have become pure act."[49]

In its most extreme moments, Emerson's prose aspires to be such pure power. In his desire to "transcend form as I do time & space" (JMN, 7:429) and to hymn the soul's capacity for attaining "a state of being and power" (CW, 1:105), Emerson strives to free himself from the humanizing but petrifying form of language altogether. He seems, at times, to want to transcend mere expression and simply generate force, energy as impalpable and transparent as light and thought ("Thought is all light, and publishes itself to the universe" [CW, 1:116]), as inchoate as "the interior fires, the molten core of the globe" (JMN, 7:540). "Speech," he said, "is power" (W, 8:92). But there was a counter urge in Emerson for a place purer than utterance, which meant, in effect, the silence of a self-extinguished non-being—essays that were also anti-essays. He praised silence as "the solvent that destroys personality, and gives us leave to be great and universal" (CW, 2:203). Light, his imagery suggests, is the pure language of power. "The original soul," if we could see it, would appear as a "jet of pure light" (CW, 2:213). The "apocalypse of the mind" takes place in that flood of light that pierces the self and makes it a "transparent eyeball"—bathed in and made receptive to pure power.

We have arrived, then, once again, at that transcendental Emerson this study has endeavored to de-emphasize. We have returned to the Will-renouncing Emerson, the Emerson usually described as "wisely passive"—the "mystic moralist" that Maeterlinck associated with Plotinus, Novalis, the hermit saint Jean van Ruysbroeck, and the tradition of Catholic mysticism. One may choose to see this strain in Emerson as exemplary of a timeless human urge to "disindividualize," to renounce and transcend the self. The imagination has often, R. P. Blackmur notes (attempting to account for the presence of an analogous tendency in Henry Adams), surrendered itself to laws that "certify its accelerating destruction." This has been done before, throughout history, in the perennial activities of "incantation, in theology, in war."[50]

I wish, in conclusion, to suggest another way of looking at this side of Emerson, an explanation more in keeping with the mid-nineteenth-century philosopher of power I have attempted to recover. Let me suggest that this impulse to transcend humanity—though it may employ a Platonic idiom, though it may resemble an ancient mysticism—is finally, in Emerson's hands, something other than mysticism or idealism, something not so easily classified, something that is more accurately understood in terms of its own, more convoluted nineteenth-century contexts. It might be better thought of not, as it usually is, in Buddhistic or pantheistic terms but as the kind of ironic recoil a philosophy of power (a psychology of self-annealing, of self-creation, a "metaphysics of Will," a "philosophy of identity," a "homocentrism") seems to make at its verge. We may call this the final tendency of a tradition of Protestant-Romantic thought or the apocalyptic, deconstructive limit toward which much post-Enlightenment thought seems to point. Whatever we call it, it is a tendency Emerson shares with many writers and philosophers of the past two centuries. Maurice Mandelbaum, for instance, locates Schopenhauer in this tradition when he observes that "[for Schopenhauer] a true grasp of the suffering which arises through the restless, unceasing striving of the Will is a form of knowledge that leads to the final annihilation of the Will itself."[51]

In its metamorphosis to pure force, Emerson's "thought" or "self" *over*reaches itself. It aims for a perfect transparency or willing abandonment of the self—a kind of martyred or ghostly freedom from the exhausting affirmation of an autonomous identity. In a posthumously published fragment ("On Truth and Lie in an Extra-Moral Sense"), Nietzsche similarly envisioned a universe cleared of all human intellect. In "The Rule of Phase Applied to History," Henry Adams foresaw a comparable apocalypse. More recently, Foucault has prophesied the destruction or drastic alteration of our conception of man and his place in the universe as the era of "the philosophy of identity" draws to its close. "The promise of the superman," he concludes (referring to a Nietzschean preoccupation that found a precursor in Emerson's hunger for a "superhumanity"), "signifies first and foremost the imminence of the death of man."[52] To identify in Emerson this impulse to efface the self is to emphasize an underlying tendency, not the main thrust of his thought. But that impulse is one paradoxical consequence of Emerson's "search after power"—as it was for writers like Nietzsche and Adams, who came later and were more conscious of it.

The choice of war as a central metaphor for the affirmation of the self attests to the longing for self-annihilation—the longing even for the death of man—that can lie submerged in a philosophy of power or identity. Emerson's incantatory theology of the self was also a theology of war. Like those other nineteenth-century poeticizings of war, like the power philosophies of Nietzsche or Adams, it seems, at times, to predict its own disappearance.

NOTES

Introduction

1. William James, "The Sentiment of Rationality," in *The Will to Believe and Other Essays in Popular Philosophy and Human Immortality* (1897, 1898; rpt. New York: Dover, 1956), 89–90. Idealism is, of course, as elusive a term as Transcendentalism. Like Transcendentalism—like my own topic, power—it is really an enormously inclusive category, an umbrella term, that attracts to itself a variety of components.

There is, consequently, certainly a way in which the Emerson I shall argue for may be regarded as a preeminent idealist. J. G. Merquior has, for example, recently attempted to clarify the term as it has been used over the past two centuries, and the definition he offers would undoubtedly include Emerson. "The first tenet of [a post-Kantian] idealist metaphysics" is, according to Merquior (who cites Maurice Mandelbaum), "the belief that 'within natural human experience one can find the clue to an understanding of the ultimate nature of reality.'" In the history of modern philosophy, the classical and Platonic aspects of idealism—as well as that tendency that would locate "our grasp of reality" in our "spiritual being"—have turned out to be far less influential than the fundamental anthropocentric component that Mandelbaum's broad definition suggests. Merquior writes:

> After the death of Hegel in 1831 the spiritual element in idealism succumbed to the assault of the pervasive secularism of nineteenth-century thought, [but] the anthropocentric viewpoint of idealist metaphysics survived vigorously, from Schopenhauer and Nietzsche to Bergson, Heidegger and the later Wittgenstein—all of them philosophers of the human experience, and interpreters of being in all-too-human terms (like Schopenhauer's Will or . . . Nietzsche's "play").

If one defines idealism in terms of this prestructuralist, "humanized view of reality," as Merquior calls it, then Emerson should undoubtedly be regarded as an idealist. But Emerson scholarship has rarely had in mind this progressive notion of a forward-looking idealism—one that defines a major, modern tradition—when it has, time after time, relegated Emerson to an idealist camp. The idealism usually ascribed to him has had far more pejorative connotations; scholars have generally linked him to what were, by the mid-nineteenth century, ancient or obsolescent points of view.

The definition William James suggests seems to me, therefore, a far more useful representation of the kind of naive or outdated idealism usually ascribed to Emerson. And it is with the kind of idealism usually ascribed to him that I am most concerned. The outlines of that traditional way of defining him should become clearer as I take issue with it in the chapters to come. See J. G. Merquior, *Foucault* (Berkeley: University of California Press, 1985), 19–20; Maurice Mandelbaum, *History, Man, and Reason: A Study in Nineteenth-Century Thought* (Baltimore, Md.: Johns Hopkins University Press, 1971), 6.

2. Martha C. Nussbaum, "Transcending Humanity," in *Love's Knowledge:*

Essays on Philosophy and Literature (New York: Oxford University Press, 1990), 379.

3. Ibid., 368, 378.

4. Ibid., 372.

5. Leavis, cited in Thomas McFarland, *Shapes of Culture* (Iowa City: University of Iowa Press, 1987), 118.

6. "Virtually every aspect of power, every use of the term 'power,' which Nietzsche refers to or employs was," George J. Stack concludes, "anticipated in Emerson's writings." "Nietzsche's 'doctrine' of a universal will to power in nature and, *a fortiori*, in man, society, culture, and history is fundamentally a completion of impressionistic conceptions that were originally forged in his mind by Emerson" (George Stack, *Nietzsche and Emerson: An Elective Affinity* [Athens: Ohio University Press, 1992], 164, 157). See my review of this important study in *Philosophy and Literature* 17 (October 1993), 396–98.

7. From Santayana's 1886 Harvard essay, "The Optimism of Ralph Waldo Emerson," in *George Santayana's America,* ed. James Ballowe (Urbana: University of Illinois Press, 1967), 72.

8. *Ralph Waldo Emerson: Selected Essays, Lectures, and Poems,* ed. Robert D. Richardson (New York: Bantam Books, 1990), 10.

9. Jonathan Bishop, *Emerson on the Soul* (Cambridge, Mass.: Harvard University Press, 1964), 133, 139; Donald E. Pease, *Visionary Compacts: American Renaissance Writings in Cultural Context* (Madison: University of Wisconsin Press, 1987), 232.

10. Richard Poirier, *The Renewal of Literature: Emersonian Reflections* (New York: Random House, 1987), 147, 141.

11. Jon P. Klancher, *The Making of English Reading Audiences, 1790–1832* (Madison: University of Wisconsin Press, 1987), 72–73.

12. Northrop Frye, "The Drunken Boat: The Revolutionary Element in Romanticism," in *Romanticism Reconsidered: Selected Papers from the English Institute,* ed. Northrop Frye (New York: Columbia University Press, 1963), 14.

13. William Ellery Channing, *Works* (Boston: n.p., 1841), vol. 1, 74.

14. Frye, "Drunken Boat," 16.

15. See the chapter on "The Worship of Force" in Walter E. Houghton, *The Victorian Frame of Mind* (New Haven, Conn.: Yale University Press, 1957), 196–217.

16. Thomas Carlyle, *A Carlyle Reader,* ed. G. B. Tennyson (New York: Cambridge University Press, 1984), 173, 42–43.

17. Jacques Barzun, *Darwin, Marx, Wagner: Critique of a Heritage,* 2nd ed. (Chicago: University of Chicago Press, 1958), 170; Bertrand Russell, *History of Western Philosophy* (New York: Simon and Schuster, 1945), 828; David Simpson's description of Schelling in *German Aesthetic and Literary Criticism: Kant, Fichte, Schelling, Schopenhauer, Hegel,* ed. David Simpson (New York: Cambridge University Press, 1984), 117; Robert C. Solomon, *In the Spirit of Hegel: A Study of G. W. F. Hegel's "Phenomenology of Spirit"* (New York: Oxford University Press, 1983), 367–68; Mandelbaum, *History, Man, and Reason,* 317, 319.

18. John Kinnaird, *William Hazlitt: Critic of Power* (New York: Columbia University Press, 1978), 89–90.

19. Ronald E. Martin, *American Literature and the Universe of Force*

(Durham, N.C.: Duke University Press, 1981), 32, 7.

20. Ibid., 3.

21. Howard Mumford Jones, *Revolution and Romanticism* (Cambridge, Mass.: Harvard University Press, 1974), 409, 412.

22. Barbara Packer, "Ralph Waldo Emerson," in *Columbia Literary History of the United States,* ed. Emory Elliott (New York: Columbia University Press, 1988), 398.

23. "Emerson is," Rosenwald writes, "a better journalist than he is an essayist." Lawrence Rosenwald, *Emerson and the Art of the Diary* (New York: Oxford University Press, 1988), 72, 62; Evelyn Barish, *Emerson: The Roots of Prophecy* (Princeton, N.J.: Princeton University Press, 1989), 256; John McAleer, *Ralph Waldo Emerson: Days of Encounter* (Boston: Little, Brown, 1984), 380.

Chapter 1: The Anti-Emerson Tradition

1. Alfred Kazin, "The Father of Us All," *New York Review of Books,* 21 January 1982, 3; Richard Poirier, *Renewal of Literature,* 141. The epigraph is from "Emersonianism," originally published in *The New Yorker,* 4 June 1984, and reprinted in John Updike, *Odd Jobs: Essays and Criticism* (New York: Knopf, 1991), 148–68.

2. Lawrence Buell, "The Emerson Industry in the 1980s: A Survey of Trends and Achievements," *ESQ: A Journal of the American Renaissance* 30 (1984):118; Kazin, "Father of Us All," 3; Harold Bloom, "Mr. America," *New York Review of Books,* 22 November 1984, 19; Richard Poirier, *A World Elsewhere: The Place of Style in American Literature* (New York: Oxford University Press, 1966), 56; Joel Porte, *Representative Man: Ralph Waldo Emerson in His Time,* 2d ed. (New York: Columbia University Press, 1988), x; Denis Donoghue, *Reading America: Essays on American Literature* (Berkeley: University of California Press, 1988), 37; Stanley Cavell, *In Quest of the Ordinary: Lines of Skepticism and Romanticism* (Chicago: University of Chicago Press, 1988), 27–28; John Michael, *Emerson and Skepticism: The Cipher of the World* (Baltimore, Md.: Johns Hopkins University Press, 1988), ix; David Bromwich, *A Choice of Inheritance: Self and Community from Edmund Burke to Robert Frost* (Cambridge, Mass.: Harvard University Press, 1989), 148.

3. Buell, "Emerson Industry," 118; Harriet Martineau, *Retrospect of Western Travel* (1838; rpt. Haskell House, 1969), vol. 2, 203; Theodore Parker, in *The Transcendentalists: An Anthology,* ed. Perry Miller (Cambridge, Mass.: Harvard University Press, 1950), 415–16; Walt Whitman, in *The Shock of Recognition,* ed. Edmund Wilson (1943; rpt. New York: Octagon Books, 1975), vol. 1, 272; James Russell Lowell, in *Literary Criticism of James Russell Lowell,* ed. Herbert Smith (Lincoln: University of Nebraska Press, 1969), 206, 213; Matthew Arnold, in *The Recognition of Ralph Waldo Emerson,* ed. Milton R. Konvitz (Ann Arbor: University of Michigan Press, 1972), 73.

4. John Dewey, "Ralph Waldo Emerson," in *Emerson: A Collection of Critical Essays,* ed. Milton Konvitz and Stephen Whicher (Englewood Cliffs, N.J.: Prentice-Hall, 1962), 29; John Jay Chapman, "Emerson," in *Shock of Recognition,* vol. 1, 596, 657; Henry James, *The American Scene* (1907; Bloomington: Indiana University Press, 1968), 264; George Woodberry, *Ralph Waldo Emerson* (1907; rpt.

New York: Haskell House, 1968), 176; T. S. Eliot, in *Shock of Recognition,* vol. 2, 855; Paul Elmer More, *Shelburne Essays in American Literature,* ed. Daniel Aaron (New York: Harcourt, Brace, and World, 1963), 173; Lewis Mumford, *The Golden Day: A Study in American Literature and Culture* (1926; New York: Dover, 1968), 45.

5. Barrett Wendell, in *Recognition of Ralph Waldo Emerson,* 118; Charles Feidelson, *Symbolism and American Literature* (Chicago: University of Chicago Press, 1953), 120; D. H. Lawrence, in *Recognition of Ralph Waldo Emerson,* 169.

6. Buell, "Emerson Industry," 117; Stanley Cavell, *This New Yet Unapproachable America: Lectures after Emerson after Wittgenstein* (Albuquerque, N.Mex.: Living Batch Press, 1989), 107; David Marr, *American Worlds Since Emerson* (Amherst: University of Massachusetts Press, 1988), 9; Peter Carafiol, "Reading Emerson: Writing History," *Centennial Review* 30 (Fall 1986), 450.

7. Joel Porte, "The Problem of Emerson," in *The Uses of Literature,* ed. Monroe Engel (Cambridge, Mass.: Harvard University Press, 1973), 94.

8. Ibid., 92–93; William Dean Howells, *Literary Friends and Acquaintances,* ed. David F. Hiatt and Edwin H. Cady (Bloomington: Indiana University Press, 1968), 56; Cavell, *This New Yet Unapproachable America,* 3.

9. David Robinson, *Apostle of Culture: Emerson As Preacher and Lecturer* (Philadelphia: University of Pennsylvania Press, 1982), 1; Kenneth Marc Harris, *Carlyle and Emerson: Their Long Debate* (Cambridge, Mass.: Harvard University Press, 1978), 170. Lawrence Buell, *Literary Transcendentalism: Style and Vision in the American Renaissance* (Ithaca, N.Y.: Cornell University Press, 1973) remains an important attempt "to find better ways of measuring the qualities of [Transcendentalist] works" (2)—though its opening page alone provides ample evidence of the usual condescension. See also, as particularly telling examples of the broad, negative presuppositions that underlie Emerson scholarship, Paul K. Conkin, *Puritans and Pragmatists: Eight Eminent American Thinkers* (New York: Dodd, Mead, 1968), 151–90, and Alfred S. Reid, "Emerson's Prose Style: An Edge to Goodness," in *Style in the American Renaissance: A Symposium,* ed. Carl Strauch (Hartford, Conn.: Transcendental Books, 1970), 37–42. Important direct denunciations of Emerson include James Truslow Adams, "Emerson Re-Read," in *Recognition of Ralph Waldo Emerson,* 182–93; Yvor Winters, "Jones Very and R. W. Emerson: Aspects of New England Mysticism" and "The Significance of *The Bridge* by Hart Crane, or What Are We to Think of Professor X?" in *In Defense of Reason* (Chicago: Swallow Press, 1937); Quentin Anderson, *The Imperial Self: An Essay in American Literary and Cultural History* (New York: Knopf, 1971); Russell Kirk, *The Conservative Mind: From Burke to Santayana* (Chicago: Henry Regnery, 1953), 209–13; A. Bartlett Giamatti, "Power, Politics and a Sense of History," in *The University and the Public Interest* (New York: Atheneum, 1981), 166–79; and John Updike, "Emersonianism."

10. Maurice Gonnaud, *An Uneasy Solitude: Individual and Society in the Work of Ralph Waldo Emerson,* trans. Lawrence Rosenwald (Princeton, N.J.: Princeton University Press, 1987), 262, 116.

11. O. W. Firkins, *Ralph Waldo Emerson* (1915; rpt. New York: Russell and Russell, 1965), 373; O. W. Firkins, "Has Emerson a Future?" in *Selected Essays* (Minneapolis: University of Minnesota Press, 1933), 80–81; Carafiol, "Reading Emerson: Writing History," 432.

12. Carafiol, "Reading Emerson: Writing History," 432.

13. Cavell, "Emerson's Aversive Thinking," in *Romantic Revolutions: Criticism and Theory*, ed. Kenneth Johnston et al. (Bloomington: Indiana University Press, 1990), 243; Brownson's essay is reprinted in *Transcendentalists: An Anthology*, 198–200; John Morley, in *Recognition of Ralph Waldo Emerson*, 76; W. C. Brownell, *American Prose Masters*, ed. Howard Mumford Jones (1909; Cambridge, Mass.: Harvard University Press, 1963), 126–27.

14. T. S. Eliot, in *Shock of Recognition*, vol. 2, 859; Perry Miller, "From Edwards to Emerson," in *Errand into the Wilderness* (Cambridge, Mass.: Harvard University Press, 1956), 186; Leslie Fiedler, "American Literature," in *Contemporary Literary Scholarship: A Critical Review*, ed. Lewis Leary (New York: Appleton-Century-Crofts, 1958), 174; Buell, *Literary Transcendentalism*, 1–2; Irving Howe, *The American Newness: Culture and Politics in the Age of Emerson* (Cambridge, Mass.: Harvard University Press, 1986), 14.

15. Howells, *Literary Friends and Acquaintances*, 56; Cavell, *This New Yet Unapproachable America*, 78.

16. Cavell, *This New Yet Unapproachable America*, 78; Dewey, "Ralph Waldo Emerson," 24; T. S. Eliot, in *Shock of Recognition*, vol. 2, 859.

17. Philip F. Gura, *The Wisdom of Words: Language, Theology, and Literature in the New England Renaissance* (Middletown, Conn.: Wesleyan University Press, 1981), 103–4; Cavell, *This New Yet Unapproachable America*, 79. See, as an example of this approach, Ellen Kappy Suckiel's recent conclusion that Emerson remains "first and foremost . . . a preacher" ("Emerson and the Virtues," in *American Philosophy: Royal Institute of Philosophy Lecture Series: 19*, ed. Marcus Singer [New York: Cambridge University Press, 1985], 152). Bruce Kuklick recommends, in the same volume, that further attempts to interpret Emerson's thought be replaced by the study of its local contexts ("Does American Philosophy Rest On a Mistake?" in *American Philosophy*, 187).

18. For Henry James Sr.'s famous response to Emerson—"Oh you man without a handle!" see F. O. Matthiessen, *The James Family* (New York: Knopf, 1961), 43; Henry James, "Emerson," in *Partial Portraits* (1888; rpt. Ann Arbor: University of Michigan Press, 1970), 25; Cavell, *This New Yet Unapproachable America*, 107; Bishop, *Emerson on the Soul*, 1.

19. See Poirier, *Renewal of Literature*, 33; George Kateb, "Thinking About Human Extinction (I) Nietzsche and Heidegger," *Raritan* 6 (Fall 1986):1–28, and "Thinking About Human Extinction (II) Emerson and Whitman," *Raritan* 6 (Winter 1987):1–22; Gura, *Wisdom of Words*, 104; Cornel West, *The American Evasion of Philosophy: A Genealogy of Pragmatism* (Madison: University of Wisconsin Press, 1989), 74.

20. Porte, "Problem of Emerson," 94.

21. Cavell, *The Senses of Walden: An Expanded Edition* (San Francisco: North Point Press, 1981), 33, 124. Joel Porte likewise apologized for an earlier anti-Emerson bias in his preface to the first edition of *Representative Man* (New York: Oxford University Press, 1979), xxi.

22. Cavell, *This New Yet Unapproachable America*, 80.

23. Giles Gunn, *The Culture of Criticism and the Criticism of Culture* (New York: Oxford University Press, 1987); Geoffrey Hartman, *Criticism in the Wilderness: The Study of Literature Today* (New Haven, Conn.: Yale University Press,

1980), 9; William Cain, *The Crisis in Criticism: Theory, Literature, and Reform in English Studies* (Baltimore, Md.: Johns Hopkins University Press, 1984), 240.

24. Kazin, "Father of Us All," 3; James Russell Lowell, "A Fable For Critics," in *Shock of Recognition,* vol. 1, 46. Emerson is, Kazin concluded in 1984, essentially "a revenant from early ages of faith—a primordial, 'aboriginal' kind of early Christian" (*An American Procession* [New York: Knopf, 1984], 39).

25. West, *American Evasion of Philosophy,* 11. Two other recent arguments for resituating Emerson in the mainstream of European thought, not simply within the confines of New England tradition, are Russell B. Goodman, *American Philosophy and the Romantic Tradition* (New York: Cambridge University Press, 1990); and Lawrence Buell, "Emerson in His Cultural Context," in *Ralph Waldo Emerson: A Collection of Critical Essays,* ed. Lawrence Buell (Englewood Cliffs, N.J.: Prentice-Hall, 1993), 48–60.

26. See Eric Cheyfitz's foreword to Gonnaud, *Uneasy Solitude,* xviii; and West, *American Evasion of Philosophy,* 10–11. Philip Rosenberg points out that Carlyle's role as cultural critic was largely unprecedented in the English tradition (*The Seventh Hero: Thomas Carlyle and the Theory of Radical Activism* [Cambridge, Mass.: Harvard University Press, 1974], vii, 33, 52–53).

27. West, *American Evasion of Philosophy,* 36. Harold Bloom makes a similar point: "The relation of Emerson to both Nietzsche and William James suggests that Emersonian Transcendentalism was already much closer to pragmatism than to Kant's metaphysical idealism" (*Agon: Towards a Theory of Revisionism* [New York: Oxford University Press, 1982], 20).

28. Carolyn Porter, *Seeing and Being: The Plight of the Participant Observer in Emerson, James, Adams, and Faulkner* (Middletown, Conn.: Wesleyan University Press, 1981), 94; Gertrude Reif Hughes, *Emerson's Demanding Optimism* (Baton Rouge: Louisiana State University Press, 1984), 162, 18; Feidelson, *Symbolism and American Literature,* 135; Poirier, *Renewal of Literature,* 171; Eric Cheyfitz, *The Trans-Parent: Sexual Politics in the Language of Emerson* (Baltimore, Md.: Johns Hopkins University Press, 1981), xi, 15; Donoghue, *Reading America,* 36; Harold Bloom, *Figures of Capable Imagination* (New York: Seabury Press, 1976), 60.

29. Bloom, "Mr. America," 20; Wilson, *Shock of Recognition,* vol. 1, 596; Richard Grusin, "Revisionism and the Structure of Emersonian Action," *American Literary History* 1 (Summer 1989), 404–31.

30. West, *American Evasion of Philosophy,* 3.

31. Maurice Mandelbaum, *History, Man, and Reason,* 5.

32. See Walter Kaufmann's discussion of the Emerson-Nietzsche relationship in his introduction to Nietzsche, *Gay Science,* 7–13; see also Frederic Ives Carpenter, *Emerson Handbook* (New York: Hendricks House, 1953), 244–49.

33. Arnold, in *Recognition of Ralph Waldo Emerson,* 70; Henry James, *Partial Portraits,* 32; William James, "Address at the Emerson Centenary in Concord," in *Emerson: A Collection of Critical Essays,* 19, 23.

34. Dewey's essay is, F. O. Matthiessen noted in 1941, "in strong opposition to the usual academic dismissal of Emerson's thought" (*American Renaissance: Art and Expression in the Age of Emerson and Whitman* [New York: Oxford University Press, 1941], 4).

35. Dewey, "Ralph Waldo Emerson," 24.

36. Ibid., 27–28.

37. Ibid.

38. Dewey, cited in West, *American Evasion of Philosophy,* 97.

39. West, *American Evasion of Philosophy,* 74, 85.

40. The "second phase of Emerson studies" is Bliss Perry's description, in *Emerson Today* (Princeton, N.J.: Princeton University Press, 1931), 5.

41. Henry James, *Partial Portraits,* 2, 7–10; the Matthiessen quotation is from *James Family,* 429.

42. Henry James, *Partial Portraits,* 8, 31, 15.

43. The Santayana quotations are from "The Genteel Tradition in American Philosophy," in *Santayana on America,* ed. Richard Lyon (New York: Harcourt, Brace, and World, 1968), 40, 45, 54; Irving Howe, "The American Voice—It Begins on a Note of Wonder," *New York Times Book Review,* 4 July 1976, 2.

44. Santayana, "The Genteel Tradition at Bay," in *Santayana on America,* 158, 138; Babbitt and Warner G. Rice, cited in René Wellek, "Irving Babbitt, Paul More, and Transcendentalism," in *Transcendentalism and Its Legacy,* ed. Myron Simon and Thornton H. Parsons (Ann Arbor: University of Michigan Press, 1966), 192–193, 197.

45. Santayana, "Emerson the Poet," in *Santayana on America,* 271; Santayana, "The Optimism of Ralph Waldo Emerson," in *George Santayana's America,* 83, 73, 81; Santayana, "Emerson," in *Santayana on America,* 267, 266, 259, 260. For the evolution of Santayana's opinion of Emerson, see Porte, *Representative Man* (1979), 16–31.

46. Santayana, *The Last Puritan: A Memoir in the Form of a Novel* (New York: Scribner's, 1936), 201, 126, 404, 445.

47. Santayana, "Emerson the Poet," 275, 271.

48. Santayana, "Dewey's Naturalistic Metaphysics," in *Santayana on America,* 111–12, 121, 116, 125.

49. Hegel, *German Aesthetic and Literary Criticism: Kant, Fichte, Schelling, Schopenhauer, Hegel,* 211. See Eugene Goodheart, *The Cult of the Ego: The Self in Modern Literature* (Chicago: University of Chicago Press, 1968), 118–19, for a discussion of Nietzsche and this German, Protestant tradition of the "I" as appropriator and consumer.

50. Santayana, *Three Philosophical Poets* (1910; rpt. New York: Cooper Square Publishers, 1970), 7–8.

51. Santayana, "Optimism of Ralph Waldo Emerson," 73.

52. John Burt Foster, *Heirs to Dionysus: A Nietzschean Current in Literary Modernism* (Princeton, N.J.: Princeton University Press, 1981), 51.

53. Santayana, "Optimism of Ralph Waldo Emerson," 73.

54. Santayana, "Emerson the Poet," 273.

55. Henry James, *Partial Portraits,* 17.

56. "Cheerful Monist" is Frost's description in *Emerson: A Collection of Critical Essays,* 12.

57. Porte, *Representative Man* (1979), 229.

58. Ibid., 258–59, 234.

59. Leo Marx, *The Machine in the Garden: Technology and the Pastoral Idea in America* (New York: Oxford University Press, 1967), 230.

60. I quote Robert Solomon's description of Heidegger's philosophy in *In*

the Spirit of Hegel, 389. The traditional description of Emerson as "a philosopher of intuition," Cavell notes, "uniformly fails to add that he is simultaneously the teacher of tuition" (*In Quest of the Ordinary,* 115).

61. Mandelbaum characterizes the "pragmatic-economical view of the human mind" as the theory that defines intelligence "in terms of its usefulness in satisfying needs." According to this view, all that we consider knowledge or truth or regard "as an order fixed by nature itself" may be defined, instead, as "a product of our own tendencies to arrange and summarize experience in a manner useful to us." See Mandelbaum, *History, Man, and Reason,* 16–17.

62. Robert Solomon suggests the shared emphasis on "action as knowledge" that links Fichte and Hegel to the pragmatism of William James and Dewey (*In the Spirit of Hegel,* 10–11).

63. Carlyle, *Carlyle Reader,* 152.

64. Johann Fichte, *The Vocation of Man,* trans. William Smith (1931; rpt. Chicago: Open Court, 1940), 94.

65. Dewey, cited in West, *American Evasion of Philosophy,* 82.

66. Dewey, "Ralph Waldo Emerson," 29.

67. West, *American Evasion of Philosophy,* 73.

68. Ibid., 211; Dewey quotations from ibid., 100–101, 104, 92, 91. Cavell approaches Wittgenstein and Emerson as "philosophers of culture" in *This New Yet Unapproachable America.*

69. William James, *The Energies of Men* (New York: Moffat, Yard, 1917), 38.

70. Henry Adams, *The Education of Henry Adams,* ed. Ernest Samuels (Boston: Houghton Mifflin, 1973), 314, 463, 461.

71. West, *American Evasion of Philosophy,* 25.

72. Poirier, *Renewal of Literature,* 59.

73. Kenneth Burke, "I, Eye, Ay—Emerson's Early Essay 'Nature': Thoughts on the Machinery of Transcendence," in *Transcendentalism and Its Legacy,* 9; Eduard Baumgarten, *Der Pragmatismus: R. W. Emerson, W. James, J. Dewey* (Frankfurt, 1938); Matthiessen, *American Renaissance,* 368; Perry Miller, *Nature's Nation* (Cambridge, Mass.: Harvard University Press, 1967), 171; Daniel Aaron, *Men of Good Hope: A Story of American Progressives* (New York: Oxford University Press, 1951), 8. Emerson, Hermann Hummel concluded in 1946, "must be regarded as the teacher and master rather than as a 'précurseur' of Nietzsche" ("Emerson and Nietzsche," *New England Quarterly,* 19 [March 1946]:84). But scholarship on the Emerson-Nietzsche connection has been sparse. The handful of articles in English, as well as European studies, are catalogued in Carpenter, *Emerson Handbook,* 254–58. See also William Salter, *Nietzsche the Thinker* (New York: Holt, 1917).

74. Aaron, *Men of Good Hope,* 8.

75. Feidelson, *Symbolism and American Literature,* 126.

76. Gonnaud, *Uneasy Solitude,* 355.

77. Matthiessen, *American Renaissance,* 367–68, 4.

78. Jon Klancher defines "master sign" as a single, totalizing concept that takes on, in the hands of a critic-seer like Carlyle, sufficient heuristic power to explain a diverse array of social, philosophical, political, and cultural problems (*Making of English Reading Audiences,* 71–73).

79. See Gonnaud's introduction to Stephen Whicher, *Freedom and Fate: An*

Inner Life of Ralph Waldo Emerson, 2d ed. (Philadelphia: University of Pennsylvania Press, 1971), x.

80. Poirier, *Renewal of Literature,* 33; Hughes, *Emerson's Demanding Optimism,* 70; Julie Ellison, "The Edge of Urbanity: Emerson's *English Traits,*" *ESQ: A Journal of the American Renaissance* 32 (1986):104.

81. Bishop, *Emerson on the Soul,* 165.

82. See, for example, Cheyfitz, foreword to Gonnaud, *Uneasy Solitude,* xv; Marr, *American Worlds Since Emerson,* 70–71; and Harold Bloom's introduction to *Modern Critical Interpretations: Henry James's 'The Portrait of a Lady'* (New York: Chelsea House, 1987), 6.

83. Whicher, *Freedom and Fate,* 172–73.

84. Ibid.; see also 179.

85. This central passage from *Freedom and Fate* is on pp. 55–56.

86. Ibid., 172.

87. See *Freedom and Fate,* 56, 53, 44; Arnold described Heinrich Heine as a "soldier in the war of liberation of humanity" (cited in Peter Allan Dale, *The Victorian Critic and the Idea of History: Carlyle, Arnold, and Pater* [Cambridge, Mass.: Harvard University Press, 1977], 63).

88. Harold Bloom, *The Ringers in the Tower: Studies in Romantic Tradition* (Chicago: University of Chicago Press, 1971), 224; Anderson, *Imperial Self,* 130; Lewis P. Simpson, *The Man of Letters in New England and the South* (Baton Rouge: Louisiana State University Press, 1973), 81, 65; Laurence Holland, cited in Eric Cheyfitz, *The Trans-Parent,* 15; Porte, *Representative Man* (1979), 209–82 and passim. Leo Marx's analysis (in *Machine in the Garden*) of the complex relationship between Transcendentalism and technological power should not be left out as an important example of this trend.

89. Dewey, cited in West, *American Evasion of Philosophy,* 103; Whicher, *Freedom and Fate,* 55–56.

90. Whicher, *Freedom and Fate,* 56; Firkins, "Has Emerson a Future?," 79.

91. Firkins, "Has Emerson a Future?" 79–81; Henry Bamford Parks, in *Emerson: A Collection of Critical Essays,* 126, 124.

92. Dewey called Emerson's ideas "versions of the Here and the Now" ("Ralph Waldo Emerson," 28); Donoghue, *Reading America,* 23, 37; Gay Wilson Allen, *Waldo Emerson* (New York: Viking, 1981), 642; Anthony J. Cascardi, "Emerson on Nature: Philosophy beyond Kant," *ESQ: A Journal of the American Renaissance* 30 (1984):202. Emerson and those in his tradition are, Russell Goodman writes, "as much 'transcendentalist' as 'pragmatic'" (*American Philosophy and the Romantic Tradition,* 33).

Chapter 2: The Doctrine of Use

1. John Jay Chapman, "Emerson," 644.

2. Fred Kaplan, *Thomas Carlyle: A Biography* (Ithaca, N.Y.: Cornell University Press, 1983), 121.

3. Emerson is paraphrasing Bacon, but he may well have in mind Goethe's insistence on action and productivity. See Gustaaf Van Cromphout, *Emerson's Modernity and the Example of Goethe* (Columbia: University of Missouri Press, 1990), 41–54.

4. "[D]eath for Emerson," Evelyn Barish notes, "remained not a true loss or

ending, but an open question, a source of possibility, for much longer than is common" (*Emerson*, 34).

5. Cf. W, 8:177; or JMN, 13:120; or Emerson's remark in *Representative Men:* "Thus we feed on genius" (CW, 4:15).

6. James M. Cox, "R. W. Emerson: The Circles of the Eye," in *Emerson: Prophecy, Metamorphosis, and Influence,* ed. David Levin (New York: Columbia University Press, 1975), 71–73; McAleer, *Ralph Waldo Emerson,* xiv (cf. McAleer's remarks on Emerson's process of "creative assimilation," pp. 7–10).

7. Bloom, *Agon,* 335; B. L. Packer, *Emerson's Fall: A New Interpretation of the Major Essays* (New York: Continuum, 1982), 51.

8. Frank Lentricchia, *Criticism and Social Change* (Chicago: University of Chicago Press, 1983), 4.

9. Packer, *Emerson's Fall,* 51; Anderson, *Imperial Self,* 87.

10. Allen, *Waldo Emerson,* 136; McAleer, *Ralph Waldo Emerson,* 92.

11. Alexander Nehamas, *Nietzsche: Life as Literature* (Cambridge, Mass.: Harvard University Press, 1985), 198, 190. Cf. Nietzsche's thesis that "everything good is the evil of former days made serviceable," his belief that we must "press everything terrible into *service,* one by one, step by step, experimentally" (WP, 1025). See Stack, *Nietzsche and Emerson,* 176–266.

12. Arthur C. Danto, *Nietzsche as Philosopher* (New York: Columbia University Press, 1965), 212; Karl Jaspers, *Nietzsche: An Introduction to the Understanding of His Philosophical Activity,* trans. Charles Wallraff and Frederick Schmitz (Tucson: University of Arizona Press, 1965), 156–57; Nehamas, *Nietzsche,* 184 and, for Nietzsche citations, 146, 191.

13. Thoreau, cited in Richard Lebeaux, *Young Man Thoreau* (New York: Harper and Row, 1978), 129; Nehamas, *Nietzsche,* 184.

14. Danto, *Nietzsche as Philosopher,* 194–95.

15. Josiah Royce, "Nietzsche," *Atlantic Monthly,* March 1917, 329. H. L. Mencken, distinguishing Nietzsche's philosophy from idealism and classical stoicism, makes the same point: "A vast difference exists between a mere denial of pain and a willingness to admit it, face it, and triumph over it" (*The Philosophy of Friedrich Nietzsche* [London: T. Fisher, 1908], 120). On Emerson's faith in the good of evil, Christopher Lasch remarks: "The statement that 'evil is good in the making' [in "Fate"—W, 6:35] does not deny the existence of evil; what it denies is the possibility that we can abolish it" (*The True and Only Heaven: Progress and Its Critics* [New York: Norton, 1991], 264).

16. Jaspers, *Nietzsche,* 160.

17. Ibid., 141; Nehamas (*Nietzsche,* 161), paraphrasing Nietzsche's Zarathustra.

18. Allan Megill, *Prophets of Extremity: Nietzsche, Heidegger, Foucault, Derrida* (Berkeley: University of California Press, 1985), 2.

19. Royce, in *American Thought: Civil War to World War I,* ed. Perry Miller (New York: Rinehart, 1954), 20–21, 23, 25; Andrew Delbanco cites Royce's essay in *The Puritan Ordeal* (Cambridge, Mass.: Harvard University Press, 1989), 71–72.

20. Delbanco, *Puritan Ordeal,* 33; Perry Miller, *The New England Mind: The Seventeenth Century* (Cambridge, Mass.: Harvard University Press, 1939), 38; John Cotton and Cotton Mather, cited in Delbanco, *Puritan Ordeal,* 71, 115; John

Cotton, in *The Puritans in America: A Narrative Anthology,* eds. Alan Heimert and Andrew Delbanco (Cambridge, Mass.: Harvard University Press, 1985), 77; Jonathan Edwards, in *Major Writers of America,* ed. Perry Miller (New York: Harcourt, Brace, and World, 1962), vol. 1, 169.

21. Stephen Donadio, *Nietzsche, Henry James, and the Artistic Will* (New York: Oxford University Press, 1978), 260; Daniel Walker Howe, *The Unitarian Conscience* (Cambridge, Mass.: Harvard University Press, 1970), 246; Tuckerman, cited in *Unitarian Conscience,* 241.

22. Howe, *Unitarian Conscience,* 261; Brownson, in *Transcendentalists,* 108.

23. Channing, cited in Andrew Delbanco, *William Ellery Channing* (Cambridge, Mass.: Harvard University Press, 1981), 31; Howe, *Unitarian Conscience,* 115.

24. Perry Miller, *The Life of the Mind in America from the Revolution to the Civil War* (New York: Harcourt, Brace, and World, 1965), 7; Timothy L. Smith, *Revivalism and Social Reform* (Baltimore, Md.: Johns Hopkins University Press, 1957), 142.

25. See Smith, *Revivalism and Social Reform,* 96–98.

26. Henry Ware Jr., *Formation of the Christian Character* (Boston: n.p., 1866), 152, 16, 150.

27. Sampson Reed, *Observations on the Growth of the Mind* (1859; rpt. New York: Arno Press, 1972), 96, 46, 56–57.

28. William Ellery Channing, in *Transcendentalists,* 22. "Our proper work," Channing writes, "is to approach God by the . . . natural unfolding of our highest powers" (p. 25).

29. Howe, *Unitarian Conscience,* 278.

30. Randolph Bourne, cited in Bromwich, *Choice of Inheritance,* 155.

31. Santayana, *Santayana on America,* .50; Santayana, "The Poetry of Barbarism," in *Essays in Literary Criticism,* ed. Irving Singer (New York: Scribner's, 1956), 172.

32. Nehamas, *Nietzsche,* 166.

33. Alan D. Hodder, *Emerson's Rhetoric of Revelation: "Nature," the Reader, and the Apocalypse Within* (University Park: Pennsylvania State University Press, 1989), 43.

34. George Santayana, *Egotism in German Philosophy* (New York: Scribner's, n.d.), 103, 69, 142, 70–72.

35. The phrase is Richard Poirier's; see *Renewal of Literature,* 182–223.

36. Thomas McFarland, *Coleridge and the Pantheist Tradition* (Oxford: Clarendon Press, 1969), 161–62. For his further reservations regarding the scholarly predilection for finding development in an author's career, see McFarland, *Shapes of Culture,* 168–74.

37. Gonnaud, *Uneasy Solitude,* 152.

38. Ibid.

39. Reed, *Observations,* 56–57.

40. Nehamas, *Nietzsche,* 47, 61.

41. Robert E. Burkholder, "The Radical Emerson: Politics in 'The American Scholar,'" *ESQ: A Journal of the American Renaissance* 34 (1988):50; Anderson, *Imperial Self,* 43–44; Jeffrey Steele, *The Representation of the Self in the American*

Renaissance (Chapel Hill: University of North Carolina Press, 1987), 184; David Simpson, *The Politics of American English, 1776–1850* (New York: Oxford University Press, 1986), 243; John Updike, "Emersonianism," 159.

42. William H. Gass, "Emerson and the Essay," in *Habitations of the Word* (New York: Simon and Schuster, 1985), 23.

43. Nehamas, *Nietzsche*, 251, n. 6.

44. William James, cited in Kenneth Burke, *Attitudes Toward History*, 3d ed. (Berkeley: University of California Press, 1984), 6.

45. Marr, *American Worlds Since Emerson*, 16; McAleer, *Ralph Waldo Emerson*, 165; Charles Simic, *Wonderful Words, Silent Truth: Essays on Poetry and a Memoir* (Ann Arbor: University of Michigan Press, 1990), 80.

46. Marr, *American Worlds Since Emerson*, 53–54, 62; Stephen Whicher, *Freedom and Fate*, 150; Simic, *Wonderful Words*, 73, 80–81.

47. Hodder, *Emerson's Rhetoric of Revelation*, 40–41; Bloom, *Agon*, 156–57.

48. Hodder, *Emerson's Rhetoric of Revelation*, 39; "It is . . . the mind that is sublime," Hazard Adams writes, summarizing Kant, "not the objects of nature" (*Philosophy of the Literary Symbolic* [Tallahassee: Florida State University Press, 1983], 43).

49. Bloom, *Ringers in the Tower*, 19–20.

50. E. R. Curtius, "Emerson," in *Essays on European Literature*, trans. Michael Kowal (Princeton, N.J.: Princeton University Press, 1973), 225, 221; Sherman Paul, *The Shores of America: Thoreau's Inward Exploration* (1958; rpt. New York: Russell and Russell, 1971), 14; Feidelson, *Symbolism and American Literature*, 150, 29.

51. Packer, "Ralph Waldo Emerson," 389.

52. Burke, "I, Eye, Ay," 19.

53. Mandelbaum, *History, Man, and Reason*, 41. "Historicism," Mandelbaum writes, "is the belief that an adequate understanding of the nature of any phenomenon . . . [is] to be gained through considering it in terms of . . . the role which it played within a process of development" (p. 42).

54. Julie Ellison, *Emerson's Romantic Style* (Princeton, N.J.: Princeton University Press, 1984), 223; Barbara Packer is cited on the same page. See also Joel Porte, *Emerson and Thoreau: Transcendentalists in Conflict* (Middletown, Conn.: Wesleyan University Press, 1966), 50.

55. Miller, *Errand into the Wilderness*, 189; Simpson, *Politics of American English*, 258, 254, 230–31; Curtius, "Emerson," 225.

56. Simpson, *Politics of American English*, 255, 257; Miller, *Life of the Mind in America*, 320–21, 318; Miller, *Errand into the Wilderness*, 186, 204–5.

57. West, *American Evasion of Philosophy*, 5; Carlyle, *Carlyle Reader*, 91. "The opposing self" is, of course, Lionel Trilling's description of a particularly modern conception of the self—see Rosenberg, *Seventh Hero*, 1.

58. Mary Kupiec Cayton, *Emerson's Emergence: Self and Society in the Transformation of New England, 1800–1845* (Chapel Hill: University of North Carolina Press, 1989), 241.

59. R. P. Blackmur, *Henry Adams*, ed. Veronica A. Makowsky (New York: Harcourt, Brace, Jovanovich, 1980), 24–25; Adams, *Education of Henry Adams*, 388. Carlyle valued the symbol-making power for similar reasons; see Dale, *Victorian Critic and the Idea of History*, 69–72.

60. Kenneth Burke, *The Philosophy of Literary Form: Studies in Symbolic Action* (New York: Vintage Books, 1957), 54.

61. The emphasis in Emerson's descriptions of thinking and symbol making often falls in the direction not of a "high" Platonism but of a "low" pragmatism. The mind contends with the potentially threatening forces of history and urbanization through the assimilative process of imaginative use: "We too shall know how to take up all this industry and empire, this Western civilization, into thought, as easily as men did when arts were few; but not by holding it high, but by holding it low. The intellect uses and is not used,—uses London and Paris and Berlin, East and West, to its end" (W, 8:74).

62. Blackmur, *Henry Adams*, 25.

63. Walt Whitman, *Complete Poetry and Collected Prose*, ed. Justin Kaplan (New York: Library of America, 1982), 15, 987.

64. McFarland, *Coleridge and the Pantheist Tradition*, 175–76; James M. Cox, "R. W. Emerson: The Circles of the Eye," 71. Emerson's essays are, Cox suggests, "in a way . . . all repetitions of *Nature*" (p. 71); "I do not see Emerson as 'developing' or 'progressing' or 'declining.' . . . [V]isions of Emerson's career in terms of crises and turning points, in ups and downs, in directions from revolution to compromise or from idealism to realism have their own distortion" (pp. 75–76).

65. For his objection to the usual, autobiographical reading of this line, see Cavell, *In Quest of the Ordinary*, 35.

66. Porte, *Representative Man* (1979), 225; David Van Leer, *Emerson's Epistemology: The Argument of the Essays* (New York: Cambridge University Press, 1986), 189. Cf. *The American Transcendentalists: Their Prose and Poetry*, ed. Perry Miller (New York: Doubleday Anchor Books, 1957), 48.

67. Whicher, *Freedom and Fate*, 150.

68. Ibid., 171.

69. Alfred Kazin, *American Procession*, 61.

70. Hughes, *Emerson's Demanding Optimism*, x.

71. Ibid., 99, x–xi.

72. Cf. Porte, *Representative Man* (1979), 181.

73. Buell, *Literary Transcendentalism*, 181–82; Mutlu Konuk Blasing, *American Poetry: The Rhetoric of Its Forms* (New Haven, Conn.: Yale University Press, 1987), 70, 72–73.

74. Henry David Thoreau, *Walden*, ed. J. Lyndon Shanley (Princeton, N.J.: Princeton University Press, 1971), 11.

75. Cf. Nehamas, *Nietzsche*, 141–69.

76. Bishop, *Emerson on the Soul*, 205–6.

77. Whicher, *Freedom and Fate*, 151.

78. See the distinction George L. Kline makes between Kierkegaardian existentialism and the Nietzschean and Marxist stress on production: "Neither [Nietzsche nor Marx] valued subjectivity, existential decision, inwardness, passion, or spiritual suffering as such. Rather, they assigned them a certain instrumental value insofar, and only insofar, as they issue in cultural products (Nietzsche) or in socio-economic products (Marx)" ("The Use and Abuse of Hegel by Nietzsche and Marx," in *Hegel and His Critics: Philosophy in the Aftermath of Hegel*, ed. William Desmond [Albany: State University of New York Press, 1989], 1.

79. Whicher, *Freedom and Fate*, 157.

80. Whitman, *Complete Poetry and Collected Prose*, 633.

Chapter 3: The Uses of Failure

1. Erich Heller, *The Importance of Nietzsche* (Chicago: University of Chicago Press, 1988), 31. The translation of Nietzsche here is Heller's.

2. Henry James Sr. characterized Emerson as "unaffectedly innocent" and "unmistakably virgin-born" (*Critical Essays on Ralph Waldo Emerson*, ed. Robert E. Burkholder and Joel Myerson [Boston: G. K. Hall, 1983], 221–25). William James classified him as a "once-born" soul, ignorant of evil, in *The Varieties of Religious Experience* (1902; New York: Penguin Books, 1982), 80–81. See also Santayana, "Genteel Tradition in American Philosophy," 43; Woodberry, *Ralph Waldo Emerson,* 152; Sidney Hook, *Pragmatism and the Tragic Sense of Life* (New York: Basic Books, 1974), 48; Kirk, *Conservative Mind,* 213.

3. McAleer, *Ralph Waldo Emerson,* 45.

4. Octavius Brooks Frothingham, *Transcendentalism in New England: A History* (1876; Philadelphia: University of Pennsylvania Press, 1959), 221–22; Barish, *Emerson,* 8–9, 35; Hodder, *Emerson's Rhetoric of Revelation,* 62.

5. Porte, *Representative Man* (1979), 167, 170.

6. William James, *Varieties of Religious Experience,* 80–81.

7. Ibid., 488.

8. Feidelson, *Symbolism and American Literature,* 35; Herman Melville, "Hawthorne and His Mosses," in *Shock of Recognition,* vol. 1, 197; Herman Melville, *Mardi,* ed. Tyrus Hillway (1849; New Haven, Conn.: College and University, 1973), 489.

9. Thoreau, in Perry Miller, *Consciousness in Concord* (Boston: Houghton Mifflin, 1958), 162.

10. Marvin Meyers, *The Jacksonian Persuasion* (Stanford, Calif.: Stanford University Press, 1957), 50, 128–29.

11. Donadio, *Nietzsche,* 7. See Peter Heller, "Reversal as Doctrine, Method, and Symptom," in *Dialectics and Nihilism: Essays on Lessing, Nietzsche, Mann, and Kafka* (Amherst: University of Massachusetts Press, 1966), 138–43.

12. Kenneth Burke, *Perspectives by Incongruity,* ed. Stanley Edgar Hyman (Bloomington: Indiana University Press, 1964), 62–63.

13. Heller, "Reversal as Doctrine," 145.

14. Carlyle, *Carlyle Reader,* 68.

15. Newton Arvin, "The House of Pain," in *Emerson: A Collection of Critical Essays,* 58; Winters, *In Defense of Reason,* 402.

16. Melville, *Mardi,* 489.

17. Donadio, *Nietzsche,* 224.

18. See Porte's discussion of the dream's biblical imagery (*Representative Man* [1979], 80–81); Evelyn Barish notes the generally abstemious household in which Emerson grew up and the connection it fostered between "self-will" and "the expression of appetite" (*Emerson,* 18–27).

Chapter 4: Extravagance

1. Bloom, *Agon,* 331.

2. Oliver Wendell Holmes, *Ralph Waldo Emerson* (1898; rpt. New York: Chelsea House, 1980), 114, 111, 184. Harriet Martineau noted the combination

Emerson presented of an earnest "tone of mind" and "exquisite spirit of humor" (*Retrospect of Western Travel,* vol. 2, 205). Cf. also Henry Demarest Lloyd, "Emerson's Wit and Humor," in *Mazzini and Other Essays* (New York: G. P. Putnam's Sons, 1910), 71–100.

3. Holmes, *Ralph Waldo Emerson,* 184; Whitman, *Shock of Recognition,* vol. 1, 272. Not everyone approved of that "secret proclivity"; Carlyle grew weary of Emerson's "sly low-voiced sarcasm" (cited in McAleer, *Ralph Waldo Emerson,* 435).

4. Packer, *Emerson's Fall,* 6–9; Warner Berthoff, "'Building Discourse': The Genesis of Emerson's *Nature,*" in *Fictions and Events* (New York: Dutton, 1971), 208–9.

5. Cavell, *In Quest of the Ordinary,* 34; Anderson, *Imperial Self,* 24; Firkins, *Ralph Waldo Emerson,* 192–93.

6. Packer, *Emerson's Fall,* 19–20.

7. Nehamas, *Nietzsche,* 31.

8. Ibid., 141–42. Eugene Goodheart suggests that "Nietzsche's love of the bold phrase" can become "an autonomous force in his work"—a tendency that makes necessary "the scholar's attempt to recall the phrase to its context and to qualify and correct its excesses" (*Cult of the Ego,* 115). Cf. Heller, *Importance of Nietzsche,* 144, and Arthur Danto's comments on Nietzsche's fundamentally "irresponsible" style in *Nietzsche as Philosopher,* 229 and 9, 97, 146, 200.

9. Poirier, *Renewal of Literature,* 65, 74.

10. See Packer, *Emerson's Fall,* 1, 5, 6, 20, 140, 19; Cavell, "Emerson's Aversive Thinking," 223, 246.

11. Giamatti, "Power, Politics, and a Sense of History," 172, 174–77.

12. Robert D. Richardson, *Henry David Thoreau: A Life of the Mind* (Berkeley: University of California Press, 1986), 56.

13. Emerson first preached on "Self-Direction and Self-Command" and "Self-Knowledge and Self-Mastery" in the fall of 1828. See Richardson, *Henry David Thoreau,* 55.

14. Donadio, *Nietzsche, Henry James, and the Artistic Will,* 138.

15. Channing, *Transcendentalists,* 25; Thoreau, *Walden,* 324; Henry David Thoreau, "Thomas Carlyle and His Works," *Early Essays and Miscellanies,* ed. Joseph Moldenhauer et al. (Princeton, N.J.: Princeton University Press, 1975), 264–265.

16. See Margaret Fuller's preface to *Woman in the Nineteenth Century* (1845; New York: Norton, 1971), 13.

17. *American Transcendentalists,* 44, 46.

18. Michael Gilmore, *American Romanticism and the Marketplace* (Chicago: University of Chicago Press, 1985), 153; Whitman, *Complete Poetry and Collected Prose,* 987, 992–93; Thoreau, *Walden,* 100–1.

19. D. H. Lawrence, *Studies in Classic American Literature* (New York: Viking, 1961), viii; Constance Rourke, *American Humor* (New York: Harcourt, Brace, Jovanovich, 1959), 157.

20. Packer, *Emerson's Fall,* 9; Joel Porte, "Transcendental Antics," in *Veins of Humor,* ed. Harry Levin (Cambridge, Mass.: Harvard University Press, 1972), 172–73.

21. Thoreau, "Thomas Carlyle," 232, 253, 226.
22. G. W. F. Hegel, *Phenomenology of Spirit,* trans. A. V. Miller (New York: Oxford University Press, 1977), 22.
23. Novalis and Schlegel, in *German Aesthetic and Literary Criticism: The Romantic Ironists and Goethe,* ed. Kathleen Wheeler (New York: Cambridge University Press, 1984),12, 63. Cf. Wheeler's excellent introduction pp. 1–27 (citations from pp. 11–12).
24. Cavell, *This New Yet Unapproachable America,* 44; Northrop Frye, cited in Hodder, *Emerson's Rhetoric of Revelation,* 124–25. See the distinction Thomas McFarland draws between those writers who aim for "relative readability" and those who seek its deliberate "impedance." Those truth-tellers, like Blake or Kant, who prefer the language of impedance do so in the belief that "the truth must be earned, not simply read" (*Shapes of Culture,* 83–95).
25. Richard Rorty, *Philosophy and the Mirror of Nature* (Princeton, N.J.: Princeton University Press, 1979), 5–6, 369; Porte, *Representative Man,* 2d ed., 15; Wheeler, *German Aesthetic and Literary Criticism,* 11; for Yvor Winters's characterization of Emerson as "a fraud and sentimentalist," see his *In Defense of Reason,* 279.
26. Stanley Cavell calls "Schopenhauer as Educator" "a transcription and elaboration of Emersonian passages" ("Emerson's Aversive Thinking," 235). George Stack notes that Nietzsche's reading of Emerson actually precedes his knowledge of Schopenhauer and that Emerson was particularly on Nietzsche's mind during the composition of *Untimely Meditations* (see *Nietzsche and Emerson,* 153, 48, 105–7).
27. Cavell, *In Quest of the Ordinary,* 19.
28. Megill, *Prophets of Extremity,* 343, 345.
29. "Happiness Pill" is Kenneth Burke's phrase ("I, Eye, Ay," 3).
30. Cavell, *Senses of Walden: An Expanded Edition,* 141–42, 157.

Chapter 5: Working and Being Worked Upon

1. Packer, *Emerson's Fall,* 120.
2. Walter Kaufmann, note to WP, 983; Nehamas, *Nietzsche,* 7. For the debt Nietzsche's idea of the overman owes to Emerson's "synthetic men," see Stack, *Nietzsche and Emerson,* 8, 212, 348, 351, and 309–61.
3. Fuller, *Woman in the Nineteenth Century,* 176–77.
4. Solomon, *In the Spirit of Hegel,* 274, 451–53.
5. Hegel, *Phenomenology of Spirit,* 241, 240, 244, 193; Goodheart, *Cult of the Ego,* 121–22; Carlyle, *Carlyle Reader,* 238, 260.
6. Thoreau, "Thomas Carlyle and His Works," 251; Elizabeth Palmer Peabody, in *Transcendentalists,* 468.
7. This shared, fundamentally aesthetic conception of their work only makes the task of interpreting Emerson and Nietzsche all the more elusive. To see one's vocation as essentially a work of art, an act of creative mythmaking, marks one's thought and one's style as essentially *extreme.* Cf. Megill, *Prophets of Extremity,* 88.
8. Danto, *Nietzsche as Philosopher,* 225.

9. Dale, *Victorian Critic,* 15–58; Solomon, *In the Spirit of Hegel,* 442–43; Hegel, *Phenomenology,* 113–14.

10. Emerson's belief in the "moral sentiment"—in "the power of the heart to discover within itself the highest good"—as Jonathan Bishop aptly summarizes it, was "a cornerstone of his faith" (*Emerson on the Soul,* 66).

11. Mandelbaum, *History, Man, and Reason,* 364. Peter Angeles describes voluntarism as the ethical belief that "the will is the fundamental and ultimate ground in . . . arriving at moral values" and the metaphysical belief that "the will is the primary and dominant factor in all human experience and in all the processes of the universe" (*Dictionary of Philosophy* [New York: Barnes and Noble, 1981], 315).

12. Donoghue, *Reading America,* 37, 36.

13. Ibid., 21, 39.

14. Arthur Schopenhauer, *The World as Will and Representation,* vol. 2, trans. E. F. J. Payne (New York: Dover, 1958), 293; John R. Reed, *Victorian Will* (Athens: Ohio University Press, 1989), 76.

15. Goodheart, *Cult of the Ego,* 121.

16. Schopenhauer, *World as Will,* vol. 2, 301, 351.

17. Rosenwald, *Emerson and the Art of the Diary,* 101; Grusin, "Revisionism," 415; Cavell, *Senses of Walden: An Expanded Edition,* 132.

18. David Robinson, "Grace and Works: Emerson's Essays in Theological Perspective," in *American Unitarianism, 1805–1865,* ed. Conrad Edick Wright (Boston: Massachusetts Historical Society and Northeastern University Press, 1989), 129.

19. Emerson preferred the energies of war, even anarchy, to "the Chinese stagnation of society" (CW, 1:198).

20. Peter Carafiol, *Transcendent Reason: James Marsh and the Forms of Romantic Thought* (Tallahassee: Florida State University Press, 1982), 180.

21. Herman Melville, *The Confidence-Man,* ed. H. Bruce Franklin (1857; Indianapolis: Bobbs-Merrill, 1967), 310–11; Lowell, "Fable for Critics," 44–45; Firkins, *Ralph Waldo Emerson,* 362; Ray Benoit, "Emerson on Plato: The Fire's Center," in *On Emerson,* ed. Edwin Cady and Louis J. Budd (Durham, N.C.: Duke University Press, 1988), 127.

22. Cavell, *This New Yet Unapproachable America,* 44.

23. Benoit, "Emerson on Plato," 127; Solomon, *In the Spirit of Hegel,* 198.

24. Bloom, *Figures of Capable Imagination,* 61, 57, 61–62.

25. Frederic I. Carpenter, "William James and Emerson," in *On Emerson,* 43–61.

26. Benoit, "Emerson on Plato," 127; Harris, *Carlyle and Emerson,* 68; Donoghue, *Reading America,* 39; Gonnaud, *An Uneasy Solitude,* 337.

27. Stephen Whicher, "Emerson's Tragic Sense," in *Interpretations of American Literature,* ed. Charles Feidelson and Paul Brodtkorb (New York: Oxford University Press, 1959), 153; Heller, *Importance of Nietzsche,* 142.

28. Cavell, *This New Yet Unapproachable America,* 78–79.

29. Benoit, "Emerson on Plato," 130, 135, 131.

30. Tilottama Rajan, *Dark Interpreter: The Discourse of Romanticism* (Ithaca, N.Y.: Cornell University Press, 1980), 18; Grusin, "Revisionism," 428.

31. William James, *Varieties of Religious Experience*, 33.

32. Firkins, "Has Emerson a Future?" 79; Sherman Paul, *Emerson's Angle of Vision* (Cambridge, Mass.: Harvard University Press, 1952), 25; Robert Pollock, "Ralph Waldo Emerson: The Single Vision," in *American Classics Reconsidered: A Christian Appraisal*, ed. Harold C. Gardiner (New York: Scribner's, 1958), 33, 57, 30.

33. Packer, *Emerson's Fall*, 138.

34. Ibid., 144; Reed, *Victorian Will*, 75, 83. "It all comes back to the same message," Reed writes: "Man's true freedom is in the abandonment of his will to God's. Once relieved of the torment of choice, the integrated self, fueled by God's power, will be able to carry out its destiny or mission which the rebellious will might have prevented" (p. 56).

35. Pollock, "Ralph Waldo Emerson," 54; Feidelson, *Symbolism and American Literature*, 126, 123, 122.

36. Adams, *Education of Henry Adams*, 34–35.

37. Herbert Schnädelbach, *Philosophy in Germany, 1831–1933* (New York: Cambridge University Press, 1984), 5. The 1830s, Schnädelbach writes, mark "the beginning of the crisis of European humanist civilization" (p. 3).

38. Richard Rorty, *Consequences of Pragmatism* (Minneapolis: University of Minnesota Press, 1982), 153.

39. Peter Carafiol, "Reading Emerson: Writing History," 447; Danto, *Nietzsche as Philosopher*, 80.

40. Mary Kupiec Cayton, "The Making of an American Prophet: Emerson, His Audiences, and the Rise of the Culture Industry in Nineteenth-Century America," *The American Historical Review* 92 (June 1987), 613, 620; Robert C. Solomon, *History and Human Nature: A Philosophical Review of European History and Culture, 1750–1850* (New York: Harcourt, Brace, Jovanovich, 1979), xiii.

41. John Edward Toews, *Hegelianism: The Path Toward Dialectical Humanism, 1805–1841* (New York: Cambridge University Press, 1980), 1.

42. Thomas McFarland, *Romanticism and the Forms of Ruin: Wordsworth, Coleridge, and Modalities of Fragmentation* (Princeton, N.J.: Princeton University Press, 1981), xi, 338; Reed, *Victorian Will*, 95.

43. Wendell V. Harris, *The Omnipresent Debate: Empiricism and Transcendentalism in Nineteenth-Century English Prose* (DeKalb: Northern Illinois University Press, 1981), 17 and passim; Reed, *Victorian Will*, 110.

44. Kaplan, *Thomas Carlyle*, 40.

45. Blackmur, *Henry Adams*, 236.

46. Mandelbaum, *History, Man, and Reason*, 16.

47. David Robinson, for example, sees the will/will-lessness, working/being-worked-upon contradiction I have been discussing as the expression of a fundamental tension within Protestant thought: the conflict between Protestantism's inherent emphasis on action (civic work, self-culture) and its "almost quietist or mystical" pietism. For Carolyn Porter, the working/being-worked-upon dichotomy in Emerson's writing represents one of the century's exemplary articulations of the "antinomies of bourgeois thought." On the one hand, Emerson attempts—by insisting that the world is mediated and obedient to man's will—to resist the central philosophical and social schism of his time: the alienation between laborer and

product. On the other hand, Emerson's visionary idealism leads to a passive, purely "contemplative stance" before the status quo. See Robinson, "Grace and Works," 125; and Porter, *Seeing and Being*, 23, 38–40.

48. Megill, *Prophets of Extremity*, 2.

49. Ibid., 343. The point I have been attempting to make—that the contradictions in Emerson's thought are neither anachronistic nor idiosyncratic but entirely representative of tensions deeply inherent in nineteenth-century Western thought—is further confirmed by Gerald N. Izenberg, *Impossible Individuality: Romanticism, Revolution, and the Origins of Modern Selfhood, 1787–1802* (Princeton, N.J.: Princeton University Press, 1992). The Romantics, Izenberg argues, "developed a new idea of the self as characterized by fundamentally opposing impulses: a drive to assert the authority of the self and expand that authority to absorb the universe, and the contradictory impulse to surrender to a greater idealized entity as the condition of the self's infinity" (from the dust jacket).

50. Holmes, *Ralph Waldo Emerson*, 132; Kazin, *American Procession*, 39.

51. John Morley, in *Recognition of Ralph Waldo Emerson*, 76.

52. Lowell, "Fable for Critics," 44; Brownson, cited in Gonnaud, *Uneasy Solitude*, 191; William James, *Varieties of Religious Experience*, 31; Winters, *In Defense of Reason*, 263, 587; Holmes, cited in Gonnaud, *Uneasy Solitude*, 192; Porte, *Emerson and Thoreau*, 82; Bloom, *Agon*, 160, 169; Anderson, *Imperial Self*, 6–8.

53. Solomon, *In the Spirit of Hegel*, 62–63.

54. Mandelbaum, *History, Man, and Reason*, 37; Kierkegaard, cited in Solomon, *In the Spirit of Hegel*, 580, 585–86; Feuerbach, cited in Rosenberg, *Seventh Hero*, 49; Green, cited in Mandelbaum, *History, Man, and Reason*, 35. For Feuerbach on Christianity, see Mandelbaum, *History, Man, and Reason*, 34.

55. Santayana, *Egotism in German Philosophy*, 23, 106–7.

56. For Emerson's early dedication of his life to the exploration of "the nature of God," see Allen, *Waldo Emerson*, 154.

57. Solomon, *In the Spirit of Hegel*, 61; Kenneth Burke, *A Grammar of Motives* (1945; Berkeley: University of California Press, 1969), 138.

58. Rosenberg, *Seventh Hero*, 50–51 (Burke, cited by Rosenberg).

59. Dale, *Victorian Critic*, 55–58.

60. Ibid., 58.

61. George Stack notes that Emerson's persistent reflections on the will to power vividly overshadow "the echo of Christian dependency" (*Nietzsche and Emerson*, 197–98).

62. For discussion of the way in which the nineteenth-century turn to "life-philosophy" implies a fully humanized God, a rejection of "traditional School-metaphysics," and a renewed acceptance of "the anthropology of the superman," see Schnädelbach, *Philosophy in Germany*, 224–32.

63. Nietzsche, cited in Danto, *Nietzsche as Philosopher*, 100.

64. Gonnaud, *Uneasy Solitude*, 276.

65. Robinson, "Grace and Works," 127.

66. Ibid., 132.

67. Barish, *Emerson*, 201; Carafiol, "Reading Emerson," 442–44.

68. Gura, *Wisdom of Words*, 104.

69. James, *Varieties of Religious Experience*, 381.

70. Danto, *Nietzsche as Philosopher,* 231–32, 29. Nietzsche's nihilism, according to Danto, is the idea "that the world is something we have made, and must remake, and it has no structure and no meaning other than what we can impose upon it" (pp. 227–28). Frederick Copleston distinguishes between an acquiescent nihilism and Nietzsche's "active nihilism" intended to "clear the way for a new dawn, for the transvaluation of values, for the emergence of a higher type of man" (*A History of Philosophy, Book III,* [New York: Doubleday, 1985], vol. 7, 405–6). A similarly "creative nihilism" characterizes Emerson's thought, both early and late.

71. Rorty, *Consequences of Pragmatism,* 164.

Chapter 6: Detranscendentalizing Emerson

1. Buell, "Emerson Industry," 123.

2. Chapman, "Emerson," 645; Ernest Hemingway, *Green Hills of Africa* (1935; New York: Collier, 1987), 21.

3. Buell, "Emerson Industry," 127, 135.

4. Carlyle, cited in Porte, *Representative Man* (1979), 1.

5. Porte, "Problem of Emerson," 86; Cavell, *Senses of Walden: An Expanded Edition,* 33; Cavell, *In Quest of the Ordinary,* 27; Cavell, "In Quest of the Ordinary: Texts of Recovery," in *Romanticism and Contemporary Criticism,* ed. Morris Eaves and Michael Fischer (Ithaca, N.Y.: Cornell University Press, 1986), 236; Poirier, *Renewal of Literature,* 19, 78.

6. Hawthorne, "The Celestial Railroad," in *Nathaniel Hawthorne: Tales and Sketches,* ed. Roy Harvey Pearce (New York: Library of America, 1982), 817; Arthur O. Lovejoy, *Essays in the History of Ideas* (Baltimore, Md.: Johns Hopkins University Press, 1948), xiii; McFarland, *Coleridge and the Pantheist Tradition,* 127.

7. Richard P. Adams, "Emerson and the Organic Metaphor," in *Interpretations of American Literature,* 140, 143.

8. Porte, "Transcendental Antics," 179. For a useful historical definition of the Transcendentalist movement see Buell, *Literary Transcendentalism,* 3–5.

9. Bromwich, *Choice of Inheritance,* 151.

10. Paul, *Emerson's Angle of Vision,* 5.

11. "Hidden fragmentations" is Paul de Man's phrase, cited in Tilottama Rajan, *Dark Interpreter,* 46. Cf. Evan Carton's analysis of Emerson's "self-parodic" tone: "Emerson's language incorporates affirmation and denial, simultaneously undercuts (but does not quite undermine) the argument it forges, shadows its own creative claims with critical counterclaims, places irreconcilable but inextricable self-images side by side" (*The Rhetoric of American Romance: Dialectic and Identity in Emerson, Dickinson, Poe, and Hawthorne* [Baltimore, Md.: Johns Hopkins University Press, 1985], 25–26).

12. See Rajan, *Dark Interpreter,* 32, 14.

13. Buell, "Emerson Industry," 127, 133; J. Hillis Miller, in *Romanticism and Contemporary Criticism,* 100–101; Donald Pease, "Emerson, *Nature,* and the Sovereignty of Influence," *Boundary 2* 8 (1980):45; Steven Mailloux, "Truth or Consequences: On Being Against Theory," in *Against Theory: Literary Studies and the New Pragmatism,* ed. W. J. T. Mitchell (Chicago: University of Chicago Press,

1985), 70; Hayden White, *Tropics of Discourse: Essays in Cultural Criticism* (Baltimore, Md.: Johns Hopkins University Press, 1978), 50.

14. Jerome J. McGann, *The Romantic Ideology: A Critical Investigation* (Chicago: University of Chicago Press, 1983), 47, 41, 37; W. J. T. Mitchell, in *Romanticism and Contemporary Criticism*, 95.

15. Rajan, *Dark Interpreter*, 14, 13, 24, 46, 16–17; Megill, *Prophets of Extremity*, 23.

16. Buell, "Emerson Industry," 127, 136.

17. Ellison, *Emerson's Romantic Style*, 76; Ellison, "Edge of Urbanity: Emerson's *English Traits*," 107.

18. Rajan, *Dark Interpreter*, 19.

19. I cite, throughout this paragraph, Megill's concise summary of the Abrams-Miller debate (*Prophets of Extremity*, 18–20).

20. McGann, *Romantic Ideology*, 17, 31.

21. Rajan, *Dark Interpreter*, 260, 16.

22. Alfred North Whitehead, cited in Thomas McFarland, *Romanticism and the Forms of Ruin*, 337.

23. Émile Bréhier, *The History of Philosophy. Vol. 6, The Nineteenth Century: Period of Systems, 1800–1850*, trans. Wade Baskin (1932; Chicago: University of Chicago Press, 1968), 5, 1; Sénancour is cited on p. 4.

24. Rajan, *Dark Interpreter*, 25, 29. "What German theory progressively brings out," Rajan notes, "through its analysis of forms that recognize the discontinuity between poetic intention and the ideal aimed at, is a naïveté in the poetics of hope of which the Romantics are always half conscious" (p. 53).

25. McFarland, *Romanticism and the Forms of Ruin*, xi.

26. Ibid., xi, xii, 365, 41; Thomas McFarland, *Romantic Cruxes: The English Essayists and the Spirit of the Age* (New York: Oxford University Press, 1987), 31; Rajan, *Dark Interpreter*, 14.

27. McFarland, *Romantic Cruxes*, 30–31.

28. McFarland, *Romanticism and the Forms of Ruin*, 338–39.

29. Eric Newton sees the advent of romantic movements as "a by-product of the decay of humanism"—what results when man is "displaced from his central position as the measure of all things and [is] involved . . . in a struggle . . . which always belittles him" (*The Romantic Rebellion* [New York: Schocken Books, 1964], 62).

30. Matthiessen, *American Renaissance*, 30, 40, 3, 56.

31. Ibid., 28, 30, 4, 5, 98.

32. Ibid., 3, 75, 52.

33. Adams, "Emerson and the Organic Metaphor," 137, 141, 150, 148, 151.

34. Ibid., 150, 151.

35. Ibid., 149, 148, 150.

36. Ibid., 146, 139, 150. Feidelson, *Symbolism and American Literature*, must be noted here as another influential study to take Emerson as a wholly monistic thinker. Like Matthiessen and Richard Adams, Feidelson finds Emerson's search for "the mirage of ideal unity" (p. 157) morally shallow and aesthetically unworkable.

37. Bloom, *Agon*, 9, 162.

38. Poirier, *Renewal of Literature*, 17, 171, 41, 73, 70.

39. Ibid., 41, 65, 181.

40. Ibid., 171; Ellison, *Emerson's Romantic Style*, 158, 86; Ellison, "Aggressive Allegory," *Raritan* 3 (Winter 1984):102.

41. Ellison, *Emerson's Romantic Style*, 76.

42. Packer, *Emerson's Fall*, 84, 7, 1, 5.

43. See the longer article from which this chapter is taken, my "De-Transcendentalizing Emerson," *ESQ: A Journal of the American Renaissance*, 34 (1988): 77–139.

44. Adams, "Emerson and the Organic Metaphor," 146.

45. Whicher, "Emerson's Tragic Sense," in *Interpretations of American Literature*, 153; Whicher, *Freedom and Fate*, 172.

46. Whicher, *Freedom and Fate*, 173; Whicher, "Emerson's Tragic Sense," 160; Bishop, *Emerson on the Soul*, 219, 205.

47. James, "Emerson," 25; Whicher, "Emerson's Tragic Sense," 153; Curtius, "Emerson," 212–13; More, *Shelburne Essays*, 192; Chapman, "Emerson," 601, 605, 606.

48. Santayana, "Emerson," 264, 266, 267.

49. See James Engell, *The Creative Imagination: Enlightenment to Romanticism* (Cambridge, Mass.: Harvard University Press, 1981), x; Jacques Barzun, *Darwin, Marx, Wagner,* 170; Toews, *Hegelianism,* 1–2. For the "humanistic 'reduction' or transformation of the Hegelian absolute"—its translation, in the writings of Strauss, Bauer, and Feuerbach, into "completely immanent, human terms as man's self-actualization"—see Toews, *Hegelianism,* 8.

50. Charles Taylor, *Hegel* (New York: Cambridge University Press, 1975), 42; Rorty, *Consequences of Pragmatism,* 224.

51. René Wellek, *Confrontations* (Princeton, N.J.: Princeton University Press, 1965), 212, 164; Hartman, *Criticism in the Wilderness,* 46, 45; Emerson, cited in Lloyd D. Easton, *Hegel's First American Followers* (Athens: Ohio University Press, 1966), 49; Matthiessen, *American Renaissance,* 54.

52. Simpson, *German Aesthetic and Literary Criticism,* 161, 80, 8.

53. Taylor, *Hegel,* 546, 561, 547.

54. Mandelbaum, *History, Man, and Reason,* 58–59.

55. The phrase "historical ecology of [Coleridge's] thought" is McFarland's (*Romanticism and the Forms of Ruin,* 308).

56. Thoreau, *Walden,* 205, 324, 98, 91. A multitude of nineteenth-century synthesizers and system makers—Cousin, Fourier, Comte, Spencer, Marx, and others—may be cited as the European background for the syncretic aims, the failed resolutions and resultant contradictions in Emerson's writing. From Margaret Fuller's vision of a new society founded on "the harmonious growth of the sexes," to Orestes Brownson's prediction of a world-wide revolution, to the radical economies instituted at Brook Farm or Walden Pond, American Transcendentalism was similarly engaged in the search for some omnisynthetic theory comprehensive enough to provide the new generalizations by which the individual and society could live. "I hope to see the time," as George Ripley put it in 1837, "when religion, philosophy, and politics will be united in a holy Trinity, for the redemption . . . of our social institutions." (The description of Fuller is from Anne C. Rose, *Transcendentalism as a Social Movement, 1830–1850* [New Haven, Conn.: Yale University Press, 1981], 60; Ripley is cited on p. 51).

57. Emerson, "Thoughts on Modern Literature" (1840); rpt. in *Essays and Lectures,* ed. Joel Porte (New York: Library of America, 1983), 1151, 1156, 1161, 1162.

58. Simpson, *German Aesthetic and Literary Criticism,* 20.

59. Toews, *Hegelianism,* 1.

60. I do not mean that Hegel's resolutions were definitive. The same tension between transcendental and anti-transcendental impulses we find in Emerson underlies Hegelian philosophy, as it does nineteenth-century thought generally. Robert Solomon notes the "confused mixture of absolute idealism and historicism" in the *Phenomenology* (*In the Spirit of Hegel,* 239). See also Henry Sussman, *The Hegelian Aftermath: Readings in Hegel, Kierkegaard, Freud, Proust, and James* (Baltimore, Md.: Johns Hopkins University Press, 1982).

61. As Charles Taylor puts it: "A subjectivity which is inspired tirelessly to create new forms is one which by definition can never achieve integral expression, can never find a form which truly expresses itself" (*Hegel,* p. 46). For the contradictions in Kant's thinking that Hegel hoped to resolve, see Taylor's introductory chapter, pp. 29–50.

62. Buell, *Literary Transcendentalism,* 165; see also pp. 181–82.

63. Walter Kaufmann, *Hegel: A Reinterpretation* (Notre Dame, Ind.: University of Notre Dame Press, 1978), 49.

64. Whicher, *Freedom and Fate,* 56.

65. Martin, *American Literature and the Universe of Force;* For Fiske's ambiguous but highly effective rhetoric, see Milton Berman, *John Fiske: The Evolution of a Popularizer* (Cambridge, Mass.: Harvard University Press, 1961) 196, 216. William James speaks of the "peace-conferring power" of the absolute in *A Pluralistic Universe* (1909; Cambridge, Mass.: Harvard University Press, 1977), 62. See also Burke, "I, Eye, Ay," 11. Cushing Strout suggests that William James's psychology was a similar mixture of tender-minded and tough-minded, "the strenuous will and the mood of 'letting go.'" The "functioning American," he notes (citing Erik Erikson), "as the heir of a history of extreme contrasts and abrupt changes, bases his final ego identity on some tentative combination of dynamic polarities" ("The Pluralistic Identity of William James: A Psychohistorical Reading of *The Varieties of Religious Experience,*" *American Quarterly* 23 (May 1971):150.

Chapter 7: The Rhetoric of War

1. Santayana, *Egotism in German Philosophy,* 72.

2. Schopenhauer, *World as Will and Representation,* vol. 2, 354.

3. Barzun, *Darwin, Marx, Wagner,* 172, 129, 92–93.

4. Lowell, *Literary Criticism,* 213.

5. Daniel Aaron, *The Unwritten War: American Writers and the Civil War* (New York: Oxford University Press, 1975), 37.

6. See Ernest Lee Tuveson, *Redeemer Nation: The Idea of America's Millennial Role* (Chicago: University of Chicago Press, 1968), 191.

7. Cited in Frank Kermode, *The Sense of an Ending* (New York: Oxford University Press, 1966), 98.

8. "The Moral Equivalent of War" was first published in 1910. I cite the version reprinted in Matthiessen, *James Family,* 636–46.

9. See Barzun, *Darwin, Marx, Wagner,* 93–94.

10. Aaron, *Unwritten War,* xiii–xv, 25–30. George M. Fredrickson, *The Inner Civil War: Northern Intellectuals and the Crisis of the Union* (New York: Harper and Row, 1965), must also be noted as an indispensable study of the ways in which Northern intellectuals came to value the war.

11. Aaron, *Unwritten War,* xviii.

12. M. H. Abrams, *Natural Supernaturalism: Tradition and Revolution in Romantic Literature* (New York: Norton, 1971), 354–55, 358.

13. Michael Walzer, *The Revolution of the Saints* (1965; New York: Atheneum, 1976), 290, 298.

14. See David Porter, *Emerson and Literary Change* (Cambridge, Mass.: Harvard University Press, 1978), 107. For "the image of the soldier" as "a virtual *leitmotif* within Emerson's writings," see Edward Stessel, "The Soldier and the Scholar: Emerson's Warring Heroes," *Journal of American Studies* 19 (August 1985):165–97.

15. Henry Thoreau, *Thoreau: People, Principles, and Politics,* ed. Milton Meltzer (New York: Hill and Wang, 1963), 197.

16. William Ellery Channing, "The Christian Warfare," *The Christian Examiner,* January-February 1824, 102–8.

17. J. F. Maclear, "The Republic and the Millennium," in *The Religion of the Republic,* ed. Elwyn A. Smith (Philadelphia: Fortress Press, 1971), 183.

18. See Tuveson, *Redeemer Nation,* 78.

19. Michel Foucault, *Discipline and Punish: The Birth of the Prison,* trans. Alan Sheridan (New York: Random House, 1979), 168–69. For American interest in military service as a model for society, see Fredrickson, *Inner Civil War,* 139–40, 98–112, 211–13.

20. Michel Foucault, *Power/Knowledge: Selected Interviews and Other Writings 1972–1977,* ed. Colin Gordon (New York: Pantheon, 1980), 188, 236, 74.

21. Foucault, *Discipline and Punish,* 102, 194.

22. Ibid., 29.

23. Ibid., 193; Michel Foucault, *The History of Sexuality,* Vol. 1, *An Introduction,* trans. Robert Hurley (New York: Random House, 1978), 123.

24. Foucault, *Discipline and Punish,* 170, 155, 165.

25. Michael Paul Rogin, *Fathers and Children: Andrew Jackson and the Subjugation of the American Indian* (New York: Random House, 1975), 136, 142.

26. See Donald Bouchard's introduction to Michel Foucault, *Language, Counter-Memory, Practice: Selected Essays and Interviews,* ed. Donald Bouchard (Ithaca, N.Y.: Cornell University Press, 1977), 23.

27. Burke, *Grammar of Motives,* 330.

28. Henry James, cited in Daniel J. Schneider, *The Crystal Cage* (Lawrence: Regents Press of Kansas, 1978), 70. See Schneider's chapter on "Warfare and Aggression" in James's fiction, pp. 70–95.

29. Foucault, *Power/Knowledge,* 114, 123.

30. For Burke's thesis that war is the modern activity that comes closest to "the totality of tribal festivals" in eliciting the response of all members of society, see *Grammar of Motives,* 328.

31. Kermode, *Sense of an Ending,* 98; Yeats is cited on the same page.

32. Cf. Walter Kaufmann, *Nietzsche: Philosopher, Psychologist, Antichrist,* 4th ed. (Princeton, N.J.: Princeton University Press, 1974), 386–90.

33. Barzun, *Darwin, Marx, Wagner,* 303.

34. Kermode, *Sense of an Ending,* esp. 46–47, 172–73.

35. William Graham Sumner, *War and Other Essays* (New Haven, Conn.: Yale University Press, 1911), 29–40.

36. Matthiessen, *American Renaissance,* 368; Maurice Gonnaud, "Introduction," in Whicher, *Freedom and Fate,* xv–xvi.

37. Feidelson, *Symbolism and American Literature,* 98; Miller, *Errand into the Wilderness,* 188.

38. Henry James, "Emerson," 25. For the history of the very real commitment Emerson did make to social activism, see Len Gougeon, *Virtue's Hero: Emerson, Antislavery, and Reform* (Athens: University of Georgia Press, 1990).

39. Porte, *Representative Man* (1979), 234.

40. Poirier, *World Elsewhere,* 56.

41. Lowell, "Fable for Critics," 44; Jane Welsh Carlyle, cited in McAleer, *Ralph Waldo Emerson,* 439; Santayana, "Emerson," 258–59; Winters, *In Defense of Reason,* 279; Feidelson, *Symbolism and American Literature,* 161.

42. Tuveson, *Redeemer Nation,* 47–48.

43. Feidelson, *Symbolism and American Literature,* 160.

44. Gilles Deleuze, "Nomad Thought," in *The New Nietzsche,* ed. David B. Allison (New York: Dell, 1977), 142; see also Allison's introduction, pp. xi–xxviii.

45. Woodberry, *Ralph Waldo Emerson,* 50.

46. I take most of my examples here from Packer, *Emerson's Fall,* 1–21.

47. The description is Whicher's (SE, xxi).

48. Porter, *Emerson and Literary Change,* 201.

49. Miller, *Consciousness in Concord,* 33.

50. Maurice Maeterlinck, *On Emerson and Other Essays,* trans. Montrose J. Moses (New York: Dodd, Mead, 1912), 44. Emerson speaks of the artist's need to "disindividualize himself" (W, 7:48). See also Blackmur, *Henry Adams,* 275.

51. Mandelbaum, *History, Man, and Reason,* 324.

52. Michel Foucault, *The Order of Things: An Archaeology of the Human Sciences* (New York: Random House, 1970), 386–87, 342, and *Language, Counter-Memory, Practice,* 139–64.

WORKS CITED

Aaron, Daniel. *Men of Good Hope: A Story of American Progressives.* New York: Oxford University Press, 1951.

———. *The Unwritten War: American Writers and the Civil War.* New York: Oxford University Press, 1975.

Abrams, M. H. *Natural Supernaturalism: Tradition and Revolution in Romantic Literature.* New York: Norton, 1971.

Adams, Hazard. *Philosophy of the Literary Symbolic.* Tallahassee: Florida State University Press, 1983.

Adams, Henry. *The Education of Henry Adams.* 1918. Edited by Ernest Samuels. Boston: Houghton Mifflin, 1973.

Adams, Richard P. "Emerson and the Organic Metaphor." In *Interpretations of American Literature,* edited by Charles Feidelson and Paul Brodtkorb, 137–52. New York: Oxford University Press, 1959.

Allen, Gay Wilson. *Waldo Emerson.* New York: Viking, 1981.

Anderson, Quentin. *The Imperial Self: An Essay in American Literary and Cultural History.* New York: Knopf, 1971.

Angeles, Peter A. *Dictionary of Philosophy.* New York: Barnes and Noble, 1981.

Arvin, Newton. "The House of Pain." In *Emerson: A Collection of Critical Essays,* edited by Milton R. Konvitz and Stephen Whicher, 46–59. Englewood Cliffs, N.J.: Prentice-Hall, 1962.

Barish, Evelyn. *Emerson: The Roots of Prophecy.* Princeton, N.J.: Princeton University Press, 1989.

Barzun, Jacques. *Darwin, Marx, Wagner: Critique of a Heritage.* 2nd ed. Chicago: University of Chicago Press, 1958.

Baumgarten, Eduard. *Der Pragmatismus: R. W. Emerson, W. James, J. Dewey.* Frankfurt, 1938.

Benoit, Ray. "Emerson on Plato: The Fire's Center." 1963. In *On Emerson,* edited by Edwin Cady and Louis J. Budd, 127–38. Durham, N.C.: Duke University Press, 1988.

Berman, Milton. *John Fiske: The Evolution of a Popularizer.* Cambridge, Mass.: Harvard University Press, 1961.

Berthoff, Warner. "`Building Discourse': The Genesis of Emerson's *Nature*." In *Fictions and Events,* 182–218. New York: Dutton, 1971.

Bishop, Jonathan. *Emerson on the Soul.* Cambridge, Mass.: Harvard University Press, 1964.

Blackmur, R. P. *Henry Adams.* Edited by Veronica A. Makowsky. New York: Harcourt, Brace, Jovanovich, 1980.

Blasing, Mutlu Konuk. *American Poetry: The Rhetoric of Its Forms.* New Haven, Conn.: Yale University Press, 1987.

Bloom, Harold. *Agon: Towards a Theory of Revisionism.* New York: Oxford University Press, 1982.

———. *Figures of Capable Imagination.* New York: Seabury Press, 1976.

———. "Mr. America." *New York Review of Books,* 22 November 1984, 19–24.

———. *The Ringers in the Tower: Studies in Romantic Tradition.* Chicago: University of Chicago Press, 1971.

————, ed. *Modern Critical Interpretations: Henry James's* The Portrait of a Lady. New York: Chelsea House, 1987.

Bréhier, Émile. *The History of Philosophy.* Vol. 6, *The Nineteenth Century: Period of Systems, 1800–1850.* Translated by Wade Baskin. 1932. Chicago: University of Chicago Press, 1968.

Bromwich, David. *A Choice of Inheritance: Self and Community from Edmund Burke to Robert Frost.* Cambridge, Mass.: Harvard University Press, 1989.

Brownell, W. C. *American Prose Masters.* 1909. Edited by Howard Mumford Jones. Cambridge, Mass.: Harvard University Press, 1963.

Buell, Lawrence. "The Emerson Industry in the 1980s: A Survey of Trends and Achievements." *ESQ: A Journal of the American Renaissance* 30 (1984):117–36.

————. *Literary Transcendentalism: Style and Vision in the American Renaissance.* Ithaca, N.Y.: Cornell University Press, 1973.

Burke, Kenneth. *Attitudes Toward History.* 3d ed. Berkeley: University of California Press, 1984.

————. *A Grammar of Motives.* 1945. Berkeley: University of California Press, 1969.

————. "I, Eye, Ay—Emerson's Early Essay 'Nature': Thoughts on the Machinery of Transcendence." In *Transcendentalism and Its Legacy,* edited by Myron Simon and Thornton H. Parsons, 3–24. Ann Arbor: University of Michigan Press, 1966.

————. *Perspectives by Incongruity.* Edited by Stanley Edgar Hyman. Bloomington: Indiana University Press, 1964.

————. *The Philosophy of Literary Form: Studies in Symbolic Action.* New York: Vintage Books, 1957.

Burkholder, Robert E. "The Radical Emerson: Politics in 'The American Scholar.'" *ESQ: A Journal of the American Renaissance* 34 (1988):37–57.

Burkholder, Robert E., and Joel Myerson, eds. *Critical Essays on Ralph Waldo Emerson.* Boston, Mass.: G. K. Hall, 1983.

Cain, William. *The Crisis in Criticism: Theory, Literature, and Reform in English Studies.* Baltimore, Md.: Johns Hopkins University Press, 1984.

Carafiol, Peter. "Reading Emerson: Writing History." *Centennial Review* 30 (Fall 1986):431–51.

————. *Transcendent Reason: James Marsh and the Forms of Romantic Thought.* Tallahassee: Florida State University Press, 1982.

Carlyle, Thomas. *A Carlyle Reader.* Edited by G. B. Tennyson. New York: Cambridge University Press, 1984.

Carpenter, Frederic Ives. *Emerson Handbook.* New York: Hendricks House, 1953.

————. "William James and Emerson." 1939. In *On Emerson,* edited by Edwin Cady and Louis J. Budd, 43–61. Durham, N.C.: Duke University Press, 1988.

Carton, Evan. *The Rhetoric of American Romance: Dialectic and Identity in Emerson, Dickinson, Poe, and Hawthorne.* Baltimore, Md.: Johns Hopkins University Press, 1985.

Cascardi, Anthony J. "Emerson on Nature: Philosophy beyond Kant." *ESQ: A Journal of the American Renaissance* 30 (1984):201–10.

Cavell, Stanley. "Emerson's Aversive Thinking." In *Romantic Revolutions: Criti-*

cism and Theory, edited by Kenneth Johnston et al., 219–49. Bloomington: Indiana University Press, 1990.

——. *In Quest of the Ordinary: Lines of Skepticism and Romanticism.* Chicago: University of Chicago Press, 1988.

——. "In Quest of the Ordinary: Texts of Recovery." In *Romanticism and Contemporary Criticism,* edited by Morris Eaves and Michael Fischer, 183–239. Ithaca, N.Y.: Cornell University Press, 1986.

——. *The Senses of Walden: An Expanded Edition.* San Francisco: North Point Press, 1981.

——. *This New Yet Unapproachable America: Lectures after Emerson after Wittgenstein.* Albuquerque, N.Mex.: Living Batch Press, 1989.

Cayton, Mary Kupiec. *Emerson's Emergence: Self and Society in the Transformation of New England, 1800–1845.* Chapel Hill: University of North Carolina Press, 1989.

——. "The Making of an American Prophet: Emerson, His Audiences, and the Rise of the Culture Industry in Nineteenth-Century America." *The American Historical Review* 92 (June 1987):597–620.

Channing, William Ellery. "The Christian Warfare." *The Christian Examiner,* January-February 1824, 103–8.

——. *Works.* Boston: n.p., 1841.

Chapman, John Jay. "Emerson." 1897. In *The Shock of Recognition,* edited by Edmund Wilson, 1:600–658. 1943. New York: Octagon Books, 1975.

Cheyfitz, Eric. *The Trans-Parent: Sexual Politics in the Language of Emerson.* Baltimore, Md.: Johns Hopkins University Press, 1981.

Copleston, Frederick. *A History of Philosophy, Book III.* New York: Doubleday, 1985.

Cox, James M. "R. W. Emerson: The Circles of the Eye." In *Emerson: Prophecy, Metamorphosis, and Influence,* edited by David Levin, 57–81. New York: Columbia University Press, 1975.

Curtius, E. R. "Emerson." In *Essays on European Literature,* translated by Michael Kowal, 211–27. Princeton, N.J.: Princeton University Press, 1973.

Dale, Peter Allan. *The Victorian Critic and the Idea of History: Carlyle, Arnold, and Pater.* Cambridge, Mass.: Harvard University Press, 1977.

Danto, Arthur. *Nietzsche as Philosopher.* New York: Columbia University Press, 1965.

Delbanco, Andrew. *The Puritan Ordeal.* Cambridge, Mass.: Harvard University Press, 1989.

——. *William Ellery Channing.* Cambridge, Mass.: Harvard University Press, 1981.

Deleuze, Gilles. "Nomad Thought." In *The New Nietzsche,* edited by David B. Allison, 142–49. New York: Dell, 1977.

Dewey, John. "Ralph Waldo Emerson." In *Emerson: A Collection of Critical Essays,* edited by Milton R. Konvitz and Stephen Whicher, 24–30. Englewood Cliffs, N.J.: Prentice-Hall, 1962.

Donadio, Stephen. *Nietzsche, Henry James, and the Artistic Will.* New York: Oxford University Press, 1978.

Donoghue, Denis. *Reading America: Essays on American Literature.* Berkeley: University of California Press, 1988.

Easton, Lloyd D. *Hegel's First American Followers*. Athens: Ohio University Press, 1966.

Eaves, Morris, and Michael Fischer, eds. *Romanticism and Contemporary Criticism*. Ithaca, N.Y.: Cornell University Press, 1986.

Ellison, Julie. "Aggressive Allegory." *Raritan* 3 (Winter 1984):100–15

———. "The Edge of Urbanity: Emerson's *English Traits*." *ESQ: A Journal of the American Renaissance* 32 (1986):96–109.

———. *Emerson's Romantic Style*. Princeton, N.J.: Princeton University Press, 1984.

Emerson, Ralph Waldo. *The Collected Works of Ralph Waldo Emerson*. Edited by Robert Spiller et al. 4 vols. Cambridge, Mass.: Harvard University Press, 1971–.

———. *The Complete Works of Ralph Waldo Emerson*. Centenary Edition. Edited by Edward Waldo Emerson. 12 vols. Boston: Houghton Mifflin, 1903–1904.

———. *The Early Lectures of Ralph Waldo Emerson*. Edited by Stephen Whicher et al. 3 vols. Cambridge, Mass.: Harvard University Press, 1959–1972.

———. *Emerson in His Journals*. Edited by Joel Porte. Cambridge, Mass.: Harvard University Press, 1982.

———. *English Traits*. Edited by Howard Mumford Jones. Cambridge, Mass.: Harvard University Press, 1966.

———. *The Journals and Miscellaneous Notebooks of Ralph Waldo Emerson*. Edited by William H. Gilman et al. 16 vols. Cambridge, Mass.: Harvard University Press, 1960–1982.

———. *The Letters of Ralph Waldo Emerson*. Edited by Ralph L. Rusk. 6 vols. New York: Columbia University Press, 1939.

———. *Ralph Waldo Emerson: Selected Essays, Lectures, and Poems*. Edited by Robert D. Richardson. New York: Bantam Books, 1990.

———. *Selections from Ralph Waldo Emerson*. Edited by Stephen Whicher. Boston: Houghton Mifflin, 1957.

———. "Thoughts on Modern Literature." 1840. In *Essays and Lectures*, edited by Joel Porte, 1147–68. New York: Library of America, 1983.

———. *The Topical Notebooks of Ralph Waldo Emerson*. Edited by Ralph H. Orth, Susan Sutton Smith, and Ronald A. Bosco. 2 vols. Columbia: University of Missouri Press, 1990–.

Engell, James. *The Creative Imagination: Enlightenment to Romanticism*. Cambridge, Mass.: Harvard University Press, 1981.

Feidelson, Charles. *Symbolism and American Literature*. Chicago: University of Chicago Press, 1953.

Fichte, Johann. *The Vocation of Man*. Translated by William Smith. [1800]; 1931. Chicago: Open Court, 1940.

Fiedler, Leslie. "American Literature." In *Contemporary Literary Scholarship: A Critical Review*, edited by Lewis Leary, 157–85. New York: Appleton-Century-Crofts, 1958.

Firkins, O. W. "Has Emerson a Future?" In *Selected Essays*, 79–93. Minneapolis: University of Minnesota Press, 1933.

———. *Ralph Waldo Emerson*. 1915. New York: Russell and Russell, 1965.

Foster, John Burt. *Heirs to Dionysus: A Nietzschean Current in Literary Modernism*. Princeton, N.J.: Princeton University Press, 1981.

Foucault, Michel. *Discipline and Punish: The Birth of the Prison*. Translated by Alan Sheridan. New York: Random House, 1979.

———. *The History of Sexuality. Vol. 1, An Introduction*. Translated by Robert Hurley. New York: Random House, 1978.

———. *Language, Counter-Memory, Practice: Selected Essays and Interviews*. Edited by Donald Bouchard. Ithaca, N.Y.: Cornell University Press, 1977.

———. *The Order of Things: An Archaeology of the Human Sciences*. New York: Random House, 1970.

———. *Power/Knowledge: Selected Interviews and Other Writings 1972–1977*. Edited by Colin Gordon. New York: Pantheon, 1980.

Fredrickson, George M. *The Inner Civil War: Northern Intellectuals and the Crisis of the Union*. New York: Harper and Row, 1965.

Frothingham, Octavius Brooks. *Transcendentalism in New England: A History*. 1876. Philadelphia: University of Pennsylvania Press, 1959.

Frye, Northrop. "The Drunken Boat: The Revolutionary Element in Romanticism." In *Romanticism Reconsidered: Selected Papers from the English Institute*, edited by Northrop Frye, 1–25. New York: Columbia University Press, 1963.

Fuller, Margaret. *Woman in the Nineteenth Century*. 1845. New York: Norton, 1971.

Gass, William H. "Emerson and the Essay." In *Habitations of the Word*, 9–49. New York: Simon and Schuster, 1985.

Giamatti, A. Bartlett. "Power, Politics and a Sense of History." In *The University and the Public Interest*, 166–79. New York: Atheneum, 1981.

Gilmore, Michael. *American Romanticism and the Marketplace*. Chicago: University of Chicago Press, 1985.

Gonnaud, Maurice. *An Uneasy Solitude: Individual and Society in the Work of Ralph Waldo Emerson*. Translated by Lawrence Rosenwald. Princeton, N.J.: Princeton University Press, 1987.

Goodheart, Eugene. *The Cult of the Ego: The Self in Modern Literature*. Chicago: University of Chicago Press, 1968.

Goodman, Russell B. *American Philosophy and the Romantic Tradition*. New York: Cambridge University Press, 1990.

Grusin, Richard. "Revisionism and the Structure of Emersonian Action." *American Literary History* 1 (Summer 1989):404–31.

Gunn, Giles. *The Culture of Criticism and the Criticism of Culture*. New York: Oxford University Press, 1987.

Gura, Philip F. *The Wisdom of Words: Language, Theology, and Literature in the New England Renaissance*. Middletown, Conn.: Wesleyan University Press, 1981.

Harris, Kenneth Marc. *Carlyle and Emerson: Their Long Debate*. Cambridge, Mass.: Harvard University Press, 1978.

Harris, Wendell V. *The Omnipresent Debate: Empiricism and Transcendentalism in Nineteenth-Century English Prose*. DeKalb: Northern Illinois University Press, 1981.

Hartman, Geoffrey. *Criticism in the Wilderness*. New Haven, Conn.: Yale University Press, 1980.

Hawthorne, Nathaniel. "The Celestial Rail-road." 1843. In *Nathaniel Hawthorne:*

Tales and Sketches, edited by Roy Harvey Pearce, 808–24. New York: Library of America, 1982.

Hegel, G. W. F. *Phenomenology of Spirit.* Translated by A. V. Miller. New York: Oxford University Press, 1977.

Heimert, Alan, and Andrew Delbanco, eds. *The Puritans in America: A Narrative Anthology.* Cambridge, Mass.: Harvard University Press, 1985.

Heller, Erich. *The Importance of Nietzsche.* Chicago: University of Chicago Press, 1988.

Heller, Peter. *Dialectics and Nihilism: Essays on Lessing, Nietzsche, Mann, and Kafka.* Amherst: University of Massachusetts Press, 1966.

Hemingway, Ernest. *Green Hills of Africa.* 1935. New York: Collier, 1987.

Hodder, Alan D. *Emerson's Rhetoric of Revelation: "Nature," the Reader, and the Apocalypse Within.* University Park: Pennsylvania State University Press, 1989.

Holmes, Oliver Wendell. *Ralph Waldo Emerson.* 1889. New York: Chelsea House, 1980.

Hook, Sidney. *Pragmatism and the Tragic Sense of Life.* New York: Basic Books, 1974.

Houghton, Walter E. *The Victorian Frame of Mind.* New Haven, Conn.: Yale University Press, 1957.

Howe, Daniel Walker. *The Unitarian Conscience.* Cambridge, Mass.: Harvard University Press, 1970.

Howe, Irving. *The American Newness: Culture and Politics in the Age of Emerson.* Cambridge, Mass.: Harvard University Press, 1986.

———. "The American Voice—It Begins on a Note of Wonder." *New York Times Book Review,* 4 July 1976, 1–3.

Howells, William Dean. *Literary Friends and Acquaintances.* Edited by David F. Hiatt and Edwin H. Cady. Bloomington: Indiana University Press, 1968.

Hughes, Gertrude Reif. *Emerson's Demanding Optimism.* Baton Rouge: Louisiana State University Press, 1984.

Hummel, Hermann. "Emerson and Nietzsche." *New England Quarterly* 19 (March 1946):63–84.

Izenberg, Gerald N. *Impossible Individuality: Romanticism, Revolution, and the Origins of Modern Selfhood, 1787–1802.* Princeton, N.J.: Princeton University Press, 1992.

James, Henry. *The American Scene.* 1907. Bloomington: Indiana University Press, 1968.

———. "Emerson." In *Partial Portraits,* 1–33. 1888. Ann Arbor: University of Michigan Press, 1970.

James, William. "Address at the Emerson Centenary in Concord." In *Emerson: A Collection of Critical Essays,* edited by Milton R. Konvitz and Stephen Whicher, 18–23. Englewood Cliffs, N.J.: Prentice-Hall, 1962.

———. *The Energies of Men.* New York: Moffat, Yard, 1917.

———. "The Moral Equivalent of War." 1910. In *The James Family,* by F. O. Matthiessen, 636–46. New York: Knopf, 1961.

———. *A Pluralistic Universe.* 1909. Cambridge, Mass.: Harvard University Press, 1977.

———. *The Varieties of Religious Experience.* 1902. New York: Penguin Books, 1982.

———. *The Will to Believe and Other Essays in Popular Philosophy and Human Immortality.* 1897, 1898. New York: Dover, 1956.

Jaspers, Karl. *Nietzsche: An Introduction to the Understanding of His Philosophical Activity.* Translated by Charles Wallraff and Frederick Schmitz. Tucson: University of Arizona Press, 1965.

Jones, Howard Mumford. *Revolution and Romanticism.* Cambridge, Mass.: Harvard University Press, 1974.

Kaplan, Fred. *Thomas Carlyle: A Biography.* Ithaca, N.Y.: Cornell University Press, 1983.

Kateb, George. "Thinking About Human Extinction (I) Nietzsche and Heidegger." *Raritan* 6 (Fall 1986):1–28.

———. "Thinking About Human Extinction (II) Emerson and Whitman." *Raritan* 6 (Winter 1987):1–22.

Kaufmann, Walter. *Hegel: A Reinterpretation.* Notre Dame, Ind.: University of Notre Dame Press, 1978.

———. *Nietzsche: Philosopher, Psychologist, Antichrist.* 4th ed. Princeton, N.J.: Princeton University Press, 1974.

Kazin, Alfred. *An American Procession.* New York: Knopf, 1984.

———. "The Father of Us All." *New York Review of Books,* 21 January 1982, 3–6.

Kermode, Frank. *The Sense of an Ending.* New York: Oxford University Press, 1966.

Kinnaird, John. *William Hazlitt: Critic of Power.* New York: Columbia University Press, 1978.

Kirk, Russell. *The Conservative Mind: From Burke to Santayana.* Chicago: Henry Regnery, 1953.

Klancher, Jon. *The Making of English Reading Audiences, 1790–1832.* Madison: University of Wisconsin Press, 1987.

Kline, George L. "The Use and Abuse of Hegel by Nietzsche and Marx." In *Hegel and His Critics: Philosophy in the Aftermath of Hegel,* edited by William Desmond, 1–34. Albany: State University of New York Press, 1989.

Konvitz, Milton R., ed. *The Recognition of Ralph Waldo Emerson.* Ann Arbor: University of Michigan Press, 1972.

Konvitz, Milton R., and Stephen Whicher, eds. *Emerson: A Collection of Critical Essays.* Englewood Cliffs, N.J.: Prentice-Hall, 1962.

Kuklick, Bruce. "Does American Philosophy Rest On a Mistake?" In *American Philosophy: Royal Institute of Philosophy Lecture Series: 19,* edited by Marcus Singer, 177–89. New York: Cambridge University Press, 1985.

Lasch, Christopher. *The True and Only Heaven: Progress and Its Critics.* New York: Norton, 1991.

Lawrence, D. H. *Studies in Classic American Literature.* 1923. New York: Viking, 1961.

Lebeaux, Richard. *Young Man Thoreau.* New York: Harper and Row, 1978.

Lentricchia, Frank. *Criticism and Social Change.* Chicago: University of Chicago Press, 1983.

Lovejoy, Arthur. *Essays in the History of Ideas.* Baltimore, Md.: Johns Hopkins University Press, 1948.

Lowell, James Russell. "A Fable for Critics." 1848. In *The Shock of Recognition,* edited by Edmund Wilson, 1:23–78. 1943. New York: Octagon Books, 1975.

————. *Literary Criticism of James Russell Lowell.* Edited by Herbert Smith. Lincoln: University of Nebraska Press, 1969.

Maclear, J. F. "The Republic and the Millennium." In *The Religion of the Republic,* edited by Elwyn A. Smith, 183–216. Philadelphia: Fortress Press, 1971.

Maeterlinck, Maurice. *On Emerson and Other Essays.* Translated by Montrose J. Moses. New York: Dodd, Mead, 1912.

Mailloux, Stephen. "Truth or Consequences: On Being Against Theory." In *Against Theory: Literary Studies and the New Pragmatism,* edited by W. J. T. Mitchell, 65–71. Chicago: University of Chicago Press, 1985.

Mandelbaum, Maurice. *History, Man, and Reason: A Study in Nineteenth-Century Thought.* Baltimore, Md.: Johns Hopkins University Press, 1971.

Marr, David. *American Worlds Since Emerson.* Amherst: University of Massachusetts Press, 1988.

Martin, Ronald E. *American Literature and the Universe of Force.* Durham, N.C.: Duke University Press, 1981.

Martineau, Harriet. *Retrospect of Western Travel.* 2 vols. 1838. New York: Haskell House, 1969.

Marx, Leo. *The Machine in the Garden: Technology and the Pastoral Idea in America.* New York: Oxford University Press, 1967.

Matthiessen, F. O. *American Renaissance: Art and Expression in the Age of Emerson and Whitman.* New York: Oxford University Press, 1941.

————. *The James Family.* New York: Knopf, 1961.

McAleer, John. *Ralph Waldo Emerson: Days of Encounter.* Boston: Little, Brown, 1984.

McFarland, Thomas. *Coleridge and the Pantheist Tradition.* Oxford: Clarendon Press, 1969.

————. *Romantic Cruxes: The English Essayists and the Spirit of the Age.* New York: Oxford University Press, 1987.

————. *Romanticism and the Forms of Ruin: Wordsworth, Coleridge, and Modalities of Fragmentation.* Princeton, N.J.: Princeton University Press, 1981.

————. *Shapes of Culture.* Iowa City: University of Iowa Press, 1987.

McGann, Jerome J. *The Romantic Ideology: A Critical Investigation.* Chicago: University of Chicago Press, 1983.

Megill, Allan. *Prophets of Extremity: Nietzsche, Heidegger, Foucault, Derrida.* Berkeley: University of California Press, 1985.

Melville, Herman. *The Confidence-Man.* 1857. Edited by H. Bruce Franklin. Indianapolis: Bobbs-Merrill, 1967.

————."Hawthorne and His Mosses." 1850. In *The Shock of Recognition,* edited by Edmund Wilson, 1:187–204. 1943. New York: Octagon Books, 1975.

————. *Mardi.* 1849. Edited by Tyrus Hillway. New Haven, Conn.: College and University, 1973.

Mencken, H. L. *The Philosophy of Friedrich Nietzsche.* London: T. Fisher, 1908.

Merquior, J. G. *Foucault.* Berkeley: University of California Press, 1985.

Meyers, Marvin. *The Jacksonian Persuasion.* Stanford, Calif.: Stanford University Press, 1957.

Michael, John. *Emerson and Skepticism: The Cipher of the World.* Baltimore, Md.: Johns Hopkins University Press, 1988.

Miller, Perry. *Consciousness in Concord.* Boston, Mass.: Houghton Mifflin, 1958.

————. *Errand into the Wilderness.* Cambridge, Mass.: Harvard University Press, 1956.

————. *The Life of the Mind in America from the Revolution to the Civil War.* New York: Harcourt, Brace, and World, 1965.

————. *Nature's Nation.* Cambridge, Mass.: Harvard University Press, 1967.

————. *The New England Mind: The Seventeenth Century.* Cambridge, Mass.: Harvard University Press, 1939.

————, ed. *American Thought: Civil War to World War I.* New York: Rinehart, 1954.

————. *The American Transcendentalists: Their Prose and Poetry.* New York: Doubleday Anchor Books, 1957.

————. *Major Writers of America.* 2 vols. New York: Harcourt, Brace, and World, 1962.

————. *The Transcendentalists: An Anthology.* Cambridge, Mass.: Harvard University Press, 1950.

More, Paul Elmer. *Shelburne Essays in American Literature.* Edited by Daniel Aaron. New York: Harcourt, Brace, and World, 1963.

Mumford, Lewis. *The Golden Day: A Study in American Literature and Culture.* 1926. New York: Dover, 1968.

Nehamas, Alexander. *Nietzsche: Life as Literature.* Cambridge, Mass.: Harvard University Press, 1985.

Newton, Eric. *The Romantic Rebellion.* New York: Schocken, 1964.

Nietzsche, Friedrich. *Basic Writings of Nietzsche.* Translated and edited by Walter Kaufmann. New York: Modern Library, 1968.

————. *Daybreak: Thoughts on the Prejudices of Morality.* Translated by R. J. Hollingdale. New York: Cambridge University Press, 1982.

————. *The Gay Science.* Translated by Walter Kaufmann. New York: Random House, 1974.

————. *Human, All Too Human: A Book for Free Spirits.* Translated by R. J. Hollingdale. New York: Cambridge University Press, 1986.

————. *The Portable Nietzsche.* Translated and edited by Walter Kaufmann. New York: Viking, 1954.

————. *Untimely Meditations.* Translated by R. J. Hollingdale. New York: Cambridge University Press, 1983.

————. *The Will to Power.* Translated by Walter Kaufmann and R. J. Hollingdale. New York: Random House, 1968.

Nussbaum, Martha C. "Transcending Humanity." In *Love's Knowledge: Essays on Philosophy and Literature,* 365–91. New York: Oxford University Press, 1990.

Packer, Barbara [B. L.]. *Emerson's Fall: A New Interpretation of the Major Essays.* New York: Continuum, 1982.

————. "Ralph Waldo Emerson." In *Columbia Literary History of the United States,* edited by Emory Elliott, 381–98. New York: Columbia University Press, 1988.

Paul, Sherman. *Emerson's Angle of Vision.* Cambridge, Mass.: Harvard University Press, 1952.

————. *The Shores of America: Thoreau's Inward Exploration.* 1958. New York: Russell and Russell, 1971.

Pease, Donald E. "Emerson, *Nature,* and the Sovereignty of Influence." *Boundary 2* 8 (1980):43–74.

———. *Visionary Compacts: American Renaissance Writings in Cultural Context.* Madison: University of Wisconsin Press, 1987.

Perry, Bliss. *Emerson Today.* Princeton, N.J.: Princeton University Press, 1931.

Poirier, Richard. *The Renewal of Literature: Emersonian Reflections.* New York: Random House, 1987.

———. *A World Elsewhere: The Place of Style in American Literature.* New York: Oxford University Press, 1966.

Pollock, Robert. "Ralph Waldo Emerson: The Single Vision." In *American Classics Reconsidered: A Christian Appraisal,* edited by Harold C. Gardiner, 15–58. New York: Scribner's, 1958.

Porte, Joel. *Emerson and Thoreau: Transcendentalists in Conflict.* Middletown, Conn.: Wesleyan University Press, 1966.

———. "The Problem of Emerson." In *The Uses of Literature,* edited by Monroe Engel, 85–114. Cambridge, Mass.: Harvard University Press, 1973.

———. *Representative Man: Ralph Waldo Emerson in His Time.* New York: Oxford University Press, 1979. 2d ed. New York: Columbia University Press, 1988.

———. "Transcendental Antics." In *Veins of Humor,* edited by Harry Levin, 167–83. Cambridge, Mass.: Harvard University Press, 1972.

Porter, Carolyn. *Seeing and Being: The Plight of the Participant Observer in Emerson, James, Adams, and Faulkner.* Middletown, Conn.: Wesleyan University Press, 1981.

Porter, David. *Emerson and Literary Change.* Cambridge, Mass.: Harvard University Press, 1978.

Rajan, Tilottama. *Dark Interpreter: The Discourse of Romanticism.* Ithaca, N.Y.: Cornell University Press, 1980.

Reed, John R. *Victorian Will.* Athens: Ohio University Press, 1989.

Reed, Sampson. *Observations on the Growth of the Mind.* 1859. New York: Arno Press, 1972.

Richardson, Robert D. *Henry David Thoreau: A Life of the Mind.* Berkeley: University of California Press, 1986.

Robinson, David. *Apostle of Culture: Emerson as Preacher and Lecturer.* Philadelphia: University of Pennsylvania Press, 1982.

———. "Grace and Works: Emerson's Essays in Theological Perspective." In *American Unitarianism, 1805–1865,* edited by Conrad Edick Wright, 121–42. Boston: Massachusetts Historical Society and Northeastern University Press, 1989.

Rogin, Michael Paul. *Fathers and Children: Andrew Jackson and the Subjugation of the American Indian.* New York: Random House, 1975.

Rorty, Richard. *Consequences of Pragmatism.* Minneapolis: University of Minnesota Press, 1982.

———. *Philosophy and the Mirror of Nature.* Princeton, N.J.: Princeton University Press, 1979.

Rose, Anne C. *Transcendentalism as a Social Movement, 1830–1850.* New Haven, Conn.: Yale University Press, 1981.

Rosenberg, Philip. *The Seventh Hero: Thomas Carlyle and the Theory of Radical*

Activism. Cambridge, Mass.: Harvard University Press, 1974.

Rosenwald, Lawrence. *Emerson and the Art of the Diary*. New York: Oxford University Press, 1988.

Rourke, Constance. *American Humor*. 1931. New York: Harcourt, Brace, Jovanovich, 1959.

Royce, Josiah. "Nietzsche." *Atlantic Monthly,* March 1917, 321–31.

Russell, Bertrand. *History of Western Philosophy*. New York: Simon and Schuster, 1945.

Santayana, George. *Egotism in German Philosophy*. 1916. New York: Scribner's, n.d.

————. *George Santayana's America*. Edited by James Ballowe. Urbana: University of Illinois Press, 1967.

————. *The Last Puritan: A Memoir in the Form of a Novel*. New York: Scribner's, 1936.

————. "The Poetry of Barbarism." In *Essays in Literary Criticism,* edited by Irving Singer, 149–78. New York: Scribner's, 1956.

————. *Santayana on America*. Edited by Richard Lyon. New York: Harcourt, Brace, and World, 1968.

————. *Three Philosophical Poets*. 1910. New York: Cooper Square Publishers, 1970.

Schnädelbach, Herbert. *Philosophy in Germany, 1831–1933*. New York: Cambridge University Press, 1984.

Schneider, Daniel J. *The Crystal Cage*. Lawrence: Regents Press of Kansas, 1978.

Schopenhauer, Arthur. *The World as Will and Representation*. 2 vols. Translated by E. F. J. Payne. New York: Dover, 1958.

Simic, Charles. *Wonderful Words, Silent Truth: Essays on Poetry and a Memoir*. Ann Arbor: University of Michigan Press, 1990.

Simpson, David. *The Politics of American English, 1776–1850*. New York: Oxford University Press, 1986.

————, ed. *German Aesthetic and Literary Criticism: Kant, Fichte, Schelling, Schopenhauer, Hegel*. New York: Cambridge University Press, 1984.

Simpson, Lewis P. *The Man of Letters in New England and the South*. Baton Rouge: Louisiana State University Press, 1973.

Slater, Joseph, ed. *The Correspondence of Emerson and Carlyle*. New York: Columbia University Press, 1964.

Smith, Timothy L. *Revivalism and Social Reform*. Baltimore, Md.: Johns Hopkins University Press, 1957.

Solomon, Robert C. *History and Human Nature: A Philosophical Review of European History and Culture, 1750–1850*. New York: Harcourt, Brace, Jovanovich, 1979.

————. *In the Spirit of Hegel: A Study of G. W. F. Hegel's "Phenomenology of Spirit."* New York: Oxford University Press, 1983.

Stack, George J. *Nietzsche and Emerson: An Elective Affinity*. Athens: Ohio University Press, 1992.

Steele, Jeffrey. *The Representation of the Self in the American Renaissance*. Chapel Hill: University of North Carolina Press, 1987.

Stessel, Edward. "The Soldier and the Scholar: Emerson's Warring Heroes." *Journal of American Studies* 19 (August 1985):165–97.

Strout, Cushing. "The Pluralistic Identity of William James: A Psychohistorical Reading of *The Varieties of Religious Experience.*" *American Quarterly* 23 (May 1971):135–52.

Suckiel, Ellen Kappy. "Emerson and the Virtues." In *American Philosophy: Royal Institute of Philosophy Lecture Series: 19,* edited by Marcus Singer, 135–52. New York: Cambridge University Press, 1985.

Sumner, William Graham. *War and Other Essays.* New Haven, Conn.: Yale University Press, 1911.

Taylor, Charles. *Hegel.* New York: Cambridge University Press, 1975.

Thoreau, Henry David. "Thomas Carlyle and His Works." In *Early Essays and Miscellanies,* edited by Joseph Moldenhauer et al., 219–67. Princeton, N.J.: Princeton University Press, 1975.

———. *Thoreau: People, Principles, and Politics.* Edited by Milton Meltzer. New York: Hill and Wang, 1963.

———. *Walden.* Edited by J. Lyndon Shanley. Princeton, N.J.: Princeton University Press, 1971.

Toews, John Edward. *Hegelianism: The Path Toward Dialectical Humanism, 1805–1841.* New York: Cambridge University Press, 1980.

Tuveson, Ernest Lee. *Redeemer Nation: The Idea of America's Millennial Role.* Chicago: University of Chicago Press, 1968.

Updike, John. "Emersonianism." In *Odd Jobs: Essays and Criticism,* 148–68. New York: Knopf, 1991.

Van Leer, David. *Emerson's Epistemology: The Argument of the Essays.* New York: Cambridge University Press, 1986.

Walzer, Michael. *The Revolution of the Saints.* 1965. New York: Atheneum, 1976.

Ware, Henry. *Formation of the Christian Character.* Boston: n.p., 1866.

Wellek, René. *Confrontations.* Princeton, N.J.: Princeton University Press, 1965.

———. "Irving Babbitt, Paul More, and Transcendentalism." In *Transcendentalism and Its Legacy,* edited by Myron Simon and Thornton H. Parsons, 185–203. Ann Arbor: University of Michigan Press, 1966.

West, Cornel. *The American Evasion of Philosophy: A Genealogy of Pragmatism.* Madison: University of Wisconsin Press, 1989.

Wheeler, Kathleen, ed. *German Aesthetic and Literary Criticism: The Romantic Ironists and Goethe.* New York: Cambridge University Press, 1984.

Whicher, Stephen. "Emerson's Tragic Sense." In *Interpretations of American Literature,* edited by Charles Feidelson and Paul Brodtkorb, 153–60. New York: Oxford University Press, 1959.

———. *Freedom and Fate: An Inner Life of Ralph Waldo Emerson.* 1953. 2d ed. Philadelphia: University of Pennsylvania Press, 1971.

White, Hayden. *Tropics of Discourse: Essays in Cultural Criticism.* Baltimore, Md.: Johns Hopkins University Press, 1978.

Whitman, Walt. *Complete Poetry and Selected Prose.* Edited by Justin Kaplan. New York: Library of America, 1982.

Wilson, Edmund, ed. *The Shock of Recognition.* 2 vols. 1943. New York: Octagon Books, 1975.

Winters, Yvor. *In Defense of Reason.* Chicago: Swallow Press, 1937.

Woodberry, George. *Ralph Waldo Emerson.* 1907. New York: Haskell House, 1968.

INDEX

Aaron, Daniel, 46, 195

Abrams, M. H., 27, 171–72, 196

Adams, Hazard, 222 n.48

Adams, Henry: on Emerson, 152; and failure, 110, 116; and power, 13, 14, 28, 45, 88, 200; on renunciation of the will, 209; and tuition, 88; *The Education,* 89; *Mont-Saint-Michel and Chartres,* 89; "The Rule of Phase Applied to History," 210

Adams, James Truslow, 214 n.9

Adams, Richard P., 176–77

"Address at the Emerson Centenary in Concord" (W. James), 32

Alcott, Bronson, 168

Allen, Gay Wilson, 52, 62, 229 n.56

Allison, David B., 235 n.44

Anderson, Quentin, 51, 61, 76, 118, 157, 214 n.9

Angeles, Peter, 227 n.11

Arnold, Matthew, 20, 30, 48, 51, 167, 219 n.87

Arvin, Newton, 113

Babbitt, Irving, 33

Bacon, Francis, 74–75

Bain, Alexander, 46

Balzac, Honoré de, 181

Barbauld, Letitia Anna, 106

Barish, Evelyn, 18, 107, 162, 219–20 n.4, 224 n. 18

"Bartleby the Scrivener" (Melville), 168

Barzun, Jacques, 11, 192, 194, 202

Baumgarten, Eduard, 46

Benoit, Ray, 146–49

Bentham, Jeremy, 67

Berkeley, George, 51, 164

Berman, Milton, 233 n.65

Berthoff, Warner, 118

Beyond Good and Evil (Nietzsche), 128–29

Bhagavid-Gita, 206

Bishop, Jonathan, 9, 25, 49, 50, 102–3, 180, 227 n.10

Blackmur, R. P., 89, 155, 209, 235 n.50

Blake, William, 11, 121, 158, 196

Bloom, Harold: on antinature tradition, 83; on compensation, 58; on Emerson and autonomy of the imagination, 51; on Emerson as dualist, 178; on Emerson as Gnostic, 157; on Emerson as humanist, 147; on Emerson's influence, 20; on Emerson and Nietzsche, 117; on Emerson and power, 29; on Emerson as pragmatist, 216 n.27; on Emerson's sense of evil, 219 n.82; on Romanticism, 27

Book of Revelation, 115

Boscovich, R. J., 187

Bostetter, Edward, 174

Bourne, Randolph, 69

Bréhier, Émile, 172, 185

Brisbane, Albert, 204

Bromwich, David, 20, 168

Brownell, W. C., 24

Brownson, Orestes, 23–24, 67, 106, 125, 156, 232 n.56

Buddha, 181

Buddhism, 35, 85, 94, 103, 104, 143, 145, 161, 167, 209

Buell, Lawrence: and anti-Emerson tradition, 23–24, 214 n.9; on detranscendentalizing Emerson, 165–67, 169–70; on the "Emerson Image," 17; on Emerson in European context, 216 n.25; on Emerson's reception, 19, 21; on *Literary Transcendentalism,* 214 n.9; on prospectiveness, 97, 188; on Transcendentalism, 230 n.8

Burke, Edmund, 11

Burke, Kenneth, 46, 85, 89, 111, 158–59, 174, 189, 200–1, 234 n.30

Caesar, Julius, 57, 134–35, 144

Camus, Albert, 130

Carafiol, Peter, 21, 22, 146, 154
Carlyle, Jane Welsh, 207
Carlyle, Thomas, 28, 208; on Emerson,
  106, 225 n.3; extravagant rhetoric
  of, 119, 124, 126, 154; and German writing, 27; and Goethe, 54,
  74; and master signs, 218 n.78;
  and Napoleon, 11; and the opposing self, 88; as philosopher of
  power, 13, 45, 90, 112, 198; on
  symbol making, 222–23 n.59; theology of, 158–59; on work, 136,
  138; *Sartor Resartus,* 42, 112, 136
Carpenter, F. I., 50, 148, 218 n.73
Carton, Evan, 230 n.11
Cascardi, Anthony J., 52
Cavell, Stanley: on anti-Emerson tradition, 23–25, 29, 31, 149, 166; on
  Emerson as cultural critic, 44, 218
  n.68; on Emerson's extravagant
  rhetoric, 118, 121, 127; on Emerson as founder of American thinking, 20, 26–27, 166; on Emerson
  and Nietzsche, 226 n.26; on Emerson as philosopher of direction,
  131; on Emerson's reception, 21;
  on Emerson as teacher of tuition,
  217–18 n.60; Emersonian thinking,
  143; and intuition, 59; and philoso-
  phy, 130; on revisor-philosophers,
  127, 147; on Romanticism, 27; *The
  Senses of Walden,* 26
Cayton, Mary Kupiec, 154
Channing, William Ellery, 11, 67, 68,
  124, 196, 205, 221 n. 28
Chapman, John Jay, 20, 53, 181
Cheyfitz, Eric, 29, 219 n.82
Church, Frederic, 7
Clausewitz, Karl von, 201
Colacurcio, Michael, 8
Cole, Thomas, 7
Coleridge, Samuel Taylor, 11, 26–27,
  91, 149, 159, 173
Columbus, Christopher, 68, 134
Comte, Auguste, 189, 232 n.56
The Confidence-Man (Melville), 125
Conkin, Paul K., 214 n.9
Cooper, James Fenimore, 86–87, 167

Copleston, Frederick, 230 n.70
Cousin, Victor, 232 n.56
Cox, James M., 58, 91, 223 n.64
Crane, Hart, 147
Crèvecoeur, J. Hector St. John, 205
Cromwell, Oliver, 7, 162
Curtius, E. R., 84, 87, 180–81

Dale, Peter Allan, 159, 222 n.59
Danto, Arthur, 63, 154, 164, 225 n.8,
  229 n.70
Darwin, Charles, 11, 45, 154, 191,
  192, 194, 202
Delbanco, Andrew, 66
Deleuze, Gilles, 208
de Man, Paul, 27, 169–70, 230 n.11
Democratic Vistas (Whitman), 90
De Quincey, Thomas, 12
Derrida, Jacques, 155, 165, 208
Descartes, René, 26, 148, 172
Dewey, John: compared to Emerson,
  34; and defense of Emerson, 24,
  30–32, 43–44, 50, 88, 146, 147,
  219 n.92; as edifying philosopher,
  127; on Emerson and democracy,
  20, 43; instrumentalism of, 69; and
  philosophy of power, 45, 90; and
  pragmatism, 42–43, 46, 52, 68,
  147, 151; *Experience and Nature,*
  34; "The Need for a Recovery of
  Philosophy," 44
Dickinson, Emily, 110, 125, 155, 166
"The Domain of Arnheim" (Poe), 204
Donadio, Stephen, 111, 115, 123–24
Donne, John, 159, 222 n.59
Donoghue, Denis, 20, 29, 52, 141,
  147–48, 151

The Education of Henry Adams, 89
Edwards, Jonathan, 51, 67, 148, 167,
  175
Eliot, T. S., 20, 24, 33, 48, 50, 176
Ellison, Julie, 48, 49, 86, 147, 170,
  179, 187
Emerson, Ralph Waldo, works of:
  "American Civilization," 53; "The

American Scholar," 42, 60, 132, 138; "Aristocracy," 45, 108; "Art," 103; "Character," 190; "Circles," 58, 95, 120, 129, 162, 186; "Civilization," 99, 102–3; "Clubs," 100; "Compensation," 132–34, 139–40, 142, 161; *The Conduct of Life,* 36–47, 71, 91, 96, 133; "The Conservative," 55–56, 77, 137; "Divinity School Address," 23; "Domestic Life," 99; early lectures (1833–36), 71–79; *English Traits,* 37, 142; *Essays: First Series,* 176; *Essays: Second Series,* 113–14; "Experience," 49, 58, 61, 94, 96, 114, 129, 177; "Fate," 90–96, 118; "Harvard Commemoration Speech," 194–95; "Lectures on the Times," 54, 162; "Literary Ethics," 73; "Manners," 77; "Man the Reformer," 138; "Natural History of Intellect," 114, 142; *Nature,* 29, 38, 41, 53, 58–61, 71–75, 78, 79–86, 87, 88, 91, 94, 101, 103, 141, 176; "Nature" (essay), 85–86; "New England Reformers," 114; "Nominalist and Realist," 56–58, 61; "Old Age," 96–99; "The Over-Soul" 162; "Perpetual Forces," 108; "The Poet," 97; "Power," 45, 47, 138; "The Relation of Man to the Globe" (lecture), 71; *Representative Men,* 60, 94–95; "Self-Reliance," 49, 128–29, 144, 161; *Society and Solitude,* 72, 96–105; "The Sovereignty of Ethics," 160–61; "Spiritual Laws," 108–9, 161; "Success," 101; "The Transcendentalist," 55, 168; "The Uses of Natural History" (lecture), 72; "The Uses of Unhappiness" (sermon), 62; "Water" (lecture), 71; "Wealth," 47; "Works and Days," 55, 100–1, 134; "Worship," 162
Emerson's Demanding Optimism (Hughes), 130
Emerson's Fall (Packer), 26

"Emerson the Poet" (Santayana), 32, 33
"The Energies of Men" (W. James), 44
Experience and Nature (Dewey), 34

Faulkner, William, 177
Feidelson, Charles, 8, 21, 28, 46, 50, 84, 110, 152, 207, 231 n.36
Feuerbach, Ludwig, 154, 158, 232 n.49
Fichte, Johann Gottlieb, 11, 12, 27, 42, 82, 154, 158, 183, 196
Fiedler, Leslie, 24
Firkins, O. W., 23, 52, 118, 146, 150
Fiske, John, 189, 233 n.65
Ford, Henry, 47, 203
Foucault, Michel, 15, 19, 29, 121, 169, 197–201, 210
Fourier, Charles, 232 n.56
Franklin, Benjamin, 67, 133
Fredrickson, George M., 234 n.10, 234 n.19
Freedom and Fate (Whicher), 47–52
Freud, Sigmund, 26, 45, 123
Frost, Robert, 38
Frothingham, O. B., 23, 107
Frye, Northrop, 11, 27
Fuller, Margaret, 12, 106, 124–25, 135, 168, 205, 232 n.56

Gass, William H., 76, 117
Giamatti, A. Bartlett, 122–23, 203, 214 n.9
Gibran, Kahlil, 122, 183
Gifford, Sanford Robinson, 7
Gilmore, Michael, 125
Goddard, H. C., 23
Goethe, Johann Wolfgang von, 34, 54, 59, 74–75, 106, 135, 145, 153, 185, 186, 219 n.3
Gonnaud, Maurice, 71, 72, 148, 160, 203
Goodheart, Eugene, 133, 217 n.49, 225 n.8
Goodman, Russell B., 216 n.25, 219 n.92
Gougeon, Len, 235 n.38
Greeley, Horace, 204

Green, T. H., 158
Grusin, Richard, 29, 143, 150
Gunn, Giles, 27
Gura, Philip F., 9, 24, 26, 162

Harris, Kenneth Marc, 148
Hartman, Geoffrey, 27, 183
Hawthorne, Nathaniel: and American
    Renaissance, 28; on Emerson, 106,
    166; and failure, 110; moral com-
    plexity of, 27; and power of black-
    ness, 112; reception of, 16, 151,
    167; romances of, 125; *The Scarlet
    Letter,* 15
Hazlitt, William, 12, 13
Heade, Martin, 7
Hegel, Georg Wilhelm Friedrich, 11,
    153; on appetitive relation to the
    external world, 35, 71; and *Aufhe-
    bung,* 185; and Christianity,
    157–59; contradictions in philoso-
    phy of, 147, 154, 182, 185–88;
    and emphasis on conflict, 139,
    189; and *Erinnerung,* 185; and ex-
    pressivism, 183–84, 187; and
    Hegelian Absolute, 154, 232 n.49;
    idealism of, 182–84, 187; and
    "Lordship and Bondage," 136; on
    master-worker relationship, 55,
    136; and philosophy of will, 183;
    and post-Hegelian philosophy,
    139, 180, 182, 184; power lan-
    guage of, 196; on subjectivity, 188,
    233 n.61; as system maker, 173,
    169, 182, 185–89; on truth as pro-
    cess, 127; and "the unhappy con-
    sciousness," 174; and work ethic,
    135–36; "Introduction to the Phi-
    losophy of Art," 169; *Phe-
    nomenology of Spirit,* 136, 189
Heidegger, Martin, 26, 27, 127, 217
    n.60
Heine, Heinrich, 219 n.87
Heller, Erich, 106, 148, 225 n.8
Heraclitus, 195, 200
Herder, J. G., 184
Hobbes, Thomas, 67

Hodder, Alan D., 69, 81, 83, 107
Holland, Laurence, 51
Holmes, Oliver Wendell, 117–18, 157,
    195
Hook, Sidney, 106
Hopkins, Vivian C., 46, 50
Houghton, Walter E., 11
Howe, Daniel Walker, 67
Howe, Irving, 24, 33
Howells, William Dean, 22, 24
Hughes, Gertrude Reif, 16, 28, 48, 95,
    96, 97, 147. *See also Emerson's
    Demanding Optimism*
Hume, David, 51, 67
Hummel, Hermann, 218 n.73

Interpretations of Poetry and Religion
    (Santayana), 33
"Introduction to the Philosophy of Art"
    (Hegel), 169
Irwin, John, 9
Izenberg, Gerald N., 229 n.49

Jackson, Andrew, 111, 199
James, Henry, Jr.: compared to Nietz-
    sche, 115; on Emerson, 20, 25,
    30–38, 50, 87, 146, 151, 177, 179,
    180, 205; and Napoleon, 11; and
    war, 200
James, Henry, Sr., 25, 106, 215 n.18,
    224 n.2
James, William: on Emerson, 30, 32,
    148, 150, 157, 166, 224 n.2; on
    mysticism, 162–63; and power, 13,
    14, 29, 44–46, 71, 88, 90, 139;
    pragmatism of, 34–35, 46, 52, 66,
    68, 69, 77, 104, 153, 188; psychol-
    ogy of, 233 n.65; "Address at the
    Emerson Centenary in Concord,"
    32; "The Energies of Men," 44;
    "The Moral Equivalent of War,"
    193–94; "The Sentiment of Ratio-
    nality," 3; *The Varieties of Reli-
    gious Experience,* 110
Jaspers, Karl, 63–65
Jesus, 57, 128, 132–35, 151, 181

Johnson, Edward, 196
Johnson, Samuel, 77–78
Jones, Howard Mumford, 14

Kant, Immanuel, 26, 27, 148, 159, 183; and conception of power, 11; contradictions in philosophy of, 154, 187; and expressivism, 183–84; and Kantian categories, 142; and Kantian idealism, 65; and noumenal world, 55; and post-Kantian philosophy, 42, 65, 152, 159, 168; on the sublime, 83
Kaufmann, Walter, 135, 216 n.32
Kazin, Alfred, 19, 27, 35, 95, 216 n.24
Kermode, Frank, 201–2
Kierkegaard, Søren, 140, 157, 165, 223 n.78
Kinnaird, John, 12–13
Kirk, Russell, 106, 214 n.9
Klancher, Jon, 218 n.78
Kline, George L., 223 n.78
Kuklick, Bruce, 8, 215 n.17

Lane, Fitz Hugh, 7
Lasch, Christopher, 220 n.15
The Last Puritan (Santayana), 33, 34
Lawrence, D. H., 21, 125
Leaves of Grass (Whitman), 90, 125, 204
Leavis, F. R., 6
Leibniz, Gottfried Wilhelm, 172
Lincoln, Abraham, 194
Literary Transcendentalism (Buell), 214 n.9
Lloyd, Henry Demarest, 225 n.2
Locke, John, 51, 67, 148, 160, 172
Lovejoy, Arthur, 167, 171
Lowell, James Russell, 20, 27, 146, 156, 166, 207
Luther, Martin, 78, 128, 196, 206

McAleer, John, 58, 107, 220 n.6
McFarland, Thomas, 71, 91, 154–55, 167, 173–74, 221 n.36, 226 n.24

McGann, Jerome J., 169, 171–72
Maeterlinck, Maurice, 209
Mandelbaum, Maurice, 12, 42, 140, 157, 210, 211 n.1, 218 n.61, 222 n.53
Mardi (Melville), 110
Marr, David, 21, 80
Martin, Ronald E., 13, 189
Martineau, Harriet, 20, 225 n.2
Marx, Karl: compared to Emerson, 28, 85–86; and contradictions in Marxism, 154; and emphasis on production, 223 n.78; and emphasis on struggle, 191–92; and Hegel, 136, 182, 184; and master-worker relationship, 55, 136; misreadings of, 123; as philosopher of power, 11, 13, 28, 45; as philosopher of will, 153; radical humanism of, 158; as system maker, 232 n.56
Marx, Leo, 41–42, 219 n.88
Mather, Cotton, 67
Matthiessen, F. O., 21, 32, 46, 47, 165, 175–77, 179, 183, 203, 216 n.34
Megill, Allan, 65, 130, 155–56, 170, 226 n.7, 231 n.19
Melville, Herman: compared to Emerson, 16, 19, 27, 28, 33, 79, 113, 151, 155, 167, 177, 207; on Emerson, 106, 146, 166; extravagant rhetoric of, 125–26; on a national literature, 205; and power, 12; and work, 138; "Bartleby the Scrivener," 168; *The Confidence-Man,* 125; *Mardi,* 110; *Moby-Dick,* 15, 110, 125
Mencken, H. L., 220 n.15
Merquior, J. G., 211 n.1
Meyers, Marvin, 111
Michael, John, 20
Michelangelo, 75, 99, 144
Miller, J. Hillis, 169, 171
Miller, Perry, 8, 13, 46, 86–88, 200, 203–4, 209
Milton, John, 77, 144
Mitchell, W. J. T., 169
Moby-Dick (Melville), 15, 110, 125
Montaigne, Michel de, 146, 206, 207

Mont-Saint-Michel and Chartres
(Adams), 89
"The Moral Equivalent of War" (W.
James), 193–94
More, Paul Elmer, 20, 181
Morley, John, 24, 50, 156
Mumford, Lewis, 21

Napoleon Bonaparte, 11, 57, 60, 69,
144, 206
The Narrative of Arthur Gordon Pym
(Poe), 125
"The Need for a Recovery of Philosophy" (Dewey), 44
Nehamas, Alexander, 63, 69, 76, 120
New Testament, 196
Newton, Eric, 231 n.29
Newton, Sir Isaac, 144, 187
Nietzsche, Friedrich: aesthetics of, 173;
aestheticist ontology of, 65,
155–56; and *amor fati,* 63; as anti-
humanist, 70, 121; apocalyptic
style of, 207–8; and Christian
other world, 5; Christian rhetoric
of, 157; compared to Emerson,
7–10, 26–28, 37–39, 44–46,
49–52, 56, 58–59, 69–71, 77, 88,
90, 93, 101, 104–5, 106, 111–13,
115, 117, 120–24, 126–31,
133–35, 139–46, 151, 153–56,
160, 162, 165, 190–93, 200–2,
207–8; as edifying philosopher,
127–28; on Emerson, 30, 120; and
emphasis on assimilation, 35, 56,
111, 133; and emphasis on production, 65–66, 105, 223 n.78;
and emphasis on struggle, 36, 105,
115, 139; and emphasis on suffering, 38, 64, 106, 112, 220 n.11;
and emphasis on tuition, 59, 104;
and emphasis on use, 63, 65,
104–5, 111, 220 n.11; and extravagant rhetoric of, 62–63, 117,
119–24, 126–31; and Goethe, 106,
135; as nihilist, 10, 65–66, 164,
230 n.70; and overcoming, 4–5,
70, 77; and overman (*Über-*

mensch), 6, 64–65, 135; as
philosopher of power, 6, 10,
13–14, 28, 44–45, 47, 58, 69, 71,
88, 90, 93, 112–13, 134, 159–60,
186; as pragmatist, 46, 153; on
war, 190–93, 200–2; and will to
power, 7, 76, 104, 140–44, 164;
Beyond Good and Evil, 128–29;
"On Truth and Lie in an Extra-
Moral Sense," 210; "Schopenhauer
as Educator," 129; *Thus Spoke
Zarathustra,* 6, 65, 83, 101, 192
Novalis, 126, 127, 156, 209
Nussbaum, Martha C., 4–5

Odysseus, 5
"The Optimism of Ralph Waldo Emerson" (Santayana), 33

Packer, Barbara: on anti-Emerson tradi-
tion, 119; on Emerson and anti-
nature tradition, 86; on Emerson
and power, 84, 133; on Emerson's
rhetoric, 118–19, 121, 126, 151,
179; on "Experience," 58, 61;
Emerson's Fall, 26
Paine, Tom, 57, 134
Parker, Theodore, 20
Parks, Henry Bamford, 52
Pascal, Blaise, 148
Paul, Sherman, 46, 50, 84, 150, 168
Peabody, Elizabeth, 138
Pease, Donald E., 9, 169
Perry, Bliss, 217 n.40
Phenomenology of Spirit (Hegel), 136,
189
Plato, 31, 60, 149, 181
Platonism, 31, 46, 51, 138, 139, 167,
181
Plotinus, 52, 145, 146, 207, 208
Poe, Edgar Allan, 12, 107, 110, 126,
204; "The Domain of Arnheim,"
204; *The Narrative of Arthur Gor-
don Pym,* 125
Poirier, Richard: on Emerson's contra-
dictions, 165, 177–79; on Emer-

son's influence, 20, 166, 206; on Emerson and Nietzsche, 121; on Emerson and power, 10, 19, 29, 178–79; on Emerson as pragmatist, 147; on Whicher, 48; on writing off the self, 202; *The Renewal of Literature,* 165, 177–78

Pollock, Robert, 150, 152

Porte, Joel: anti-Emerson bias, 215 n.21; on Emerson and antinature tradition, 222 n.54; on Emerson and Christian ethics, 157; on Emerson's extravagant rhetoric, 26, 126, 128, 168; on Emerson image, 166, 176; on Emerson's influence, 20; on Emerson as Transcendentalist, 21–22; on Emerson and power, 40–41, 51; on "Spiritual Laws," 109; *Representative Man,* 26, 215 n.21, 224 n.18

Porter, Carolyn, 28, 147, 228–29 n. 47

Porter, David, 208

Porter, Noah, 202

Pound, Ezra, 51

Rajan, Tilottama, 170–74, 231 n.24

Reed, John, 151–52, 228 n.34

Reed, Sampson, 68, 74

Reid, Alfred S., 214 n.9

Reid, Thomas, 67

The Renewal of Literature (Poirier), 165, 177–78

Representative Man (Porte), 26, 215 n.21, 224 n.18

Richardson, Robert D., 8, 122–23, 225 n.13

Richter, Jean Paul, 126

Ripley, George, 232 n.56

Robinson, David, 22, 144, 161, 228–29 n.47

Rogin, Michael Paul, 199

Rorty, Richard, 127–28, 153, 164, 182

Rose, Anne C., 232 n.56

Rosenberg, Philip, 158–59, 216 n.26, 222 n.57

Rosenwald, Lawrence, 18, 143, 213 n.23

Rourke, Constance, 126

Rousseau, Jean-Jacques, 123, 147

Royce, Josiah, 64, 66

"The Rule of Phase Applied to History" (Adams), 210

Rusk, Ralph, 50

Russell, Bertrand, 11

Ruysbroeck, Jean van, 209

Sainte-Beuve, Charles Augustin, 33

Salter, William, 218 n.73

Santayana, George: on Emerson, 6, 8, 32–38, 43, 50, 87, 106, 146, 151, 181, 207; on pragmatism, 34–35, 69; on Protestant-Romantic tradition, 15, 35–36, 70, 158, 190; "Emerson the Poet," 32, 33; *Interpretations of Poetry and Religion,* 33; *The Last Puritan,* 33, 34; "The Optimism of Ralph Waldo Emerson," 33; *Three Philosophical Poets,* 35

Sartor Resartus (Carlyle), 42, 112, 136

The Scarlet Letter (Hawthorne), 15

Schelling, Friedrich W. J., 9, 153, 154, 158, 182, 183

Schiller, Johann Christoph Friedrich, 173

Schlegel, August Wilhelm, 126

Schlegel, Friedrich, 126, 127, 172

Schnädelbach, Herbert, 228 n.37, 229 n.62

Schneider, Daniel J., 234 n.28

Schopenhauer, Arthur: aesthetics of, 173; Christian rhetoric of, 157; compared to Emerson, 94; and emphasis on struggle, 191; as philosopher of will, 12, 140, 141, 143, 153, 154, 183, 210; on self-extinction, 161, 210

"Schopenhauer as Educator" (Nietzsche), 129

Sénancour, 172

The Senses of Walden (Cavell), 26

"The Sentiment of Rationality" (W. James), 3

Shakespeare, William, 49, 78–79, 99, 132–35, 144

Shelley, Percy Bysshe, 158
Simic, Charles, 80
Simpson, David, 76, 86–87, 183, 185
Simpson, Lewis P., 51
Smith, Adam, 136
Solger, Karl, 126
Solomon, Robert C., 11, 135–36, 139, 147, 154, 157, 217 n.6, 218 n.62, 233 n.60
Spencer, Herbert, 11, 189, 194, 202, 232 n.56
Spengler, Oswald, 26
Spinoza, 52, 156, 172
Stack, George J., 212 n.6, 226 n.2, 226 n.26, 229 n.61
Steele, Jeffrey, 76
Steinmetz, S. R., 193
Stessel, Edward, 234 n.14
Stewart, Dugald, 67, 160
Stowe, Harriet Beecher, 138
Strout, Cushing, 233 n.65
Suckiel, Ellen Kappy, 215 n.17
Sumner, William Graham, 202–3
Sussman, Henry, 233 n.60
Swedenborg, Emanuel, 88, 167, 183, 187, 206

Taylor, Charles, 184, 233 n.61
"Thomas Carlyle" (Thoreau), 138
Thoreau, Henry David: apocalyptic style of, 185, 207; on Carlyle, 126; Christian rhetoric of, 158; compared to Emerson, 20, 26, 28, 112, 175–76, 205; contradictions of, 147; on Emerson, 166; extravagant rhetoric of, 124, 168, 196, 207; and failure, 110; and prospectiveness, 188; and self-culture, 63; and transcendence of experience, 208–9; and work, 138; "Thomas Carlyle," 138; *Walden,* 99
Three Philosophical Poets (Santayana), 35
Thus Spoke Zarathustra (Nietzsche), 6, 65, 83, 101, 192
Tieck, Ludwig, 126
Toews, John Edward, 182, 232 n.49

"On Truth and Lie in an Extra-Moral Sense" (Nietzsche), 210
Tuckerman, Joseph, 67
Tuveson, Ernest Lee, 207
Twain, Mark, 33
"Twilight" (Whitman), 105

Updike, John, 19, 76, 214 n.9

Van Cromphout, Gustaaf, 219 n.3
The Varieties of Religious Experience (W. James), 110

Walden (Thoreau), 99
Walker, James, 67
Walzer, Michael, 196
Ward, Samuel Gray, 114
Ware, Henry, Jr., 68, 204
Weber, Max, 158
Wellek, René, 171–72, 183
Wendell, Barrett, 21
West, Cornel, 26, 28, 43, 44, 45, 88, 147
Wheeler, Kathleen, 226 n.23
Whicher, Stephen, 146; and anti-Emerson tradition, 8, 148, 180; and developmental approach to Emerson, 71; on Emerson and power, 7, 50–52, 105, 151; on late Emerson, 80, 92, 94, 95, 96, 103, 105, 170; *Freedom and Fate,* 47–52
White, Hayden, 169
Whitehead, Alfred North, 172
Whitman, Walt: and antinature tradition, 83; apocalyptic style of, 207; and Christianity, 157, 158; compared to Emerson, 19, 28, 147, 204, 205; on Emerson, 20, 118, 166; extravagant rhetoric of, 124, 126, 168, 207; as healthy minded soul, 110; and Hegel, 186; and power, 6, 12–13; and symbols, 90; and work, 138; *Democratic Vistas,* 90; *Leaves of Grass,* 90, 125, 204; "Twilight," 105
Wilson, Edmund, 29

Winters, Yvor, 113, 128, 157, 207, 214
        n.9, 226 n.25
Wittgenstein, Ludwig, 26, 127
Woodberry, George, 20, 106, 208
Wordsworth, William, 83, 91, 149, 158

Yeats, William Butler, 193, 201